# Veiled Leadership

# Veiled Leadership

## Katharine Drexel, the Sisters of the Blessed Sacrament, and Catholic Race Relations

Amanda Bresie

The Catholic University of America Press
Washington, DC

Copyright © 2023
The Catholic University of America Press
All rights reserved.

Cataloging-in-Publication Data is available from the
Library of Congress.
ISBN: 978-0-8132-3723-7
eISBN: 978-0-8132-3724-4

# Contents

Acknowledgments ................................ vii

Introduction. "A New Virility": The Sisters of the Blessed Sacrament and a New Catholic Mission ....... 1

1. "Go Ye Forth and Teach All Nations": Mother Katharine Drexel's Challenge to the Catholic Church .................................. 17

2. "Received from Other Sources": Mother Katharine Drexel and the Bureau of Catholic Indian Missions ... 45

3. "Souls! Souls! Should Be Our Cry, Our Ambition, Our Only Aim": SBS Administration of Indigenous Schools .................................. 85

4. Intent and Impact: Assessing SBS Indigenous Missions . 113

5. Human Rights and Sacramental Rites: SBS Missions in Black Communities ......................... 135

6. Navigating Race and Religion in Jim Crow Louisiana . 169

7. The Catholic Rosenwald: Mother Katharine Schools in Rural Louisiana ........................... 207

8. From Spiritual to Temporal Needs: The Evolution of the Sisters of the Blessed Sacrament and Catholic Social Justice ............................... 227

9. "These Kluxes Are All Wrought Up": Battling the "Catholic Problem" and Conflicting Visions of America .................................. 251

Conclusion ..................................... 273

Bibliography ................................... 281

# Tables

Table 2-1. Aid to Non-SBS Indian Missions ............ 56

Table 2-2. Drexel Subsidies to Lenten Collection
1887–1924 .................................. 62

Table 5-1. SBS Schools for Black Students, 1891–1935 .... 160

Table 7-1. SBS Rural Schools ....................... 218

# Acknowledgments

DESPITE THE MANY HOURS I have spent squirreled away in my office or hiding in the library reading, writing, and thinking, this manuscript is the product of community, not solitude. I extend my deep gratitude to the many people whose support and cooperation have made the project possible.

This book was born at Texas Christian University, and I am grateful that I found an intellectual home there. I owe many thanks to Rebecca Sharpless, who patiently listened to a thousand ideas, followed me on long tangents, and read endless drafts. Her guidance turned a mess of anecdotes and facts into an argument. She made me a better writer, thinker, teacher, and feminist.

Additionally, Jodi Campbell, Gregg Cantrell, and Todd Kerstetter were instrumental in helping me clarify my thoughts. This book owes much to their patient editing and thoughtful criticism. Many of the ideas in this book came out of an independent study with Jeff Williams and Lisa Barnett at Brite School of Divinity, who pushed me to figure out why Katharine Drexel matters.

My work would not have been possible without the help of archivists and librarians. At the Archives of the Sisters of the Blessed Sacrament I am indebted to the help of Stephanie Morris. I am also grateful for the companionship and aid of Sister Roland Lagarde and Sister Damian Widmeier. Mark Thiel at Marquette University Special Collections was instrumental in my research. His help navigating the Bureau of Catholic Indian Missions Collection was invaluable. Xavier University's Lester Sullivan made my trip to New Orleans productive and enjoyable. The Interlibrary Loan staff at Texas Christian University gathered far-flung resources. Without them, the research on this book would have been impossible.

Trevor Lipscombe at the Catholic University of America Press rescued this manuscript from obscurity and encouraged me to revise it for publication. He believed in it long after I had given up on it. The entire team at the Catholic University of America Press has made this book a pleasure to work on. The readers' thoughtful critiques improved this book, and I appreciate them challenging me to think more critically about the Sisters of the Blessed Sacrament and to reframe some of my arguments.

The Texas Catholic Historical Society welcomed me when I was a graduate student, and through them I have gotten to work with some of the smartest and kindest historians in Texas. I have enjoyed working with this group of impressive scholars of Catholic history and culture. Richard Fossey invited me into the organization and has been a source of support for many years. He published my first essay and never stopped encouraging me or asking about Katharine Drexel. Many thanks to Claudia Anderson, Marian Barber, Matthew Butler, and Selena Aleman for their support as well.

For the past nine years I have taught and chaired the History Department at Greenhill School. I could not ask for a better community. My Greenhill family has given me a place to thrive. Every day I get to do what I love—engage students and build community. The school has also backed my research and helped me grow as a historian and a teacher. I am particularly grateful to my colleagues in the History Department: Genie Burke, Scott Cotton, Ron Frankland, Sidrah Khan, Justin Solonick, and Jason Yaffe. They have all helped me practice conference papers and edit essays. Librarian Abby Harrison has not only supported my research but that of everyone on campus. Melissa Battis, Laura Hudec, Monsie Muñoz and Andy Mercurio have made me a better teacher and human. They have my heart. My students keep me curious and teach me as much as I teach them. Each year I am amazed that I get to share a classroom with young people who ask important questions, dare me to think bigger, and dazzle me with their empathy. I love going to work every day, and they are the reason. Finally, the Cross Country team has shown me the power of hard work and determination;the best ideas in this book came to me while running with them.

I owe my greatest debt to my family. My mother, Susan Kasten, provided childcare so I could pursue my research, and she read early drafts of book chapters. She is the reason I know where to put a comma. Daniel Kasten, my father, did not live to see the publication of this book, but he taught me to write and think, and so his spirit is on every page and in everything I do. I am deeply thankful for my sister Jennifer Turner, who has been my sounding board, my staunch ally, and my closest friend. Jay, Zoey, and Nora Turner provided many fun distractions while I worked on this manuscript, and I'm just thankful that they exist. The whole extended Bresie clan has supported me and helped in any way they could. Much love to Don, Maria, and Chris Bresie, Lisa, Robert, and Jon Meegan, and to Katie, Joseph, and Mia Parnell. I want to extend my sincere thanks to the entire family—and, yes, I will get a new topic of conversation now.

Eric Bresie, my husband, aided this project in a thousand ways. He has patiently formatted tables, battled pagination problems, held my hand while I cried with frustration, walked thousands of miles by my side as I talked out problems in the text, listened to presentations, booked vacations around my research agenda, given back rubs, made tea, poured wine, and loved me. While the words are mine, this book has been a team effort. This is for him. My son Leo was born when I began this research, and he has grown up with this book. He pulled me away from this project for a long time and delayed its publication by years. But he made my heart explode with love, and I have no regrets.

INTRODUCTION

# "A New Virility"

## The Sisters of the Blessed Sacrament and a New Catholic Mission

> Resolve: Generously with no half-hearted, timorous dread of the opinions of the church and men to manifest my mission. To speak only and when it pleases God; but to lose no opportunity of speaking before priests and bearded men. Manifest yourself. You have no time to occupy your thoughts with that complacency of consideration of what others will think. Your business is simply, "What will my Father in Heaven think?"
>
> —Katharine Drexel, 1889

WHEN DESIGNING THE MOTHERHOUSE of the Sisters of the Blessed Sacrament, Mother Katharine Drexel issued a challenge to the Roman Catholic Church and American Society. On the cornerstone she invoked Romans 9:26, "And it shall be in the place where it was said unto them, you are not my people; there they shall be called the sons of the living God." The cornerstone called out a nation that had treated Black and Indigenous populations with scorn and reminded the church that it was supposed to treat all people as children of God. By extending Catholic doctrine to racial minorities, the thirteen sisters who moved into the convent in 1892 challenged the religious, political, and educational status quo. The Sisters of the Blessed Sacrament for Indians and Colored People (SBS) founded dozens of schools and social settlements across the country, and they helped finance the majority of Catholic schools for Black and Indigenous students in the United States. The story of Drexel and the SBS sheds light on Catholic

---

Quoted in Consuela Marie Duffy, SBS, *Katharine Drexel: A Biography* (Bensalem, PA: Peter Reilly Company, 1966), 246.

attempts to challenge Protestant American hegemony and on previously unexplored interracial endeavors. Further, the work of the SBS demonstrates that despite limitations imposed by a patriarchal church, religious women had the power to influence social policy.

## "A New Era of Missionary Endeavor"

Led by Mother Katharine Drexel, a wealthy Philadelphia heiress, the Sisters of the Blessed Sacrament for Indians and Colored People used traditional church teachings to challenge the existing social order.[1] While the congregation's annals and publications overflow with talk of giving succor to "pagan" souls and bringing the "poor heathens" the light of the world, they accomplished these religious goals through keen business practices and political wheedling and by venturing to places others feared to travel. In founding a new religious congregation dedicated to aiding Black and Indigenous people, Mother Katharine gave the Protestant practice of organizing home missions a uniquely Catholic context. Mother Katharine recognized that she and the SBS were spearheading a new type of Catholic evangelization; indeed, years later she noted, "A new era of missionary endeavor has been apparent in the Church of America during the past twenty years.... It would seem as if, in casting off the swaddling clothes of its infancy, a new virility began to manifest itself and the impulse of this new life gave birth to a new spirit."[2] Drexel was one of the first Catholic women to recognize the power of the church to transform American society.

Mother Katharine Drexel and the Sisters of the Blessed Sacrament tried to lead souls to God while addressing societal inequality. The nuns' understanding of religious doctrine lay at the center

---

1 Though canon law distinguishes between religious sisters and nuns depending on whether they swear simple or solemn vows, I will use the terms interchangeably; likewise, I will also use *order* and *congregation* to mean a group of religious sisters or brothers. In addition, when Katharine Drexel entered religious life, she took on the title Mother Katharine. For the sixty-four years she lived as a religious sister, she answered to this name. Therefore, when referring to her after her profession, I will use *Drexel* and *Mother Katharine* interchangeably.

2 Mother Katharine Drexel, "Foreword," *Mission Fields at Home*, October 1928, 1.

of their teaching, their neighborhood outreach, their voting, and their petitioning. A sister best summed up the SBS mission in their magazine in 1934: "Driven on by the realization that all men are potential members of the Mystical Christ, the Church, *with divine daring they push on, striving always to extend and expand and intensify the Kingdom of Christ among these million*."[3] Here the "Kingdom of Christ" reflects Protestant Social Gospel ideals that challenged society to blunt the injustices and inequalities caused by the industrial economy. The sisters adapted Social Gospel language ("the Kingdom of Christ") to a distinctly Catholic idiom (the "Mystical Christ"). Further, while many Progressive Era reformers shied away from racial issues, the SBS asserted the Catholic Church's place in transforming race relations.[4] This book examines the Sisters of the Blessed Sacrament from their 1891 founding through the end of Mother Katharine Drexel's active ministry in 1935. While no study of the SBS would be complete without studying the life of Mother Katharine, this book is not a biography of a saint. Instead, it explores the groundbreaking work of the congregation she led.

Why produce another work on missionaries, who have been accused of leading ethnocentric campaigns of cultural genocide?[5] Missionaries make twenty-first-century historians squeamish. The

---

3 "Auxiliaries of the Sisters of the Blessed Sacrament," *Mission Fields at Home*, September 1934, 170.

4 Michael McGerr has identified "The Shield of Segregation" as a key element of Progressive Era ideology. Segregation became a method of conflict avoidance for many during the time period. Historians have concluded that both Indigenous and Black people lost ground during the Progressive movement as whites emphasized a vigorous, muscular, Caucasian Christianity. McGerr, *A Fierce Discontent: The Rise and Fall of the Progressive Movement in America, 1870–1920* (New York: Oxford University Press, 2003), 182–220; Jackson Lears, *Rebirth of a Nation: The Making of Modern America, 1877–1920* (New York: HarperPerennial, 2009), 92–132.

5 See, for example, Margaret Jacobs, *White Mother to a Dark Race: Settler Colonialism, Maternalism, and the Removal of Indigenous Children in the American West and Australia, 1880–1940* (Lincoln: University of Nebraska Press, 2009); Lawrence Lucas, *Black Priest/White Church: Catholics and Racism* (New York: Random House, 1970); and George Tinker, *Missionary Conquest: The Gospel and Native American Cultural Genocide* (Minneapolis: Fortress Press, 1993).

last few years have seen new, horrible information come to light about Catholic education for Indigenous people. The world has watched the discovery of mass graves in Canada that reveal the human toll of residential boarding schools.[6] Additionally, in the wake of the murder of George Floyd in 2020, it is hard to read about outreach missions to Black communities that emphasized assimilation into white society more than equity. The sisters had absolute faith in the justness of their cause and the primacy of the Catholic Church, but scholars have since documented the cultural damage their actions caused. While the sisters claimed to appreciate Indigenous cultures and Black achievements, they tried to instill the values of middle-class, white America in their students of color. Why, then, add to the literature of white women trying to "save" Black and Indigenous people by forcing them to accept new cultural values? The sisters peppered their writings with phrases such as "little heathens" and "poor darkeys." Their use of terms such as "savage" and "pagan" to describe Indigenous peoples and their emphasis on the necessity of "civilizing" and "Christianizing" strikes modern readers as racist and patronizing. The missionary goal of Americanization is rooted in white supremacy. Ironically, the people missionaries sought to Americanize had been in the United States for many more generations than the missionaries themselves.

This does not mean historians should ignore the work of missionaries, however. The question should not be *How could they?* But rather *Why did they? What do their choices say about American society?* Historian Anne Firor Scott has cautioned against dismissing missionaries: "We must never forget that the efforts to 'bring people to Christ' or to save them from sin were enormously energizing concepts for women in missionary, moral reform, temperance, and antislavery societies. It is important to remember that the earliest white efforts to cross the racial barrier came from women in religion-based associations."[7] Missionaries like the SBS

---

6 Ian Austen, "Horrible History: Mass Grave of Indigenous Children Reported in Canada," *New York Times*, October 5, 2021, https://www.nytimes.com/2021/05/28/world/canada/kamloops-mass-grave-residential-schools.html.

7 Anne Firor Scott, *Natural Allies: Women's Associations in American History* (Urbana: University of Illinois Press, 1991), 182.

had paternalistic and racist ideas, but they also engaged in complex cross-cultural relationships that are worth exploring. Unlike male missionaries who fulfilled clerical roles and administered the sacraments, Catholic sisters spent time getting to know children and families through classroom interactions and home visits. The sisters were on the front lines of cultural mediation, often helping their students and families navigate social services and engaging in dialogue over the nature of American citizenship. Impact is always more important than intent, but it is essential to understand what the SBS set out to achieve. The Sisters of the Blessed Sacrament took part in the destruction of cultures, though they believed they offered Black and Indigenous people more palatable paths to assimilation than their Protestant counterparts. Nevertheless, the sisters' work harmed the communities they sought to help. Navigating this territory is murky but necessary.

Reformers and philanthropists who worked with Black and Indigenous people during the Progressive Era, such as the Friends of the Indian, the Indian Rights Association, and the American Missionary Association, championed education and Americanization—the process of indoctrinating ethnic groups into middle-class white culture. The same reform organizations cast aspersions on whether Roman Catholics, many of whom immigrated in the nineteenth century, could truly adapt to American life, and they decried Catholic efforts to work with Black and Indigenous populations. Formed during a period of virulent anti-Catholicism, the Sisters of the Blessed Sacrament envisioned the Americanization process as one intertwined with Roman Catholic spiritual instruction. The SBS harbored ambiguous feelings about the relationship between church and state, often simultaneously pleading for federal money and opposing governmental regulation. Drexel's sisters sought to "Win America for Christ," but they also challenged traditional notions about who could be an American and what constituted a Christian nation. Since their efforts do not fit neatly into existing narratives on women and reform movements, their work has largely gone unheralded.

Though the literature on women, religion, and social reform in the late nineteenth and early twentieth centuries in the United States is vast, Catholic women typically appear as aid recipients, not reformers.[8] Important scholarship has chronicled the efforts of white, native-born, middle-class women who formed what historians have labeled the American Protestant Empire.[9] This work has added depth to the historical understanding of women as cultural agents and has challenged traditional ideas about domesticity, but much remains to be studied on Catholic women, and nuns in particular, whose profession of vows of poverty, chastity, and obedience precluded the hallmarks of womanhood: motherhood and homemaking. What did it mean to young women "to love them [Indigenous People and African Americans] with the natural love of a woman, and the supernatural love of a spouse of Christ? To love them, as it were with mothers' hearts in virgins' bosoms?"[10] The Sisters of the Blessed Sacrament took popular tropes about women in reform and translated them to a Catholic context.

Unlike Protestant women's groups that borrowed their theological underpinnings from the Social Gospel movement, Drexel and other Catholic women took their cues from Leo XIII's

---

8  Space only permits a few examples of the literature, but some of the most important works on the topic include Wendy J. Deichmann Edwards and Carolyn De Swarte Gifford, eds., *Gender and the Social Gospel* (Urbana and Chicago: University of Illinois Press, 2003); Carolyn De Swarte Gifford, ed., *The American Deaconess Movement in the Early Twentieth Century* (New York: Garland, 1987); Jacquelyn Dowd Hall, *Revolt against Chivalry: Jessie Daniel Ames and the Women's Campaign against Lynching* (New York: Columbia University Press, 1979); Patricia Hill, *The World Their Household: The American Woman's Foreign Mission Movement and Cultural Transformation, 1870–1920* (Ann Arbor: University of Michigan Press, 1985); Peggy Pascoe, *Relations of Rescue: The Search for Female Moral Authority in the American West, 1874–1939* (New York: Oxford University Press, 1990); Joe M. Richardson, *Christian Reconstruction: The American Missionary Association and Southern Blacks, 1861–1890* (Athens: University of Georgia Press, 1986); Scott, *Natural Allies*; Rhonda Ann Semple, *Missionary Women: Gender, Professionalism and the Victorian Idea of Christian Mission* (Suffolk, UK: Boydell Press 2003); Susan A. Yohn, *A Contest of Faiths: Missionary Women and Pluralism in the American Southwest* (Ithaca, NY: Cornell University Press, 1995).

9  Barbara Reeves-Ellington, Kathryn Kish Sklar, and Connie A. Shemo, eds., *Competing Kingdoms: Women, Mission, Nation, and the American Protestant Empire, 1812–1960* (Durham, NC: Duke University Press, 2010), 4.

10  Father Anselm Weber, "The Sisters of the Blessed Sacrament for Indians and Colored People," *St. Anthony's Messenger*, January 1899, 267–69.

groundbreaking encyclical *Rerum Novarum: On Capital and Labor*. The document issued in 1891, the same year as Mother Katharine founded the Sisters of the Blessed Sacrament, affirmed that the church had a role to play in social justice and human rights. It attacked both liberal capitalism and socialism and demanded that Catholics work for justice within the auspices of the Catholic Church.[11] The document affirmed that the answer to social ills could be found through a "return to the Christian life and Christian institutions."[12] Specifically, it called for Catholic groups to form to address the casualties of unfettered capitalism. Forty years later Pius XI would reaffirm the church's commitment to social justice and the suffering poor in his encyclical *Quadragesimo Anno*.[13] Both of these documents were essential to groups that wanted to engage with issues of human rights, as it gave them uniquely Catholic theological language to describe their work and to separate them from their Protestant peers. It is not clear whether Drexel read either document, but the SBS's actions show a commitment to using the church to solve social problems. The Sisters of the Blessed Sacrament felt the need to defend their students from three perils: public schools, Protestant missions, and paganism. They used a militant tone to describe their work: "We are engaged in mighty warfare for the souls of the Indians and Colored. . . . He, our Lord and Master, bids us go forth to all parts of the earth where there is a soul of Black or Red and tell them of His redeeming love; show them the wiles and tricks of the infernal enemy; tell them how the sacred Heart yearns for them." Continuing the martial metaphor, the sisters asserted, "The Standard of Christ is the royal insignia of their races—POVERTY, HUMILITY, CONTEMPT."[14] They viewed their enemy as Satan acting through a sanitized public Protestantism. While these views fit with the

---

11   Leo XIII, *Rerum Novarum: Encyclical Letter of Our Holy Father by Diving Providence Pope Leo XIII on the Condition of Labor*, 1891, in David J. O'Brien and Thomas A. Shannon, *Catholic Social Thought: The Documentary Heritage*, 10th ed. (Maryknoll, NY: Orbis, 2003), 14–39.

12   Leo XIII, *Rerum Novarum*, 24.

13   Pius XI, *Quadragesimo Anno Encyclical Letter of His Holiness Pius XI by Divine Providence Pope*, 1931, in O'Brien and Shannon, *Catholic Social Thought*, 42–79.

14   "The Sisters of the Blessed Sacrament for Indians and Colored People," *Indian Sentinel*, 1907, 14–15.

American Catholic worldview at the time, their insistence on acting upon these ideas was unusual.

Catholic women, often from lower-class, immigrant households, did not meet the standards of middle-class American womanhood set by Protestant elites, so scholars have assumed that Catholic women failed to participate in social reform movements. Aaron Abell has concluded, "To some Protestants the words 'Catholic' and 'reform' were contradictory terms, the juxtaposition of which provoked hilarity and mirth."[15] Like Protestants, Catholic women considered themselves the spiritual centers of their families, but they did not often use their role as religious guardians to gain positions of authority.[16] They did not lack interest in social justice; rather, they had limited courses of action open to them. Catholic women joined fewer civic causes, containing their activities under the umbrella of the church, which restricted the involvement of lay women. By 1910 Catholic women participated in more than 1,200 social service organizations, but clerics held virtually all positions of power.[17] Priests encouraged religious fervor and an increased reception of the sacraments but did not support women taking leadership roles in social reform work. Some members of the church hierarchy warned their female followers to stay true to the tenets of their faith and resist becoming "New Women "who exerted themselves in the public and professional arena. Cardinal James Gibbons, for example, condemned the "Restless Woman" in a 1902 article in *Ladies Home Journal*, saying, "Who enters the political arena is sure to be soiled by its mud. As soon as woman thrusts herself into politics and mingles with the crowd to deposit her vote, she must expect to be handed roughly . . . the more woman gains in the political arena, the more she loses in the domestic kingdom." He urged women to turn away from the New Woman and look instead to a more appropri-

---

15  Aaron Abell, *American Catholicism and Social Action: A Search for Social Justice 1865–1950* (Garden City, NY: Hanover House, 1960), 91.

16  Colleen McDannell, *The Christian Home in Victorian America, 1840–1900* (Bloomington: Indiana University Press, 1986), 52–76.

17  Debra Campbell, "Reformers and Activists," in *American Catholic Women: A Historical Exploration*, ed. Karen Kennelly, CSJ (New York: Macmillan, 1989), 169.

ate model, "Mary, the Mother of Christ."[18] In the twentieth century, as other denominations became more ecumenical, Catholics developed increasingly insular institutions and sought social change through the Roman Catholic Church rather than secular organizations.[19] Groups such as the Sisters of the Blessed Sacrament could be seen as parallel, counter-organizations to Protestant and secular reform societies.

## Sisters as Missionaries

While some Catholic women served in their own communities, they had few opportunities to engage in mission work. They lagged several decades behind their Protestant counterparts, in part because the Vatican considered United States a foreign mission field until 1908. The mission field status meant that the United States was under the authority of the Propaganda Fide and that it received mission funding and clergy from Europe. The Roman Curia, or governing body of the church, viewed America as a Catholic backwater. Conditioned to receive the attention of missionaries, few American Catholics thought of doing their own proselytizing. Katharine Drexel told a story that, in an audience with Pope Leo XIII, she pleaded with him to send European missionaries to the American West, and she was shocked when he asked her why she did not become a missionary herself. Missionaries did not come out of American Catholic churches in the late nineteenth century, and they certainly were not women. In 1890, the year before the Sisters of the Blessed Sacrament foundation, Mother Frances Cabrini fought to get permission to use the feminine form of missionary in the name of her congregation, the Missionary Sisters of the Sacred Heart of Jesus.[20] Because the church did not acknowledge female missionaries during this time, most scholars have not, either.

---

18   James Cardinal Gibbons, "The Restless Woman," *Ladies Home Journal*, January 1902, 6.

19   William M. Halsey, *The Survival of American Innocence: Catholicism in the Era of Disillusionment, 1920–1940* (Notre Dame, IN: University of Notre Dame Press, 1980), 57.

20   Kathleen Sprows Cummings, *A Saint of Our Own: How the Quest for a Holy Hero Helped Catholics Become American* (Chapel Hill: University of North Carolina Press, 2019), 107.

In the last few decades, however, new scholarship has challenged traditional ideas about Catholic women, missionaries, and social work.²¹ Many historians now view nuns as women able to move outside the limits of culturally acceptable female occupations of wife and mother or spinster. Anne M. Butler has stated, "Nuns and sisters . . . were neither silent nor secluded, disinterested nor ingenuous, warped nor winsome. Rather, they were movers and shakers in the religious and secular spheres."²² Joining a religious order provided Catholic women the opportunity to engage in meaningful work, travel the world, and advance professionally. Catholic nuns ran schools, hospitals, and managed complex financial empires.²³ In 1894, a female commentator for *Catholic World* captured the spirit of the sisters, insisting, "Sisters are before the world as representative women in its best sense, not as relics of a buried past, as fossils for spiritual geologists to examine, classify, and put behind glass doors to be labeled 'Footprints of Creation'—the first, perhaps after the Azoic age." The writer suggested instead that they should be seen as "the incarnate idea of the Golden Rule, the eleventh Commandment clothed in flesh and blood."²⁴ Nuns, in other words, took theology to the streets.

---

21  Mary J. Oates, *The Catholic Philanthropic Tradition in America* (Bloomington: Indiana University Press, 1995); Dorothy M. Brown and Elizabeth McKeown, *The Poor Belong to Us: Catholic Charities and American Welfare* (Cambridge, MA: Harvard University Press, 1997).

22  Anne M. Butler, *Across God's Frontiers: Catholic Sisters in the American West, 1850–1920* (Chapel Hill: University of North Carolina Press, 2012), xiv.

23  For example, see Emily Clark, *Masterless Mistresses: The New Orleans Ursulines and the Development of a New World Society, 1727–1820* (Chapel Hill: University of North Carolina Press, 2007); Carol K. Coburn and Martha Smith, *Spirited Lives: How Nuns Shaped Catholic Culture and American Life, 1836–1920* (Chapel Hill: University of North Carolina Press, 1999); Mary Ann Donovan, SC, *Sisterhood as Power: The Past and Passion of Ecclesial Women* (New York: Crossroad, 1989); Suellen Hoy, *Good Hearts: Catholic Sisters in Chicago's Past* (Urbana: University of Illinois Press, 2006); James J. Kenneally, *The History of American Catholic Women* (New York: Crossroad, 1990); Jo Ann Kay McNamara, *Sisters in Arms: Catholic Nuns through Two Millennia* (Cambridge, MA: Harvard University Press, 1996).

24  F. Edselas, "Woman's Work in Religious Communities," *Catholic World*, January 1894, 511.

Prior to Vatican II, nearly 90 percent of nuns taught in some capacity.[25] While many congregations expressed an interest in teaching Black and Indigenous students, bishops often insisted the sisters spend their time ministering to the Catholic immigrants flooding American cities instead.[26] Additionally, many sisters who emigrated from countries such as France, Italy, or Germany had language barriers that limited their ability to engage American society. Thus, the work of many nineteenth-century Catholic nuns focused on serving the needs of their immediate neighborhood parishes. They ran schools, hospitals, and social settlements and acted as cultural intermediaries, easing immigrants' transition into mainstream culture. As Kathleen Sprows Cummings has shown, Catholic women could be "New Women," too.[27] Despite the limitations imposed by their subordinate status, some Catholic sisters including Drexel and the Sisters of the Blessed Sacrament embraced the progressive missionary impulse. The Sisters of the Blessed Sacrament stand out because Mother Katharine's wealth and influence enabled them to dictate their own mission agenda.

While the so-called race problem occupied many thinkers and writers in the late nineteenth century, Mother Katharine herself did not dwell on theories of race, preferring to act rather than to pontificate. She saw problems and set out to solve them using the tools of her day: education and evangelization. Nuns occupied a unique position in society, but they ultimately remained under the control of a patriarchal hierarchy that policed women. As Drexel founded the Sisters of the Blessed Sacrament, she could not but have been aware of the church's censorship of Mother Mary Francis Cusack and her congregation, the Saint Joseph Sisters of Peace, who actively pursued social justice in the 1880s. Archbishop Michael

---

25 Patricia Wittenberg, *The Rise and Fall of Catholic Religious Orders: A Social Movement Perspective* (Albany: State University of New York Press, 1994), 40, 48.

26 For further explanation on why Catholic women were slow to join in missionary endeavors, see Dana L. Robert, *American Women in Mission: A Social History of Their Thought and Practice* (Macon, GA: Mercer University Press, 1996), 318–29.

27 Kathleen Sprows Cummings, *New Women of the Old Faith: Gender and Catholicism in the Progressive Era* (Chapel Hill: University of North Carolina Press, 2007), 3.

Corrigan of New York City nursed a grudge against Cusack, an outspoken proponent of reform, and had her blackballed from every diocese in the country. Cusack left the congregation, and later she rejected Catholicism.[28] Her book written about the controversy caused a stir in 1889 just as Drexel made the decision to take up the home mission cause.[29] Cusack's case was not unique. Those like Drexel who wished to pursue social justice had to tread carefully. Despite a seemingly innocuous plan to extend Catholic schooling and charity to the disfranchised, the SBS challenged the church to live up to its principles of universality.

Though they considered themselves missionaries, the Sisters of the Blessed Sacrament offered more than catechism classes and rosaries; rather, they used social settlement work and political pressure to institute societal change. In the late nineteenth century, Drexel paid for a California tribe to file court cases to prevent whites from encroaching on their land, and she lobbied Congress through the Bureau of Catholic Indian Missions to preserve native water rights in Arizona and New Mexico. Over time, the SBS grew increasingly active in what Drexel would have termed "temporal" concerns. During the 1920s and 1930s, the SBS partnered with the National Association for the Advancement of Colored People (NAACP) on several early civil rights campaigns. Drexel donated to the Scottsboro Boys Defense Fund and joined the Scottsboro Defense Committee. The SBS also funded and helped plan a NAACP investigation into labor conditions on the Mississippi Flood Control Project and lobbied President Franklin Roosevelt for a more equitable Contractor's Code. In addition, sisters agitated for the Costigan-Wagner Anti-Lynching Act. The SBS maintained that social and economic justice would lead people to God and further the missionary cause. The sisters' canny use of politi-

---

28 For a biography of Cusack, see Dorothy Vidulich, *Peace Pays a Price: A Study of Margaret Anna Cusack, Nun of Kenmare* (Teaneck, NJ: Garden State University Press, 1975).

29 Mary Francis Cusack, *The Nun of Kenmare: An Autobiography* (London: Hodder and Stoughton, 1889). Cusack's book tours took her to both Pittsburgh and Philadelphia in 1889 and 1890. While Drexel was in the Sisters of Mercy convent and would not have heard her speak, the local paper would have been full of reports on Cusack and the scandal. The sisters would have discussed the topic.

cal means to achieve spiritual ends complicates issues of church and state separation. Previous studies of the Sisters of the Blessed Sacrament have glossed over the sisters' unique marriage of the sacred and the worldly. SBS attitudes both reflected and differed from mainstream middle-class American views on race, culture, and education.[30] By placing the emphasis on the activities of religious sisters who affected the daily lives of those they pledged to serve far more than the bishops and priests who waxed eloquently on the subject of the "Indian Plight" or the "Negro Problem," this book examines the differences between lived religion and dogma. In other words, what do dense Latin encyclicals mean on the streets of New Orleans or in hogans on Navajo land?

## Beyond Sanctity: A Need for Honest Appraisal of the SBS

As a canonized Catholic saint, Drexel has attracted several biographers. These works emphasize her holiness and sacrifice.[31] Especially in her lifetime, much of the writing on Mother Katharine and the Sisters of the Blessed Sacrament exalted Drexel's disbursement of her vast fortune but failed to acknowledge her financial and political acumen. A poem in the *Indian Sentinel*, the official magazine of the Bureau of Catholic Indian Missions, epitomizes this tendency:

> She [Drexel] saw it all [the world of privilege], and smiling,
>     turned away
> To those dark souls that sought their deities
> In the weird whispers of the swaying trees
> And led them into light, and taught to pray.

---

30  This book builds on studies by Cyprian David and Christopher Vecsey. While these scholars have delivered a big picture of the relationship of the church and minority populations, much remains to explore, especially in the realm of education: Davis, *The History of Black Catholics in the United States* (New York: Crossroad, 1991); Vecsey, *On the Padres' Trail* (Notre Dame, IN: University of Notre Dame Press, 1996); Vecsey, *The Paths of Kateri's Kin* (Notre Dame, IN: University of Notre Dame Press, 1997); Vecsey, *Where the Two Roads Meet* (Notre Dame, IN: University of Notre Dame Press, 1999).

31  For example, Cheryl C. D. Hughes, *Katharine Drexel: The Riches-to-Rags Story of an American Catholic* Saint (Grand Rapids, MI: Eerdmans, 2014);

Poet Hall Stoner Lusk concluded that change in the treatment of Black and Indigenous people would come about "not by famous deeds / Far heralded; but through the quiet lives / Of those who labor in the common ways, / And follow Love, in patience, where She leads."[32] This idealized vision of a woman who cast aside money to quietly offer religious training to minorities ignores the true nature of what Mother Katharine and the Sisters of the Blessed Sacrament attempted.

The lives of Drexel and her congregation need context. They worked within specific societal constructs of race, religion, reform, and national identity. Unlike many stories about missionaries, in the case of the SBS, the culture that missionaries tried to impose on their students differed from the dominant national culture. As outliers themselves—the SBS were semi-cloistered Catholic women from primarily immigrant backgrounds in society that regarded their lifestyles as alien and unnatural—their attempts to Americanize Black and Indigenous groups complicates our understanding of cultural hegemony. The nuns' vision of Americanization, which stressed loyalty to the traditions of the Roman Catholic Church, contrasted with that of most Americans. The Sisters of the Blessed Sacrament joined traditional religious rhetoric with modern philanthropic practices and political lobbying to reshape the debate on who could claim rights as Catholics and as Americans.

This work features the voices of the sisters' students and their families wherever possible, but it primarily tells the story of the Sisters of the Blessed Sacrament as they struggled to ameliorate the conditions of Black and Indigenous Catholics. Their efforts reflected their conception of the Catholic Church as the Mystical

---

Duffy, *Katharine Drexel*; Katherine Burton, *The Golden Door: The Life of Katharine Drexel* (New York: P. J. Kenedy & Sons, 1957); Ellen Tarry, *Katharine Drexel, Friend of the Oppressed* (San Francisco: Ignatius Press, 1958); Patricia Lynch, SBS, *Sharing the Bread in Service: The Sisters of the Blessed Sacrament, 1891–1991*, 2 vols. (Bensalem, PA: Sisters of the Blessed Sacrament, 1998); Lou Baldwin, *Saint Katharine Drexel: Apostle to the Oppressed* (Philadelphia: Catholic Standard and Times, 2000); and Daniel McSheffery, *Saint Katharine Drexel: Pioneer for Human Rights* (Totowa, NJ: Resurrection Press, 2002).

32   Hall Stoner Lusk, "Mother Katharine," *Indian Sentinel*, 1907, 3.

Body of Christ. While they sometimes copied the techniques of their Protestant counterparts, the sisters had their own ideological framework that guided their actions. The nuns' understanding of religious doctrine lay at the center of their teaching, their visitations, their voting, and their petitioning. A sister best summed up the SBS mission in their magazine: "Driven on by the realization that all men are potential members of the Mystical Christ, the Church, *with divine* daring they push on, striving always to extend and expand and intensify the Kingdom of Christ among these million."[33] The theological conflicts the nuns had with both Protestant Home Mission leaders and government agents led to differences in how the Catholic sisters ran schools, visited the sick, and even campaigned for voting and labor rights.

The year 1891, when Mother Katharine founded the Sisters of the Blessed Sacrament, was filled with debates about racial and social policy both within and outside of the Catholic Church. That year Pope Leo XIII published his encyclical *Rerum Novarum*, which outlined the church's ideas about a just society. It also marked the ordination of Reverend Charles Uncles, SSJ, the first African American to receive Holy Orders in the United States, although he never led a parish because bishops feared to install black priests. Drexel took her vows at roughly the same time Father Francis Craft began the American Congregation of the Order of Saint Benedict, a short-lived, all-Indigenous congregation. The first SBS sisters gathered in their new convent just after the first Mohonk Conference on the Negro Question and in the height of the popularity of the yearly Mohonk Friends of the Indian Conferences. The year before had seen slaughter at Wounded Knee. Relations between whites and both Black and Indigenous people had reached their nadir. The frontier, as Frederick Jackson Turner would report two years later, had closed. American society, both Catholic and otherwise, was at a crossroads. Katharine Drexel responded to the turmoil by asserting a role for Catholic women in the debates. She took the ideas espoused by the papal authorities in Rome and translated them to address specifically American problems in a way that made many

---

33 "Auxiliaries of the Sisters of the Blessed Sacrament," *Mission Fields at Home*, September 1934, 170.

in the church uncomfortable. In forming the Sisters of the Blessed Sacrament, Drexel challenged the church to live up to its ideals. This radical adherence to the tenets of faith combined with Drexel's ample war chest helped the SBS reshape the American Catholic landscape.

CHAPTER 1

# "Go Ye Forth and Teach All Nations"

## Mother Katharine Drexel's Challenge to the Catholic Church

THOUGH A PETITE WOMAN, barely five feet tall, Mother Katharine Drexel's vivacious personality and steely determination made her a transformative figure in American Catholicism. Her leadership defined the congregation she founded, and her long life, spanning nearly a century, enabled her to directly affect each woman who professed vows as a Sister of the Blessed Sacrament for the first fifty years of its existence. In addition, her fortune bankrolled not only the missions of the SBS but also almost every school for Black and Indigenous people in the nation. In a hierarchical system that silenced women, her views on race, education, and home missions shaped church policy.

### Educated for Service

Drexel defies easy characterization. Unlike most Catholic sisters in the United States, who hailed from middle- and working-class families, Katharine Drexel was a member of Philadelphia's upper crust. Her father, Francis Anthony Drexel, was an international financier, a partner in the Houses of Drexel and Morgan, and her mother, Hannah Jane Langstroth Drexel, descended from one of Pennsylvania's founding families. Drexel would later use the financial acumen she learned from her banker father to stretch the budgets of the schools and organizations she supported. Born November 26, 1858, Katharine led a privileged early life filled with private tutors, summer homes, and extensive travel.[1] Despite

---

1 Drexel, named after her paternal grandmother, was christened Catharine Mary. When she entered religious life she took the name Mary Katharine and signed all of her letters "Mother M. Katharine." To avoid confusion, I will refer to her by her religious name throughout.

the family's wealth, however, the Drexels lived relatively simply. Their house at 1503 Walnut Street, just blocks away from tony Rittenhouse Square, was elegant but not as large or as elaborate as their fortune could have purchased, and the girls wore plain, though well-made, clothing. Francis Drexel, the son of an Austrian immigrant, professed a deep commitment to Catholicism. He built a private oratory, or small chapel, in the family's home and spent hours each day in prayer. The elaborate altar, which had previously belonged to the Convent of the Madames de Sacred Heart, became a focal point for the household. Francis also occasionally filled in as the organist at the nearby cathedral.[2]

The example of her parents helped Drexel forge a philanthropic model based equally on professionalism and piety. Katharine's mother, Hannah, a Baptist Quaker, died shortly after her birth. Though she never knew her mother, Katharine and her older sister, Elizabeth, maintained contact with the Langstroth family. Drexel's early experience of navigating her relationship with her Protestant family members proved a substantial advantage when she later ministered to non-Catholics. An early biographer tells a charming anecdote about young Katharine and her sisters struggling with how to participate in the Protestant prayer life at their grandmother's house while remaining loyal to the Catholic Church. Their childish solution was to hold up rosaries while they prayed with the Protestant ministers so everyone would know they were Catholic. While the brandishing of rosaries became a family joke, it demonstrates Drexel's concern with how to be respectful of others and true to one's own beliefs.[3]

In 1860, her father remarried, taking Emma Bouvier as his wife, yoking two powerful and wealthy Catholic families.[4] Katharine and her older sister, Elizabeth, welcomed a third sibling, Louise, in 1863. Francis and Emma Drexel believed in using their wealth for the benefit of society and for the glory of the

---

2 Burton, *Golden Door*, 16–17.
3 Duffy, *Katharine Drexel*, 35.
4 Emma Bouvier Drexel's nephew, John Vernou Bouvier Jr., was the grandfather of Jacqueline Bouvier Kennedy. On their honeymoon John F. Kennedy and his new bride stopped at the convent for Mother Katharine's blessing.

church. Francis exhorted his wife to do good works: "God has also bestowed on us abundance. Continue your charities in His name. Be the dispenser of His gifts and let us also extend the charity of thought toward those who offend us."[5] Both heeded the call to service.

Despite her marriage to a multimillionaire, Emma Bouvier Drexel kept a well-appointed but simple house and taught her daughters to serve their community. Mrs. Drexel established a home-based charity she called The Dorcas, after the woman in the book of Acts who performed good deeds, and she earned the nickname "Lady Bountiful." Every week people gathered outside the gates of the family home eager for her assistance. Katharine Drexel reported that her stepmother did not simply dole out cash but rather kept careful records of her spending. Like many nineteenth-century philanthropists, she had a well-defined sense of the worthy and unworthy poor.[6] She hired Mary Bilger as a caseworker to investigate claims and to make sure recipients used the aid properly. If the caseworker found legitimate need, she would issue a ticket to the beneficiary. This ticket could then be taken to Emma Drexel, who would "try to devise a means of giving the needed help right then and there—a grocery order or an order for coal or rent, or shoes." She also kept meticulous records documenting her gifts. Reflecting on her mother's charity, Drexel noted that when the same people repeatedly returned for help, "Mama would be able to inquire and the records gave her the information she needed. In this way Mama took a personal interest in them. And they knew it and she was able to direct them. She got to know them and know their needs. And her sympathy was unwearying."[7] Emma Drexel spent as much as $30,000 per year on her Dorcas

---

    5    Duffy, *Katharine Drexel*, 37.

    6    Many Charity Organization Societies (COS) spent considerable time differentiating between the worthy and unworthy poor, often based on adherence to white middle-class values systems. While Emma Drexel operated on her own, she was clearly influenced by COS policies. For more, see Brent Ruswick, *Almost Worthy: The Poor, Paupers, and the Science of Charity in America, 1877–1917* (Bloomington: Indiana University Press, 2013).

    7    Katharine Drexel, "Oral Memoir, November 29, 1935," quoted in Mary J. Oates, *The Catholic Philanthropic Tradition in America* (Bloomington: Indiana University Press, 1995), 126.

work.[8] Shortly before her death in 1883, Emma Drexel told her daughters she expected them to continue her philanthropic work and firmly reminded them, "Don't let the poor have cold feet."[9] Drexel carefully observed her parents and incorporated both their eagerness to offer assistance and their dislike of profligate spending into her own philanthropic style. From them she developed a belief in systematic charity and demanded full accountability, occasionally irritating priests and nuns unused to philanthropists who required receipts.

In addition to valuing piety and charity, Drexel's family emphasized education. Instructed by private tutors, young Katharine studied logic, moral philosophy, literature, art, music, religion, and history and learned how to read classical Latin as well as literary French. She read classics by Chaucer, Shakespeare, Pope, and Tolstoy and studied American and European history.[10] Emma Bouvier Drexel also insisted that her daughters share their education. For many years, the three sisters organized a Sunday school for the poor as well as the children of their household servants. An early biographer told a story of young Katharine selecting prizes for the Sunday School students but refusing to give them to those who had not put in enough effort to satisfy her. Even as a child she took accountability and efficiency seriously.[11]

As befitted an elite young woman, Drexel augmented her education with overseas travel. The family crossed the Atlantic several times, combining the Grand Tour with pilgrimages to Catholic holy sites. Drexel also took extensive trips across the American West. During these journeys she witnessed the plight of the Indigenous population. She read Helen Hunt Jackson's *Century of Dishonor* and Stanley Pumphery's "Indian Civilization," which fur-

---

[8] Cheryl C. D. Hughes, *Katharine Drexel: The Riches-to-Rags Story of an American Saint* (Grand Rapids, MI: Eerdmans, 2014), 25.

[9] "The Sisters of the Blessed Sacrament for Indians and Colored People," *Indian Sentinel*, 1907, 6.

[10] Nicole Farmer Hurd, "Master Art of a Saint" (Ph.D. diss., University of Virginia), 84–89, and Lynch, *Sharing the Bread in Service*, 1:10–12.

[11] Ellen Tarry, *St. Katharine Drexel: Friend of the Oppressed* (San Francisco: Ignatius Press, 1958), 29.

ther cemented her interest in Indigenous ministry.[12] In the early 1890s, people in the Catholic community compared Drexel to Helen Hunt Jackson, stating, "She walks in Mrs. Jackson's shoes, and fills them too."[13] When she spoke to the Catholic Students Mission Crusade at their convention in Dayton, Ohio, in 1921, she explained her call to service: "Was it when turning over the pages of U.S. History to learn as you of the landing of the Spaniards, the English & the French in our country and their trade with the Indians; or was it when, later on, I read of the Negro kidnapped & brought to this country against his will that my soul questioned was there no real obligation incumbent on a Xian [Christian] people—amongst whom I was one—to evangelize these pagans in whose midst a Divine Providence had placed us?" Turning from civics to religion, she continued, "Or, was it at the High Mass on Sundays in the Cathedral of St. Peter and Paul's in Philadelphia when my eyes rested on the huge gilt letters over the rear arch 'Thou art a vessel of election to carry My name amongst the gentiles'?" Drexel further pressed the students at the Crusade convention to explore what their religion said about racial difference, when she wondered, "Or was it in reading the Sunday gospel, 'Go ye forth and teach all nations' *all nations*, & therefore the Indian and Negro—that the grace of God touched my young heart as it has touched yours, with a sense of the privilege it is to have any part in bringing the Sacred Heart to the World and the World to the Sacred Heart?"[14]

Her experience first reading about and then viewing firsthand the effects of colonization and slavery profoundly shaped her worldview. She believed whites owed a debt to Indigenous and

---

12   Helen Hunt Jackson, *Century of Dishonor: A Sketch of the U.S. Government's Dealings with Some of the Tribes* (1889; repr. Boston: Roberts Brothers, 1895); Stanley Pumphery, *Indian Civilization: A Lecture by Stanley Pumphery with an Introduction by John G. Whittier* (Philadelphia: Bible and Tract Distributing Society, 1877; repr. Ann Arbor: University of Michigan Library, 2005). Information on Drexel's reading comes from Hurd, "Master Art of a Saint," 89.

13   F. M. Edselas, "Visit to Ramona's Home: A Typical Ranch," *Catholic World*, September 1893, 790.

14   Mother Katharine Drexel, MMK Writings 21, no. 3058, Archives of the Sisters of the Blessed Sacrament, Bensalem, Pennsylvania (hereafter ASBS).

Black Americans that could be repaid through Catholic education.[15] That Black and Indigenous people would have preferred land, money, and the overhaul of societal structures that contributed to their oppression is without question, but Drexel believed that her faith was the greatest gift she could bestow.

### Early Philanthropy

Encouraged by her parents to embark on philanthropic work of her own, she began supporting the efforts of Catholic missionaries on Indian reservations. One of her first behests, made when she was twenty-five, illustrated her belief that the poor deserved beauty and quality. During an 1883 trip to the West, she noticed that the Our Lady of Grace Chapel in Tacoma lacked a statue of the Blessed Mother. Upon her return to Philadelphia, she sent a large statue worth $100, more than a working-class family would earn in a month, to the mission. Father Hylebos, the priest, thought the statue too fine for the chapel. General Red Spot, one of the Puyallup who attended Our Lady of Grace, disagreed and responded, "No, this big statue will speak better to our hearts than a little statue, and now we can think better of Our Mother in Heaven."[16]

What began as sporadic donations turned into a philanthropic career after Francis Drexel's 1885 death. His passing made Katharine and her sisters some of the nation's wealthiest heiresses, and all three dedicated the money to charitable causes. Francis Drexel's will contained several unusual stipulations that would affect the future of Sisters of the Blessed Sacrament. He died with a fortune valued at roughly $15.6 million.[17] The estate immediately distributed $1.5 million to various, primarily Catholic, charities, and the remainder went into a trust for the three sisters. Each received a third of the income of the fund each year, but they

---

15 Gwen Bristow, "Little Girl of Long Ago Grows Up to Be Revered Founder of Religious Order," *New Orleans Times Picayune*, October 15, 1932, 1.
16 Quoted in Baldwin, *Saint Katharine Drexel*, 50.
17 In 2022 dollars, this would have been the equivalent of roughly $438,000,000—calculated by multiplying the original sum by the percentage increase of the Consumer Price Index. As the money was put in trust with the daughters drawing only interest, it increased substantially over the course of Drexel's life.

could not draw upon the principal. Aimed at repelling gold-digging suitors, the will specified that if there were no heirs upon the death of the last sister, the money would revert to the charities named in the will. This did, in fact, occur.[18]

With the money from their father's estate, Katharine, Elizabeth, and Louise established a Chair of Moral Theology at the Catholic University of America in honor of Francis Drexel. In addition, they built St. Francis Industrial School in Eddington, Pennsylvania, with the goal of training older orphan boys, both white and black, in a trade. Drexel's older sister, Elizabeth, kept close tabs on St. Francis Industrial School, and her younger sister, Louise, started funding Catholic missionary work to Black Americans, primarily through the Society of Saint Joseph, or the Josephites, a congregation of priests dedicated to serving Black communities. Katharine Drexel first chose to work with the embryonic Bureau of Catholic Indian Missions (BCIM), and later Louise convinced her to expand her charitable focus to include Black Americans.

### Discerning a Vocation

At the same time, Drexel experienced a call to religious life. In 1887, while on a European tour, the Drexel sisters had an audience with Pope Leo XIII, who nudged her toward a religious vocation. As she pled with the pope to send missionaries to the American West, Leo XIII looked at her and replied, "Why not become a missionary yourself, my child?"[19] His words troubled her. Later she credited this conversation with being "the germ which gave life to the Sisters of the Blessed Sacrament," but at the time, Katharine Drexel told no one except for her spiritual director, Bishop James O'Connor of Nebraska, whom she had first met when he presided

---

18  Drexel's older sister, Elizabeth Drexel Smith, died in childbirth in 1890, and her younger sister, Louise Drexel Morrell, died childless in 1943. After Mother Katharine Drexel's death, the Sisters of the Blessed Sacrament lost much of their dependable funding; indeed, it was for this reason that Drexel put the clause "If I live" upon all financial contracts she entered.

19  Mother Katharine Drexel, "Carroll Club Talk, February 1923," MMK Talks, H10A box 30, folder 14, ASBS.

over a parish near her family's summer home near Torresdale, Pennsylvania.[20] For several years they corresponded as she wrestled with her vocation. O'Connor repeatedly dissuaded her from entering the convent and instead encouraged her to make her own private vow of chastity while continuing her public philanthropy. The bishop claimed she could do more good outside of the convent. On March 5, 1887, he wrote, "You are making bountiful provision for the most abandoned and forlorn of God's creatures on this continent. You have the means, you have the brains, you have the freedom of action necessary to do this work well." He believed that subjecting herself to the discipline of convent life would thwart her plans to aid home missions. O'Connor cautioned, "In religion, you could direct your income to this or some other good purpose, but your talents and your energies would be directed by others."[21] Anne M. Butler has argued that his reluctance to see Drexel enter a congregation stemmed from the fact that he did not want the Bureau of Catholic Indian Missions to lose her contributions.[22] Traditionally women who entered the religious life had to appoint an administrator for their worldly affairs. Before changes to canon law in 1908, new sisters relinquished any money they brought into the convent, such as a dowry, into a common fund controlled by the Superior General.[23] Had Drexel entered an existing congregation of sisters, as she originally wanted to do, she would have lost control of her fortune. To O'Connor and other clergy who relied on her generosity, Drexel's decision to enter a convent might have proved financially disastrous.

After wavering for several years, Drexel finally wrote her mentor on November 26, 1888, asserting her autonomy: "It appears to me, Reverend Father, that I am not obliged to *submit* my judgment to yours, as I have been doing for two years, for I

---

20  Ibid.

21  James O'Connor to Katharine Drexel (March 5, 1887), quoted in Duffy, *Katharine Drexel*, 127.

22  Anne Butler, "Mother Katharine Drexel: Spiritual Visionary for the West," in *By Grit and Grace: Eleven Women Who Shaped the American West*, ed. Glenda Riley and Richard W. Etulain (Golden, CO: Fulcrum, 1997), 198–220.

23  For a more detailed explanation of nun's fiduciary rights, see Fintan Geser, OSB, *The Canon Law Governing Communities of Sisters* (St. Louis: B. Herder, 1938), 211–30.

feel so sad in doing it, because the world cannot give me peace, so restless because my heart is not rested in God."[24] O'Connor acquiesced to her desire to enter the religious life, but he insisted that rather than join an existing group she should found her own institute for the benefit of Black and Indigenous people. At first Drexel resisted. She still felt called to the contemplative life, especially because those congregations received Communion every day, a rarity among active orders.[25] O'Connor countered that she could institute daily Communion into the rule of the new order and assured her, "An order established for the Negroes and Colored people will make a more direct and economical use of your money than the Indian Bureau could. Even as a foundress, you will have your faults, but God, not you, will do the work."[26] With these reassurances, Drexel acquiesced. Working in conjunction with Archbishop Patrick John Ryan of Philadelphia, O'Connor and Drexel drew up plans for the Sisters of the Blessed Sacrament for Indians and Colored People.[27]

On May 6, 1889, Drexel took the first step into her new life by entering the Sisters of Mercy Convent in Pittsburgh. After a six-month postulancy, a probationary period mandated by canon law, she began her novitiate following an elaborate reception ceremony on November 7, 1889. Wearing a sumptuous cream satin wedding dress with a train that had to be carried by two children and an exquisitely cut diamond ring, she took her first vows and trained for the role of Superior General of a new congregation.[28] The elab-

---

24 Katherine Drexel to James O'Connor, November 26, 1888, quoted in Duffy, *Katharine Drexel*, 129.

25 Contemplative nuns spend their time in prayer rather than working as teachers or nurses. These sisters often live cloistered lives, limiting their exposure to the outside world. Prior to reforms in 1901, canon law held contemplative sisters to be the only true nuns. Women belonging to active orders that did not observe cloister were considered sisters, rather than nuns.

26 Drexel to O'Connor, February 24, 1889, quotation in Hurd, "Master Art of a Saint," 75. O'Connor to Drexel, February 28, 1889, quoted in Hurd, "Master Art of a Saint," 77.

27 Archbishop Patrick John Ryan (1831–1911) served as a mentor for Drexel, especially during the early years of the congregation's formation.

28 Until the approval of the SBS Rule in 1907, Drexel was known as the Mother Superior of the congregation, but after receiving papal approbation, she

orate profession, followed by a banquet for three hundred guests, drew attention from the nation's secular and religious press.[29]

A few days after Drexel's reception into the convent, Archbishop Ryan addressed a crowd of priests and bishops gathered in Baltimore to celebrate the one-hundred-year anniversary of the establishment of the American hierarchy, a commemoration of the century that had passed since U.S. Catholics were granted their own bishop, rather than relying on foreign governance. In his speech, he condemned the poor treatment of Black and Indigenous people, calling it "the two great blots upon American civilization," and he proposed that the church "resolve to make reparation for these shortcomings of the past." Ryan believed that Drexel's entrance into religious life offered the Catholic Church a way to atone for not doing more to end slavery or to protect Indigenous people from losing their land. As he described Drexel's reception ceremony, he made her a symbol of self-sacrifice: "She knelt before the illumined altar of the God of all the races of men, and offered her great fortune, her life, her love, her hopes, that until the grave shall receive her, all she possess now or shall possess in the future may belong to God and to the Indian and Colored Races." He added, "She seemed the prophetess of reparation and conciliation between the races. Silently she offered her young heart to God and only sighed that he may accept the sacrifice, and that, until the grave shall receive her, all she possesses or shall possess may belong to God and to His despised and neglected ones."[30] Ryan's emphasis on Mother Katharine's financial sacrifices is typical for male clergy of the period. Drexel, on the other hand, never focused on the fortune she donated. She stressed that she merely gave up what all sisters were called to sacrifice: everything. She would have considered her call to service in home mis-

---

was known as the Superior General. Drexel, always looking for ways to reuse material, had her reception wedding dress turned into priest's vestments for holy days. These vestments are stored in the Archives of the Sisters of the Blessed Sacrament.

29   "Took the White Veil: Miss Drexel Enters the Convent of the Sisters of Mercy," *New York Times*, November 8, 1889, 1.

30   "The Sisters of the Blessed Sacrament for Indians and Colored People," *Queen's Work*, March 1919, 61–62.

sions far more important and more radical than giving up a life of luxury, and she bristled when newspapers referred to her as the "millionaire nun." Despite public misconceptions, she threw herself into the establishment of a new missionary congregation.

## Founding a New Order

On February 12, 1891, in honor of Lincoln's birthday, Drexel took her vows as the head of the Sisters of the Blessed Sacrament for Indians and Colored People. She originally suggested the name the Sisters of the Blessed Sacrament, but Archbishop Ryan added *for Indians and Colored People* to clarify their mission.[31] The Sisters of the Blessed Sacrament operated as a diocesan congregation under the Archdiocese of Philadelphia until their Rule received Roman approbation in 1907 and it was recognized as a canonical congregation subject to Roman, rather than diocesan, control.[32] The name reflects Mother Katharine's passion for the Eucharist and her intention to spread the sacrament to all people. The Eucharist, according to Drexel, had to be shared. In her vows, she swore "to be the mother and servant of the Indian and Negro races according to the rule of the Sisters of the Blessed Sacrament; and not to undertake any work which would lead to the neglect or abandonment of the Indian and Colored races."[33] The rule of the congregation stipulated that in addition to working on their own spiritual perfection all sisters "shall, by an apostolate of prayer and work, zealously endeavor to procure, through Jesus in the Blessed Sacrament, living temples for His Divinity amongst the Indian and Negro races."[34] Drexel also stated that she and her fellow sisters were to "train the youth of these races, without distinction of religion, to become self-sustaining men

---

31 Because they later dropped "For Indians and Colored People," for clarity I refer to the organization as simply the Sisters of the Blessed Sacrament.

32 Becoming a canonical congregation meant that the sisters answered directly to Rome and were not subject to the whims of local bishops. In general, this meant that they had less male oversight. Many congregations sought canonical status as a way of maintaining autonomy. See James J. Kenneally, *The History of American Catholic Women* (New York: Crossroad, 1990), 43.

33 Duffy, *Katharine Drexel*, 169.

34 John Tracy Ellis, ed., *Documents of American Catholic History* (Wilmington, DE: Michael Glazier, 1987), 2:575.

and women."[35] Cloaked in traditional theological language, this rule offered something radically new. While some of the novelty can be attributed to the spirit of reform sweeping the nation as well as a nascent Catholic revivalism, the boldness of the SBS stemmed from Drexel herself, who had both the audacity and the means to realize her vision. This cross-cultural mission set the Sisters of the Blessed Sacrament apart from other women religious. While some other groups had founded schools for Black students, most did it as a supplement to their work with white children. Many of the schools set up to educate Black students lasted only a short time; for example, the Sisters of St. Joseph of Carandolet established a school for freed slaves in St. Louis in 1836, but they had to close it shortly afterward amidst pressure from the white community. In fact, most nuns could only afford to educate poor or non-white students if they also operated academies for the children of the elite or if they taught music and offered art lessons on the side.[36] Drexel's fortune allowed the Sisters of the Blessed Sacrament to put their entire focus on the most needy student populations. The promise to serve young people regardless of their religious preference created a stir with some in the hierarchy who wanted to reserve Catholic education for Catholics. The clause about wishing to empower "self-sustaining men and women" would eventually lead the SBS to fight for economic justice.

Another factor differentiated the SBS from others who worked in Black and Indigenous communities: the congregation did not form as a subsidiary to a male order. For example, the

---

35 "American Foundation of Religious Orders: The Congregation of the Sisters of the Blessed Sacrament for Indians and Colored People," *American Ecclesiastical Review* 8 (January 1898): 7.

36 The first Ursuline sisters who arrived in New Orleans in 1727 offered classes to African Americans and Indians in the evenings after conducting their classes for the white girls. While many groups such as the Sisters of St. Joseph, Sisters of the Sacred Heart, and Sisters of Mercy did operate schools for minorities, this work did not provide enough financial support to the sisters for them to devote themselves to it full time. In addition, particularly after Reconstruction, the work could bring threats of physical violence or financial ruin. See Emily Clark, *Masterless Mistresses: The New Orleans Ursulines and the Development of a New World Society, 1727–1834* (Chapel Hill: University of North Carolina Press, 2007), and Coburn and Smith, *Spirited Lives*.

Josephite Fathers brought the Franciscan Sisters of Mill Hill to the United States to share in their work in Black churches and school, but the sisters remained in many ways tied to the order of priests. The German missionaries the Society of the Divine Word (SVD) also worked with the Missionary Congregation Servants of the Holy Spirit, a group of nuns that was founded in 1889 by the SVD Superior Arnold Janssen to provide laborers for Divine Word missions.[37] The Servants of the Holy Spirit did not obtain independence from the SVD until well into the twentieth century. Drexel's congregation, on the other hand, had both the freedom and the financial security to make their own decisions about which mission fields to enter, though they still had to rely on the good will of the local bishops.[38]

## Personalism, Not Punditry

Though she dedicated her life and fortune to aiding Black and Indigenous people, Mother Katharine's own thoughts on race prove elusive. As the Superior General of the Sisters of the Blessed Sacrament, she filled her days with the minutiae of administering dozens of schools for minority students, and she left pontificating to others. Her vast correspondence includes details about the best type of stuffing for the mattresses at boarding schools, insurance regulations, fire safety, and proper methods of ridding a school of rats, but it lacks a concrete explanation of her racial ideology. Still, while her ideas on race were not revolutionary, they repre-

---

37 For a history of the Society of the Divine Word in the United States, see Ernest Brandewie, *In the Light of the Word: Divine Word Missionaries in North America* (Maryknoll, NY: Orbis, 2000).

38 Though the SBS became a canonical institution, subject to the pope rather than to a diocesan ordinary, the bishops of each diocese had control over which religious congregations operated in their domain. Local bishops had to invite the sisters in and ultimately retained control over decisions about building new churches and oratories. The bishop also had the authority to make visitations and to express concern about internal governance. Thus, while Drexel's money gave her a degree of freedom, she still had to make sure she had the support of the hierarchy in order to implement her ambitious plans. For details on the authority of bishops over sisters, see D. I. Lanslots, OSB, *Handbook of Canon Law for Congregations of Women under Simple Vows* (New York: Fr. Pustet, 1909), 20, 57, 137–49.

sented a new departure for the Catholic Church. Mother Katharine was one of the first to apply Catholic social teaching to minority communities, and her wealth helped her ideas gain greater acceptance in the church.

Mother Katharine addressed religion more than race in her correspondence; she believed both Black and Indigenous people needed education and evangelization. She repeatedly called the sisters "instruments of God in the Christianization of these people."[39] She also frequently referred to owing a debt of service to Black Americans who had been thrust into slavery. She wrote, "The 12 million Colored in the U.S. are here just simply because about 4 generations ago white men iniquitously kidnapped them from their native Africa, huddled them into slave ships and sold them here into bondage." In response, she believed, "Surely we Americans of the true Church owe this dark Race that which God in His mercy gave to us, the knowledge of the True Church. Our Lord's own words are: 'Go Ye forth and teach all nations.' It is true these words were said by our Lord to the Apostles; but we can all be co-operator with it in the salvation of Souls, of these souls."[40] She liked to use this verse from Matthew's Gospel to explain her mission, stressing that teaching *all nations* meant extending Catholic education to racial minorities.[41]

Drexel wanted to save souls, but there is evidence that she also saw the missions as a means of radical racial assimilation. In 1935, she wrote, "If the people in the United States knew of the possibilities of these missions. . . . The Indians as such will pass away—red, less red, less red, white. The same of the Colored, black, less black, less black, white. As in myself there is some Anglo-Saxon, some Roman. There are not so many pure blood

---

[39] Mother Katharine Drexel, "Since the Beginning," Collated Writings, 1922 or later, H 10J86, vol. 28, fol. 1, ASBS.

[40] Mother Katharine Drexel, "A Short Note on Needing Sisters to Bring Knowledge of the True Church to the Negro," MMK Talks, 1920, H10J 8b, vol. 28, fol. 112–13, ASBS.

[41] The full verse of Matthew 28:19 reads, "Go, therefore, and make disciples of all nations, baptizing them in the name of the Father, and of the Son, and of the Holy Spirit, teaching them to observe all that I have commanded you. And behold, I am with you always, until the end of the age": *New American Bible*.

people of any one race. Our ancestors were, but they are dead, and yours are too."[42] This statement belies the fact that she spent many years of her life trying to preserve the culture of Black and Indigenous groups, but her advocacy of interracial marriage highlights her fundamental (and highly radical for the 1930s) belief in the inherent equality of the soul and the unifying power of the sacrament. Not even her fellow Catholic supporters on racial issues such as Jesuit John LaFarge or Josephite John T. Gillard would have argued for intermarriage.[43] In a similar vein, in 1902, she wrote about her desire to educate Indigenous people "so that they too may be fit to intermarry with good Catholic whites, and not the worst white element." She wanted them to be "mingled as Normans and Saxons were, so that future generations may not be able to discern difference of Nationality but that mingled into one Nation all may serve God on earth and praise Him eternally in heaven."[44] This statement would have been highly controversial—indeed illegal in many states—for the first years of the twentieth century. Most likely her words are less a plan to form one unified race than a reflection on the SBS belief that "everyone has an immortal soul made to the image and likeness of God" and "shares in the common dignity of a human being regardless of his nationality or race."[45]

---

42   Mother Katharine Drexel, "Talk to Sisters," ca. 1935, H 10A, box 30, fol. 16, ASBS.

43   LaFarge took pains to point out that while the Catholic Church did not technically oppose intermarriage, it cautioned couples to avoid it because of the possibility for family and legal tensions. He also suggested that most African Americans had no interest in marrying whites. See John LaFarge, SJ, *The Race Question and the Negro: A Study of the Catholic Doctrine on Interracial Justice* (New York: Longmans, Green, 1943). Gillard, ironically, did not favor intermarriage but talked about the superiority of mulattoes. John T. Gillard, SSJ, *The Catholic Church and the American Negro* (Baltimore: St. Joseph's Society Press, 1929), 253.

44   Mother Katharine Drexel, SBS, to My very dear daughters in the B[lessed] S[acrament], October 15, 1902, in *Writings of Katharine Drexel*, vol. 2, no. 144, ASBS, quoted in Anne M. Butler, Michael E. Engh, SJ, and Thomas W. Spalding, CFX, eds., *The Frontiers and Catholic Identities* (Maryknoll, NY: Orbis, 1999), 71.

45   Mother Katharine Drexel to Sister M. Dolores, *Annals of the SBS*, vol. 27, 1932, 177, ASBS.

In any event, Mother Katharine favored a personalist approach to racial issues. She and those in her congregation identified needs, and, if money and personnel allowed, they acted. For much of the congregation's existence, the sisters aimed not at restructuring society but at combating and ameliorating the effects of racism. They saw problems and addressed them, leaving lengthy discussion for others. For example, in 1920, when the Divine Word Fathers proposed building a seminary for Black men who wished to study for the priesthood, male clerics hemmed and hawed and discussed theological ramifications. Archbishop Giovanni Bonzano, the apostolic delegate to the United States, refused to commit to the proposal. Cardinal James Gibbons expressed only limited sympathy. Father John Dorsey, a Black priest, declined to endorse the endeavor because of his hatred for segregation and his worries about the theological implications of the move. Katharine Drexel, on the other hand, pledged $2,000 for the project, insisting that the Divine Word Missionaries (DVM) open within the year. They broke ground in Greenville, Mississippi, and the seminary opened its doors on Drexel's schedule. In 1923, when prejudice forced the seminary out of town, Drexel provided much of the funding to move it to Bay St. Louis, Mississippi. When it looked like white priests and bishops would be unwilling to employ the first graduating class of priests, Mother Katharine provided most of the funds to build the priests their own church, Immaculate Heart of Mary, in the Diocese of Lafayette.[46] Some have viewed this practicality as acquiescence to Jim Crow. For example, James B. Bennett asserts that the SBS "contributed to the segregated and inferior position of the black church members."[47] As a woman in a male-dominated, hierarchical institution, however, Mother Katharine did not have the ability to integrate seminaries. She did, however, have the money and influence to make sure that Black men had the opportunity to enter the priesthood at a time when most Catholics balked at the proposition.

---

46 Stephen Ochs, *Desegregating the Altar: The Josephites and the Struggle for Black Priests, 1871–1960* (Baton Rouge: Louisiana State University Press, 1990), 249. For more on the seminary itself, see Brandewie, *In the Light of the Word*, 216–23.

47 James B. Bennett, *Religion and the Rise of Jim Crow in New Orleans* (Princeton, NJ: Princeton University Press, 2005), 200.

## The First Sisters

To accomplish her goals, Drexel needed to attract women to the cause. On November 9, 1889, Archbishop Ryan announced Drexel's plans at a bishops' meeting in Baltimore and asked his fellow bishops to advertise the SBS in their dioceses. Drexel personally corresponded with each potential applicant and gathered sacramental certificates, medical information, and letters of recommendation for the young women. According to canon law, all potential sisters had to be at least fifteen years old, the product of a legitimate birth, and in possession of good morals.[48] The SBS also refused to consider sisters over the age of thirty, as the work would be physically demanding. In addition to professing a true vocation, those women interested in joining had to possess a "zeal for the Indian and Colored races."[49] Mother Katharine asked applicants two important questions: whether they would "object to tending and washing Indian and colored children" or nursing them if they were contagious. Those who had problems with those tasks were summarily dismissed. When selecting sisters, she carefully noted, "If there is any prejudice in the mind we must uproot it, or it will pull us down."[50]

Unlike Drexel, who grew up in the top tier of Philadelphia society, the first sisters who joined her hailed from less gilded surroundings. Several of the first community members came from the Sisters of Mercy's Pittsburgh house where Drexel had completed her novitiate. The Sisters of Mercy loaned the fledgling congregation the novice mistress Mother Inez Casey and another sister, the cook.[51] They began with ten novices (Sr. Magdalen, Sr. Joseph, Sr. Aloysius Kavanaugh, Sr. Evangelist Gillespie, Sr. Margaret Mary

---

48  Geser, *Canon Law Governing Communities of Sisters*, 195–209.
49  "Sisters of the Blessed Sacrament for Indians and Colored People," *Indian Sentinel*, 1907, 12.
50  Hoy, *Good Hearts: Catholic Sisters in Chicago's Past*, 89.
51  The novice mistress has the critical job of training novices in religious life. For the two-year period of the novitiate, the novice mistress makes sure the young women under her charge learn the congregation's rule and master course work in theology and education. The novice mistress also makes sure the novices truly understand their vocations; Geser, *Canon Law Governing Communities of Sisters*, 225.

Thomas, Sr. Bechmans Duffy, Sr. M. Patrick Flaherty, Sr. Francis Xavier McCann, Sr. M. James Ottis, and Sr. Veronica Gallagher), who had started their training with the Sisters of Mercy, and three postulants, who had not yet received the habit (Agnes Gillen, Margaret de Boben, and Margaret Butler).[52] Only after a rigorous three-year novitiate could sisters profess their first temporary vows. Following these first vows the newly professed would enter a five-year probationary period before taking perpetual vows.[53] This lengthy trial period surpassed the recommended novitiate of one to two years and allowed novices to gain thorough training in both religious life and teaching methods.[54]

In the first formative years of the SBS, forty-one women entered, but only twenty-two made perpetual vows. These women ranged in age from eighteen to thirty-three and came primarily from Irish and German immigrant families, though only three of them had been born abroad themselves. Roughly 60 percent of the women had held jobs prior to entering the convent, and only one had a college degree. Two had worked in stores, five had been live-in servants for families, two had labored in mills, and four had earned money as seamstresses. Though Mother Katharine made sure they came from respectable, churchgoing, families, as a group they hailed from the middling classes.[55]

At first Drexel did not insist on rigorous academic preparation for the sisters. In 1889, she wrote Bishop O'Connor, "It does not require a high order or education to teach Indians. Indeed, I think *good* and simple souls with humble pious, solid faith do best in

---

52  Lynch, *Sharing the Bread in Service*, 1:50.

53  Elinor Tong Dehey, *Religious Orders of Women in the United States: Accounts of Their Origin and of Their Most Important Institutions* (Hammond, IN: W. Conkey, 1913), 298–306.

54  According to a study done in the 1940s, sister training before WWII was frequently far too brief, and novice teachers were sent out woefully unprepared with "most of her professional training acquired by learning to do by doing." See Sr. Bertrande Meyers, *The Education of Sisters: A Plan for Integrating the Religious, Social, Cultural and Professional Training of Sisters* (New York: Sheed and Ward, 1941), 6–14.

55  Patricia Lynch, "Collective Biography: Founding Women of the Sisters of the Blessed Sacrament," *U.S. Catholic Historian* 10, nos. 1/2 (1991/1992): 102.

these missions."[56] She did, however, enroll sisters in courses at the Drexel Institute, an industrial college founded by her uncle, Anthony Drexel.[57] The first SBS took basic normal (teacher-training) courses in addition to classes in domestic art and science. In general, with the exception of Drexel and one or two others who had attended academies, the early sisters did not have advanced academic preparation and seemed content to rely on good hearts to reach their students.[58] In this respect, however, they did not differ from other nineteenth-century women setting out to teach, particularly in frontier locations, very few of whom had high school diplomas, much less college degrees. As late as 1910, only 5 percent of teachers had more than a high school education.[59] With the creation of the Sisters' College attached to the Catholic University of America, Drexel took new interest in advanced education. She attended classes for several years at the new college and sent many of the sisters. By the 1920s, most sisters pursued both secondary and tertiary education.

Though the first sisters did not have a lot of formal education, Mother Katharine made it clear that she sought high-quality sisters. The work demanded "the most refined qualities of temper and intelligence" and women who were "animated by the lowly spirit of Christ."[60] In a call for SBS vocations printed in a Franciscan magazine, Father Anselm Weber mocked the notion that nuns were meant to teach in fancy academies, asking potential novices to consider, "Do you really believe it to be so immensely pleasing to God to teach these distinguished ladies to speak Italian, and to

---

56  Drexel to O'Connor, November 30, 1889, quoted in Hurd, "The Master Art of a Saint," 99.

57  The Drexel Institute featured a College of Home Economics where students took classes in nutrition, food preparation and handling, and other fields preparing women for service to "the kitchen, children, and Church." For more on the Institute, see A. Creese, *A. J. Drexel (1826–1893) and His Industrial University* (Princeton, NJ: Newcomen Society, 1949).

58  Hurd, "Master Art of a Saint," 100–111.

59  Mary Hurlbut Cordier, *Schoolwomen of the Prairies and Plains: Personal Narratives from Iowa, Kansas, and Nebraska, 1860s–1920s* (Albuquerque: University of New Mexico Press, 1992), 46.

60  Anselm Weber, "The Sisters of the Blessed Sacrament for Indians and Colored People," *St. Anthony's Messenger*, January 1899, 266.

pray in French? To teach them natural history, physics, psychology, logic and the geography of Father India?"[61] Instead, he suggested, serving with the Sisters of the Blessed Sacrament served a more crucial purpose in the church. Though they lacked accomplishments such as Italian and French, the first sisters possessed an interest in teaching and learning. Ironically, Mother Katharine herself struggled in the classroom. During her novitiate with the Sisters of Mercy she had difficulty controlling her students. In 1890 she wrote an account of a particularly disastrous lesson when a little boy continually blew a whistle as she tried to talk and then ran away from her when she attempted to restore order. Sensing her lowered guard, the entire class belted out a loud hymn. With the young nun's attention diverted, another child kindled a small fire in the classroom. A more experienced sister had to rush in to calm the storm.[62] Despite Mother Katharine's own difficulties in classroom management, however, most sisters left St. Elizabeth's convent with solid pedagogical training.

The first Sisters of the Blessed Sacrament claimed disparate backgrounds and different spiritual gifts, but they all had one thing in common: they were all white. Drexel originally considered forming an integrated congregation, but after discussions with her sister Louise, her brother-in-law Edward Morrell, and Archbishop Ryan, she came to the conclusion that it would be too difficult, especially as laws in the South prevented whites and Black people from occupying the same buildings. She also feared that discipline could get awkward with members of different races judging one another.[63] Drexel did, however, support the idea that Black and Indigenous women could participate fully in religious life, something hotly debated in the late nineteenth century. When the head of the Josephites, Father John Slattery, echoed old myths about Black women's alleged hypersexuality and suggested that Black women had neither the discipline nor the moral fiber to enter the state of religious life, Drexel fired back, "They are sent to do the work of the religious, without the graces or protection

---

61  Ibid., 267.
62  Drexel to O'Connor, January 14, 1890, quotation in Duffy, *Katharine Drexel*, 154–56.
63  Lynch, *Sharing the Bread in Service*, 1:41–42, 68–70.

of the religious. It is too much work without the spiritual merit and protection the religious life affords. If it be possible—as seems to be the case—that the Colored girl may live in religion, why should she not do so, and enjoy its advantages?"[64]

As early as 1893, the Sisters of the Blessed Sacrament accepted their first Indigenous novice, Sister Elizabeth Burton, a Seneca, and they continued to accept the occasional Indigenous applicant. They also aided in the establishment of the Oblate Sisters of the Blessed Sacrament, a congregation of Indigenous women located at their mission in Marty, South Dakota, in 1935. The congregation did not accept Black novices until 1950, though occasional Black women, typically members of the Oblate Sisters of Providence or the Holy Family Sisters, spent prolonged periods of time at the convent. The inability (or unwillingness) to run an integrated congregation kept the SBS from expanding as rapidly as other orders that recruited primarily from their students. Monsignor Joseph Stephan went so far as to say, "Your subjects are Indians and negroes, from whom you cannot recruit postulants. These must be recruited from the whites, or your Order will not be able to continue its work."[65] A few other congregations accepted the occasional light-skinned postulant, often without realizing it; however, the church did not officially have any integrated orders. Black women wishing to profess religious vows had to choose among the Oblate Sisters of Providence, the Holy Family Sisters, or the Handmaids of Mary.[66] There is some evidence that Drexel also did not accept Black women into the SBS

---

64 Mother Katharine Drexel to Father John Slattery, December 12, 1898, quoted in Hurd, *Master Art of a Saint*, 34. Drexel refers to the idea, popular until the Second Vatican Council, that nuns occupied a rarified plane and were closer to God than the laity. Before the Council, Canon Law stipulated, "Profession of the three essential vows, made in the state of grace, can remit all punishment due to sin"; Lanslots, *Handbook of Canon Law*, 85.

65 Joseph A. Stephan to Mother Katharine Drexel, September 28, 1899, BCIM records, series 1, box 38, folder 1, Marquette University Archives, Milwaukee, WI (hereafter MUA).

66 See Margaret Susan Thompson, "Philemon's Dilemma: Nuns and the Black Community in Nineteenth-Century America: Some Findings," in *The American Catholic Religious Life: Selected Historical Essays*, ed. Joseph M. White (New York: Garland, 1988), 81–96.

because she did not want to take candidates from these orders. During her canonization process, several members of the Oblates and Holy Family Sisters came forward to support this claim and to defend Drexel against claims of racism.[67]

While the first Sisters of the Blessed Sacrament, with the exception of Mother Katharine, had no previous experience with Indigenous people, several young women had worked with Black students. A few of them had taught Sunday school at the local Black parishes in Philadelphia, especially at St. Peter Claver, which had been funded by the Drexel family. Sister Mary of Lourdes, who entered in 1908, explained that she used to have one of the Black families at her church sit in her family's pew because she was afraid others would shun them.[68] Most of the sisters who joined in the congregation's first years said they felt called to do so because of the opportunity to engage in perpetual adoration of the sacrament while also performing important corporal works. In her application, Sr. Evangelista wrote to Drexel that she longed "to live day and night in the same house with the Blessed Sacrament, to have recourse to it, the only source from which real strength can come."[69] Some also yearned for the adventure of visiting far-off reservations and encountering different cultures.

When Mother Katharine formed the Sisters of the Blessed Sacrament, the foreign mission field had not yet opened to American Catholic women. The first congregation of foreign missionaries, the Mary Knoll Sisters, did not organize until 1920 and did not attempt a foreign mission until 1925. Drexel's financial independence gave the early SBS applicants one of their only opportunities to serve in a cross-cultural mission field.[70] Some sisters experienced disappointment, however, when their visions of adventure clashed with the reality of running parochial schools. As one sister teaching at Holy Providence School told visiting Jesuit writer Daniel Lord in 1924, "Mother Drexel really meant us to be mis-

---

67 Cummings, *A Saint of Our Own*, 189–90.
68 Oral History Project, Sisters of the Blessed Sacrament, 1971, ASBS.
69 Quoted in Lynch, *Sharing the Bread in Service*, 1:63.
70 For more on the lack of opportunities for American Catholic foreign missionaries, see Robert, *American Women in Mission*, 318–29.

sionary Sisters but we soon found that nothing permanent can be done for the colored race without educating them. . . . So instead of finding myself on a mission, as I had thought to do, I find myself in a classroom with all the regular work of grammar school."[71] For the SBS, fulfilling the traditional role of Catholic school teacher was cutting-edge mission work as sisters extended traditional parish school to Black and Indigenous students.

Drexel's vivacious personality, her unique position in society, and her advocacy of home missions drew other young women to the fledgling congregation. Historian Dana L. Robert asserts, "Although American women had undertaken cross-cultural work within the United States in connection with other religious institutes, it was Drexel's status as an heiress and as a native-born American Mother Superior that legitimated the ability of American women to engage in home missions."[72] Though novices entered for disparate reasons, choosing to join an unproven, upstart congregation was a daring move, especially as their work engendered protest and contempt.

## Body of Christ as Call to Action

The Sisters of the Blessed Sacrament tapped into a late nineteenth-century sacramental revival that guided their missionary impulse. As historian Jay P. Dolan has explained, the revival drove most Catholics to a personal search for salvation, but Drexel and others were inspired to save the nation.[73] They grounded their call to action in the sacraments. Prior to Pius X's *Sacra Tridentina Synodus*, which encouraged daily Communion, most Catholics approached the altar rail only a few times a year. According to Catholic theology, frequent Communion affected not only the individual who partook of the sacrament, but also the greater community. Pius X urged those who received Communion to go out and eradicate social ills, for "reform of the person leads to reform of the

---

71 Daniel Lord, SJ, *Our Nuns: Their Varied and Vital Service for God and Country* (New York: Benziger Brothers, 1924), 74.
72 Robert, *American Women in Mission*, 334.
73 Jay P. Dolan, *Catholic Revivalism: The American Experience, 1830–1900* (Notre Dame, IN: University of Notre Dame, 1978), 159–63.

world."⁷⁴ As Catholics believe that the Eucharist is the literal body and blood of Jesus Christ, the ingestion of the sacrament imparts holiness and power. Reform-minded Catholic women believed that the Eucharist fueled their efforts at social change. Mother Katharine credited the Eucharistic renewal with forming her mission ideology. In fact, during the last years of her life she always kept a picture of Pius X in her hands, praying over it for hours at a time.⁷⁵

In addition to empowering women to act and engage in the sanctification of the community, the SBS emphasis on the role of the Eucharist reflects the Catholic idea that the sacrament unites all peoples in the Mystical Body of Christ. The Mystical Body of Christ refers to the church on earth, sometimes called the Church Militant. The doctrine stemmed from the Apostle Paul's New Testament writings and stated that members of the Mystical Body of Christ were connected to each other through the sacraments, particularly baptism and the Eucharist. Membership in the church, then, meant a link between Christ and all Catholics who participated in the sacrament. One became a part of the Body of Christ through baptism and renewed the connection by receiving Communion. According to the doctrine, all baptized members, both living and dead, are united by the Holy Spirit. Theologian Fulton Sheen explained, "In his earthly Life, *He* [Christ] possessed the fullness of the Godhead; in His Mystical Life, *we* receive of Its fullness."⁷⁶ Paul Hanly Furfey, a sociologist at the Catholic University of America, saw further implications and suggested, "A priest in Burma is overwhelmed by the difficulties of his position, but he suddenly finds his burden lifted because a peasant girl in Belgium has made a good Communion. A despairing man in Paris is saved from suicide because a woman in Brazil gives some money to a beggar. Something like this—if we were permitted to see it—would be the activity of the Mystical Body of Christ."⁷⁷

---

74  Joseph P. Chinnici, OFM, *Living Stones: The History and Structure of Catholic Spiritual Life in the United States* (New York: Macmillan, 1989), 155; A Redemptorist Father, "The Social Value of Frequent Communion," *Emmanual*, September 1928, 227–34.

75  Burton, *Golden Door*, 298.

76  Fulton J. Sheen, *The Mystical Body of Christ* (London: Sheed and Ward, 1935), 25.

77  Paul Hanly Furfey, *Fire on the Earth* (New York: Macmillan, 1936), 48.

First used as a rallying cry to Catholic Church membership and triumphalism in the late nineteenth century, the Mystical Body imagery was co-opted by socially conscious Catholics such as Katharine Drexel and the Sisters of the Blessed Sacrament to undermine racism. Their reception of the sacraments gave women the gumption to engage in activities foreign to the church, such as creating the American church's first real home mission society or leaping into political activism. The Sisters of the Blessed Sacrament used sacramental language to explain their mission to Black and Indigenous people. Mother Katharine urged her sisters, "See them—these redeemed souls streaming with the cleansing Blood. I want you to save them—you my sacramental Sisters; you whose bodies are my living ciboriums—I want you to go forth and make of these souls living tabernacles of My Divinity."[78] When they spoke and wrote pamphlets for white audiences, they pointed out that Black and Indigenous souls shared in the divinity of Christ and thus should receive equal rights. Each issue of their mission magazine, *Mission Fields at Home*, contained a reflection on the Eucharist next to stories about their schools and community centers. They justified their pioneering practices by relating them to the central tenets of Catholicism.

The sisters kept the Eucharist at the center of their lives and work. Drexel described the altar as the centerpiece of SBS training, explaining, "Here she [the novice] immolates herself to God by vows which are promised before this altar. At this altar she received during the time of her preparation inspirations of grace." She added, "Here the young virginal heart pours out its love and receives from Her Eucharistic spouse the zeal and fortitude and strength which she will need for her future work."[79] At the motherhouse in Bensalem, Pennsylvania, the sisters practiced perpetual adoration of the Eucharist, which meant that they remained in prayer before the tabernacle at all times. They also had permission to receive daily Communion, a rarity since, during that time period, most Catholics only received the sacrament on a monthly basis. The power of the Eucharist, the sisters believed, would

---

78   *Original Annals of the SBS 1904–1905*, 37, ASBS.
79   Mother Katharine Drexel, "Since the Beginning," 1922 or later, MMK Talks, H10J86 box 28, fol. 1, ASBS.

strengthen the connections between members of the body of Christ. A writer for the *Mission Fields at Home* explained, "From the Eucharistic Heart of Jesus Hostia goes forth the dynamic energy that pulses through the arteries of the Congregation, the current that carries the elements of the real life, the spiritual and ideal into the yearning souls of men."[80] Not only did the Eucharist prepare the novice for work outside the convent, but Drexel insisted, "Each adorer is a missionary."[81] A life of prayer was a life of action. She believed that a sister on a Navajo reservation in Arizona could be spiritually and even physically aided by a prayer uttered before the altar in Pennsylvania. In her writings, Mother Katharine repeatedly stressed the importance of putting the Blessed Sacrament into action, telling the sisters to say a prayer from Song of Songs: "Put me as a seal upon Thy heart and on thine arm." She added, "The heart signifies interior life and the arm active life. My heart is most necessary but my arm is necessary also."[82]

The centrality of the Eucharist had further importance for the congregation. Not only did it supply the sisters with the energy to build missions throughout the country, but it also united them with those they sought to aid. Despite using language like "heathens" and "pagans," they believed that the Catholic sacraments had the power to unify all believers, eradicating differences in race and class. An editorial from *Mission Fields at Home* summarized: "After all, if we look the facts clearly in the face we must admit that from the viewpoint of complete Catholicism there is no race problem. We are children of the one Father, creatures of the one Creator forming part of His Mystical Body in the Church Militant here below, and destined to continue that membership in the Church Triumphant above."[83] The Sisters of the Blessed Sacrament believed that all those who received the sacraments became "living temples of His Divinity" and thus deserved respect and justice.

---

80 Both quotations are from "The Heart of the Congregation," *Mission Fields at Home*, October 1928, 9.
81 Ibid.
82 Mother Katharine Drexel, "Reading the Spirit of the Apostolate," Collated Writings, MMK Talks, H10J8B, vol. 28, fol. 9, ASBS.
83 "This Race Problem," *Mission Fields at Home*, March–April 1940, 4.

Though Drexel prioritized the sisters' spiritual mission to Black and Indigenous people, she also sought to ameliorate their social and economic conditions. Like most other reformers of the time period, she believed education would lead to advancement. Today scholars take umbrage with this approach, which failed to tackle discrimination and instead focused on "playing up what was wrong with Black people."[84] Yet, the SBS believed their best chance of success lay in preparing Black and Indigenous people for "effective citizenship of this world and of the next."[85] Thus they built churches, settlement homes, community centers, and schools all over the country. At the time of Mother Katharine's death in 1955, the SBS operated fifty-one convents, forty-nine elementary schools, twelve high schools, and one university, and they financed hundreds more institutions. The Sisters of the Blessed Sacrament sought to win souls, but to do that, they had to address more worldly concerns. The dignity of the human soul necessitated adequate education, financial stability, and basic civil rights. They believed that through education, specifically Roman Catholic education, Black and Indigenous people could advance socially and economically even within a racist society.

The sisters were not the only teachers who descended on reservations, Southern towns, and Northern inner cities in the late nineteenth and early twentieth centuries. The Black community prided itself on self-help and provided the majority of teachers in Black schools. Of the aid that came from outside the community, most educational funding came from government. Three things, however, differentiated the Sisters of the Blessed Sacrament from these other sources of aid: their outsider status, their insistence on centrality of the Catholic Church to the educational process, and their financial ability to act without popular support. The Sisters of the Blessed Sacrament set out to fill the void between dogma and action.

---

84 Ibram X. Kendi, *Stamped from the Beginning: The Definitive History of Racist Ideas in America* (New York: Nation, 2016), 279.
85 Duffy, *Katharine Drexel*, 231.

CHAPTER 2

# "Received from Other Sources"

## Mother Katharine Drexel and the Bureau of Catholic Indian Missions

IN 1904, REV. WILLIAM KETCHAM, the Bureau of Catholic Indian Missions' director, complained, "Had it not been for one devoted woman, raised up by Almighty God for the edification of the American people, and for the succor of poor abandoned races, the whole system of Catholic Indian schools would have collapsed and the Indian children been given over to schools decidedly anti-Catholic in all their tendencies."[1] He referred, of course, to Drexel, who donated more than $100,000 a year each year to build and maintain Catholic Indian schools and to support missionaries. Between her initial gifts in 1885 to her retirement from active duty in 1935, no one had a larger impact on the Catholic mission to educate and evangelize Indigenous Americans. Because she preferred to donate anonymously, tracing her monetary contributions is difficult, but she spent an estimated $15 to $20 million on Indigenous mission projects. In an era of stiff competition between Catholics and Protestants, Mother Katharine provided the means to keep Catholic schools open even as they faced opposition from the federal government. Generous contributions tell only part of the story, however. Through shrewd business practices, political acumen, and steely resolve, Drexel shaped Catholic Indian policy for nearly five decades.

### Following the Drexel Model

Her considerable financial investments meant clergy had to adapt to her philanthropic business model—one that held clerics

---

1 Bureau of Catholic Indian Missions, *Report of the Director of the Bureau of Catholic Indian Missions for 1903–1904* (Washington, DC: Bureau of Catholic Indian Missions, 1904), 2–3.

accountable and tried to serve as many students as possible. In addition to funding dozens of mission schools, churches, and convents for the Bureau of Catholic Indian Missions, her reach extended to government-run schools, where she paid priests and sisters to provide religious education. Through her contacts on reservations, she developed an interest in Indigenous rights causes, and she wielded considerable lobbying power in Washington. In an age when few women, particularly Catholic women, exercised authority, Mother Katharine Drexel controlled millions of dollars and made the church hierarchy solicit her opinions. Though church officials did not always agree with the wealthy nun, without her fiscal and policy contributions the church's mission program would not have been implemented.

While historians have acknowledged some of Drexel's financial contributions, neither their magnitude nor her influence on policy has come to light. For example, in his important study of Indigenous missions, Jesuit historian Francis Paul Prucha mentioned Mother Katharine only in passing, noting, "This work of the Drexels was coordinated and directed by the officers of the Bureau of Catholic Indian Missions and the members of the hierarchy who had missions within their dioceses."[2] His assessment underrepresents her importance to the entire home mission endeavor. This lacuna has been further complicated by her 2000 canonization. Using the language of sanctity to describe Mother Katharine makes her more palatable to a church that is still struggling to define proper channels for women's authority. During her lifetime and even after, many in the hierarchy were uncomfortable with Mother Katharine's outsized influence on policy, and they frequently chose to downplay her ability to shape the church's mission work. The BCIM did not coordinate Drexel's work; she decided the future of BCIM enterprises.

The glossing over of Drexel's contributions is symptomatic of a larger absence of women religious in the missionary narrative. School and mission centers paid for by Mother Katharine and predominantly staffed by nuns are most often remembered for their

---

2 Prucha, *The Churches and the Indian Schools, 1888–1912* (Lincoln: University of Nebraska Press, 1979), 3.

connection to male priests. Franciscans Anselm Weber and Berard Haile deserve praise for their linguistic and ethnographic work at St. Michael's on the Navajo Reservation in Arizona, but Mother Katharine bought their land, paid their salaries, and financed the publication of their books. Sisters labored in the school, cooked, cleaned, and did the priests' laundry. They worked on the front lines of the church with no recognition then and little today.[3] Rev. William Ketcham understood her significance far more than his contemporaries when he declared, "The fate of our Indian missions hangs in the balance; it depends, apparently on the life of one true Catholic woman—Mother M. Katharine Drexel."[4]

### The Catholic "Indian Question"

Mother Katharine did not pioneer missions to Indigenous peoples; rather, she helped systemize a tradition started by French and Spanish Jesuits and Franciscans in the sixteenth century.[5] Despite a lengthy history of Catholic missionary activity, by the nineteenth century zeal for Indigenous conversions took a back seat to the American church's institutional expansion.[6] Most bishops snug in their urban residences had neither the time nor the inclination to consider the needs of Indigenous people. When the Second Provisional Council convened in Baltimore in 1833, the prelates decided to turn all work on Indigenous missions over to

---

   3   Recent scholarship has begun to correct this gap. Anne Butler's *Across God's Frontiers* covers a wide range of women religious' activities in the American West, including on Indian missions (233–46). Other important works on nuns and Catholic Indian missions include James T. Carroll, *Seeds of Faith: Catholic Indian Boarding Schools* (New York: Garland, 2000); Irene Mahoney, OSU, *Lady Blackrobes: Missionaries in the Heart of Indian Country* (Golden, Colo.: Fulcrum, 2006); and Susan Peterson, "A Widening Horizon: Catholic Sisterhoods on the Northern Plains, 1874–1910," *Great Plains Quarterly* 5, no. 3 (Spring 1985): 125–32.
   4   Rev. Wm. H. Ketcham, *Our Catholic Indian Missions: A Paper Read before the Catholic Missionary Congress, Chicago, November 16, 1908* (Washington, DC: Byron S. Adams, 1908), 15.
   5   See, for example, Christopher Vecsey, *On the Padres' Trail*; *The Paths of Kateri's Kin*; and *Where the Two Roads Meet*.
   6   Jay P. Dolan, *The American Catholic Experience: A History from Colonial Times to the Present* (Garden City, NY: Doubleday, 1985), 135.

the Jesuits. By foisting the responsibility onto the Jesuits, the hierarchy could wash their hands of the issue while patting themselves on the back for their benevolence. Despite episcopal neglect, during the early nineteenth century, religious orders established mission communities amongst dozens of Indigenous groups. The situation might have continued with Catholics making small but steady gains had it not been for burgeoning interest in the "Indian Question" following the Civil War.

Throughout the nineteenth century, the government sponsored plans to solve the "Indian Problem" through the primer and the hoe. In 1885, William Strong promised his fellow reformers at the Lake Mohonk Conference, "If we could take these 50,000 Indian children, and put them in schools at an expense of some millions of dollars to the United States, teaching them the trades and employments of civilized life, and then send them back to their homes, the Indian problem would be solved."[7] According to these reformers, if Indigenous youth could be made to see the righteousness of the white American, then they would "turn away from the blanket," melt into white society, and cease to be an impediment to progress. They believed that educated Indigenous tribes could aid American economic expansion. Indian Commissioner Thomas Jefferson Morgan explained, "A wild Indian requires a thousand acres to roam over, while an intelligent man will find a comfortable support for his family on a very small tract. When the rising generation of Indians have become civilized and have learned how to utilize the land they live on, a vast domain now useless can be thrown open to settlement." He concluded, "Barbarism is costly, wasteful and extravagant. Intelligence promotes thrift and increases prosperity."[8]

Other reformers believed that offering Indigenous youth an American-style education could atone for, in Helen Hunt Jack-

---

7 William Strong, "Remarks on Indian Reform," *Proceedings of the Third Annual Meeting of the Lake Mohonk Conference* (1885), quoted in Francis Paul Prucha, *Americanizing the American Indians: Writings of the "Friends of the Indian" 1880–1900* (Cambridge, MA: Harvard University Press, 1973), 41.

8 Quoted in David Wallace Adams, *Education for Extinction: American Indians and the Boarding School Experience, 1875–1928* (Lawrence: University of Kansas Press, 1995), 20.

son's words, a "Century of Dishonor." In its *Twelfth Annual Report*, the Board of Indian Commissioners concluded, "If the common school is the glory and boast of our American civilization, why not extend its blessings to the 50,000 benighted children of the red men of our country, that they too may share its benefits and speedily emerge from the ignorance of centuries."[9] Seen as the great equalizer, education, according to leading Protestant and secular thinkers, offered Indigenous people their best chance of escaping the poverty of the reservation and gaining the precious accoutrements of white civilization. It went without saying, however, that American-style schooling would tear asunder the fabric of Indigenous society and kin systems. Though reformers fired no weapons, they were, in fact, continuing to wage war against the Indigenous. Merrill Gates, chairman of the U.S. Board of Indian Commissioners, reminded his fellow Friends of the Indian, "We are going to conquer the Indians by a standing army of school teachers, armed with ideas, winning victories by industrial training, and by the gospel of love and the gospel of work."[10]

While the government had operated a handful of day schools located on reservations since the early nineteenth century, by the 1880s boarding schools, particularly those located a distance from reservations, gained in popularity. The off-reservation schools were modeled on the work of Richard Henry Pratt, a former military officer, at Carlisle, Pennsylvania. Pratt aimed to "kill the Indian in him and save the man."[11] Pleased with Pratt's work at Carlisle, the government built twenty-five off-reservation boarding schools across the country between 1879 and 1902.[12] Assimi-

---

9   Board of Indian Commissioners, "Indian Education," *Twelfth Annual Report of the Board of Indian Commissioners* (1880), quoted in Prucha, *Americanizing the American Indians*, 196.
10   Quoted in Adams, *Education for Extinction*, 27.
11   Richard H. Pratt, "The Advantages of Mingling Indians with Whites," *Official Report of the Nineteenth Annual Conference of Charities and Correction*, 1892, quoted in Prucha, *Americanizing the American Indians*, 260–61.
12   While Pratt located his school in Carlisle, Pennsylvania, the others sprouted up in the West. Schools appeared in Chemawa, Oregon; Chilocco, Oklahoma; Genoa, Nebraska; Albuquerque, New Mexico; Lawrence, Kansas; Grand Junction, Colorado; Santa Fe, New Mexico; Fort Mojave, Arizona; Carson, Nevada; Pierre, South Dakota; Phoenix, Arizona; Fort Lewis, Colorado; Fort

lation became the key word for all interested in solving the pernicious problem of Indigenous people who insisted on preserving their cultures and lands.

Since a military solution had not worked, a Christian one, reformers agreed, should be tested. What version of the Christian message Indigenous people should receive remained highly contentious as Protestants and Catholics squared off for the right to operate missions. Much of the hostility stemmed from the ironically named Peace Policy, which used mission work as a federal tool to maintain order. President Ulysses S. Grant's plan to pacify the Plains united religious reformers with government bureaucracy. As a result of Grant's strategy, government money for mission schools rose from $75,000 to more than $2 million each year.[13] In addition to Grant's belief that religious groups might succeed where troops had failed, the president also hoped to save money by utilizing an existing ecclesiastical infrastructure. Grant neglected to specify exactly how the missions would be divided, thus dooming the plan to collapse under the weight of sectarian squabbling.

The first Board of Indian Commissioners, an all-Protestant group, denied Catholics a voice.[14] Given their centuries of mission work, the exclusion of Roman Catholics from the board triggered uproar in the Catholic press. Between their lack of representation on the board and the fact that they only received eight (later reduced

---

Shaw, Montana; Flandreau, South Dakota; Pipestone, Minnesota; Mount Pleasant, Michigan; Tomah, Wisconsin; Wittenberg, Wisconsin; Greenville, California; Morris, Minnesota; Chamberlain, South Dakota; Rapid City, South Dakota; and Riverside, California. The location of these schools meant that some students lived relatively close to the boarding schools, while others traveled hundreds, if not thousands, of miles to school.

13  Carroll, *Seeds of Faith*, 4.

14  While much of the exclusion can be blamed on anti-Catholic sentiment, it should be noted that the board also shunned other non-mainstream groups, especially the Moravians, the Mormons, and the southern branches of the Baptist and Methodist Episcopal and Presbyterian churches. In addition, the omission of Catholics might not have been entirely the fault of a prejudiced government, as most of the American hierarchy had gone to Rome for the First Vatican Council between 1869 and 1870 and would not have been able to respond to a government summons. Robert H. Keller, *American Protestantism and United States Indian Policy, 1869–82* (Lincoln: University of Nebraska Press, 1983), 72–73.

to seven) of the thirty-eight Indian agencies they had historically operated, Catholics claimed discrimination. Their ire increased in 1874, when the Department of the Interior granted exclusionary rights to the denomination in charge of each agency, meaning Catholics could not send missionaries to a Protestant agency, even when the tribes identified as Catholics. While the Catholic press printed enraged editorials, those actively involved in Catholic Indian missions realized they needed to establish an organization to lobby in Washington. The policy of granting exclusionary mission rights, Catholic activists claimed, robbed Indigenous people of their right to freedom of religion. That these groups might have wished to use their freedom of religion to practice their own religions likely never occurred to the zealous missionaries. On January 2, 1874, J. Roosevelt Bayley, the archbishop of Baltimore, appointed General Charles Ewing to serve as the commissioner for Catholic Bishops in Washington. This job entailed pressuring the government to support Catholic missionary work. Ewing's lobbying paid off, and by 1877 the church ran eleven boarding schools and seventeen day schools and employed 137 teachers. Archbishop Bayley authorized the creation of the Bureau of Catholic Indian Missions (BCIM) in 1879 under the leadership of Rev. Joseph A. Stephan. The bureau, which was fully sanctioned at the Third Plenary Council of Baltimore in 1884, provided the church with a centralized means of organizing its missions amongst Indigenous people.

In 1882, Henry Teller, secretary of the Interior under Chester A. Arthur, ended the contentious Peace Policy.[15] Though Catholics and Protestants had bickered during the thirteen years of Grant's Peace Policy, all had agreed that missionaries were the answer to the "Indian Problem." After the collapse of the Peace Policy, however, ideological debates grew increasingly acrimonious. Protestant and secular reformers advocated the dissolution of the reservation system, the increase of individual rather than tribal land ownership, the citizenship of Indigenous people, and the creation of a universal government-run school system.[16] Rather than continue to press for religious education, reformers championed the Dawes

---

15 Peter J. Rahill, *The Catholic Indian Missions and Grant's Peace Policy, 1870–1884* (Washington, DC: The Catholic University of America Press, 1953), 323.

16 Prucha, *Americanizing the American Indians*, 8.

Severalty Act in 1887. The Dawes Act, which President Grover Cleveland signed on February 8, 1887, proposed dismantling reservations and giving individuals land allotments. Heads of households were to receive 160 acres, single persons over eighteen and orphans under eighteen received eighty acres, and other single persons under eighteen were to receive forty acres. Land ownership was supposed to speed the process of assimilation, but the Dawes Act led to a collapse of tribal unity and millions of acres of land leaving Indigenous control.[17] While many mainstream Protestant groups abandoned the idea of mission work in favor of government programs, Catholics like Drexel continued to see a special role for the church in education and evangelization.

## The ATM of Catholic Indian Missions

While the BCIM received some funding from federal government subsidies and the Lenten Collection for Indian and African American Missions, the Drexel family financed the bulk of the late nineteenth-century construction boom. The Lenten Collection never raised more than a pittance. The first collection in 1887 brought in only $81,898, and it dwindled for the remainder of the century.[18] Though it modestly increased in the twentieth century, the Lenten Collection never amounted to more than a few pennies per Catholic per year. Other sources of money, such as the Society for the Preservation of the Faith among Indian Children, the Association of Holy Childhood, and the Marquette League, also failed to bring in substantial funds. For example, in 1906, the Preservation Society raised $14,957.21, the Marquette League $2,200, and the Association of Holy Childhood $4,000; Mother Katharine supplied over $100,000.[19] Drexel's money thus proved essential for Catholic mission work.

---

17 Francis Paul Prucha, *The Great Father: The United States Government and the American Indians* (Lincoln: University of Nebraska Press, 1984), 2:666–81.

18 Bureau of Catholic Indian Missions, *The Bureau of Catholic Indian Missions 1874–1895* (Washington, DC: Church News, 1895), 20.

19 Bureau of Catholic Indian Missions, *Report of the Director of the Bureau of Catholic Indian Missions for 1905–1906* (Washington, DC: BCIM, 1906), and *Report of the Director of the Bureau of Catholic Indian Missions for 1906* (Washington, DC: BCIM, 1906), 29, 78.

Her interest in Indigenous missions began when she was still a teenager. In 1876, Katharine Drexel began corresponding with Bishop James O'Connor about Catholic Indian missions, and the Drexel family took several extended tours of the West in the 1880s, where they visited schools and mission outposts. Drexel reported that the Indigenous people she met on her western tours, including Red Cloud, asked for Catholic schools. As Anne M. Butler has pointed out, Drexel took this request to be a crying out for the Catholic faith rather than a search for "any advantage a receptive listener might provide." Butler suggests, "For Indians mired in the misfortunes of the reservation, the proximity of white visitors offered a chance of reaching absent administrators, whether of church or state."[20] The Northern Plains chiefs whom Mother Katharine met had ulterior motives for requesting Catholic schools. Red Cloud had a French-Canadian son-in-law who advocated for Jesuit missionaries. Sitting Bull viewed the pope as a global peace-broker. Consequently, several chiefs became Catholic converts and demanded "Black Robe" (i.e., Roman Catholic) schools for their reservations to facilitate a lasting peace with the government. While she might not have understood the underlying political motivations of the Indigenous people she met, these western encounters fueled Drexel's interest in mission work.

Fathers Martin Marty, OSB, and Joseph A. Stephan also pressured Drexel to invest in Indigenous missions.[21] In 1885, shortly

---

20  Butler, *Across God's Frontiers*, 199.

21  Martin Marty, OSB (1836–96) was born in Switzerland, where he joined the Benedictine order in 1855. He came to the United States to head the Abby at St. Meinrad, Indiana, in 1859. In the 1870s he became an important advocate for Indigenous missions and started the work at Fort Yates. He later became vicar apostolic of the Dakota Territory and in 1889 was named the bishop of Sioux Falls. He also worked with the government as an Indian commissioner from 1889 to his death in 1896. Reverend Joseph A. Stephan (1822–1901) originally hailed from Germany. While he began his theological training in Germany, he immigrated to the United States in 1847, where he received ordination in the Diocese of Cincinnati. Stephan served in various positions along the American frontier and grew increasingly interested in Indigenous missions. He served as an Indian agent for Standing Rock starting in 1878. He became head of the Bureau of Catholic Indian Missions in 1884. For more complete biographical

after Francis Drexel's death, the priests arrived unannounced at the Drexels's Philadelphia home looking for a handout. They could not have anticipated that their begging mission would produce a new business partner. In their first decade of partnership, Katharine Drexel donated close to one million dollars to the Bureau of Catholic Indian Missions, established a $50,000 fund for BCIM operations, and constructed dozens of schools.[22] Drexel and the priests at the BCIM wanted to offer a Catholic alternative everywhere the government sought to Americanize Indigenous children. By the time she entered religious life in 1889, Drexel had become an integral part of the bureau's affairs. She so frequently wrote to priests, bishops, and archbishops offering her suggestions on how to best operate the BCIM that her sister Elizabeth jested, "Kate, you ought to be a St. Simon Stylites and preach from your pillar to the Bishops and priests of the United States."[23] The comparison with St. Simon Stylites, an early fifth-century ascetic who lived on a small platform on the top of a tall column, was apt. The holy man tried to leave the world, but his actions and his reputation of sanctity attracted high-ranking clerics who wished to consult with him. Similarly, Drexel's removal from the world through her religious vows brought her increased power and influence. During her novitiate with the Sisters of Mercy, the nuns allowed her several hours each day to manage the voluminous correspondence necessary to continue her work with the BCIM, while her brother-in-law Edward Morrell handled her finances.[24] By the time she made her vows as Mother Superior of the Sisters of the Blessed Sacrament in 1891, Katharine Drexel had become integral to the survival of most of the nation's Catholic Indian missions.

The Drexel fortune built schools all over the West. Her generosity became such a trope that in 1914 a priest could offhandedly

---

information, see "Bishop Martin Marty, OSB, Apostle of the Sioux," *Indian Sentinel*, January 1920, 7–10, and Kevin Abing, "Directors of the Bureau of Catholic Indian Missions, 2. Joseph A. Stephan, 1884–1901," explanatory note, Bureau of Catholic Indian Mission Papers, MUA.

22   Bureau of Catholic Indian Missions, *Bureau of Catholic Indian Missions 1874–1895*, 19.
23   Quotation in Lynch, *Sharing the Bread in Service*, 1:29.
24   Consuela Marie Duffy, *Katharine Drexel*, 145.

report, "It should be noted in passing that in one particular this school shares the history of most other Catholic Indian schools, namely that it was made possible chiefly by the generosity of Mother Katharine Drexel."[25] It is difficult to discern exactly how many schools Mother Katharine built, as she liked to keep her involvement a secret, but she was at least partly responsible for dozens. The following list pieced together from SBS and BCIM sources should be viewed as a best estimate. For some schools, such as St. Boniface in Banning, California, she bought the land, paid construction costs, purchased the animals for the industrial education, and contributed money each year for the school's support.[26] For other schools and mission centers, particularly as the work of her own congregation spread, Mother Katharine contributed more modestly, such as advancing a $10,000 loan to finance the construction of St. Anthony's in New Mexico's Zuni Pueblo.[27]

In addition to providing construction costs and aiding missionaries, for years Drexel also covered the insurance policies for schools supported by the BCIM. Fire frequently ravaged isolated mission schools, which often relied upon dangerous wood-burning stoves for heat. Since the impoverished missions could not afford the premiums, Drexel supplied the money. She often had to remind the bureau to renew the policies. When she sent the money for Holy Rosary Mission in South Dakota in 1894, she urged haste, cautioning Stephan, "Suppose it were to burn today."[28] She had reason for caution, as she saw several of the schools she supported go up in flames. For example, she built St. Louis Industrial School for Osage Girls in 1889 only to have to reconstruct it when fire consumed it the same year.[29] She faced similar losses with the

---

25 "Sacred Heart Institute in Vinita, Oklahoma," *Indian Sentinel*, 1914, 15.
26 Tanya Rathbun, "Hail Mary: The Catholic Experience at St. Boniface," in *Boarding School Blues: Revisiting America Indian Educational Experiences*, ed. Clifford Traafzer, Jean A. Keller, and Loene Sisquoc (Lincoln: University of Nebraska Press, 2006), 156.
27 Mother Katharine Drexel to Charles Lusk, January 19, 1923, BCIM correspondence, series 1–1, reel 114, MUA.
28 Mother Katharine Drexel to J. A. Stephan, undated 1894, BCIM records, series 1–1, box 32, folder 23, MUA.
29 "Catholic Indian Schools, St. Louis Industrial School for Osage Girls," *Indian Sentinel*, 1910, 6–7.

TABLE 2-1. Aid to Non-SBS Indian Missions

| Name | Location | Date Established |
|---|---|---|
| St. Mary's | Odanah, Wisconsin | 1883 |
| St. Benedict | White Earth, Minnesota | 1884 |
| St. Mary Academy | Graceville, Minnesota | 1885 |
| Holy Childhood of Jesus | Harbor Springs, Michigan | 1886 |
| St. Francis | Rosebud Agency, South Dakota | 1886 |
| St. Francis Mission | Corn Creek, South Dakota | 1886 |
| St. Stephen's Mission | Wyoming | 1886 |
| Immaculate Conception | Crow Creek, South Dakota | 1887 |
| St. Ann's | Turtle Mountain, North Dakota | 1887 |
| St. Catherine's Mission | Santa Fe, New Mexico | 1887 |
| St. Louis | Pawhuska, Oklahoma | 1887 |
| St. Paul's Mission | Montana | 1887 |
| St. Xavier's Mission | Montana | 1887 |
| St. Bede | Standing Rock, South Dakota | 1887 |
| Holy Rosary Mission | Pine Ridge Agency, South Dakota | 1888 |
| San Xavier del Bac | Arizona | 1888 |
| St. Ann's | Umatilla, Oregon | 1888 |
| St. Francis Xavier | North Yakima, Washington | 1888 |
| St. George | Takoma, Washington | 1888 |
| St. Mary's | Red Lake, Minnesota | 1888 |
| St. Paul's Mission | Fort Belknap, Montana | 1888 |
| St. Elizabeth's | Purcell, Oklahoma | 1888 |
| Sacred Heart Mission | Elbowoods, South Dakota | 1889 |
| St. John's School | Oklahoma | 1889 |
| Holy Family | Blackfoot Reservation | 1890 |
| Holy Family Mission | Montana | 1890 |
| St. Anthony | San Diego, California | 1890 |
| St. Ignatius | Flathead, Montana | 1890 |
| St. Peter's Mission | Montana | 1890 |
| St. Stanislas | Lewiston, Idaho | 1890 |
| St. Aloysious | Standing Rock, South Dakota | 1890 |
| Cheyenne River Mission | South Dakota | 1892 |
| St. Benedict's | White Earth, Minnesota | 1892 |
| St. Jerome's | Fort Totten, North Dakota | 1892 |
| St. Mary's | Quapaw, Oklahoma | 1893 |
| Hominy Station | Hominy Creek, Oklahoma | 1894 |
| Lac de Flambeau | Lac de Flambeau, Wisconsin | 1896 |
| St. Boniface | Banning, California | 1896 |
| St. Catherine's | Bad River, South Dakota | 1896 |
| Holy Cross School | Cross Village, Michigan | 1897 |

*continued on next page*

TABLE 2-1. (*continued*)

| Name | Location | Date Established |
|---|---|---|
| St. Agnes School | Antlers, Oklahoma | 1897 |
| St. John the Baptist | Gila Crossing, Arizona | 1897 |
| St. Michael the Archangel | Grande Ronde, Oregon | 1898 |
| St. Michael's Mission | La Cienga, Arizona | 1898 |
| St. Joseph's | Chickasha, Oklahoma | 1899 |
| Holy Family | Bayfield, Wisconsin | 1900 |
| St. Joseph's | Kehena, Wisconsin | 1900 |
| St. Joseph's | Old Town, Florida | 1900 |
| St. Joseph's Mission | Slickapoo, Idaho | 1902 |
| St. Patrick's | Anadarko, Oklahoma | 1902 |
| Sacred Heart Institute | Vinita, Oklahoma | 1903 |
| St. Joseph's School | Muskogee, Oklahoma | 1903 |
| Chin Lee Mission | Chin Lee, Arizona | 1905 |
| Our Lady of Guadalupe | Jemez Pueblo, New Mexico | 1906 |
| Our Lady of Mercy | Hogansburg, New York | 1906 |
| St. John's | Saint Louis, Missouri | 1907 |
| St. Augustine | Winnebago, Nebraska | 1908 |
| St. Catherine Mission | Topawa, Arizona | 1908 |
| St. William's | Boswell, Oklahoma | 1909 |
| Lukachukai Chapel | Lukachukai, Arizona | 1910 |
| Loretto School | Bernalillo, New Mexico | 1911 |
| St. Joseph's | Oneida, Wisconsin | 1913 |
| St. Mary's | Tohatchi, New Mexico | 1914 |
| Lourdes | Papago Reservation, Arizona | 1915 |
| St. Elizabeth's | Cocklebur, Arizona | 1915 |
| Topawa | Papago Reservation, Arizona | 1915 |
| St. John the Baptist | Komatke, Arizona | 1922 |
| St. Anthony's | Gallup, New Mexico | 1923 |
| St. Paul's | Marty, South Dakota | 1923 |
| St. Bernard's | Fort Yates, North Dakota | 1924 |
| St. Clare's | Anegan, Arizona | 1927 |
| San Esteban del Rey | Acoma Pueblo, New Mexico | 1930 |
| San Jose Mission | Pisenemo, Arizona | 1930 |
| Catherine Tekakwitha Mission | Houck, Arizona | 1932 |
| St. Joseph's | Laguna Pueblo, New Mexico | 1935 |

Holy Family School on the Blackfoot Reservation, where the buildings she erected burned in 1898.[30] While she reminded her sisters to fully rely on God, she refused to construct wooden buildings and kept insurance premiums up to date—after all, she believed God helps those who help themselves.

## "A Friend of the Missions"

Drexel's work building and supporting mission schools through gifts large and small brought her and the BCIM into conflict with a formidable foe at the end of the nineteenth century: the United States government. In the 1890s, Protestant missionary groups joined the chorus calling for government-run Indigenous schools and gradually pulled out of the mission field. The Protestant exodus meant Catholics began receiving a greater proportion of the government contracts given to religious schools. In 1874 the church received only $8,000 for Indigenous school contracts, but by 1890, Catholics took in $500,000.[31] As Catholics obtained a greater portion of the federal school money, sectarian tensions rose. When Thomas Jefferson Morgan was appointed commissioner of Indian Affairs and Daniel Dorchester named superintendent of Indian Schools, the situation erupted as Catholics believed both men held anti-Catholic prejudice. BCIM director Joseph Stephan's vitriolic protests about these appointments caused Morgan to sever ties between the Bureau of Indian Affairs and the Bureau of Catholic Indian Missions in 1891.[32] While they eventually restored relations, bickering and sniping continued. It became clear that followers of the Roman Church had a different vision of Americanization than their Protestant counterparts.

To nineteenth-century reformers, civilization meant Christianity. Secular schools had religious agendas. For example, Richard Henry Pratt, who founded the influential Carlisle Indian School in

---

30 "Editorials," *Indian Sentinel*, 1912, 20.
31 Mark Clatterbuck, *Demons, Saints, and Patriots: Catholic Visions of Native America through the "Indian Sentinel," 1902–1962* (Milwaukee: Marquette University Press, 2009), 39.
32 Prucha, *Churches and the Indian Schools*, 10–24; also see Carroll, *Seeds of Faith*, 86–88.

1879, made religion a central part of his goal of assimilation into white "civilization."[33] At Carlisle, students attended prayer services during the week and church on Sunday, for the gospel and plow, the two supposed pillars of civilization, were inextricably intertwined. The fusion of the interests of church and state created problems for those not adhering to Protestant republican ideology. As Father Ketcham of the BCIM put it, "It would be just as reasonable to expect a man to live in an Arkansas swamp and breathe for [a] year a poisoned atmosphere without contracting malaria as to expect a Catholic child in a Government school to escape perversion."[34] The government mandated prayers and chapel attendance at all federally run schools, leading Father Ketcham to ask in exasperation, "As to Government Indian boarding schools, what are they but seminaries of Protestantism?"[35] Facing Protestants who began to champion "non-sectarian" government-run education that would deliver a basic Protestant Christian message without delving into the doctrinal differences separating the various branches of Protestantism, the BCIM vowed to fight to preserve the partnership that they had cultivated for thirty years. The ensuing struggle created anti-Catholic backlash.[36] Between the 1890s and the start of World War I, Protestants and Catholics engaged in a battle for funding and cultural hegemony. In this struggle, Drexel became the Catholic Church's most valuable asset.

Catholicism with its mystique of "otherness" threatened reform groups that aimed to assimilate Indigenous people into white American culture. President Grover Cleveland's 1892 appointment of Daniel M. Browning as Indian commissioner turned the tide against Catholic missions. In 1896, Browning got Congress to slash con-

---

33 William Henry Pratt, *Battlefield & Classroom: Four Decades with the American Indian, 1867–1904*, ed. Robert M. Utley (Norman: University of Oklahoma Press, 2003), 283.

34 Bureau of Catholic Indian Missions, *Report of the Bureau of Catholic Indian Mission for 1900–01 and 1901–02* (Washington, DC: Bureau of Catholic Indian Missions, 1902), 28.

35 "Editorial," *Indian Sentinel*, 1905–6, 36.

36 Prucha, *Churches and the Indian Schools*, 26–41. For anti-Catholicism during the time period, see Justin Nordstrom, *Danger on the Doorstep: Anti-Catholicism and American Print Culture in the Progressive Era* (Notre Dame, IN: University of Notre Dame Press, 2006), 1–18.

tracts to Catholic schools by 20 percent. He also mandated that Indigenous children had to go to a government school if there was one close to their home. Catholics resented his pronouncement, which later became known as the Browning Ruling, that "the Indian parents have no right to designate which school their children shall attend." By the turn of the century, the amount of money that Catholic schools received from the government had dropped 85 percent from the 1895 contract amount.[37] Congress also eliminated food rations for Indigenous students at mission schools, though these were restored in 1904. By the end of the century, it was clear that Catholic missions could no longer rely on the government for funding.

Not ready to give up, BCIM director Rev. Ketcham lobbied in Washington to use tribal funds, money owed by the government to each tribe according to treaty arrangements, to pay for Catholic schools. The Supreme Court upheld this policy in the 1906 ruling *Quick Bear v. Leupp*. The tribal fund policy required missionaries to gather signatures to determine the number of Indigenous people who supported the church. The more signatures the church received, the more it got paid. Getting signatures become an intense competition between Catholics and government agents. It is difficult to discern what percentage of the Indigenous population considered itself Catholic, since often the religious preference of schoolchildren depended on which missionary had reached an isolated settlement first or even on what they offered the tribes in exchange for their signatures. In 1889 the church claimed 39,490 Indigenous Catholic; the number had more than doubled to 88,801 by 1910. After 1911 the annual mission report stopped printing a head count, but by the 1930s the BCIM estimated more than 100,000 Indigenous Catholics.[38] While tribal funds helped support the missions, the money never covered all expenses. To compensate, some schools shifted from boarding to day schools.

---

37 Prucha, *Churches and the Indian Schools*, 40.

38 *Mission Work among the Negroes and the Indians: What Is Being Accomplished by Means of the Annual Collection Taken Up for Our Missions* (Baltimore: Sun Book and Job Printing Office, 1889), 9; *Mission Work among the Negroes and the Indians: What Is Being Accomplished by Means of the Annual Collection Taken up for Our Missions* (Clayton, DE: Press of St. Joseph Industrial School, 1910), 14.

Others rented Catholic school buildings to the government with the proviso that the Catholic teachers would remain but would refrain from religious instruction during school hours.[39] Primarily, however, the Bureau of Catholic Indian Missions relied on cash infusions from Mother Katharine Drexel.

In 1898, Mother Katharine developed a complicated subsidy system that paid schools the difference between their original government contracts and the reduced rates if they maintained a specified number of students.[40] In 1899, Drexel paid $92,046 in subsidies.[41] She contributed, on average, $20,000 each quarter, though the amount lessened in the 1930s as many of the schools either closed or became more self-sufficient. Between 1895 and 1928, Drexel estimated that she had given the BCIM $5,913,558 for buildings, maintenance, and subsidies.[42] In return for this aid, she required the schools to carry additional students (beyond the number they had government contracts for) without compensation. She believed this would motivate missionaries to increase their efforts to recruit students.

Though Drexel supported more than fifty schools, her involvement was supposed to be a secret. Schools received a stipend each quarter with the designation "From a Friend of the Indian Missions," but everyone understood the money came from the heiress nun's coffers. Still, when Ketcham put together his annual report for 1907, Drexel asked that he not print her name in the publication; instead, she requested he label the income as

---

39   This plan was not novel. The Grey Nuns at Fort Totten, for example, had joined the Civil Service in 1874 and had been paid by the government to staff the school there. Sisters also served as government employees at the school at Fort Yates, founded in 1882. Catholic congregations liked the government support. The pay for sisters at government-run Fort Totten ranged between $360 and $900 per year, while the BCIM could only pay between $150 and $175 per year. For more, see Carroll, *Seeds of Faith*.

40   Mother Katharine Drexel to J. Stephan, August 1, 1898, BCIM records, series 1–1, box 36, folder 31, MUA.

41   J. Stephan to Mother Katharine Drexel, June 10, 1899, BCIM records, series 1–1, box 38, folder 1, MUA.

42   Mother Katharine Drexel to J. B. Tennelly, July 24, 1928, BCIM records, series 1–1, roll 151, MUA.

TABLE 2-2. Drexel Subsidies to Lenten Collection 1887–1924

| Year | Lenten Collection | Drexel Subsidies |
|---|---|---|
| 1887 | $81,898.01 | |
| 1888 | $76,175.30 | |
| 1889 | $69,408.73 | |
| 1890 | $70,330.81 | |
| 1891 | $63,386.84 | |
| 1892 | $66,068.09 | |
| 1893 | $66,014.13 | |
| 1894 | $57,840.49 | |
| 1895 | $58,001.80 | |
| 1896 | $61,939.63 | |
| 1897 | $65,385.76 | |
| 1898 | $64,242.75 | |
| 1899 | $60,880.47 | |
| 1900 | $79,853.42 | $231,096.87 (between 1898 and 1901) |
| 1901 | $82,798.20 | $82,333.65 |
| 1902 | $119,687 | $83,827.48 |
| 1903 | $121,206.61 | $86,003.25 |
| 1904 | $87,175.18 | $84,548.49 |
| 1905 | $148,672.31 | $73,839.51 |
| 1906 | $171,816.76 | $79,980.96 |
| 1907 | $103,415.62 | $89,255.94 |
| 1908 | $89,162.72 | $70,604.87 |
| 1909 | $97,358.38 | $57,564.78 |
| 1910 | $92,520.23 | $73,316.82 |
| 1911 | $113,309.86 | $73,260.27 |
| 1912 | $109,549.35 | $41,031.39 |
| 1913 | $117,446.96 | $70,024.31 |
| 1914 | $112,668.53 | $51,166.29 |
| 1915 | $109,354.04 | $48,746.62 |
| 1916 | $144,705.13 | $46,722.13 |
| 1917 | $135,013.61 | $44,873.72 |
| 1918 | $147,617.81 | $39,481.71 |
| 1919 | $155,971.40 | $41,263.70 |
| 1920 | $210,717.64 | $42,292.02 |
| 1921 | $196,242.22 | $39,784.43 |
| 1922 | $215,190.35 | $38,938.75 |
| 1923 | $231,047.05 | $39,518.25 |
| 1924 | $273,241.53 | $39,862.35 |

\* Starting in 1905 some Catholic schools started receiving additional funding by accessing Indian Tribal Funds. As both tribal funding and the Lenten collection rose, Mother Katharine's subsidies fell.

Table compiled from *Reports on Mission Work among the Negroes and the Indians: What Is Being Accomplished by Means of the Annual Collection Taken up for Our Missions, 1887–1925*, BCIM records, series 7-2, reel 1, MUA.

"received from other sources."⁴³ She believed that if people saw the Drexel name, they would think they did not need to contribute as well. She explained, "So many of the priests engaged in Colored Work have this experience and they fear having it known that aid is received from us simply because the faithful think if Mother Katharine assists the mission it is not in very great need."⁴⁴

## Time, Talent, and Treasure

In addition to subsidizing mission schools, Drexel aided the Bureau of Catholic Missions in myriad ways. She provided an estimated $1,277,410 to construct churches, schools, convents, and rectories between 1895 and 1928. She also financed the daily activities of the BCIM. Drexel purchased the BCIM headquarters in Washington, D.C., in 1888, gave the bureau a quarterly stipend, and covered travel expenses of the director until 1933, when the Depression forced her to cut spending.⁴⁵ In 1920, the SBS purchased a second residence near the BCIM headquarters and sent three sisters to administer bureau business. The sisters assigned to Tekakwitha House handled correspondence for the Society for the Preservation of the Faith Among Indian Children, the fundraising arm of the bureau, performed administrative tasks such as typing and processing the payroll, and edited the *Indian Sentinel*, the society's magazine.⁴⁶ For many years the bureau

---

43 Mother Katharine Drexel to Rev. William Ketcham, March 27, 1907, BCIM records, series 1–1, box 55, folder 6. When he put her name in the report despite her insistence otherwise, she penned a rather cross missive, informing him, "I am sorry, however that you put my name in it" and accused him of going back on their agreement. See Mother Katharine Drexel to Rev. William Ketcham, May 3, 1908, BCIM records, series 1–1, box 59, folder 5.
44 Mother Katharine Drexel to Rev. William Ketcham, March 27, 1909, BCIM records, series 1–1, box 63, folder 8.
45 Mother Katharine Drexel to Rev. William Hughes, January 5, 1933, BCIM records, series 1–1, reel 186, MUA.
46 Ketcham organized the Society for the Preservation of the Faith among Indian Children in 1901 as a way to supplement the income of the bureau. Members paid dues and in return received an indulgence. The *Indian Sentinel*, the society's magazine, began as an annual in 1902. In 1916 it began quarterly publication. The magazine chronicled the history of Indian missions, gave updates on schools, printed obituaries of missionaries, and connected needs and donors.

owed its existence to the talents and treasure of the Sisters of the Blessed Sacrament. While attaching her own sisters to the BCIM helped the bureau, it also gave Drexel unfettered access to the center of power. Through her sisters, she gained key information about missionaries' work, the legitimacy of monetary requests, and any potential sources of conflict. SBS editing of the *Sentinel* also helped her shape the public conversation about the missions. Mother Katharine asserted control over the bureau while professing to be its most humble servant.

## Government School Cooperation

Mother Katharine, like most Catholics, believed church-affiliated mission schools such as the ones her own sisters operated held the key to the "Indian Problem," but she did not ignore the reality that most Indigenous students attended government schools. In 1916, the BCIM noted that more than five thousand Indigenous Catholics attended government-run boarding schools.[47] Mother Katharine and her cohorts at the bureau feared Protestant influence.[48] A letter printed in the 1902 BCIM report from an Indigenous Catholic boy to a sister highlighted the supposed danger of government education: "I am getting to be an infidel. I'll tell why. Since I have entered the Government school, they teach various beliefs and have various preachers come to school, who preach this and that, and sometimes debate on other denominations, which leads me to darkness and unbelief." The child concluded, "They dispute against the Catholic religion, saying this and that—that the priest has no more right than a common person to hear people's faults, and that they know the very character of a person. So I am at a point of standstill. I have not gone to confession for two years."[49] Those interested in the missionary cause imagined this story magnified thousands of times over. To combat this leakage of the faith, Mother Katharine financed Catholic instruction at government institutions.

---

47 "Catholic Instruction in Government Boarding Schools," *Indian Sentinel*, Winter 1916, 20.

48 Mother Katharine Drexel, "MMK Talks to Tekakwitha Club February 28, 1933," H10A box 30, folder 16, ASBS.

49 *Report of the Bureau of Catholic Indian Missions for 1900–01 and 1901–02*, 28.

SBS sisters took responsibility for the religious education of the students at many government schools, including the Carlisle Indian School in Pennsylvania and the Santa Fe Indian School in New Mexico, as well as Fort Defiance and Chin Lee (now Chinle) in Arizona. This entailed traveling to the schools on Sundays, assisting the priests at Mass, and conducting catechism classes. They also prepared students to receive the sacraments. Sometimes they sponsored Communion breakfasts for hungry students after Mass, as canon law prohibited ingesting food or water after midnight the night preceding the reception of the sacraments. For example, in March 1900, Mother Katharine provided a lavish breakfast banquet for Carlisle students at the local opera house.[50] They looked for ways to counter the Protestant culture at government schools.

At some government schools, such as Carlisle, the sisters also played a role in shaping policy, as they put in place guidelines for Catholic students in the "outing" program. Outing, one of the cornerstones of Pratt's educational theory, placed Indigenous students in white homes to work and learn about American customs and family life.[51] The sisters, working in conjunction with Rev. Henry Ganss, forced Carlisle to adopt supplementary rules for Catholic students. In this system, all applications from families wishing to hire indigenous Catholics had to go through the priest or the sisters. In addition, Catholic applicants had to provide a recommendation written by a priest and had to promise students would attend weekly Mass. They insisted that "the Catholic patrons should realize that the Indian pupils come to the family not merely in the capacity of a servant, to do the drudgery and servile work of the house, but as members of an unfortunate race, to be taught the ways of civilized life." Accordingly, "they should be treated with firmness, kindness, forbearance and patience. Every innocent method to contribute to their comfort, health, pleasure and advancement should be adopted." The sisters admonished, "Great care should be exercised in the choice of companions, playmates, or friends of the pupil. Every effort

---

50   *Red Man and Helper*, March 9, 1900, 1.
51   Adams, *Education for Extinction: American Indians and the Boarding School Experience, 1875–1928* (Lawrence: University of Kansas Press, 1995), 157–62.

should be made to give them a pleasant home, cheerful surroundings, and above all the society of good, exemplary Catholic companionship."[52] The sisters did not find their efforts to save students from treatment as menial servants successful, and in later years they opposed outing plans because "Catholic families made little drudges out of the children, did not feed them sufficiently and the training received in some of the families was not satisfactory at all."[53] This treatment was normal for outing programs, which opened vulnerable students to exploitation and abuse.

While the Sisters of the Blessed Sacrament had more influence over policy at Carlisle than they did at some other government schools, they played prominent roles at the schools they visited. In addition, the sisters sometimes brought government students to the missions for religious retreats.[54] The sisters also used their time with government school students to advocate for marrying within the church, a sacrament Indigenous people adopted with less frequency than baptism and Communion. For example, in 1906 at St. Michael's in Arizona, the SBS reported thirty-four baptisms and 229 Communions but no marriages. By 1915 the number of marriages had risen to nine, but it remained a small proportion of total sacraments administered.[55] To entice more students, sisters made sure the weddings at government schools were accompanied by great fanfare. At Fort Defiance, for example, the sisters brought a choir of eighteen St. Michael's students to provide the music for the first Catholic Navajo wedding held in January 1913.[56]

Since the SBS did not have enough sisters to visit every government school, Mother Katharine built chapels near the schools and hired priests to provide sacraments. By the 1920s, she spent

---

52 Rules found in *Report of the Director of the Bureau of Catholic Indian Missions for 1906* (Washington, DC: BCIM, 1906), 52.

53 Mother Katharine Drexel to Rev. William Hughes, January 10, 1928, BCIM correspondence files, series 1–1, reel 151, MUA.

54 Father Egbert Fischer, "The Fort Defiance School," *Indian Sentinel*, 1914, 42–46.

55 *Report of Catholic Indian Missions for 1906*, St. Michael's, St. Michael's Arizona, *Report of Catholic Indian Missions for 1915*, St. Michal's, St. Michael's Arizona, BCIM records, series 2/2: mission reports, reel 2, MUA.

56 Fischer, "The Fort Defiance School," *Indian Sentinel*, 1914, 46.

more than $7,000 each year on salaries for priests to say masses at government schools including Flandreau, Pierre, Pipestone, Chilocco, Seneca, Genoa, Rapid City, Chemawa, Mescalero, Lodge Grass, and Haskell.[57] Some priests, such as Father Gall Eugster, OSB, whom Drexel paid to serve Chemawa in Oregon, took their jobs as religious liaisons seriously. Eugster spent Saturday and Sunday at the school each week.[58] Others, such as the priest at Genoa Indian School in Nebraska, said Mass only a few times per month.[59] As relations between priests and government schools were often fraught, Drexel stressed that the priests she paid should be zealous "and *prudent* as well." The ideal priest "understands that he can't gather the Catholic Indian children of an institution like Haskell at *any* time *he* chooses to call."[60]

In addition to paying for priests to supply religious instruction, she also sent stipends for clerics to gather signatures of Indigenous parents to ensure that their children would receive Catholic education while attending government schools.[61] Federal policy dictated that to receive religious education from a particular denomination, the parents had to sign a paper stating their religious preference. This stipulation launched frenzied missionaries deep into reservation territory hunting for signatures. As Mother Katharine informed the American Board for Catholic Missions, "One never knows how many miles are implied in the lift of an Indian's chin."[62] Often parents would sign the petition of the first cleric to reach them, so these signatures cannot be read as support

---

57 *Quarter Ending December 29, 1929*, BCIM records, series 1-1, reel 151, MUA.

58 "Catholic Instruction in Government Schools: United States Indian School, Chemawa, Oregon," *Indian Sentinel*, April 1917, 30–31.

59 "Catholic Instruction in Government Schools, U.S. Indian School, Genoa, Nebraska," *Indian Sentinel*, Winter 1916, 20–21.

60 Mother Katharine Drexel to Rev. William Ketcham, November 17, 1905, BCIM records, series 1-1, box 49, folder 2, MUA.

61 Rev. William Hughes to Rev. Marcellus Troester, OFM, March 8, 1923; Rev. Marcellus Troester to Mother Catherine, March 3, 1923; Fr. Brendan Haile, OFM, to Mother Katharine Drexel, April 9, 1923, BCIM records, series 1-1, reel 110, MUA.

62 Mother Katharine Drexel, "Report 1935 to American Board for Catholic Missions," MMK talks, box 30, folder 16, ASBS.

for Catholicism. Drexel's gifts worked on the presumption that money was best spent when it could affect the greatest number of people, so while she believed, as did all Catholic missionaries, that religious schools represented the best option for Indigenous students, she also worked to spread the faith in secular institutions.[63] If the purpose of government schools was to Americanize Indigenous populations, Drexel used her money to insure that part of that Americanization included Catholic religious instruction.

It is unclear how students at government schools regarded Drexel's efforts. Adam Fortunate Eagle, who attended Pipestone in Minnesota, remembered being confused about church. He recalled, "Every Sunday we all have to go to Church. Church is something I don't understand. My Aunt Anna told me my father was Evangelical, my brother Curtis is Catholic, and my mother and other three older brothers and sisters are Episcopalian. On Sunday morning Mrs. Burns asks me what faith I belong to, I say, 'Chippewa.'"[64] Some priests cynically reported that the students only came to them when they provided a meal or entertainment. Some students might have attended Catholic services out of genuine religious devotion; others attended because they were forced to, and some came for the free food.

## Business of Sanctity

While historians have noted Mother Katharine's hefty donations, they have not examined her business practices or the difficulty the male hierarchy had in bending themselves to Drexel's agenda. Clerics had to meet Mother Katharine's exacting standards or risk losing her money. These tensions, combined with Mother Katharine's own financial woes and personnel disagreements, eventually led to her lessening influence at the Bureau of Catholic Indian Missions. Everyone involved in Indigenous missions knew the money issued from Drexel & Co. Bank came with

---

63 H. Leduc to William Ketcham, October 26, 1920, and William Ketcham to H. Leduc, November 2, 1920, BCIM records, series 1-1, reel 97, MUA.

64 Adam Fortunate Eagle, *Pipestone: My Life in an Indian Boarding School* (Norman: University of Oklahoma Press, 2010), 31.

strings attached. Mother Katharine kept detailed records and demanded accountability. Anyone who accepted her money had to sign a contract stating the money would be used exclusively to benefit Indigenous people. If the schools closed or ceased to be used for Indigenous education, she demanded the return of her investment. Those who did not agree to her rules received nothing. She told an uncooperative priest who wanted her help in building a chapel for the Crows, "I do not wish to force you into anything you do not approve of, only without such a contract I cannot conscientiously help you." Drexel warned, "Other Indians in the United States require help as urgently as the poor Crows. I shall look about me for an Order who will bind itself to such a perpetual contract & help these other Indians whose souls are as precious in God's sight as are the Crows."[65]

Mother Katharine never wavered from including this stipulation in her contracts, even when clerics explicitly told her to forgo it. For example, when she financed the purchase of a home for a priest in Antlers, Oklahoma, she made it contingent on the bishop signing an agreement promising to forfeit her investment if it were not used for Indigenous education. Father Ketcham asked her not to make the bishop sign, but she sent the agreement to the prelate anyway, informing Ketcham, "As he has signed papers of this kind before, I do not think he will hesitate about this. As soon as he returns the papers duly signed I hope if I live to be able to send you the money as promised."[66] When she reported that the bishop had completed the paperwork, all Ketcham could say was, "Since your experiment turned out so nicely, I am only too happy you took the initiative and did what you did."[67] She had a similar confrontation in 1923 with then BCIM director Rev. William Hughes when she demanded, over his objections, that a donor sign a note for a loan because it was "a little more businesslike."[68]

---

65 Mother Katharine Drexel, *Writings 3161*, ASBS.
66 Mother Katharine Drexel to Father William Ketcham, November 20, 1917, BCIM records, series 1-1, reel 84, MUA.
67 Rev. William Ketcham to Mother Katharine Drexel, December 1, 1917, BCIM records, series 1-1, reel 84, MUA.
68 Father William Hughes to Norine Prudom, January 7, 1923, BCIM records, series 1-1, reel 111, MUA.

She also only funded projects that she felt could flourish. Missionaries knew that their ability to gain funding from the BCIM depended on Mother Katharine's stamp of approval.[69] Drexel did not believe in frivolity and did not commit funds to priests and sisters unless she had vetted them. When she received requests from priests with whom she did not have a working relationship, she always ran their names by the bureau to ensure that they were doing quality work. For example, when Fr. E. Lapointe begged her for money, she dashed off a note to Charles Lusk, the bureau's longtime secretary, to ask "if the Father is really working among the Indians and if his cause is a deserving one."[70] Drexel was wary of writing checks to unproven causes. When Sister Ignatius, an Ursuline working at St. Labre in Montana, wrote to Drexel asking her to build a new schoolhouse, Father Stephan wrote back explaining, "The idea you appear to have that Miss Drexel will assist in the building of large, costly school-houses is an erroneous one. . . . She is willing to help, as far as she can, all the Indian Missions. . . . She has, it is true, given to a few Indian Missions considerable sums for building purposes, but as the money has not always been judiciously applied and has resulted in a demand for more money, she has naturally become more careful."[71] Her scientific management distinguished Drexel from other do-gooders who simply issued checks based on emotion or obligation. Drexel counted every penny and demanded it be used, as she often put it, *ad maiorem Dei gloriam*, for the greater glory of God.

The daughter of a banking tycoon, Katharine Drexel demanded painstaking recordkeeping in a church setting that was not comfortable with a woman dictating the terms of business. At the same time as Drexel insisted that clerics sign her agreements,

---

69 For example, before appealing for money from the Negro and Indian Mission Board, Father Sylvester Eisenman and Father William Hughes made sure the committee led by Cardinal Dougherty saw Mother Katharine's letters of approval for the mission in Marty, South Dakota. Rev. William Hughes to Father Sylvester Eiseneman, September 18, 1923, and Father Sylvester Eisenman to Rev. William Hughes, October 9, 1923, BCIM records, series 1–1, reel 111, MUA.

70 Mother Katharine Drexel to Charles Lusk, January 19, 1923, BCIM records, series 1–1, reel 114, MUA.

71 Father James Stephan to McFarland, February 18, 1888, BCIM records, series 1, reel 17, MUA.

canon law gave bishops the authority to suppress diocesan congregations and the right to examine postulants and novices and to preside over the elections of superiors. Those congregations that had papal approbation had more independence from the local ordinary, but they were still subject to visitations from the bishops, and ultimately the bishop had to grant or refuse permission to build new churches or other prayer structures within his diocese. They had the right to exercise arbitrary power, as Bishop William G. McCloskey did in 1896 when he ejected the Sisters of Notre Dame from the Diocese of Louisville. The same man also stripped the leader of the Louisville Ursulines of her rights as superior because she crossed the Ohio River without his direct approval.[72] As Carol K. Coburn and Martha Smith have pointed out, "Women religious who challenged male authority often found themselves ostracized and labeled 'unladylike' and their very sanity questioned."[73] The fact that the loss of Drexel's support would bring the entire Catholic Indian mission system to a halt meant that priests and bishops, unused to consulting with women and hesitant to treat them as equals, had to swallow their pride to get Mother Katharine's assistance.

Used to snapping orders at nuns, priests and members of the hierarchy had difficulty acknowledging her ability to shape the work of the church. For example, in 1928, when Mother Katharine sent an item in to add to the agenda of the meeting of the Negro and Indian Mission Board, the secretary, Rev. J. B. Tennelly, first sent word to Cardinal Dennis Dougherty, stating, "Mother Katharine says nothing in the letter which accompanies these documents (regarding SBS contributions to home missions) which would lead me to infer that she had consulted Your Eminence in regard to laying her request before the Board. For this reason I thought that it would be only proper for me first to ask if I have Your Eminence's authorization to include the matter."[74]

---

72 James M. Woods, *A History of the Catholic Church in the American South, 1513–1900* (Gainesville: University Press of Florida, 2011), 307.

73 Coburn and Smith, *Spirited Lives*, 94.

74 Rev. J. Tennelly to His Eminence Dennis Cardinal Dougherty, November 1, 1928, BCIM records, series 1–1, reel 151, MUA. Tennelly later became the director of the BCIM after Hughes resigned in 1935.

While Dougherty urged Tennelly to add the item to the agenda, Tennelly's need to double-check demonstrates the clergy's hesitance to acknowledge Drexel's policy contributions.[75] Though she signed letters to bishops and cardinals with fawning statements such as, "Kneeling to kiss the sacred Purple and to beg the blessing of Your Eminence," Mother Katharine Drexel held the upper hand in negotiations.[76] Perhaps resentment led the church hierarchy to praise her generosity and her holiness but refuse to acknowledge her financial acuity.

## Details and Disagreements

Mother Katharine's insistence on control could cause conflict. She liked to handle details personally and wanted to be included in all phases of a project. When reporting on a visit from Mother Katharine, Father Sylvester Eisenman, a priest in Marty, South Dakota, joked about her fastidiousness: "Of course she admires everything. She even admired St. Paul's Mission from the cellar all the way to the garret."[77] While her attention to detail amused Father Eisenman, it could create hardship for the missions. Before signing checks, Mother Katharine double-checked paperwork. When she was away from the convent, schools had to wait for payment, creating problems for those needing to purchase food and supplies. In 1922, her long absence caused BCIM Secretary Charles Lusk to send plaintive letters to the schools explaining that he hoped to send their checks soon, but the money depended on Mother Katharine's return.[78]

While her own travels occasionally delayed payments, she held missionaries accountable to the terms in her contracts and demanded stringent recordkeeping. In 1899, she informed Rev.

---

75 Cardinal Dougherty to Rev. J. Tennelly, November 2, 1928, BCIM records, series 1–1, reel 151, MUA.

76 Mother Katharine Drexel to His Eminence Dennis Cardinal Dougherty, November 4, 1932, BCIM records, series 1–1, reel 180, MUA.

77 Father Sylvester Eisenman to Father William Hughes, November 3, 1922, BCIM records, series 1–1, reel 105, MUA.

78 Charles Lusk to Rt. Rev. Eis, August 14, 1922, BCIM records, series 1–1, reel 105, MUA.

Stephan that several of the schools she had agreed to subsidize had not supported the agreed-upon number of students and pointed out discrepancies in their reports. She threatened to cut off support to any school or mission that did not promptly file its paperwork.[79] In 1904, tired of chronically late or incorrectly completed reports from two schools, she delayed payments to make a point. She explained to Ketcham that the reports to the two schools came after she had already written a check covering the others, and she noted, "It seems to me that Mother Francis said last year when these reports were delinquent without *any good reason* they would have to wait until the next quarter, and as she was in retreat when these came, and had previously sent the cheque for those which were received *on time* I simply made no response on the matter."[80] Mother Katharine did send the money, but she wanted her displeasure noted.

Ever the banker's daughter, she checked reports and crunched numbers multiple times. Letters to the bureau frequently began with phrases such as, "According to my calculations there is a slight discrepancy. . . ." or "would you please look into. . . ." She also followed up her donations with visits to ensure that work was being carried out properly. While canon law required her to visit SBS schools and convents, Drexel also inspected those schools she funded.[81] While travel put strains on Mother Katharine's time and body, she performed these visits until a massive 1935 heart attack forced her into retirement. Those who wanted a handout had to follow her rules and submit to her inspection.

This system did not always work smoothly. In 1917, Father Thomas Grant, SJ, a priest who served at St. Labre in Montana, complained to Father Ketcham, "You require us to carry 55 children in order to get the full pay for the 17 provided for by the Bureau and the 28 provided for by Mother Catherine. But you

---

79  Mother Katharine Drexel to J. Stephan, September 1, 1899, BCIM records, series 1-1, box 38, folder 1, MUA.

80  Mother Katharine Drexel to William Ketcham, August 18, 1904, BCIM records, series 1-1, box 46, folder 10, MUA.

81  Robert Fossey and Stephanie Morris, "St. Katharine Drexel and St. Patrick's Missions to the Indians of the Southern Plains: A Study in Saintly Administration," *Catholic Southwest* 18, no. 1 (2007): 61–82.

make no provision in your contract for any in excess of this number while you expressly cut down the payment when the number falls below 55." He continued his polemic, adding, "Moreover, you only consider the Bureau bound to the contract on the condition that it can get the funds. A contract to be square should work both ways, namely, when the number goes below and pay is reduced on that account, it should also be increased when the number goes above the number called for."[82] While the bureau director agreed with the frazzled priest and responded that a more equitable system would indeed pay per student, he added, "The system we have is an arrangement between the Bureau and Mother Katharine, whose contribution is a matter of absolute necessity and which I understand she promised on condition that this system should be carried out. So it appears to be a choice between forfeiting her contribution or retaining the system."[83] Her rules forced missions to attract and retain students, but the complicated subsidy system gave school administrators headaches.

## Limited Resources, Unlimited Needs

No matter how generously Mother Katharine spread her fortune, missionaries demanded more. By the early twentieth century, letters from the missions she had built decades earlier complained of deteriorating physical plants and poor conditions. Students did not have enough to eat. Some schools crumbled into disuse.[84] Poverty was endemic. In one particularly pitiful letter, a priest lamented that he did not even have the money to buy his constipated assistant a laxative.[85] Others wrote of forgoing running water and furniture while eking out a living from the small stipends from the BCIM and Mother Katharine.[86] As Drexel built

---

82   Father Thomas Grant to William Ketcham, March 8, 1917, BCIM records, series 1-1, reel 84, MUA.

83   Father William Ketcham to Father Thomas Grant, March 19, 1917, BCIM records, series 1-1, reel 84, MUA.

84   Mahoney, *Lady Blackrobes*, 246.

85   Father Francis Redman to Father William Hughes, September 12, 1923, BCIM records, series 1-1, reel 110, MUA.

86   Hubert A. Van Rechem to Joseph H. Fargis, January 18, 1906, BCIM records, series 1-1, box 53, folder 6, MUA.

many of the missions, priests and sisters believed it fell to her and the bureau to complete repairs, despite the fact that she made it clear on all her contracts that her support could only be guaranteed "while I live" and never made promises of continued support. When she began her charitable work in the 1880s, Drexel believed the schools would eventually support themselves through their industrial work. As Rev. William Ketcham pointed out in 1912, however, "Experience shows that no Indian school ever became self-supporting, and I have given up the idea that any ever will."[87] Thus Mother Katharine found herself besieged with more requests than even her ample coffers could handle.

The St. Louis Industrial School for Osage Girls in Pawhuska, Oklahoma, highlights this tension. Before entering the convent, Mother Katharine purchased the 160 acres of land, built the school, and placed the Sisters of St. Francis of Glen Riddle in charge. In 1915, after more than a quarter of a century, the Sisters of St. Francis turned operations of the school over to the Sisters of Loretto. The BCIM secured a contract to use Osage tribal funds to pay the sisters one hundred dollars per student. The SBS also paid one hundred dollars each for up to twenty-five non-Osage students. While the SBS retained the title to the land and subsidized students, the school was supposed to support itself. Nevertheless, the Sisters of Loretto repeatedly appealed to Mother Katharine for financial help.

In 1918, Mother Magdalene, the sister in charge of the school, asked for $1,500 for repairs. Drexel sent the money, but she also encouraged the sisters to reach out into the community to attract more paying students to the school.[88] In 1922, the sisters again pleaded with Mother Katharine to repair a leaky roof, as the costs were driving them into debt.[89] The following year, a visiting priest reported the physical plant, by then thirty-three years old, in

---

87   Father William Ketcham to Hubert Post, September 13, 1912, BCIM records, series 1–1, reel 62, MUA.
88   Father William Ketcham to Mother Magdalene, February 20, 1918, BCIM records, series 1–1, reel 98, MUA.
89   Mother Agnita to Father William Hughes, October 10, 1922, BCIM records, series 1–1, reel 106, MUA.

increasing disrepair, noting crumbling cement between the stones, a crooked porch, inadequate blackboards, and a cellar "full of water eight inches deep." He estimated between three and five thousand dollars for the needed repairs.[90] Everyone looked to Mother Katharine to foot the bill. By 1924, tensions had erupted between the local superior, Sr. M. Scholastica of the Sisters of Loretto, and the SBS. Sister Scholastica sent multiple letters to Father Hughes, asserting, "I wrote to Mother Catherine and asked her to help us pay the bill [$1,000 to pump water out of the basement], but she did not even answer my letter."[91] Mother Katharine did, in fact, send $300 as a gift and offered to give an advance on the $750 per quarter they received for non-Osage students, but the Sisters of Loretto felt abandoned and desperate. As Sr. Scholastica told Father Hughes, "We cannot live on air, neither can we live any longer on credit."[92]

For her part, Mother Katharine must have felt pressed beyond even her considerable means, especially when, the following year, the Pawhuska school once more begged her to bail them out of financial disaster. In April 1925, the local fire inspector visited the school and stated that to meet city codes the sisters had to re-roof the school, install a new septic tank, and add fire escapes. Drexel offered to pay for the new septic tank ($450) and the repair of broken plastering ($840), but she drew the line at paying for new fire escapes. Drexel, ever practical, suggested the sisters "experiment by a fire drill how long it will take to empty all at once your 23 beds occupied in the attic and the 40 beds occupied downstairs. You can make experiments with imaginary fires in different part of the house and report how long it takes in each case. I think 3 minutes would do it if the children were properly drilled."[93] Drexel believed the fire marshal had political motivations for put-

---

90 Father William Huffer to Father William Hughes, August 8, 1923, BCIM records, series 1–1, reel 114, MUA.
91 Sister M. Scholastica to Father William Hughes, February 8, 1924, BCIM records, series 1–1, reel 118, MUA.
92 Sister M. Scholastica to Father William Hughes, October 31, 1924, BCIM records, series 1–1, reel 118, MUA.
93 Mother Katharine Drexel to Sister M. Scholastica, May 26, 1925, BCIM records, series 1–1, reel 125, MUA.

ting this burden on the nuns, and she tried to get the BCIM director to use his clout to get the fire marshal's orders rescinded.[94] She set aside some of the money she had promised to pay for non-Osage students to aid with the repairs, but she offered subtle criticism, suggesting the Sisters of Loretto were not engaging the community and winning the hearts and minds of the Osage: "Dear Mother, these past years you were so bound by circumstances you did not feel free, I think, to have mothers' meetings, gatherings of your former pupils to go out into the camp, teach Sunday School, etc." She added, "The Osage love the Sisters of St. Francis [who previously staffed the school], and I am sure the devotedness of the Sisters of Loretto has won the confidence of the Osages and will more and more win them."[95] In other words, if they just tried harder, success would come. It is not hard to understand how such a position would aggravate the sisters, who taught with grumbling stomachs in a dilapidated building.

The Osage, whose tribal funds paid for most of the school's upkeep, also resented the arrangement. In 1924 students complained of hunger and loneliness, though Mother Scholastica quipped, "I do not think they have any reason to complain about eating, for we are feeding them beyond the money we are getting in."[96] The Osage expressed their disapproval by withdrawing support. Despite a government contract for seventy-five students, by the 1928–29 school year only seven full-blood and twelve mixed-blood students remained. The Osage, who had a lot of money due to the discovery of oil on their land, offered to improve the property by adding a new gymnasium, swimming pool, and dorms, but only if Drexel agreed to deed them back the 160 acres of school land.[97] When she did not comply, the Osage refused to sign the

---

94   Rev. William Hughes to Rt. Rev. Francis C. Kelley, DD, Bishop of Oklahoma, March 25, 1925, BCIM records, series 1–1, reel 129, MUA; Rev. William Hughes to Rt. Rev. Francis C. Kelley, May 29, 1925, BCIM records, series 1–1, reel 129, MUA.

95   Mother Katharine Drexel to Mother M. Scholastica, February 21, 1925, BCIM records, series 1–1, reel 128, MUA.

96   M. Scholastica to Father William Hughes, December 5, 1924, BCIM records, series 1–1, reel 118, MUA.

97   Robert Stuart to Mother Katharine Drexel, February 12, 1929, BCIM records, series 1–1, reel 159, MUA.

government contract in 1930, though some students continued at their own expense. The misadventures at Pawhuska show some of the pitfalls of a business model that emphasized reaching as many students as possible. In many cases, Drexel displayed impressive business acumen, but in spreading herself too thin, she listened more to her heart than her head. For Drexel, reaching more children meant growing the Mystical Body of Christ, something she considered more pressing than fire escapes and septic tanks. Those who had to live in crumbling facilities lacking basic safety features likely did not see it the same way.[98]

Mother Katharine's philanthropic model and missionaries' continual demand for more money strained Drexel's resources. As per the instructions of her father's will, she received half of the interest on a trust of roughly $15 million. By the 1920s this was roughly $220,000 per year.[99] Still, it was never enough to meet demands, especially as she continually pushed to increase the scope of the work. As early as 1899 Rev. Stephan had urged her to make "provisions for the traditional 'rainy day,'" but Drexel refused and swore to devote her entire income to the missions.[100] As SBS schools proliferated, money for BCIM schools grew scarce. Despite this, she dismissed critics who warned against opening more missions. In 1904, when Ketcham wrote her such a letter, she responded, "You must pardon me, Father, when I tell you that the vision of no less than your venerable self waxing warm on the prospect of new schools . . . was too much for my gravity, and although I was very busy, I actually had to take the time to laugh." She added, "Never mind, Father, all these things will come to an end," and she urged him to trust in Divine Providence.[101]

---

[98] In 1942 the SBS took over administration of St. Louis when the Sisters of the Loretto withdrew. Though they tried to increase enrollment, Osage girls preferred to attend white schools, where they were not subject to rigid Catholic discipline. The SBS closed the school in 1949. Lynch, *Sharing the Bread in Service*, 2:19–21.

[99] Butler, *Across God's Frontiers*, 216.

[100] James Stephan to Mother Katharine Drexel, September 1, 1899, BCIM records, series 1-1, box 38, folder 1, MUA.

[101] Mother Katharine Drexel to Father William Ketcham, December 12, 1904, BCIM records, series 1-1, box 46, folder 11, MUA.

Providence, however, could not protect her from financial difficulties. The federal income tax instituted in 1913, combined with overextension in the mission field, created considerable financial strain. By 1920, with post–World War I inflation causing soaring prices, the situation was dire, and the BCIM had to lend Drexel money to help her cover expenses at SBS schools.[102] When an Ursuline sister wrote Ketcham asking for a raise in her school's stipend, he reported, "She [Drexel] cannot do anything because the high prices have crippled her institutions likewise and the income tax has eaten into her funds so that it will be impossible to expect any further help from her—that is more than she is giving." He further mused, "In fact, I wonder that she has been able to keep up as well as she has. I know that she has stinted herself and her own institutions."[103] In 1923, when the BCIM requested money to help with its Christmas appeal, Drexel provided a loan rather than a donation, complaining that she did not have even six dollars to give. She blamed the income tax, remarking, "It requires some degree of resignation to render cheerfully 'to Caesar the things that are Caesars.'"[104] The situation brightened in 1924 when Pennsylvania Senator George Wharton Pepper moved a tax exemption through Congress for people who donated more than 90 percent of their income for the previous ten years to charity. This exemption, which at the time applied only to Drexel, saved roughly $100,000 per year.[105]

As early as 1924, though she continued to support BCIM missions, she began asking for money from the bureau when she petitioned for $5,000 to build an addition school on the Navajo reservation.[106] In 1928, the congregation began drawing money from the annual Lenten collection, something it had previously

---

102 Father Ketcham to Rt. Rev. Mathias C. Lenihan, bishop of Great Falls Montana, April 28, 1920, BCIM records, series 1–1, reel 97, MUA.
103 Father Ketcham to Sr. M. Loyola, May 20, 1920, BCIM records, series 1–1, reel 98, MUA.
104 Mother Katharine Drexel to Father William Hughes, October 19, 1923, BCIM records, series 1–1, reel 114, MUA.
105 "Income Tax Exemption for Mother Katharine Drexel," *Indian Sentinel*, July 1924, 102.
106 Father William Hughes to Rev. Daniel J. Geroke, bishop of Tucson, March 19, 1924, BCIM records, series 1–1, reel 117, MUA.

avoided.[107] While Mother Katharine continued to assist the BCIM through the 1930s (over $100,000 each year), she could no longer singlehandedly bankroll operations. In 1933, she informed BCIM director Rev. William Hughes, "We have been accustomed in the past to give all the financial help we could possibly afford to missionary works outside of our Congregation, but we have finally reached the limits of our resources."[108]

## Fading Cooperation with the BCIM

Her shrinking ability to dispense funds well as personal tensions with the BCIM director Rev. William Hughes, who had taken over from Ketcham in 1922, made her less central to bureau operations and limited her influence on policy during the 1930s. While always professional and polite, the letters between Drexel and Hughes contain little of the warmth of those between Mother Katharine and his predecessors Joseph Stephan and William Ketcham.[109] Hughes consulted her on fewer projects, though he continued to ask for money and to utilize SBS talent in his office. One source of disagreement between Drexel and Hughes arose when increasing numbers of Indigenous students began attending day schools. The 1928 publication of the Merriam Report, which harshly condemned boarding schools as overly institutional, unsafe, cruel, places, accused missionaries of destroying indige-

---

107 Drexel requested the Board of Catholic Missions for Indians and Negroes grant the SBS $25,000 in perpetuity. Her influence was so great that during the Depression the SBS continued to get its full allotment, while other allocations were reduced by 10 percent in 1933 and an additional 25 percent in 1934. J. Tennelly to His Eminence Dennis Cardinal Dougherty, January 18, 1933, BCIM records, series 1-1, reel 186, MUA; J. Tennelly to Most Rev. John W. Shaw, DD, November 28, 1933, BCIM records, series 1-1, reel 186, MUA.

108 Mother Katharine Drexel to Rev. William Hughes, December 11, 1933, BCIM records, series 1-1, reel 186, MUA.

109 Drexel enjoyed personal relationships with the first two directors of the BCIM. When Stephan retired in 1901, he spent his last months at the SBS motherhouse. His grave is located on their grounds. Mother Katharine also had a strong relationship with Father Ketcham, with whom she conferred regularly. Upon learning of his death in 1921, Mother Katharine immediately jumped on a train to Oklahoma, where he died, to comfort his family and help with his funeral arrangements. "Monsignor Ketcham," *Indian Sentinel*, January 1922, 402–10.

nous religion and rightly pointed out that too many of them were in poor physical condition.[110] This led to changes in federal policies that affected boarding school attendance. During the 1930s the government, pressured by John Collier, President Roosevelt's commissioner of Indian Affairs, built more than forty day schools. In 1934, Congress passed the Johnson-O'Malley Act, which eased Indigenous children into public schools.[111] Hughes embraced the new government policy, while Mother Katharine believed it threatened her life's work.

When the government announced that it planned to build additional day schools in the New Mexico pueblos, Drexel warned Hughes, "I consider that if acted upon this would be detrimental to the Catholicity of the Pueblo Indians." She anticipated that Hughes would instruct the SBS to close St. Catherine's and teach in the pueblos instead, something that would have required more money and personnel than she had available. Mother Katharine begged for reassurance.[112] In a testy response, Hughes claimed attendance at St. Catherine's would not fall, but he pushed her to consider the value of day schools, explaining that each St. Catherine's student cost roughly $113.20 per year to educate, while the same student at a day school could be taught for $18.[113] Not willing to accept Hughes's approval of the government plan, Drexel went behind his back and contacted U.S. Indian Commissioner John Sullivan, asking him to lobby Congress against the day school plan.[114] Hughes rebuked her, expressing doubt that the church could stop the government plan. He insisted

---

110 Lewis Meriam, *The Problem of Indian Administration*, Institute for Government Research (Baltimore: Johns Hopkins University Press, 1928); see especially 815–47.

111 Margaret Connell Szaz, *Education and the American Indian: The Road to Self-Determination since 1928* (Albuquerque: University of New Mexico Press, 1974), 63–91.

112 Mother Katharine Drexel to Rev. William Hughes, January 17, 1931, BCIM records, series 1-1, reel 173, MUA.

113 William Hughes to Mother Katharine Drexel, January 28, 1931, and William Hughes to Mother Katharine Drexel, February 13, 1931, BCIM records, series 1-1, reel 173, MUA.

114 Mother Katharine Drexel to William Hughes, February 28, 1931, BCIM records, series 1-1, reel 173, MUA.

that the government and the church were working for the same objective: "the bringing of the Indians, where possible, into her ordinary (which is to say parochial) organization."[115] He believed day schools and cooperation with the government were the future of mission work.

Despite her protests in this exchange, Drexel did support day schools. In 1933 she gave a speech at the Tekakwitha Club in Washington, D.C., where she stated, "It is the ideal of Catholic education to have day schools for the children whence they may return at night to the family circle, and, what is particularly desirable in the case of a pagan people, the children may carry into the home the lessons of faith and morality learned in the classroom."[116] This spat with Hughes, then, stemmed not from ideological differences over the efficacy of day schools but rather from the fear of having to shutter her beloved institutions. While this heated debate between Mother Katharine and Hughes did not sever their relationship, it marked a cooling in their correspondence. Though Mother Katharine blamed budget shortfalls, this disagreement likely led to the withdrawal of SBS from BCIM office work in the winter of 1932.[117]

The more Hughes stressed government cooperation and the transition to day schools, the more Drexel insisted upon the validity of her approach. This clash rose to a head over St. Mary's School in Miami, Oklahoma, which had been sitting empty for years. Hughes wanted to sell the property and use the money elsewhere, but Mother Katharine hesitated. She explained that she hoped to attract missionaries to reopen the school and told Hughes of a boy who got his start at St. Mary's and then boarded

---

115 William Hughes to Mother Katharine Drexel, March 31, 1931, BCIM records, series 1–1, reel 173, MUA.

116 Mother Katharine Drexel, "MMK Talks to Tekakwitha Club 28 February 1933," H 10A, box 30, folder 16, ASBS.

117 Mother Katharine Drexel to William Hughes, March 1932, BCIM records, series 1–1, reel 180, MUA. For more on Hughes's support of Collier, see William Hughes, "What of the New Indian Bill?," *Indian Sentinel*, Spring 1934, 30–36; William Hughes, "Collier Indian Bill Passes," *Indian Sentinel*, Summer 1934, 54–55, 65; and William Hughes, *Indians on a New Trail*, pamphlet (July 1934), BCIM records, series 4/2 and 3, reel 2, MUA.

at St. Catherine's while attending St. Michael's College in Santa Fe. She used the story as "proof that the Faith implanted in the heart of the child at school will assert itself later on in life, and make the boy or girl realize what a gift it is and it will lead them right."[118] Instead of retreating from that section of Oklahoma, she proposed paying a missionary priest to visit local families or conduct a summer school to attract students. Though a gifted businesswoman, her religious fervor sometimes clouded her vision.

By the time a massive heart attack forced her into retirement in 1935, Drexel's influence at the BCIM had waned. The SBS continued to operate their schools, some into the twenty-first century, but many schools closed. In 1931 Indigenous students in Catholic schools peaked at 7,500; by the late 1930s the BCIM ministered to only 4,582 pupils. This number has continued to drop. Many former students applauded when the priests and sisters deconsecrated churches and pulled out of schools because they were painful reminders of a colonial past. Some remember the mission sites Mother Katharine funded as places of abuse and neglect. In other places, Indigenous communities have worked with religious congregations to create schools that are models of cooperation and cultural enrichment. The transformation of Holy Rosary Mission on the Pine Ridge Reservation into Red Cloud Indian School epitomizes this trend.[119] While this chapter has dealt with funding and administration details, chapter 3 will explore the sisters' approach to mission schools and their complicated legacies.

For fifty years, Mother Katharine was at the center of all Bureau of Catholic Indian Missions activities, and her influence goes far beyond her padded pocketbook. Exploring Drexel's contributions—both financial and philosophical—enriches a historical understanding of both the administration of the missions and the male/female power dynamics in the church. The SBS superior general never hesitated to offer the hierarchy her opinions. When the church failed to act, she forged ahead. An exacting business-

---

118 Mother Katharine Drexel to William Hughes, January 27, 1934, BCIM records, series 1–1, reel 192, MUA.

119 Christopher Vecsey, *Where the Two Roads Meet* (Notre Dame, IN: University of Notre Dame Press, 1999), 10, 21–22, 69–78.

woman and powerful force for change in an era when the church welcomed neither, Mother Katharine Drexel carved out a unique and unprecedented role as the chief operating officer of a benevolent empire: she balanced dollars and souls.

CHAPTER 3

## "Souls! Souls! Should Be Our Cry, Our Ambition, Our Only Aim"

### SBS Administration of Indigenous Schools

WHILE DREXEL AND THE SBS financially supported dozens of schools for Indigenous Catholics, they administered only a handful of institutions. Between 1891 and 1935, the SBS staffed St. Catherine's, St. Michael's in Arizona, St. Augustine's in Winnebago, Nebraska, and St. Paul's in Marty, South Dakota.[1] The sisters viewed their work with Indigenous students as an adventure and wrote about their forays into the West with great excitement, telling stories of vivid new landscapes, material privations, adventure, encounters with "those 'other' brethren,"[2] and the opportunity to fulfill their vocation, "the very vocation of Our Lord Himself—the salvation of souls!"[3] In their roles as educators, social workers, and nurses, the sisters acted as cultural intermediaries as they worked to bring their uniquely Catholic ideas of Americanization to their reservation

---

    1  The SBS operated St. Catherine's from 1894 to 1998, St. Michael's from 1902 to the present, St. Augustine from 1909 to1945, and St. Paul's from 1922 to 1980. While the tribes they served have their own names to describe themselves, I will use the terms that the sisters used. For example, while Navajo call themselves *Diné*, I will use the Americanized spelling found in the nuns' letters.
    2  "Saint Catherine's Indian School, Santa Fe, New Mexico," *Indian Sentinel*, 1903–4, 13.
    3  Mother Katharine Drexel to the Sisters of the Blessed Sacrament, April 14, 1894, quotation in S.M.D., "Our Great Adventure," *Mission Fields at Home*, November 1928, 19.
    4  Historian Anne M. Butler has suggested that nuns operated as "culture brokers," which is a particularly apt description. Butler, *Across God's Frontiers*, 19, 227. The term was earlier explored by Margaret Connell Szaz, who used it to examine Indians who moved between white and Indian worlds. Szaz, "Introduction," in *Between Indian and White Worlds: The Culture Broker* (Norman: University of Oklahoma Press, 1994), 3–30.

schools.[4] At first the SBS ran their schools as Catholic versions of government schools, just adding sacramental preparation and Mass to the prescribed curriculum. Over time, however, they branched out to allow for more Indigenous self-expression. Like all schools designed for Indigenous students, the SBS schools robbed students of their native languages and took them away from their families. Despite this, they were popular in the communities they served. The sisters attributed their popularity to an enthusiastic embrace of Catholicism, but more likely it is because as the position of Indigenous people in the country deteriorated, the SBS schools provided goods and services they would not have gotten otherwise. To some communities, they were the less bad choice.

## St. Catharine's: The First Mission

"Westward, farther westward, in sight of rolling lands and pleasing scenic beauty, we find ourselves borne along over mountains with majestic forests, while Dame Nature seems to delight in unfolding gradually her more striking and stupendous works. Varied and inexpressible are the thoughts which possess one taking this journey."[5] This anonymous Sister of the Blessed Sacrament's description of the journey west highlights the fact that when the SBS first began staffing western Indigenous missions, they stepped into a new world for which their East Coast backgrounds had not prepared them. In 1894, only three years after the congregation's founding, the first group of missionary sisters set off for Santa Fe to reopen St. Catharine's, a school that Mother Katharine had constructed for Pueblo students in 1887.

Since its founding, the school had suffered from chronic instability. First the Sisters of Loretto operated St. Catharine's, then Benedictine Fathers from Kansas, and finally lay teachers took over, all in the span of four years. The government withdrew its contract in 1893 because the school lacked an industrial curriculum. The rocky soil surrounding Santa Fe made it very difficult to implement the sort of farming courses recommended by the U.S.

---

5 "Saint Catherine's Indian School, Santa Fe, New Mexico," *Indian Sentinel*, 1903–4, 12.

government.[6] Sister Blandina Segale, a Sister of Charity who spent twenty years in the Southwest, blamed the instability on the bishop's choice of a supervising priest "whose sympathies were not with the Indians."[7] The Sisters of Charity refused the post because they believed he would be difficult to deal with. She also blamed him for the Sisters of Loretto's hasty exit. When Mother Katharine negotiated to take over the school in 1894, she and BCIM director Monsignor Stephan made sure that the sisters, rather than a priest, would have final say in school administration. This policy gave the nuns complete control of their own affairs, and they made sure priests associated with their schools understood their place. In 1935 Rev. Garcia pled ignorance to affairs at the school in his official missionary priest report, explaining, "They [the SBS] are in charge of the school, I am just a Chaplain."[8] Asserting their authority gave the SBS the chance to design a different kind of school.

On the train ride west, the sisters learned that their new home operated by different rules than their eastern convent. Despite Frederick Jackson Turner's proclamation of the death of the frontier made the previous year, the SBS operated on the outer limits of American Catholicism. Their experiences in Philadelphia had not prepared them for this new world and its dangers. In June 1894, the second group of sisters to make the trip were removed from their train during a railroad strike in Dodge City, Kansas. The sisters caught another train, but they were waylaid for three days, forced to sleep on the rail cars. When they resumed the journey, they heard rumors that the strikers had set large kegs of dynamite to explode when the train passed through the Raton Tunnel near the Colorado/New Mexico border. Still, the eager nuns refused to wait until the danger had passed.[9] When they made it through the tunnel, the sisters attempted to telegraph the motherhouse with the

---

6   Connie Sze, "Gone but Not Forgotten: St. Catherine's Industrial Indian School," *Bulletin of the Historic Santa Fe Foundation*, Summer 2003, 11.
7   Sister Blandina Segale, *At the End of the Santa Fe Trail* (Milwaukee: Bruce, 1948), 271.
8   *Report of Catholic Indian Missions in the U.S. for Year Ending June 30, 1935*, BCIM records, series 2/2: Mission reports, reel 5.
9   Quotation in S. M. D., "Our Great Adventure," *Mission Fields at Home*, November 1928, 21.

news of their safe passage. Soldiers who witnessed the nuns at the telegraph station detained them, however. The soldiers feared the sisters were either union men or criminals using the habit as a disguise. The harrowing trip was a baptism by fire for the sisters, who had to make their traditional ideas about parochial schools fit into a new and sometimes hostile environment.

## St. Michael's: A Difficult Sell

At the turn of the twentieth century, no environment was less disposed to Catholic missionaries than the Navajo Reservation, which encompassed parts of Arizona, New Mexico, and Utah. While many Catholic Indian missions built on the work of earlier generations of Jesuits and Franciscans, the Navajo did not have a tradition of Catholicism and were skeptical of priests and sisters. The nomadic structure of Navajo society had hindered previous missionary activity. Permanent pueblo structures in New Mexico made missionary activity relatively easy, but Navajos disappeared into the desert whenever clerics made forays into their territory. In addition, the Navajo reservation boasted challenging terrain and a climate with "almost all the different stages between Switzerland and purgatory."[10] While they broiled in the summer, temperatures could reach thirty degrees below zero in the winter.

Despite these pitfalls, however, Drexel worked with Franciscan fathers based out of Cincinnati to establish a Catholic stronghold in the Navajo nation. In 1895, Mother Katharine toured the site of the future St. Michael's, just six miles south of Fort Defiance, Arizona, with BCIM director Monsignor Stephan, and began the arduous process of obtaining land rights. In 1897, Mother Katharine traveled to Cincinnati to urge the Franciscans to take on the mission, and she promised to open a boarding school as soon as she had enough personnel. The SBS financed the Franciscan mission, constructing the buildings and paying salaries for the priests and brothers who ventured to Arizona.[11] Franciscan

---

10 "The Navajo Indians and Saint Michael's Indian Mission," *Indian Sentinel*, April 1918, 9.

11 Robert L. Wilken, *Anselm Weber, O.F.M.: Missionary to the Navaho, 1898–1921* (Milwaukee: Bruce, 1955), 24–37.

operations began in 1898, though the SBS did not open St. Michael's School until 1902. At first met with suspicion, the missionaries became part of the Navajo survival strategy. In later years, the school and mission centers served as hospitals, thrift shops, and burial grounds.

## St. Augustine's and St. Paul's: Different Administrative Models

While St. Catherine's and St. Michael's went on to become large regional centers, attracting several hundred students each, St. Augustine's, the Winnebago school, remained small. Located in northeastern Nebraska, the Winnebago Reservation occupies 1,800 acres, making it considerably smaller than the nineteen pueblos that fed into St. Catherine's or the 27,425 square miles belonging to the Navajo. In the late nineteenth century, the Winnebago reservation had fallen under the pastoral care of Mother Katharine's spiritual advisor Bishop James O'Connor, but his successor, Bishop Richard Scannel, delayed opening a mission there.[12] Finally, in 1909 the SBS began construction of a day school, but during the first year they decided a boarding school would be necessary because of the inclement weather and the impassibility of roads in the winter. The school did not experience the same growth as the southwestern institutions, and the student population never topped sixty students.

Although the Sisters of the Blessed Sacrament typically constructed and financed their own schools, retaining tight control of their administration, in 1922 an opportunity presented itself in the form of a gregarious Benedictine priest named Father Sylvester Eisenman, who begged them to join his mission to the Yankton Sioux. Eisenman, originally an itinerant missionary, received requests from elders on the Yankton Reservation to start a school in Marty, South Dakota. While he began a small day school in 1919, he decided that the harsh South Dakota winters precluded a day school. By 1921, he questioned, "What about those children who lived twenty, and even thirty miles from the mission? The roads were dirt only. In wet weather, they were impassible; like-

---

12   Lynch, *Sharing the Bread in Service*, 1:129–30.

wise in winter, as deep snowdrifts blocked all traffic."[13] Lacking teachers, he journeyed to Pennsylvania to petition Mother Katharine in person. The SBS had no personnel to spare, but Eisenman refused to take "no" for an answer. He addressed the entire community, and he was so persuasive that upon finishing an impassioned speech, he asked how many sisters would like to go, and every sister held up her hand; some held up both.[14] Mother Katharine shuffled teaching assignments, and sisters arrived in Marty a few months later. The always colorful Eisenman explained to Rev. William Hughes, "Mother Katharine 'busted something' and let me have four Sisters."[15] While Mother Katharine contributed modestly to the school and provided the priest a car to traverse the reservation, Eisenman had fiscal responsibility for the school. The SBS served, for the most part, as staff rather than proprietors of St. Paul's. The school quickly grew, and as many as fifteen sisters worked at the school each year, making it one of the sisters' largest projects.

## Hustling for Students

The law favored government schools, so priests and sisters had to work hard to attract students. In March 1891, Congress authorized the commissioner of Indian Affairs "to make and enforce by proper means such rules and regulations as will secure the attendance of Indian children of suitable age and health at schools established and maintained for their benefit" and gave him the authority in 1893 to "withhold rations, clothing, and other annuities from Indigenous parents or guardians who refuse or neglect to send and keep their children of proper school age in some school a reasonable portion of each year."[16] This strong-arming enraged the Indigenous population, who sometimes chose

---

13 Mary Eisenman Carson, *Blackrobe for the Yankton Sioux: Fr. Sylvester Eisenman, OSB (1891–1941)* (Chamberlain, SD: Tipi Press, 1989), 103.
14 Mother Katharine Drexel, "Carroll Club Talk, February 1923," H 10A, box 30, folder 14, ASBS.
15 Father Sylvester Eisenman, OSB, to William Hughes, March 27, 1922, BCIM records, series 1-1, reel 105, MUA.
16 *The Statutes at Large of the United States of America*, 26:1,014; 27:635.

Catholic schools to defy the government. Knowing this, Mother Katharine encouraged sisters to insert themselves into the community to gain the trust of parents so they would elect to send their children to SBS schools.

Trust was a valuable currency to people accustomed to broken promises. When overseeing the construction of the school in Winnebago, Mother Katharine made it a point to meet all the families in town. She also wrote detailed letters to the sisters about each family so they could get to know students and parents more quickly upon arrival.[17] Within days of their arrival in Marty, sisters began visiting all corners of the reservation. Bernard J. Mahoney, the bishop of Sioux Falls, noted that they "enter into almost every detail of the life of the Indians and bring encouragement and consolation wherever they go."[18] The nuns met with both Catholics and non-Catholics to win goodwill. The trips into less well-traveled areas of the reservation also proved educational for the sisters. Mother Katharine reflected on a trip to convince Navajo students to enroll in their school: "Here we met them in their simple homes; here despite their poverty we knew them to be rich in scenic beauty and their own native culture."[19] Their willingness to venture deep into reservations differentiated them from many Protestant missionary women, who were more closely bound to their homes and children. It also flew in the face of rules of enclosure set by the church. Visitations were a central part of their praxis for the first fifty years of SBS existence.[20]

Despite their willingness to meet with families, when they first took over St. Catherine's, the sisters had difficulty convincing the Pueblo to send children, especially their girls. Under previous

---

17  Lynch, *Sharing the Bread in Service*, 1:132.

18  Bernard J. Mahoney to William Hughes, July 27, 1923, BCIM records, series 1–1, reel 111, MUA.

19  Sisters of the Blessed Sacrament, *Navajo Adventure* (Cornwells Heights, PA: Sisters of the Blessed Sacrament, 1952), 28.

20  Over time, visitations became less central to the SBS culture. Sister Francis Mary Riggs wrote a dissertation in 1967 that argued that by that time they seldom interacted with students' families. Sister Francis Mary Riggs, SBS, "Attitudes of Missionary Sisters toward American Indian Acculturation" (Ph.D. diss., Catholic University of America, 1967).

management, the school had taught only boys, but the SBS championed co-education and retooled the property to house both sexes. As at most mission schools (and Catholic schools, for that matter), boys and girls attended the same academic classes but were otherwise segregated, with separate dining and recreation facilities. Only on special occasions did the SBS open the door between the dining facilities and allow students to greet one another.[21] Still, when the SBS arrived, they described Pueblo parents as harboring "a feeling bordering on suspicion as to the wisdom of sending the girls."[22] They managed to convince parents to educate their daughters by allowing mothers and fathers to stay on campus until they were satisfied that the nuns would treat their daughters with kindness.

The SBS won over skeptical parents with a commitment to hospitality. They provided visitors hay for their horses, food, and a comfortable place to camp. St. Catherine's typically housed ten to twenty Indigenous visitors at any given time.[23] Knowing they could check in on their children likely assuaged the broken hearts of parents who left their young ones at the boarding school. A sister described a father making a panicked journey from Isleta Pueblo to Santa Fe late at night because he had heard rumors that his child cried continuously. Despite the hour, the sisters welcomed him to the school and, "to his relief he found that little Juan had long since ceased crying, had become attached to his new home and was quite happy. With his five little children around him, the father spent a very happy day, returning to his home with a lighter heart."[24] This open-door policy created a favorable impression on a group that was typically treated with hostility when visiting government schools. Only a few years before the SBS opened St. Catharine's, H. Beadle, the superintendent of the Crow Boarding School, wrote the commissioner of Indian Affairs

---

21 Sze, "Gone but Not Forgotten," 18.
22 "Saint Catherine's Indian School, Santa Fe, New Mexico," *Indian Sentinel*, 1903–4, 15.
23 "The Sisters of the Blessed Sacrament for Indians and Colored People," *Indian Sentinel*, 1907, 16.
24 SBS, "A Visit to Our Western Missions," *Mission Fields at Home*, April 1930, 102.

begging him to erect a twelve-foot-tall board fence around the school buildings because "every Indian the camp who wishes to, can converse with the pupils, and it cannot be prevented." The new fence would make sure students were "separated almost entirely from the demoralizing influences of the camp."[25] Hospitality also distinguished SBS schools from other Catholic missions, where priests protested Indians settling near school grounds because "their dancing, howling, campfire antics and the pupils running to and fro would be an intolerable detriment to the school."[26] Despite the SBS commitment to hospitality, though, in some cases years passed before families reunited. For example, Sreceay "Henry" Whitmore arrived at St. Catherine's at the age of six and did not see his family again until he was seventeen because it too far from his home in Winslow, Arizona, and his family could not afford to make the trip.[27] His lengthy absence from his family must have caused trauma.

Opening St. Michael's required even more finesse than the sisters employed at St. Catherine's, since the Navajo made it clear that they did not want a school. In 1900, Franciscan missionary Father Anselm Weber organized a meeting between Mother Katharine, Mother Evangelist, then the superior at St. Catherine's, and tribal leaders on the Navajo reservation. The meeting occurred during the Mountain Chant, a nine-day healing ceremony, which took place at Red Lake. To soften up the Navajo, Mother Katharine paid for a feast of mutton and pan bread at the dance. When they sat down to speak, several Navajo expressed concern that schooling ruined their children; one suggested that students who returned from places such as the Fort Defiance Government School were "just more malicious, more shifty, and more

---

25 H. Beadle to General H. Williamson, August 30, 1877, quotation in *Talking Back to Civilization: Indian Voices from the Progressive Era*, ed. Frederick Hoxie (Boston: Bedford St. Martin's, 2001), 10.

26 Rev. Fred Eberschweiler to Fr. James Stephan, March 15, 1888, BCIM records, series 1–1, box 21, folder 20, MUA. Later the same priest got the Indian agent to mark a line below the mission on a map and forbade Indians to camp or settle within the line.

27 Brian S. Collier, "St. Catherine Indian School, Santa Fe, 1887–2006: Catholic Indian Education in New Mexico" (Ph.D. diss., Arizona State University, 2007), 113.

dishonest than the others."[28] In many boarding schools, hunger forced students to steal, and the antagonistic relationship between teachers and students produced bitterness and anger.[29] Furthermore, he argued that the school curriculum had no relevance to reservation life.[30] Other men complained that students who fell ill at school did not have recourse to healing rituals.

After everyone had spoken, Mother Katharine promised to design the curriculum with the goal of making students useful citizens of the reservation. She did not, however, give in on the question of sending ill children back to medicine men.[31] By engaging in dialogue and creating a space where Navajo could express their frustrations, Mother Katharine differentiated herself from government agents who alternated threats of force with bribery. In addition, when they expressed continued reservations, she gave them a tour of the school site, explaining the purpose of each room and detailing her intentions. Her methods clashed with government agents who "waited until the men went off to work, and then they entered the hogan and simply took the children away by force and brought them into school."[32] Father Anselm Weber pointed out that when the government applied force, Indigenous parents chose Catholic schools: "The school at Fort Defiance has never seen any of their children (he refers specifically to people of Red Rock, whose children government agents attempted to kidnap in 1892), but they have sent twenty-

---

28 For an eyewitness description of the ritual, see Washington Matthews, "The Mountain Chant: A Navajo Ceremony," U.S. Bureau of American Ethnology Fifth Annual Report, 1883–1884 (Washington, DC: Smithsonian Institution, 1887).

29 Adams, *Education for Extinction*, 229–38.

30 Anselm Weber, "Fall 1900: Students to Santa Fe, Headmen to Cienga," in *The Navajo as Seen by the Franciscans 1898–1921: A Sourcebook*, ed. Howard M. Bahr (Lanham, MD: Scarecrow Press), 82. This complaint has been frequently leveled at Indian schools. What good did learning how to farm do on the arid, non-arable Navajo Reservation? For more on this debate, see Adams, *Education for Extinction*, 273–306.

31 Adams, *Education for Extinction*, 84.

32 Fr. Murray Bodo, *Tales of an Endishodi: Father Berard Haile and the Navahos, 1900–1961* (Albuquerque: University of New Mexico Press, 1998), 51, 95.

one children to our school even in the very first year of its existence."[33] When she spoke to the Navajo leaders, Drexel offered parents some input on their children's education. It is not clear that she actually incorporated Navajo ideas into the curriculum at St. Michael's, but she listened to their concerns, which made the SBS the lesser of two evils in the eyes of some Navajo. Enrollment steadily increased. By 1925, it was the Navajo who asked the SBS to expand St. Michael's.[34] This should not be read as approval of the SBS school so much as disapproval of the government alternative. While the decision to send a child to a mission school was difficult for parents, it was nothing compared to the culture shock that awaited students once they arrived.

## Student Intake Experiences

Arrival at SBS schools must have bewildered students. Like their counterparts in government schools, the sisters' first task was to reimagine students' appearances and remake them in the image of white children. They developed a "cleaning process" that consisted of "bathing and cutting and arranging their hair till they looked like very different little children."[35] Missionaries described these processes using patronizing and paternalistic language. At St. Paul's in South Dakota, the priest reported that the cleaning procedures were necessary because "some of the little ones look upon a broom or a bar of soap as a strange article at first. They do not even know how to wash their faces."[36] In addition to scrubbing with soap and water, the sisters used blue ointment and a fine-toothed comb to delouse students. In the early 1920s, Mother Katharine described the intake of a new five-year-old boy who entered St. Michael's wearing traditional garments and a silver necklace: "Then the disciplinarian (male advisor), in a matter-of-fact way, took off the necklace and gave it to the father, and conducted the small pupil to the bathroom for him first Amer-

---

33 Weber, "Opening at St. Michael's School—Indians attack at Round Rock," in Bodo, *Tales of an Endishodi*, 188.
34 Mother M. Berchmans, "Children Cry for It," *Indian Sentinel*, July 1926, 110.
35 Sisters of the Blessed Sacrament, *Navajo Adventure*, 30.
36 Father Sylvester Eisenman, *Little Bronzed Angel*, February 1925, 1.

ican-style bath, the father following him."[37] Memoirs written by students who attended Indigenous boarding schools invariably describe the intake process, particularly the haircut, as terrifying. Adam Fortunate Eagle, who attended Pipestone, a government-run school, in the 1930s, recalled his first-day feelings: "We're lonely, bald-headed, our clothes don't fit, and we smell awful."[38] Betty J. Eadie remembered how scared she was on the first day at a Catholic boarding school (not SBS); she recalled, "We stood by our beds until Sister blew a whistle. Then we got promptly in bed, the light was clicked off, and the door was locked from the outside. Being locked inside this big, darkened room horrified me. In the dark I waited in terror until sleep finally, gratefully overcame me."[39] The horror of this intake process is a common theme in Indigenous writings, but if the sisters had qualms about how they welcomed students, they do not appear in their writings. To them the goal of Americanization required students to part with the accoutrements of their culture, a process that scarred the children, whose identities were stripped away and, literally and figuratively, thrown out with the bathwater.

As at government schools, SBS students dressed in American-style clothes and haircuts whether they wanted to or not. Based on memoirs from other Indigenous schools, students must have felt uncomfortable donning European dress. For example, former Carlisle teacher and Indigenous activist Gertrude Bonin, who published under the name Zitkala Ša, reported her horror at the form-revealing dresses the supposedly morally superior matrons put on the students. She wrote, "I looked hard at the Indian girls, who seemed not to care that they were even more immodestly dressed than I, in their tightly fitting clothes."[40] The garments at the sisters' schools typically came from donation boxes sent in by readers of the *Indian Sentinel*. Clothing often either hung comically

---

37 "Mother Katharine Drexel's Visitation of Missions," *Indian Sentinel*, January 1923, 7.
38 Fortunate Eagle, *Pipestone*, 8.
39 Betty J. Eadie, *Embraced by the Light* (Placerville, Calif.: Gold Leaf Press, 1992), 8.
40 Zitkala Ša, "The School Days of an Indian Girl," *Atlantic Monthly*, February 1900, 186.

loose or encased limbs like sausages. Insisting that students dress according to white fashion caused trauma. There is some evidence, though, that the sisters tried to soften the blow. The sisters tried to make over the items in the thrift bins so student did not feel like they were wearing cast-off rags.[41] They taught the older girls to create more stylish and custom-fit pieces. After producing new looks from secondhand clothes, the superior of St. Michael's held a fashion show. She noted, "I am sure that the donor would be surprised that such fine garments can be produced from the old clothes sent us."[42] Despite the care they took to dress students attractively, the shift to uncomfortable and constricting Western dress was unwelcome. Most students would have preferred their traditional clothing to the new finery.

As at most Indigenous schools, the sisters gave students "Christian" names when they were baptized. The name selection process was arbitrary. In the case of the aforementioned young student who had his first bath at the school, the priest gave word that his name would be Venard because he enrolled on that saint's feast day. A few days later, a little girl arrived at St. Michael's on the anniversary of the death of Mother Katharine's sister Elizabeth, nicknamed Lisa, so the little girl was given the baptismal name Lisa.[43] Students had no say in their own names. While many Catholic schools gave students new baptismal names, the SBS had a unique practice of raising money by selling naming rights to donors. Sisters allowed benefactors who paid for students' baptismal outfits to select their names. They advertised in the *Indian Sentinel* and informed would-be donors that for five dollars they could name a student. Following baptism, the donor would receive two pictures—one with a student in native dress and one in the new baptismal clothes.[44] Sponsors also received handwritten thank-you notes from the students. Some donors liked to see pictures before they decided to name a child. One such donor, a wealthy Osage named Norine Prudom, asked for

---

41 "Old Clothes Made New by Sisters, St. Michael's Navajo School, Arizona," *Indian Sentinel*, July 1925, 144.
42 M. Berchmans, "Mission Show Window," *Indian Sentinel*, 1928, 87.
43 "Mother Katharine Drexel's Visitation of Missions," *Indian Sentinel*, January 1922, 7.
44 "The Lay Missionary at Home," *Indian Sentinel*, April 1922, 72.

"a real talented boy and girl (good looking.)"[45] Sometimes clubs and classes at Catholic schools sponsored baptisms and named Indigenous children.[46] In mission schools, student identities could be bought and sold.

The reimagining of the students' identities mirrored the sisters' own process of joining a religious order. Upon their religious receptions, postulants cut their hair, exchanged their own clothing for the uniformity of the habit, and received new names. Many sisters chose their religious names, though not always. They also divested themselves of their possessions; even their clothing did not belong to them but rather was "the habit of my use." Entrance into a convent separated them from their families and friends. SBS sisters could receive visits from family but did not have permission to visit their homes once they spoke their vows. They cast off their individual identities as they entered religious life. It is probable that the sisters who staffed Indigenous schools understood, at least to some extent, the homesickness and bewilderment of their students. The difference is that nuns were consenting adults who willingly surrendered their identities, while Indigenous students had no choice.

Many sisters noticed student reticence and fear upon arrival. The sisters reported that they tried to make the school atmosphere "homelike," but they acknowledged that the children and their parents sacrificed their ideas of "home" in sending children to school.[47] The shock students experienced must have been magnified by the language barrier. The sisters noted that "the little ones come to school with absolutely no knowledge of the language, very timid and fearful of ridicule if they misuse or mispronounce the words they laboriously learn."[48] A teacher at St. Michael's recalled, "The children were not only shy; they were almost

---

45 Father William Hughes to Mother M. Josephine at St. Michael's Mission, April 1923, BCIM correspondence files, series 1-1, reel 110, MUA.

46 Father William Hughes to Mother M. Josephine, April 27, 1923, BCIM records, series 1-1, reel 110, MUA; Father William Hughes to M. Josephine, May 3, 1923, BCIM records, series 1-1, reel 110, MUA.

47 Father Sylvester Eisenman, *Little Bronzed Angel*, November 1934, 1.

48 "A Visit to Our Western Missions," *Mission Fields at Home*, February 1930, 75.

mute."[49] To help students acclimate, two sisters slept in cubicles in the girls' dormitories, and they hired male "disciplinarians," later dubbed "advisors," to perform the same service for boys. In the early days of the St. Michael's mission, the job of helping students adjust fell to Sr. Celestine Wolff and Sr. Honora Griffin, who taught new students the routines and tucked them in at night. New arrivals stayed with these sisters, "holding their hands or the cord of the habit" for a few weeks, and they did not go to classes until they had enough rudimentary English to feel somewhat comfortable.[50] From their writings, it seems that sisters attempted to soften the intake process, though the schools, much like the sisters' convents, remained places of harsh order and must have been terrifying for students.

## School Days

The discordant clang of bells chopped up the long school days. Students had to adjust to a schedule that kept them active from before sunrise to bedtime. At Marty, students rose at 5:45 a.m. to get ready for Mass at 6:30. After Mass students had breakfast and performed chores such as bedmaking, dishwashing, sweeping, and room cleaning until 9:00 a.m., when they reported for their first classes. Students attended academic classes in the morning and industrial classes after lunch. In the evening they sometimes had time for playing games or for rehearsing musical programs. At 7:30 p.m. students attended the benediction of the Blessed Sacrament followed by the Litany of the Little Flower, evening prayers, and bed.[51] Pupils followed similar schedules at other SBS boarding schools. A former St. Catherine's student noted, "When you left the dormitory in the morning, you didn't see your bed again all day until it was bedtime." Though he liked the sisters, that student later transferred to a government school with a more relaxed schedule.[52]

---

49 Sisters of the Blessed Sacrament, *Navajo Adventure*, 29.
50 Lynch, *Sharing the Bread in Service*, 1:124.
51 Father Sylvester Eisenman, "Around the Clock at Marty," *Little Bronzed Angel*, April 1935, 6.
52 Corinne P. Sze, "'Roots That Are Very Deep': Excerpts from an Interview with Patrick Toya," *Bulletin of the Historic Santa Fe Foundation*, Summer 2003, 32.

While the sisters provided recreational activities, the grueling schedule must have overwhelmed students. One of the biggest adjustment problems came with the industrialization of time. Students were unused to days regimented and ruled by bells and horns.[53] Zitkala-Ša, who worked at Carlisle, recalled trouble adjusting to the noisy routine: "A large bell rang for breakfast, its loud metallic voice crashing through the belfry overhead and into our sensitive ears. The annoying clatter of shoes on bare floors gave us no peace. The constant clash of harsh noises, with an undercurrent of many voices murmuring an unknown tongue, made a bedlam within which I was securely tied."[54] The sisters, who kept strict schedules and routines, saying the Little Office—a schedule of prayers to be said at certain times throughout the day—might not have understood that the imposed regimentation, which to them was a symbol of holiness, caused trauma to their students.

SBS students also had to accustom themselves to a martial atmosphere. The blast of "a bugle like those used in Alpine mountains" called children to meals and directed them to classes. Captains organized the students into companies and marched them to meals, repeating, "right, left, right, left."[55] When Mother Katharine visited Saint Michael's in 1930, she was greeted with a military-style spectacle: "The band began to play, the battalions marched and countermarched, drilled in amazing unison, and in perfect formation escorted us to the house. A joy to behold!"[56] What purpose such military drills might have had on the reservation is unclear. While a former SBS student recalled the drill with fondness, suggesting, "It did me good when I went into the mili-

---

[53] Spanish missionaries often used bells, songs, and other auditory cues to impose social control on the Indians—they effectively reordered time and space. Since the earliest days of contact, then, these practices became a standard tool of missionaries. See Kristen Dutcher Mann, *The Power of Song: Music and Dance in Mission Communities of Northern New Spain, 1590–1810* (Stanford, CA: Stanford University Press, 2010), 179.

[54] Zitkala-Ša, *American Indian Stories* (Washington, DC: Hayworth, 1921), 23.

[55] "Mother Katharine Drexel's Visitation of Missions," *Indian Sentinel*, January 1923, 5.

[56] SBS, "A Visit to Our Western Missions," *Mission Fields at Home*, February 1930, 75.

tary. It is doing me good now," memoirs from students at other Indigenous schools suggest that students resented the military atmosphere.[57] Because it was the norm at government schools, the nuns who frequently had to answer detractors who labeled Catholics un-American wanted to demonstrate that they too could create the ideal, muscular American.[58] The sisters valued discipline, which could also explain the affinity for martial education. As a student at St. Catherine's recalled, "First, we learn to say, 'Yes, Sister,' and 'Thank you, Sister,' and then we learn to speak English fluently."[59]

## Discipline and Resistance

Not all students accepted the sisters' discipline, and many expressed their displeasure with their feet. The sisters did not keep official tallies on the numbers of students who ran away, but it was a common theme in their writings. In a speech on the works of the congregation, Mother Katharine described a picnic when the sisters discovered that four girls and two boys had run away. At once some of the older students mounted horses and searched for the students until 1 a.m., when they returned with "the little truants."[60] At St. Paul's some students repeatedly resisted the missionaries and lit out whenever they saw an opportunity, leading the priest to dub a group of them "outlaws."[61] Marty's isolated location, however, meant that runaways usually showed up after a few days, after "a day or two on the prairie, a night in a hay stack, and a very empty stomach."[62] Some St. Catherine's students grew tired of the school and forged a letter from a priest that authorized them to work at the Santa Fe Railroad. They wanted

---

57 Sze, "'Roots That Are Very, Very Deep,'" 28. See, for example, Mary Crow Dog and Richard Erodes, *Lakota Woman* (New York: HarperPerennial, 1991). Mary Crow Dog attended St. Francis Boarding School and compared it to a prison.
58 See Adams, *Education for Extinction*, 117–21.
59 Nat Chavez, "Pueblo Boy Writes for the Indian Sentinel," *Indian Sentinel*, July 1923, 114.
60 Mother Katharine Drexel, "Since the Beginning," ca. 1922, collated writings, H10J86, vol. 28, folder 1, ASBS.
61 Eisenman, *Little Bronzed Angel*, November 1934, 2.
62 Eisenman, *Little Bronzed Angel*, October 1936, 1.

to "be working instead of at school learning about working."⁶³ Repeated flights from the sisters' schools demonstrates that while they may have made efforts to soften the boarding school experience, many students resented them.

Many who attended Indigenous boarding schools reported harsh discipline, including corporal punishment. Tim Giago, who attended Holy Rosary Mission School (funded by Drexel but not SBS-affiliated), reported severe beatings with a leather strap.⁶⁴ Betty Eadie remembered sisters keeping order in Mass by using a long pole with a rubber ball on the end to hit misbehaving students.⁶⁵ Some punishments described by students at Indigenous schools sound sadistic. When Sister Laura caught Adam Fortunate Eagle speaking English, she threw him down the steps of a root cellar, put his hand in the door, and smashed his fingers in the door jamb.⁶⁶ A student at St. Francis at Rosebud explained that when a young girl at the school wet the bed, the sisters wrapped her up in wet sheets and threw her down the outdoor fire escape tunnel.⁶⁷ Mary Crow Dog's grandmother dared to play jacks in church, and she was taken to a dark boarded attic, where "they left ... her ... with only bread and water for nourishment." Her grandmother ran away after this treatment, but when she and her friends were found, the nuns "stripped them naked and whipped them. They used a horse buggy whip on my grandmother."⁶⁸ At Rainy Mountain Boarding School in Oklahoma, Clyde Ellis recalled that punishments included "being shackled to a ball and chain, forced to stand on tiptoe with arms outstretched, whipped across the palms of the hand, and made to kneel on two-by-four boards for extended periods." He also recalled a runaway being forced to eat his own vomit after having

---

63   Collier, "St. Catherine Indian School," 146.
64   Tim Giago, *The Aboriginal Sin: Reflections on the Holy Rosary Indian Missions School/Red Cloud Indian School* (San Francisco: Indian History Press, 1978), 2.
65   Eadie, *Embraced by the Light*, 8.
66   Fortunate Eagle, *Pipestone*, 47.
67   Debra K. S. Barker, "Kill the Indian, Save the Child: Cultural Genocide and the Boarding School," in *American Indian Studies: An Interdisciplinary Approach to Contemporary Issues*, ed. Dane Morrison (New York: Peter Lang, 1997), 48.
68   Crow Dog and Erdoes, *Lakota Woman*, 32.

to eat a meal of spoiled food.[69] Indigenous boarding schools were often brutal places of punishment and fear.

Official SBS policy prevented sisters from using corporal punishment without special approval from Mother Katharine herself, though it is difficult to say whether this ban held up in practice. Father Anselm's biographer mentions that one of the nuns at St. Michael's, the sister of boxer Jack O'Brien, was "inclined toward demonstrating the family prowess with some of the obstreperous older Navaho," but Anselm prevented her.[70] Other former SBS students deny receiving corporal punishment, saying, rather, that "they [the sisters] sat you down and they talked to you to make you understand what you are doing when you go wrong."[71] If the SBS truly did not employ corporal punishment it would have differentiated them from both mission and government-run schools. This policy might help to explain some of the popularity of SBS schools.

From the scant evidence, it seems that the sisters employed more positive discipline. Father Anselm reported an incident in 1900 when he visited St. Catherine's with five Navajo children. When a young Navajo boy loudly hummed a song during a lesson and received a reprimand from the sister, he threw a slate pencil at her face; another boy cried hysterically during the lesson. Mother Katharine assessed the situation and took all the Navajo boys to an open space behind the school, and she set up an old metal can as a target and began throwing stones at it. Soon the students "joined in the sport with excitement, and the poor can was bombarded from all sides."[72] Sometimes when a student had

---

69 Clyde Ellis, "'We Had a Lot of Fun, but of Course, That Wasn't the School Part': Life at the Rainy Mountain Boarding School, 1893–1920," in *Boarding School Blues: Revisiting American Indian Educational Experiences*, ed. Clifford Traafzer, Jean A. Keller, and Leone Sisquoc (Lincoln: University of Nebraska Press, 2006), 76–77.
70 Wilken, *Anselm Weber, O.F.M.*, 105. Given the popularity of the O'Brien surname, it is difficult to ascertain which sisters these were, since three O'Briens served concurrently. The sister could have been Sr. M. Brendan, Sr. M. Tarcisius, or Sr. M. Tecla.
71 Sze, "'Roots That Are Very, Very Deep,'" 31.
72 Anselm Weber, OFM, "Fall 1900: Students to Santa Fe, Headmen to Cienega," in *The Navajos as Seen by the Franciscans, 1898–1921: A Sourcebook*, ed. Howard M. Bahr (Lanham, MD: Scarecrow, 2004), 73–74.

difficulty adjusting to the school, the sisters tried to ascertain and focus on the pupil's strengths. In the 1930s, for example, the sisters reported that an unhappy student ran away, but after Mother Katharine watched him draw and repeatedly complimented him on it, the boy's attitude changed. He took a new interest in school, and the sisters claimed, "Something awoke in the soul of the boy."[73] Despite a preference for redirecting students' turbulent emotions, it is also clear that the sisters made offending students perform heavy manual labor as punishment. In one instance, four runaways from St. Michael's had to spend an entire day shoveling coal screenings to make room for a new supply of coal.[74] Since most of the evidence comes from the sisters' accounts, it is difficult to ascertain whether their official disavowal of corporal punishment held up in practice. Even without corporal punishment, however, students still had to adjust to the stark institutional order foisted upon them.

**Curriculum**

Much like in a convent, students practiced *ora et labora*, or prayer and work. Neither of these would have been new to Indigenous children, but the strict regimentation must have shocked them. Students' days consisted of academic study, work, and spiritual exercises. Since they followed the federal model, SBS schools offered a half academic, half industrial curriculum. Academic offerings included arithmetic, English (reading, spelling, memory lessons, composition, penmanship, and grammar), U.S. history and geography (including map drawing), music, natural sciences, and catechism. English proved difficult for many students, and the sisters estimated that it took at least four years of instruction to reach proficiency, though by the upper grades, students communicated without difficulty.[75] While the SBS typically gave academic instruction in English, at St. Paul's, Father Sylvester Eisenman preached in Sioux and led the rosary alternating in Sioux and Eng-

---

73 "Little Indian Stephen," *News Bulletin of Missions Fields at Home*, January–February 1935, 3.
74 SBS, "A Visit to Our Western Missions," *Mission Fields at Home*, February 1930, 77.
75 Ibid., 75.

lish. St. Michael's missionary Father Anselm taught religion in Navajo.[76] Sometimes older students also translated for younger ones during catechism lessons. The sisters did not develop linguistic skills to the same extent as the priests, though Mother Katharine paid to print catechisms in Choctaw, Navajo, and several other Indigenous languages.

In addition to academic work, SBS students took industrial courses. The government mandated this emphasis on industrial education to urge students to accept their allotments authorized under the Dawes Act of 1887. The sisters do not seem to have questioned these directives. Unlike at some of the wealthier government schools such as Carlisle and Haskell, however, most Catholic mission schools lacked resources to teach students useful trades. Girls learned traditional home economics subjects including plain sewing, dressmaking, laundry, cooking, table setting, and elementary nursing. At St. Michael's girls also took blanket weaving classes taught by Navajo experts. Boys learned farming, gardening, masonry, tailoring, silversmithing, and carpentry. They also worked in the school laundry and at the bakery.[77] Only at Marty, where the students operated a printing press, did SBS pupils learn a skill that would translate to the modern economy. In general, SBS schools offered little practical industrial training. Despite Mother Katharine's promises to tribal leadership that she wanted to make students useful tribal citizens, it is unclear how much use fancy sewing or tailoring would have on the reservation. Instead, students primarily performed work essential to the cost-efficient operation of the school.[78] Educational goals blurred with mission needs, as Sister M. Liguori

---

76 This was part of the BCIM's policy, which stated, "The key to an Indian's heart is his mother tongue"; "Editorials," *Indian Sentinel*, January 1917, 20.

77 Anselm Weber, "Catholic Indian Schools, St. Michael's Mission and School for the Navajo Indians," *Indian Sentinel*, 1908, 24–25.

78 Tanya L. Rathburn has made a similar point in her study on St. Boniface Indian School (also founded by Drexel) in Banning, California. She points out, "Based on the school's curriculum, the boys could learn to work in farm labor or masonry, and the girls could become maids or laundresses"; Rathburn, "Hail Mary: The Catholic Experience at St. Boniface Indian School," in Traafzer, Keller, and Siquoc, *Boarding School Blues*, 160.

reported students at St. Paul's practicing "muscular movement with the scrubbing brush."[79]

Despite the drudgery, some students claimed to enjoy the industrial classes. Margaret Grant, an eighth-grade student at St. Paul's, described the cooking course as her "Favorite Charge." Girls who took the class cleaned the kitchen and prepped for supper from 1:00 to 3:00 p.m., and then they returned at 4:30 to finish cooking for supper service at 6:00. Grant explained, "Among the things in the course we are taught, perhaps the best is to be economical in the use of foods, the right method of waiting on tables with manners and politeness, proper care for all kitchen utensils and dining room facilities." She added, "We are glad to be given the privilege to learn these things."[80] Grant wrote this essay under the supervision of sisters, so she might have hidden her real feelings about the work. Nat Chavez, first a graduate then later an employee of St. Catherine's, also appreciated industrial education. He boasted, "I wish you could see the fine rolls and nice fat bread the bakers make," and he added, "The middle sized boys would make a Chinese laundry man sit down and take notice."[81] Though learning new skills might have brought some pleasure to the students, the courses at SBS schools did not prepare them for successful careers, either on the reservation or in cities. In later years, the schools added advanced academic courses and provided teaching and nursing training.

### Recreation and Extracurricular Activities

The sisters understood that English lessons and rosaries would not win the hearts and minds of students. Students needed recreation. In 1927 Mother Katharine wrote to the nuns at St. Michael's, urging them to "get little entertainments" for the students. She acknowledged that it meant extra work but knew that if they did

---

79   Sister M. Liguori, SBS, "A Worker in Quills," *Indian Sentinel*, October 1924, 200.

80   Margaret Grant, "Essay by Margaret Grant, 8th Grader," *Little Bronze Angel*, November 1934, 7.

81   Nat Chavez, "Pueblo Boy Writes for the Indian Sentinel," *Indian Sentinel*, July 1923, 114.

not, the students would "go off." On the other hand, she explained, "If we get them to love school they'll stay. We want older boys and girls because they are the future teachers. We want the fruit."[82] Accordingly, the sisters offered many extracurriculars; however, organized and supervised play time was sometimes a burden to students who attended Indigenous schools. K. Tisianina Lomawaima points out that students resented the constant supervision and attempts to "civilize" them.[83] Father Eisenman at St. Paul's, however, assured readers of his monthly magazine, "It isn't always just classes or workshop; there is plenty of time for play. Right now outside my window, I can see a game of marbles, a happy group around the teeter-totter, and a half a dozen girls taking turns on a pair of roller skates."[84] Sometimes recreation came in the form of walks through the countryside. During these outings, students taught the sisters about the land or hunted to bring special treats back to school. Starting in the late 1920s, the schools screened movies. During the same period, they also encouraged students to participate in musicals and dramas.

The SBS touted their students' musical accomplishments. As at other Catholic schools, they judged their success by how well the choir could perform. They bragged that their non-native English speakers mastered the tricky Latin chants for High Mass. In addition to liturgical music, students performed at festivals such as National Music Week in Santa Fe, where the boys' choir sang "Regina Coeli" with a "snap, volume and timbre that evoked an unusual measure of applause."[85] Boys also played in brass bands at each school; in fact, a St. Catherine's employee crowed, "The Seniors play like regular professionals."[86] In addition, sisters directed performances of plays such as "Coaina: The Rose of the Algonquia" or "My Irish Rose." By the 1930s, SBS student performances more often reflected their heritage. For example, in

---
82  Mother Katharine Drexel to Sisters at St. Michael's School, September 1927, quotation in Hurd, "Master Art of a Saint," 136.
83  K. Tisianina Lomawaima, *They Called It Prairie Light: The Story of Chilocco Indian School* (Lincoln: University of Nebraska Press, 1994), 124.
84  Eisenman, "Around the Clock at Marty," 6.
85  "Indian Boys Good Singers," *Indian Sentinel*, April 1925, 126.
86  Chavez, "Pueblo Boy Writes for the Indian Sentinel," 114.

Marty the students presented a program of Indigenous dances. One of the sisters commented upon a particular little boy named Buttercup Joe who captured her imagination: "With his war bonnet and exquisitely beaded war club, he presented a charming picture as he danced after the manner of his forbearers [sic]."[87] In 1935, students at St. Catherine's also put on an elaborate pageant, which they opened up to all Santa Fe residents.[88] The sisters tried to exhibit their students in an effort to demonstrate that they were as good as any white children. What students thought about being pawns in this game is unclear.

## On the Athletic Field

As at other Indigenous schools, SBS students fielded multiple sports teams.[89] As former student Nat Chavez put it, "As for sports, Oh boy!"[90] David Wallace Adams has suggested that the athletic field gave students a chance to play out frustrations with whites in a socially acceptable manner. Adams has noted that athletics drew students to boarding schools who might otherwise have avoided them. Drexel seems to have understood this. When St. Michael's expanded its campus in 1918, the new building included a large basketball court.[91] By 1925, they had to construct more courts because they could not keep up with demand. Mother Berchmans Crowe, then superior at St. Michael's, jested, "If they work out their salvation as strenuously as they work at their new past time, they should surely reach the goal."[92] Students also played baseball, football, and track and field. Male students had more athletic opportunities, but girls played basketball. A visiting sister was impressed by a high-scoring basketball game between

---

87  SBS, "A Visit to Our Western Missions," *Mission Fields at Home*, May 1930, 119.

88  "Mission Briefs," *News Bulletin of Mission Fields at Home*, January–February 1935, 4.

89  David Wallace Adams, "Beyond Bleakness: The Brighter Side of Indian Boarding Schools, 1870–1940," in Traafzer, Keller, and Sisquoc, *Boarding School Blues*, 35–64.

90  Chavez, "Pueblo Boy Writes for Indian Sentinel," 114.

91  "Student's Chapter—St. Michael's," *Indian Sentinel*, April 1918, 38.

92  Mother M. Berchmans, SBS, "Navajo Basket Ball Fans," *Indian Sentinel*, July 1925, 137.

the smaller girls at St. Michael's and noted in amazement, "They made one basket after another." All the athletes received uniforms made by one of the sisters from reclaimed charity box items.[93]

Both sisters and students had a competitive spirit. The St. Michael's sisters boasted of their students' victories over their Presbyterian rivals in nearby Ganado, Arizona, exclaiming that their track and field team really "brought home the bacon in the running and jumping feats."[94] Almost every issue of the sister's publication *Mission Fields at Home* printed sports scores for their school teams and included features on their athletes. In a 1929 request for donations to enable St. Michael's to build a new gym, Mother Berchmans called sports a necessity because the boys were "all live wires and needing much room for play."[95] To the sisters, sports might have been a control mechanism, but athletics allowed students release from the rigors of an institutional setting. The sisters used sports to assert the rigorous Americanism of their students. When SBS teams played government schools, they sought to demonstrate that Catholics could assimilate and Americanize students just as thoroughly as their Protestant and secular allies. The SBS viewed education and extracurricular activities as tools for evangelization. If basketball made students happy, the nuns reasoned, they would continue at school, soak up the religious atmosphere, and bring it back to their homes.

## Illness and Death at the Missions

Religious conflict erupted between missionaries and parents when students became ill. The sisters contacted parents when their children were sick, but they tried to prevent them from taking children home or from bringing a medicine man to the school. Indigenous parents often blamed schools when their loved ones died. They had good reason to do so. According to the Merriam Report issued in

---

93 Mary Torpey, "Travelog—In Navajo-Land," *Mission Fields at Home*, December 1933, 47.
94 "Along the Highways and Pathways of the Mission Fields," *Mission Fields at Home*, August 1929, 164.
95 Mother M. Berchmans, SBS, "Navajo Games," *Indian Sentinel*, Spring 1929, 81.

1928, boarding schools were unhealthy institutions.[96] Overcrowding and unsanitary conditions meant that infectious diseases could run rampant. During St. Michael's inaugural year, six out of eighty-seven students, or nearly 7 percent, perished from various illnesses, including tuberculosis and scrofula—a swelling of lymph nodes in the neck—and parents threatened to pull their students so they could receive the attentions of the medicine man. Father Anselm Weber threatened to get the Indian agent involved to keep students in place.[97] In response, the Navajo dubbed the missionaries "wizards" and accused them of not caring for the students except "to have them baptized, and then let them die."[98] Weber claimed Protestants were behind such talk, but in truth, the schools lost many students to illness. The missionaries praised Western medicine, but their infirmaries failed to keep students alive. For example, when three Cochiti students suffered from pneumonia in the St. Catherine's infirmary, the parents demanded their children back. Adelaido, the boy, was almost dead, and the nuns unsuccessfully begged his parents not to take him. Despite the nuns' assurances that children would receive better care in the school infirmary, Teresita, one of Adelaido's sisters who stayed with the nuns, perished. The sisters later marveled that Adelaido, who they believed should have reached Cochiti as a corpse, returned to St. Catherine's in the spring, a chubby, healthy little boy.[99]

Despite losing many students, the SBS counseled parents against removing their sick children because they believed they had a duty to both body and soul. Sisters published articles about students heroically passing away in their infirmaries after receiving the sacraments, highlighting their belief in the importance of a good Catholic death. Catholics believed that the dying had to receive the sacraments of reconciliation and the anointing of the sick to reduce time in purgatory. To most Catholics, particularly before Vatican II, a "good death" was an essential tenet of the

---

96 Lewis, *Problem of Indian Administration*, 314–30.

97 Weber, "Time in the Saddle: Students and the Sacraments," in Bahr, *Navajo as Seen by the Franciscans*, 200.

98 Anselm Weber to Father Ketcham, October 20, 1905, BCIM records, series 1, box 48, folder 3, MUA.

99 SMD, "Our Pueblos," *Mission Fields at Home*, December 1928, 38.

faith. The sisters told stories of students' deaths in a way that emphasized the children's holiness and faith rather than the tragedy of the loss of life. For example, they related the story of George Raphael Shuysua, a Moqui boy the sisters brought to St. Catherine's with consumption. When they told the story, they emphasized reviving power of the Eucharist and George's religious sentiment as he admonished a weeping nun, "I am going to see my Father, and you cry!"[100] George, they claimed, preferred to die in the school infirmary with access to the sacraments than to be at home. Another story about Josephine Weatua, a St. Catherine's student from the Pueblo of Laguna and Acoma, explained that as the girl lay dying of influenza, she told her little sister Anna that she was happy she was ill "with the good Sisters" rather than at home where she could not have received the sacraments, particularly the Anointing of the Sick.[101] These pious stories might have assuaged the sisters' guilt over the deaths of young students. Sickroom tensions between parents and the sisters could cause uncomfortable misunderstandings. Shortly after a student died, fifteen Indigenous people from the same region arrived at St. Michael's; the overimaginative Sister Bridget Buckley believed they came for revenge. In a panic, she shoved the visitors aside and sprinted upstairs to warn the other sisters of the impending attack. Someone with a cooler head calmed her down and sent her back downstairs to serve the guests a hearty lunch. The missionaries later chuckled over the incident, but the account brings to life the real strains surrounding the infirmary—a place where parents and sisters fought over the bodies and souls of students.[102]

On the Navajo reservation, funerary rites became spiritually contested spaces. Navajos preferred not to touch the bodies or even the possessions of the dead. Even when sisters and priests failed to reach the souls of the living, they found themselves custodians of the dead. Mission logs report many occasions when

---

100 A Sister of the Blessed Sacrament, "Letters from Indian Missionaries: From Darkness to Light (True Story of a Moqui Indian Boy)," *Indian Sentinel*, 1907, 41.
101 Frindolin Schuster, "Indian Voice: Little Josephine Weatua," *Indian Sentinel*, October 1918, 34.
102 Weber, "Time in the Saddle: Students and the Sacraments," 200–201.

Navajo asked the religious to bury the deceased. The sisters described receiving notes reading, "Our father (or mother, or brother, as the case may be) has died. Send for his body, make a coffin and dig a grave for him."[103] The story of Michael Chappo, a Navajo boy, illustrates the complexities involved in life and death on the reservation. Lightning struck the boy, likely killing him instantly, but despite the pleas of the priest, his body was sent to the medicine man who attempted revival. Only after trying traditional healing techniques did family members send for missionaries to bury him.[104] The sisters reported another case in which the Navajo had built a hogan for a dying baby and had conducted traditional rites, for when the sisters came the baby's face had been painted red, and a band with a feather encircled the child's forehead. Again, the family did not request a Catholic presence until after the baby had died, at which point they asked the sisters to take the corpse to the school for burial.[105] Often the families of the deceased gave the missionaries detailed instructions on how to position the body and what to include in the coffin, thus involving them in hybrid burial ceremonies.[106] These stories show that the Navajo, despite the efforts of the SBS and the Franciscans, continued their own religious practices, but they also demonstrate the complex web of community the SBS created in indigenous communities. Chapter 4 will assess the extent to which the sisters accomplished their aims and the effects of the schools on the Indigenous community.

---

103   SBS, "St. Michael's Indian School, Navajo Reservation, Arizona," *Mission Fields at Home*, December 1930, 48.

104   SBS, "A Visit to Our Western Missions," *Mission Fields at Home*, February 1930, 77.

105   M. Letterhouse, "Hogans and Summer Homes," *Mission Fields at Home*, November 1930, 21.

106   Berard Haile, OSF, "Some Mortuary Customs of the Navajo," in Bodo, *Tales of an Endishodi*, 159–61.

CHAPTER 4

# Intent and Impact

## Assessing SBS Indigenous Missions

A DEFINITIVE EVALUATION of the impact of the SBS-run schools on Indigenous students is impossible. As David Wallace Adams has pointed out, "Over the course of several years, a single year, or even a single day, a given student might experience a range of emotions and respond in a range of ways, running the gamut from active accommodation, to bewilderment, to ambivalence, or overt resistance."[1] The fact that the sisters and their fellow missionaries wrote or approved most sources further complicates the task. The missionaries had a vested interest in portraying happy, healthy children well-integrated into a large school family rather than scared and overwhelmed kids lost in a bleak institutional setting—a picture the latest research into Indigenous boarding schools paints. Since the 1980s, scholars have viewed Indigenous boarding schools as places of oppression and broken promises. In the 1990s, studies such as Robert A. Trennert Jr.'s exploration of the Phoenix Indian School and K. Tsianina Lomawaima's study of Chilocco have characterized these schools as harsh institutions where students were bullied, stripped of their identities, and made to feel inferior. Indigenous scholars such as Debra K. S. Barker have used personal experiences to inform their academic research and have labeled the boarding schools "an instrument that emotionally scarred generations of Indigenous children, leaving them and their children, as well, victims of institutionalized cultural genocide." More recent scholarship has acknowledged the futility of trying to capture the single definitive

---

1 David Wallace Adams, "Beyond Bleakness: The Brighter Side of Indian Boarding Schools, 1870–1940," in *Boarding School Blues: Revisiting American Indian Educational Experiences*, ed. Clifford Traafzer, Jean A. Keller, and Loene Sisquoc (Lincoln: University of Nebraska Press, 2006), 37.

Indigenous school experience. Between the work of historians and the activism of Indigenous people that attended these schools, it is clear that boarding schools attempted to strip away Indigenous culture and were often dreary and repressive institutions.[2] New evidence of mass graves at school sites in Canada has brought increasing public awareness to the issue and led to Pope Francis issuing an apology to former students in July 2022 as part of his "Pilgrimage of Penance." It is now clear that many of these schools set out to silence Indigenous voices or to use them for their own purposes. Despite the bias implicit in the sources, however, it is possible to draw some conclusions about SBS schools.

## SBS Definitions of Success

The sisters measured success by the number of sacraments administered. In the battle for souls, numbers mattered. Each year, the missionaries enumerated how many people they served, how many were Catholics, how many adult and child baptisms they administered, and how many Communions, marriages, and burials they presided over. Students prayed from dawn to dusk attending morning Mass and benediction every day. During Lent, they participated in the Stations of the Cross—a devotional practice involving symbolically retracing Jesus' steps on the last day of his life—each Friday and Sunday night.[3] They also spent hours each week studying the catechism. Thomas J. Morgan, the commissioner of Indian Affairs from 1889 to 1893, suggested, "In them [Catholic Indian schools] the Roman Catholic catechism occupies the first and principal place, and the aim of the schools is, prima-

---

2  See Sally McBeth, *Ethnic Identity and the Boarding School Experience of West Central Oklahoma American Indians* (Washington, DC: University Press of America, 1983); Robert A. Trennert, *The Phoenix Indian School: Forced Assimilation in Arizona, 1891–1935* (Norman: University of Oklahoma Press, 1988); Lomawaima, *They Called It Prairie Light*; Barker, "Kill the Indian, Save the Child," 47–78; Adams, *Education for Extinction*; Brenda Child, *Boarding School Seasons: American Indian Families, 1900–1940* (Lincoln: University of Nebraska Press, 1998); and Clifford E. Traafzer, Jean A. Keller, and Lorene Sisquoc, *Boarding School Blues: Revisiting American Indian Educational Experiences* (Lincoln: University of Nebraska Press, 2006).

3  Peter J. Delorme, "Essay on Lent by 10th Grade Student Peter J. Delorme," *Little Bronzed Angel*, March 1935, 6.

rily, to propagate the Catholic faith and to induce its acceptance by the Indians."[4] While Morgan intended to insult Catholic schools, the priests and nuns would have agreed with him.

In addition to formal religious training, students also enrolled in sodalities, or religious social organizations. At St. Catherine's, for example, boys joined the Holy Name Society, which met once a month to receive Communion. By 1923 the organization boasted more than seventy members and elected officers. Girls could join the Sodality of Mary, which provided them with fellowship and opportunities to hone leadership skills.[5] St. Marty's in Yankton offered membership to the St. Joseph and St. Mary's Societies.[6] These clubs shaped the social fabric of the schools, and they also served as tools for social control. The behavior guidelines and mandatory sacramental reception kept students in line as participation depended upon good behavior.[7] The SBS did not originate this practice; rather, the pre–Vatican II church made sodalities and control of children universal priorities.[8]

While the sisters prepared students to receive the sacraments, they had ulterior motives. Unlike Pratt, who sought to insert Indigenous students into towns and cities, the sisters wanted their students to return to their homes and spread Catholicism (along with European-style clothing and housing) in their villages.[9] Sisters called their schools a "sermon to our Indian people." Students

---

[4] Thomas J. Morgan, "Article for Newspaper," 1892, quoted in Carroll, *Seeds of Faith*, 86.

[5] Chavez, "Pueblo Boy Writes for the Indian Sentinel," 115.

[6] Mother Katharine Drexel, "Mother Katharine Drexel at Yankton," *Indian Sentinel*, January 1924, 21.

[7] Mary Peckham Magray, *The Transforming Power of Nuns: Women, Religion, and Cultural Change in Ireland, 1750–1900* (New York: Oxford University Press, 1998), 101.

[8] Part of the American Catholic Church was the molding of young Christians who would be the outward sign of Catholic respectability and Americanism. Robert Orsi, *Between Heaven and Earth: The Religious Worlds People Make and the Scholars Who Study Them* (Princeton, NJ: Princeton University Press, 2005), 99.

[9] Pratt told supporters, "We make our greatest mistake in feeding our civilization to the Indians instead of feeding the Indians to our civilization." Quoted in Adams, *Education for Extinction*, 53.

were "carriers of grace" expected to convert their parents.[10] The sisters must have been thrilled to receive the following report from a student about her summer vacation: "I told my brother about the school and about God. Then he wanted to come to school, so I came back with him. I think he is glad now because he came to school. I tell my folks about God."[11] More often students failed to convert their relatives. One girl recounted, "My heart did become very sorrowful and I did weep sad tears because he [the girl's father] would not love our Lord Jesus Christ."[12]

Priests and missionary sisters in far-flung villages counted on boarding school alumni to assist at Mass and to draw people to the church celebrations. In 1919, Wilber Hunt, a student at St. Catherine's, wrote to his local priest, Father Fridolin Schuster at Acoma Pueblo, promising that he would learn to serve Mass so he could help the priest when he returned.[13] The sisters also requested hymnals and organists to help train their students as musicians who could lead the singing at home.[14] In addition to serving at regular Sunday masses, former St. Catherine's students played important roles in pueblo festivals. A student from Encinal Village, part of the Laguna Pueblo, wrote a letter to the sisters about the pueblo's feast day in 1932, explaining that the St. Catherine's students took Communion together and the girls sang the High Mass. Another St. Catherine's school student played the organ.[15] Students opened new fields to missionaries. For example, at Santa Domingo Pueblo, it was a St. Catherine's student, Laurentia Senora, who became the first person to receive the sacraments in the village in 1924. Prior to her decision, the Pueblos allowed the mission priest to say Mass, but no one partook in

---

10 "Little Indians, Carriers of Grace," *Little Bronzed Angel*, April 1935, 3.
11 "Along the Highways and Pathways of the Mission Field," *Mission Fields at Home*, February 1932, 75.
12 "Saint Catherine's Indian School, Santa Fe, New Mexico," *Indian Sentinel*, 1903–4, 16.
13 "Student's Chapter," *Indian Sentinel*, July 1919, 45.
14 "Missionary Needs Supplied—And Not Supplied," *Indian Sentinel*, Summer 1929, 130; Mother M. Berchmans, "Wanted: Organists," *Indian Sentinel*, Winter 1930–31, 38.
15 "Along the Highways and Pathways of the Mission Field," *Mission Fields at Home*, February 1932, 74.

Communion.[16] Following Laurentia's example, twenty-five students from Santa Domingo enrolled in St. Catherine's. Incidents such as this led the sisters to dub their students "crusaders."[17]

Catholic students faced conflict, both spiritual and physical, when they returned to their non-Catholic villages. The sisters urged students to avoid traditional dances and to shun the medicine men of their villages.[18] This prohibition put students in awkward positions. In 1904, the sisters at St. Catherine's reported that their students would go to great lengths to avoid dances "which they feared savored of idolatry," and they "left the pueblo under cover of night and walked miles to received sacramental absolution and be fortified with the Bread of the Strong." This allowed the students "to remain firm under the pressure of repeated solicitation and long standing custom."[19] The sisters' writings do not acknowledge how their prohibitions created turmoil and strained family relationships. Gertrude Kinlichini, a student at St. Michael's, wrote a letter to the *Sentinel* describing the summer dances, but she felt compelled to add, "There are many other dances I have never seen because I am a school girl and do not attend them." She noted that when children returned home from school, many parents sent them to the medicine man for special ceremonies called "Holy Prayers," but she added, "Many children refuse to take part in this ceremony but are compelled by their parents to submit." She assured the readers, "Of course the Catholic children have no faith in this ceremony."[20] Given this letter's appearance in a missionary magazine, it is likely that Kinlichini reported what the white missionaries wanted to hear. Most

---

16 Sr. Martha, SBS, "I Want to Do This for God," *Indian Sentinel*, April 1924, 72–73.

17 "Navajo Crusaders," *Indian Sentinel*, April 1926, 92.

18 Some missionaries condemned all dancing and protested when Indians "drum and sing and dance and howl," but others tried to find positive aspects in the dancing. This tension is never wholly resolved in the missionary community. For a negative response to dancing, see J. B. Carroll, SJ, "The Fourth of July Dishonored," *Indian Sentinel*, 1910, 28–33.

19 "Saint Catherine's Indian School, Santa, Fe, New Mexico," *Indian Sentinel*, 1903–4, 15.

20 "Students' Chapter St. Michael's School, Arizona," *Indian Sentinel*, October 1917, 34.

students from Catholic schools participated in both Catholic and tribal rituals, and many felt conflicted. In 1922, a sister at St. Michael's reported a student preparing to receive baptism calling out to her mother, "Oh, Mamma, I have only one half of a day more to be a pagan."[21] One can only imagine the mother's feelings upon hearing those words. The missionaries' religious instruction led to parent-child schisms—a rich irony as they taught students the fifth commandment: Honor thy mother and father.

Students also faced ridicule from those who continued to practice the traditional religion. Mother Katharine noted that they could not recruit students from San Solano in Arizona because the village medicine man would tease and torment the students as they walked to school.[22] Sometimes tensions had more serious consequences. Zitkala-Ša published a dramatic story of the consequences of converting to Christianity called, "The Soft-Hearted Sioux" in her book *American Indian Stories*. The story followed a young man who became a missionary after going to a Christian school. When he returned to his parents with "the white man's tender heart in my breast" he was unable to provide meat for his father, who then succumbed to illness. Before he died, his father claimed that "your soft heart has unfitted you for everything!"[23] In the story, the former boarding school student was abandoned by the rest of the tribe. Accepting the sisters' teachings had serious consequences for students. Speaking in the 1920s, Mother Katharine told the story of Juan, a St. Catherine's student from Tesque Pueblo who resisted his father's efforts to initiate him into tribal customs. When Juan refused, as the sisters taught him to, his father beat him, so Juan ran away to St. Catherine's. After he returned home, he reported that tribal elders had tortured him. Juan escaped and contacted the sisters, who hid him, found him a job, and secured his safe passage to Colorado.[24] The boy's bias and the sisters' lack of understanding of pueblo life muddy this story, but

---

21 "Every Child a Catholic," *Indian Sentinel*, July 1922, 533.
22 "Through the Papago Desert: Sisters of the Blessed Sacrament Visit Mission Schools of Arizona," *Indian Sentinel*, July 1917, 14.
23 Zitkala-Ša, *American Indian Stories*, 53–62.
24 Mother Katharine Drexel, "Since the Beginning," 1922 or later, Collated Writings, H10J86, vol. 28, fol. 1, ASBS.

without doubt the boy's Christianity caused strife in his home. Similarly, in 1928, the sisters at St. Michael's reported that one of their graduates, Zita Flizigai, was turned out of her house with her newborn baby because she would not allow the medicine man to perform ceremonies over the child. Flizigai died of exposure after a fifty-mile horse ride. The SBS declared her a martyr for her faith and saw her death as a sign of the progress they were making in their goal of spreading Catholicism.[25] Though no record of their response exists, rather than a sign of holiness, Indigenous families must have seen the situation as a needless tragedy.

## SBS Schools as Third Way

Given the overwhelmingly negative literature about Indigenous schools, it is certain that some students resented the SBS schools and the sisters who ran them. Despite the sisters' professed desire to preserve some aspects of Indigenous culture, the congregation's mission was to remake Indigenous students in a Euro-American image. Kinder, gentler cultural genocide is still cultural genocide. Logic dictates that students fought against the institutional destruction of their culture and language even if their resistance was not recorded in mission archives. That said, some students spoke fondly of their time at SBS schools. For example, a Moqui boy named George Raphael Shuysua, a student at Albuquerque Government School, met a former SBS student who would "repeat some of the many things the Sisters had taught him about our Lord." Shuysua began corresponding with the sisters and asked for baptism in 1901. He tried to transfer to St. Catherine's, but a government agent denied his request. In response, he sold his bicycle to purchase a ticket to Santa Fe, where he could join the sisters.[26] While less dramatic, other students seemed to have

---

25 "Along the Highways and Pathways of the Mission Fields," *Mission Fields at Home*, December 1928, 51.

26 When George Raphael Shuysua arrived in Santa Fe, the government agent took him and sent him to a government school once again, but after he developed a lung disorder, the SBS arranged to bring him to Santa Fe, where they took care of him for several months before his death. Fifteen SBS sisters marched in his funeral procession. "Letters from Indian Missionaries: From Darkness to Light (True Story of a Moqui Indian Boy)," *Indian Sentinel*, 1907, 37–40.

appreciated the kindness of the sisters. María Montoya Martínez, later known simply as María the Potter of San Ildefonso, attended St. Catherine's from 1897 to 1899 and recalled feeling special when the sisters helped the girls make their own individualized confirmation dresses.[27] When the pueblo council voted to send María and her sisters back to St. Catherine's the following year, she considered it a reward rather than a punishment.

Others seem to have considered SBS schools the lesser of two evils compared to government-run institutions. The SBS bragged that generations of families sent their children to SBS schools. Sisters viewed increasing enrollment as acceptance of the Catholic mission. In reality, economic necessity forced many parents to send their children to boarding school. Tim Giago made this point in his reflections on his experience at Holy Rosary Indian Mission School (not SBS-run). Increasing numbers, in Giago's opinion, did not mean the schools were doing well; rather, the large enrollments merely highlighted the economic injustice inflicted on Indigenous people.[28] Vine Deloria made a similar argument, insisting, "No missionary ever realized that it was less the reality of his religion and more the threat of extinction that brought converts to him. Or if he did realize it, he never acknowledged it."[29] It is no accident that school attendance numbers shot up during the Great Depression when families were incapable of feeding their children on their own. While the sisters did not acknowledge this point, they did write about the necessity to address endemic poverty in order to lead souls to God.

## Spiritual Centers and Material Aid

At many schools and outposts, nuns acted as cultural intermediaries, giving Indigenous families aid and helping them access social services. The SBS mission extended beyond running educational facilities; rather, in the Progressive tradition of settlement

---

27  Alice Lee Marriot, *María: The Potter of San Ildefonso* (Norman: University of Oklahoma Press, 1948), 88.
28  Giago, *Aboriginal Sin*, 2.
29  Vine Deloria Jr., *Custer Died for Your Sins: An Indian Manifesto* (New York: Macmillan, 1969), 107.

houses, SBS schools doubled as food pantries, thrift stores, hospitals, and mortuaries. Sisters used material goods to make inroads into the communities they served. For example, during the 1930s the sisters opened a soup kitchen at the school at Marty, feeding between one hundred and two hundred families each day.[30] In the winter, schools provided families with basic needs such as blankets, clothing, and shoes.[31] Operating budgets did not include this type of charity, so the sisters begged readers of the *Indian Sentinel* to provide them with used clothing and shoes. Before heading to spend the summer at Lukachukai, a missionary outpost on the Navajo reservation, Sr. Honora Griffin pleaded with the readers of the *Sentinel* to send clothing that she felt would improve her reception.[32] It is unclear whether indigenous parents accepted the sisters' spiritual message—most likely they did not—but hot meals and warm clothing started conversations.

In addition to food, the schools and missions provided basic medical care to the community. SBS schools all had infirmaries staffed by sisters trained in nursing. Although built to serve ill students, the infirmaries also dispensed aid to tribal members who arrived on the doorstep. The school infirmaries were often the closest and cheapest places Indigenous families could access Western medicine. At Marty, for example, Sister Ambrose Lawlor ran a drugstore at the school where children "come to be doctored."[33] The sisters and missionary priests frequently received calls to attend to the sick on reservations. They also quizzed visitors to the school on the health of people on the reservation, so they could dispatch aid—either in the form of medicine or baptism.[34] By providing this care they tried to disrupt trust in traditional medicine.

---

30 Father Sylvester Eisenman, "Doings at Marty," *Little Bronzed Angel*, September 1933, 3.
31 Mother M. Berchmans, "Missionaries Encouraged, *Indian Sentinel*, Winter 1927–28, 37; Mother M. Berchmans, "Comfort for a Baby," *Indian Sentinel*, Fall 1928, 189.
32 Sr. Honora, SBS, "Help Wanted," *Indian Sentinel*, Summer 1928, 122.
33 Father Sylvester Eisenman, "Help Wanted, Doctors, Nurses, Druggists," *Indian Sentinel*, Spring 1930, 92.
34 Mother M. Berchmans, "Medicine Man's Good Medicine," *Indian Sentinel*, Fall 1929, 171.

Increased demand for health care led the SBS to open medical mission outposts.[35] In the 1930s they launched medical missions in Luckchukai and in Houck, both located on the Navajo reservation in Arizona. The clinic in Lukachukai averaged 640 visitors per month during the 1930s, making it an important center for Navajo health.[36] The sisters found that treating ill Navajo had other benefits. One sister reported, "The kindly care given to such sufferers, making them at least comparatively comfortable, has made many sick Navajos beg to be taken to the school."[37] Mother Katharine best summed up her intentions when she suggested the clinics could be a means of "healing the afflictions of their souls as well as their bodies."[38]

The poverty on the reservations caused by generations of governmental misrule and myopic policies created a situation where Indigenous people had to rely on missionaries for support. This need caused rapid growth in SBS schools. Attendance at St. Michael's and St. Catherine's became family traditions. In 1917, Navajo student Gertrude Kinlichini reported, "The first girl student [at St. Michael's] was named Mary, after our Blessed Mother, and now she has one child called Mary."[39] By the 1920s, the sisters were educating the grandchildren of their first students. The sisters do not seem to have considered whether families truly wanted their students to receive a Catholic education or if economic injustice and hardship—partially created by the missionaries themselves—forced them to send their children away to schools. They viewed growth as a sign of God's grace.

---

35 Mother M. Berchmans, "Medical Missions Needed," *Indian Sentinel*, Summer 1929, 130.

36 SMV, "With the Navajos in Arizona," *Mission Fields at Home*, December 1929, 42.

37 Joan Meyer, "Lukachukai," *Mission Fields at Home*, July–August 1929, 163.

38 Mother Katharine Drexel to William Hughes, December 6, 1928, BCIM records, series 1–1, reel 151, MUA.

39 "Students' Chapter, St. Michael's School, Arizona," *Indian Sentinel*, October 1917, 34.

## Conversion of Missionaries?

The sisters journeyed west intent on changing lives and saving souls. The mission changed them, as well. They could not, as their Rule charged, "become the mother of the lonely, poor and most forsaken" and remain the same.[40] As historian Mark Clatterbuck has noted, "Indians have been making converts of missionaries for as long as zealous priests and sisters have been claiming indigenous converts for themselves."[41] In their attempts to educate and evangelize, they acted as intermediaries between the Indigenous and Anglo-American culture. As Thomas Tweed has stated, "Religions mark and traverse not just the boundaries of the natural terrain and the limits of embodied life but also the *ultimate horizon*."[42] In their missionary work sisters not only physically traversed the United States, they also crossed cultural boundaries. Rather than retreating into their convents, the SBS explored the far reaches of the reservations, getting to know families' needs and concerns. In fact, they acknowledged that the ordered life of the convent did not translate to western missions.[43] They learned to adapt their semi-cloistered lifestyle to frontier conditions. For example, the first sisters at St. Michael's noted that their new dwelling place "seemed very little like a convent" as men rushed about them trying to complete the school and the Navajo came to stare at the strange arrivals. They continued to "live our regular community life as much as we possibly could," but they also valued flexibility.[44] The sisters participated in dances and cultural celebrations on the reser-

---

40 Anselm Weber, OSF, "The Sisters of the Blessed Sacrament for Indians and Colored People," *St. Anthony Messenger*, January 1901, 267–68.

41 Mark Clatterbuck, *Demons, Saints, and Patriots*, 8.

42 Thomas A. Tweed, *A Crossing and Dwelling: A Theory of Religion* (Cambridge, MA: Harvard University Press, 2006), 76.

43 Several scholars have stressed the role of the West in breaking traditional notions of cloister. Anne Butler has argued, "Nuns and sisters . . . were neither silent nor secluded, disinterested nor ingenuous, warped nor winsome. Rather, they were movers and shakers in the religious and secular spheres." Butler, *Across God's Frontiers*, xiv. Carol K. Coburn and Martha Smith have also pointed out that the scarcity of priests in the West forced nuns to act as surrogate priests and take on more active roles than those in eastern cities were used to. Coburn and Smith, *Spirited Lives*, 99.

44 SBS, *Navajo Adventure*, 53.

vations, causing them to reassess their preconceived notions about the "pagan souls" they had come to save.

While they never renounced their belief in the superiority of the Roman Catholic faith or Euro-American values, close contact caused the sisters to rethink stereotypes. They used Catholic media such as the *Indian Sentinel* and *Mission Fields at Home* to defend Indigenous life to white and middle-class readers. In 1924, SBS sisters took over as editors of the magazine, a role they continued until 1932. The SBS launched *Mission Fields at Home*, a monthly magazine, in October 1928 to raise funds and awareness. While most articles were written by sisters, their rule prohibited them from taking credit for the work, so they signed articles with pseudonyms for the first decade of the publication. They wrote primarily to solicit funds for their missionary work, but the publications helped readers interpret Indigenous culture. Anne M. Butler's assessment that "nuns served as conduits in the shaping of institutions and in the exchange of culture between indigenous and invading peoples" seems particularly appropriate when applied to the SBS.[45] The sisters' writings show this cultural exchange developed in fits and starts. They went west expecting to save heathens, but over time they grew to value Indigenous cultures.

### Early Writings: In the Battle for Souls

Early accounts of SBS visits to Indigenous homes accentuate the poverty they witnessed. To modern readers, these reports come across as patronizing. In the novitiate, prospective sisters learned that they were called "to labor for the despised and lowly," and they tended to highlight the lowliness of those to whom they ministered. Likely, they belabored the poverty of the Indian communities to fundraise. Additionally, the sisters sometimes blamed traditional religious practices for holding Indigenous people back. For example, a 1904 article praised the "simple, primitive innocence" of the Pueblo Indians, but added, "Attached to their anti-Christian customs and firm in their adherence to their old traditions, these poor deluded people, in their ignorance, know not

---

45 Butler, *Across God's Frontiers*, 11.

that their heathenish practices keep them far from the narrow path which leads to Life Everlasting."[46] According to this article, the SBS saw themselves as mighty warriors fighting for the souls of the Pueblo people. They wondered, "Will not the Divine Master's voice be hearkened to by noble souls, who will go forth to the battle—the battle with Satan and long-standing customs—and by the help of his grace, make the effort to penetrate the deep reserve, which, like a shadowy mantle, envelops the dusky Christian, and make of him a true temple of the living God?"[47] Similarly, artwork in the first issues of the mission magazines shows Indigenous people looking miserable and downtrodden. A 1907 illustration asked for divine intervention to help the SBS to "rescue the Children who sit in darkness and in the shadow of Death!"[48] Early missionary sisters believed they had to root out traditional practices to save souls and create good Americans.

Later writings stress the "progress" Indigenous peoples had made and made much of their potential as full Americans. On a 1916 tour of Papago villages, Mother Katharine reported on the pains the Papago took in their preparation for the Feast of St. Francis and pointed out, "All of this is by a people who six years ago, at the coming of their first missionaries, were living in the darkness of paganism and many of whom wore no clothing." She painted a rich picture of what she considered signs of progress: "Now the Papago farmer appears in blue overalls, shirt and suspenders, and the women's full skirts are made of tinted Calico with bodice of the same, and on their heads they wear the long scarf of blue or pink or lavender, the ends of which hang loosely at the back and are now and again caught by the light breeze and float about the dusky sunburnt face."[49] Further, recalling a 1922 trip to western missions, Mother Katharine highlighted the "civilized" elements of the Indigenous people she interacted with, drawing attention to their judicious use of land: "The Indian men

---

46 "St. Catherine's Indian School, Santa Fe, New Mexico," *Indian Sentinel*, 1903–4, 18.
47 Ibid., 19.
48 "Frontispiece," *Indian Sentinel*, 1907, 2.
49 "Through the Papago Desert: Sisters of the Blessed Sacrament Visit Mission Schools of Arizona," *Indian Sentinel*, July 1917, 11.

in blue overalls and white shirts were at work in the field, driving their cattle or jogging along in their low hay carts. The corn had already been gathered in, and only the stumps were in evidence."[50] Though the belief that progress meant adaptation to Western styles is indicative of a belief in white cultural supremacy, the articles were intended to silence critics, speculators, and farmers who sought to open reservations to white settlement.

### Educating White Readers

By the mid-1920s, SBS stories went beyond lauding Indigenous people for picking up white customs; instead, they praised native traditions and sought to educate readers about the tribes' rich history. This shift stemmed from a broader cultural resurgence in interest in Indigenous culture in the 1920s. Catholics preserved Indigenous material culture, and in 1923 the Benedictines established the Indian Art Center at St. Patrick's Boarding School on the Kiowa Reservation.[51] In 1926, missionaries founded the Catholic Anthropological Conference based at the Catholic University of America. The SBS picked up on these trends as they subscribed to the Anthropological Conference's magazine. These shifts influenced the sisters to change the way they wrote about Indigenous culture; however, their appreciation for native arts and traditions also came as a result of living together and forming relationships. When sisters visited Amos Yellow Eyes and his wife, Lucy, on the Yankton reservation, they gushed about Amos's turkey feather war bonnet, which was "quite startling in its grandeur," and Lucy's beautifully crafted dress covered with bright beads and quills.[52] The sisters stationed in Marty also wrote about visiting Mrs. White Tallow's collection of Indigenous costumes, taking pains to acclaim the workmanship.[53] Some sisters on western missions fell in love with the landscapes and people.

---

50 "Mother Katharine Drexel's Visitation of Missions," *Indian Sentinel*, January 1923, 4.

51 Clatterbuck, *Demons, Saints, and Patriots*, 142.

52 Mother Katharine Drexel, "Sisters Visit Indian Homes," *Indian Sentinel*, April 1924, 66.

53 Sister M. Liguori, SBS, "A Worker in Quills," *Indian Sentinel*, October 1924, 200.

In addition to appreciating Indigenous dress and beadwork, the Sisters of the Blessed Sacrament began attending dances and religious rituals. In 1923, sisters from St. Michael's escorted their students to the Inter-Tribal Indian Ceremonial and reported excitedly on the Hopi Stone Race, bronco riding, pony racing, and the Navajo War Dance. The St. Michael's boys' bands performed European-style music on the grandstand for the festivities, adding to the melding of cultures.[54] In another border crossing, Sister Philip Neri and a companion attended the Medicine Lodge initiation ceremony near their school in Winnebago, and she produced an ethnographic description in the *Indian Sentinel* that captured the colors, sounds, and movements of the dance. She noted, "The downcast eyes and reverent deportment might be an interesting and instructing lesson to Christians in their devotions."[55] As tempting as the nun found it to draw comparisons between the Medicine Dance and the Mass, however, she added that a feast followed the festivities and noted, "To this repast we aliens were not invited."[56] Despite some efforts to understand Indigenous culture, the sisters were strangers in a strange land. What is worth noting is Sister Philip Neri's description of the nuns as the aliens, not the Winnebago.

## *Mission Fields* Magazine

When the SBS began publishing its own magazine in 1928, they used it as a medium to disseminate information about Indigenous cultures. Just as they crossed physical borders on the western missions, their publications helped readers make similar voyages of discovery. Starting with the third issue in December 1928, the sisters ran a series of articles describing aspects of Indigenous life in New Mexico, Arizona, Nebraska, and South Dakota. These articles stressed the beautiful and "civilized" features of Indigenous culture and debunked stereotypes. The first article on the pueblos praised Indigenous family structure: "Certainly, if loving care and attention on the part of parents, and trustful response of children can repro-

---

54    Mother Katharine Drexel, *Writings Number 3067*, ASBS.
55    Sr. Philip Neri, "The Medicine Dance," *Indian Sentinel*, October 1925, 157.
56    Ibid., 158.

duce pristine happiness, the pueblos are replicas of Eden." The sisters also took care to refute the trope that Indigenous men mistreated women, insisting instead, "The Pueblo woman is not, never was, a menial nor a drudge."[57] The sisters bragged about the architectural and cultural achievements of the Pueblo, calling the pueblos "the American Pyramids" and noting, "Centuries before the fathers dew up our constitutions the Pueblo Indians had devised a democratic form of government which has worked well even to this day."[58] They praised what they called an "instinct for beauty." The articles were written as love letters for the places and people the sisters had found on their "great adventure."

The sisters believed in the idea of the "Vanishing Indian," and many of the articles expressed both an admiration for native ways of life and the fear that they might soon disappear. An April 1929 article mused, "Native art and native symbolism is [sic] ruthlessly swept away by our blind worship of efficiency. The colorful life of the Amerind must be submerged by the drab hideousness of our civilization ere we will recognize him as a useful factor in our scheme of life."[59] This fear of a disappearing lifestyle is ironic, considering that the SBS schools stripped away native dress and pulled students away from the "colorful life" in favor of a drab institutional one. The SBS magazine lauded some aspects of Indigenous culture, but noted it was "hopelessly out of step in the onward march of civilization."[60] The magazine shows that the sisters struggled with the costs of "civilization," at times regarding westernization as a positive but at other points wondering what would be lost if Indigenous culture were eradicated. As early as 1909 Mother Katharine mused, "And so the little Navajos are learning to crochet baby caps and baby sacks and dressing their dolls in European Costumes!! When in the days in the far future you, as old ladies in religious, have the Navajos who are now at St. Michael's bring

---

57 SMD, "Our Pueblos," *Mission Fields at Home*, December 1928, 37.

58 SMD, "Pueblo Homes and Churches," *Mission Fields at Home*, January 1929, 60; SMD, "Pueblo Government," *Mission Fields at Home*, February 1929, 75.

59 SMD, "The Pueblo Woman as Artist," *Mission Fields at Home*, April 1929, 107.

60 SMD, "Pueblo Babies," *Mission Fields at Home*, May 1929, 125.

their children's children to see you, will they wear the European or the Navajo costume?" She brushed off the question of physical dress, however, stating, "May their souls be clothed in the beautiful white baptismal robe and then what matters it as to the covering used for this mortal frame, provided it be neat and clean?"[61] In 1928, the sisters mused that the traditional Pueblo garb is "a thing of beauty to the artist's eye," especially when compared to the younger men and women who were "adopting civilized dress, ugly and drab as it is when contrasted with the colorful artistic garment of their older women."[62] By 1930, these questions grew increasingly urgent. In an article on the Navajo, M. D. Letterhouse mused, "In settling down to a social life in civic communities, the Navajo would no doubt lose much of his tribal distinctiveness." She continued, "Regarding some superstitious rites and practices this might be a blessing, but many sterling characteristics and much picturesque beauty would also fall by the wayside, which would be a pity."[63] The sisters showed no compunction about destroying aspects of Indigenous culture that clashed with Roman Catholicism, but they expressed some regrets about whitewashing their students. Perhaps this was a product of their own retention of ancient religious traditions and garb and their insistence that such things could be thoroughly American.

This ambiguity played out in the discussions of religion, as well. Even though in public speeches Mother Katharine often referred to saving "the souls of pagans who still sit in darkness and the shadow of death," the real relationship between the sisters and Indigenous religious customs was more nuanced.[64] *Mission Fields at Home* detailed aspects of religious life, including descriptions of rain songs, Ktsina ceremonies, and Corn Dances, to help readers understand the richness and complexity of native religious and social systems. They did this to explain "his apathy toward

---

61 Mother Katharine Drexel to Sisters at St. Michael's, May 1909, *Annals of the SBS* 10, quotation in Hurd, "Master Art of a Saint," 133.
62 SMD, "Our Pueblos," *Mission Fields at Home*, December 1928, 36.
63 M. Letterhouse, "Hogans and Summer Homes," *Mission Fields at Home*, November 1930, 21.
64 Mother Katharine Drexel, "Undated Talk to E[ucharistic] H[eart] Confrat, Feb. 12, 1928," Collated Writings, H 10J 8b, vol. 28, folder 5, 6, ASBS.

modern civilization and his low response to many well-intentioned efforts to improve his condition."[65] One article suggested the need to adopt "an open minded, sympathetic attitude toward Indian ceremonialism," which would reveal that Indigenous dances and rites are all "expressions of thanksgiving or petition to the Deity."[66] Another article described the dancing at the Feast of St. Bonaventure as "the tangible presentation, the poetic utterance of deepest and most sacred thought and prayer."[67] This conflation of Indigenous religious practices with Catholicism oversimplified the complex process of resistance and accommodation that both sides employed. Still, the statement was a sea change for the women, who had previously vowed to rescue pagans from the shadow of death.

While not advocating syncretism—the blending of belief systems—in the 1930s, articles written by Sisters of the Blessed Sacrament acknowledged the importance of mixing Catholic and Indigenous religious traditions.[68] For example, they offered lavish descriptions of Christmas prayer dances that they considered "a wise concession on the part of the Spanish friars in attempting to Christianize the pagan practices of their neophytes" to bring harmony to two systems of belief.[69] Another article addressed the

---

65 SMD, "Rain Songs and Prayers," *Mission Fields at Home*, June 1929, 141. In addition to explorations of the Pueblo people, the SBS also ran lengthy series on the Navajo, the Winnebago, the Hopi, and the Osage.

66 Joan Meyer, "Vocal Prayer of the Indian," *Mission Fields at Home*, April 1932, 99.

67 SMD, "Baile de la tablita," *Mission Fields at Home*, July–August 1929, 157.

68 This interest in Indian culture seems to have lessened between the 1930s and 1967, when Sister Francis Mary Riggs wrote a dissertation on SBS conceptions of Indian culture and acculturation. In her sociological study, she found that few sisters had much knowledge about Indian cultures. By the 1960s, the Indian missions occupied a smaller percentage of the SBS work (only 10 percent), and many sisters preferred to serve in urban schools than on isolated reservations. She also noted that as the boarding schools increased in size, it became more difficult for sisters to continue their visitation work in the villages. She suggested sisters needed further training in Indian cultures. Riggs, "Attitudes of Missionary Sisters toward American Indian Acculturation."

69 Anne McFadden, "Yuletide in the Southwest," *Mission Fields at Home*, January 1930, 52.

merging of Christmas customs. In it, a young, mission-educated boy explained why his people performed a dance immediately following Midnight Mass: "This is the way we pray to Him, by dancing and singing."[70] This both/and approach reflects the attitude of the sisters in the 1930s. If their students participated in Catholic sacraments, the sisters could accept them also worshiping in ways foreign to the church. Like the Spanish before them, the SBS also appropriated Indigenous customs and tried to put them in a Catholic context. For example, when a sister realized that fasting was an important part of a native culture, she explained Christian fast days to them, thus "sanctify[ing] their superstitions" and making "of a guilty fast a meritorious one."[71] When urging students to accept Catholic Christianity, they spoke of the importance of distinguishing between "the principle and the mere accessories and outward ornamentation of observances."[72] In other words, they began recognizing the difference between accepting the Catholic faith and bowing down to Euro-American tradition.

Despite efforts to learn more about Indigenous religion, the sisters and fellow missionaries continued to see the Medicine Men as anathema. One article by a priest the SBS worked with described a Navajo Medicine Man as "one of the ugliest persons that I have ever met" who tried to cure disease with "hideous shrieks" and "liberal applications of red and black paint."[73] They did make some attempts to figure out the appeal of the Medicine Man, however. One article explained, "Sickness is consequently the result of some evil spirit which must be expelled, or counteracted. It is this, to us strange mentality, which endows the *medicine man* with this great power. His duty is not only to cure the sick but to protect from harm and to counteract all evil." The writer called the Medicine Man "the embryo masseur and chiropractor, as well as the

---

70  John Christopher Stephen, "The Buffalo Dance," *Mission Fields at Home*, December 1930, 43.

71  Marie Augustin, "Fasts Among the Indians," *Mission Fields at Home*, March 1931, 93.

72  SBS, "Catholic Day Schools for Navajos," *Mission Fields at Home*, June 1932, 132.

73  Matthias Heile, "The Warriors of St. Michael's," *Mission Fields at Home*, October 1928, 13.

psychopathist of our advanced medical practice."[74] Despite their continued distrust of Indigenous medical practices, over time, they adopted some aspects of Indigenous practices.

By the 1930s, the sisters began incorporating Indigenous prayers into their religious lives. The February 1930 *Mission Fields at Home* featured a Navajo prayer, part of the Mountain Chant, on the cover, and the July–August issue of the same year featured the "Prayer of the Nahuatl Singer." They promoted rites and ceremonies that they felt had important messages about God's grace. For example, an article on the Hako, a prayer popular in Pawnee culture, explained that the ceremony imparts "lofty ideals of the beauty of man's relation to, and dependence on, supernatural powers and on the necessity of the family tie for the gifts of people, joy, and contentment of life."[75] What Catholic, the article suggests, could err by adopting these sentiments? While the stories employed a paternalistic tone, they also represented an attempt to understand native cultures.

**Final Assessments**

Ultimately the SBS's "Great Adventure" in Indian Territory brought both education and eradication to the Indigenous people. It appears that the SBS sought a way to make a destructive process more humane, but like all Indigenous boarding schools, they robbed students of their own culture and language. Their efforts to prove that Catholics could produce vibrant American citizens had many unintended consequences. Rather than addressing the political and economic systems that kept Indigenous populations impoverished, the sisters believed that the solution to the "Indian Problem" lay in Catholic sacraments. Though they never backed away from their mission to save souls, over time they came to value Indigenous customs and even aspects of their religion. This came to full fruition at Drexel's beatification Mass at the Vatican ceremony when former student Marie Tso Allen read interces-

---

74 SMD, "Medicine and the Medicine Man," *Mission Fields at Home*, October 1929, 3.
75 Joan Meyer, "The Hako," *Mission Fields at Home*, May 1931, 117.

sional prayers in Navajo and dancers from Laguna Pueblo performed an Eagle Dance.[76]

The Sisters of the Blessed Sacrament left their Philadelphia convent in 1894 looking for a great adventure, sure that their efforts would grow the Mystical Body of Christ and create a more harmonious nation. After decades of crossing boundaries and building communities in the West, the mission became more nuanced, and the sisters began to question the need to eradicate native cultures. While their work with Black students and their families differed from their western missions, the SBS had to overcome similar resistance from multiple fronts. That work will be the subject of the next three chapters.

---

[76] Clyde Habermans, "Pope Beatifies Philadelphia Nun Who Educated Blacks and Indians: Mother Katharine Drexel Is a Step Away from Sainthood," *New York Times*, November 21, 1988, B 14.

CHAPTER 5

# Human Rights and Sacramental Rites

## SBS Missions in Black Communities

"AT THIS TIME I also became aware that not only was knowledge of the three R's being imparted but a slow constant discipline of my will was taking place." In her autobiography, Sister Mary Gabriella Guidry, a Holy Family Sister, recalled her time at Sacred Heart School in Lake Charles in the 1920s. Weekly math facts drills, drama programs, and English lessons left a deep impression on Guidry. Her memoirs detail her delight when she reached Sacred Heart's Normal School and the sisters insisted that the children address her as "Miss Guidry," a break with a culture that denied Black women titles of respect. Watching the sisters work, Guidry discerned her own calling, so the SBS helped her enter the Sisters of the Holy Family after she finished at Sacred Heart.[1] Guidry's academic success and her entrance into the religious life epitomize the SBS's aims for their work in the Black community. The nuns sought to educate and empower within a specifically Roman Catholic context, and they viewed their brand of Catholic education as a third way in the heated educational debates of the late nineteenth and early twentieth centuries.

### The Church in Black and White

Despite a history of abuse and neglect, by the end of the nineteenth century, self-satisfied Catholic theologians touted Catholicism as the perfect religion for Black Americans because of its focus on the unifying power of Christ through the Eucharist.[2]

---

1  Mary Gabriella Guidry, *The Southern Negro Nun* (New York: Exposition Press, 1974), 16–21.
2  The church is only now starting to deal with its legacy of slaveholding and white supremacy. Catholic universities such as Georgetown have taken steps

Laypeople, too, considered the Catholic Church a force for improving the lives of the oppressed. In 1890, Daniel Rudd, the Black editor of the *American Catholic Tribune*, announced, "The Church must and will solve the American Negro problem, and that is hardly a problem to her."[3]

Despite lofty claims, however, the church served only a small fraction of the Black population. Determining the number of Black Catholics during this time period is difficult, but in 1906 the census reported thirty-one parishes that were predominantly Black, making up roughly .1 percent of the total Catholic population. This number is artificially low, though, as it did not account for the fact that during that period most Black Catholics worshipped in white parishes. It also did not consider people baptized into the church but who might not belong to a parish. The 1916 Census of Religious Bodies reported an increase to ninety Black parishes, a jump of nearly 15 percent. This figure does not represent a surge in Black Catholics but rather the emergence of more segregated parishes in the twentieth century. The 1926 report found 147 separate churches (out of 18,940 total Catholic churches). Ten years later, the religious census also showed growth reporting 178 predominantly Black parishes. This census put the Black Catholic population at 137,684, but, again, this is likely low. In 1929, Josephite researcher John Gillard made a more generous estimate of 203,986 Black Catholics. While exact numbers prove difficult to pinpoint, Black Catholics represented a small fraction of the total Roman Catholic population.[4]

---

to apologize for their role in slavery and have started making reparations. Scholars like Maureen O'Connell have called for Catholics to engage in anti-racism work to undo some of the damage. O'Connell, *Undoing the Knots: Five Generations of American Catholic Anti-Blackness* (Boston: Beacon Press, 2021). Robert P. Jones has researched how white supremacy has shaped American Christianity and has advocated for a theology of racial justice. Jones, *White Too Long: The Legacy of White Supremacy in American Christianity* (New York: Simon and Schuster Paperbacks, 2020).

3 Dan A. Rudd, "The Church Must and Will Solve," *American Catholic Tribune*, February 15, 1890, 1.

4 Bureau of the Census, *Special Reports, Religious Bodies: 1906*, part 1, *Summary and General Tables* (Washington, DC: Government Printing Office, 1910), 137; Department of Commerce, Bureau of the Census, *Religious Bodies*

While some white theologians affirmed the spiritual equality of all people and claimed that God was color-blind, the church treated Black Catholics differently. The church labeled all Black communities as mission sites, even in such places as Baltimore or New Orleans, where generations of Black Catholics had attended Mass. Black and Indigenous parishes on American soil were grouped with missions to foreign countries in reports to the Society for the Propagation of the Faith. In 1904, Father Charles D. Carroll gave a speech outlining the church's acceptance of racial stereotypes even as it sought to gain Black followers. He asserted, "The Catholic Church alone can solve the Negro problem. She alone can teach the Negro his duties as a man and a Christian sanctify his home and teach him self-restraint." He added, "The Catholic Church is as morally necessary to the Negro race as the sun in the heavens is to the physical world. Why should not the Negro make a good Catholic? God never made a race that his church could not uplift and save."[5] Priests like Carroll spoke of the universal love of God extended to all people, but then reinforced tropes of absent fathers, broken homes, and laziness in the Black community.

Southern prelates sought to use the church as social control. In 1900, Bishop Anthony Durier of Natchitoches, Louisiana, bragged that the seven schools built for Black children in his diocese focused on teaching the children "how to respect God—so little respected in other quarters; they teach them how to respect their neighbors, especially the whites, who are after all their best friends; and they teach them how to respect themselves by being moral and honest before God and men."[6] In the 1904 Lenten Collection

---

*1916*, part 1, *Summary and General Tables* (Washington, DC: Government Printing Office: 1919), 132; United States Department of Commerce, Bureau of the Census, *Religious Bodies: 1926*, vol. 1, *Summary and Detailed Tables* (Washington, DC: Government Printing Office, 1930), 708; Bureau of the Census, *Religious Bodies 1936*, vol. 1, *Summary and Detailed Tables* (Washington, DC: Government Printing Office, 1941), 882; Gillard, *Catholic Church and the American Negro*, 50.

5   "Catholic Church and the Negro: Interesting Subject Discussed by Rev. Charles D. Carroll at Catholic University," *(Baltimore) Afro American*, April 16, 1904, 4.

6   Bishop Anthony Durier, *Report on Mission Work among the Negroes and the Indians: What Is Being Accomplished by Means of the Annual Collection Taken Up for our Missions* (Clayton, DE: Press of St. Joseph's Industrial School, 1900), 18.

Appeal, Bishop Thomas S. Byrne of Nashville made a similar claim: "There is only one influence that can control the Negro, make him amenable to laws, observant of the charities of Christian civilization, and docile to the best instincts of our nature, and that influence is the faith of Christ. The fear of God is the beginning of wisdom, and to control the Negro he must be inspired with the fear of God."[7] Rather than embracing a theology of equality, most white Catholics viewed Black Catholics as exotic others who needed uplift in the form of social control. Still, the transition from inclusive to segregated parishes was lengthy, contested, and never fully completed. Historian Dolores Labbé has suggested, "When society chose Jim Crow, the Church, too, chose Jim Crow."[8] Though this assessment has merit, the process was complicated.

The massive influx of immigrant Catholics to the United States in the last quarter of the nineteenth century occupied most of the attention of the institutional church. By 1916, immigrants accounted for 75 percent of the Catholic population.[9] These immigrant communities built churches and community centers that provided safe spaces in a new country. Catholics saw the national parish as a solution to social problems caused by large-scale immigration. French, German, Polish, Czech, and Italian Catholics all attended separate national ethnic parishes, preferring to associate with their fellow countrymen. Mother Katharine, who grew up attending Holy Trinity, the traditionally German parish in Philadelphia, because her grandfather had emigrated from Austria, would not have viewed establishing separate churches for Black and Indigenous people as a tool of bigotry. Many Black parishioners saw the situation differently.

Some Black worshippers disliked segregated churches and accused Catholic clergy of bowing to Jim Crow, while others preferred separate parishes where their children could act as altar

---

7 Bishop Thomas S. Byrne, "An Appeal in Behalf of the Negro and Indian Missions of the United States," in *Report on Mission Work Among the Negroes and the Indians*, 6.

8 Dolores Egger Labbé, *Jim Crow Comes to Church* (New York: Arno Press, 1978), 69.

9 Dolan, *American Catholic Experience*, 135.

servers, they could sit wherever they liked, and they could create vibrant clubs and sodalities. In the 1910s and 1920s, Black Catholics in places such as Chicago, Illinois; Cleveland, Ohio; and St. Augustine, Florida, petitioned bishops for churches of their own where they might have autonomy. Though Catholic newspaper publisher Daniel Rudd praised the lack of a color line in the Catholic Church in the 1890s, he walked more than a mile every Sunday to attend a predominately Black Catholic church in Cincinnati rather than the mostly white one closer to his house.[10]

In the early twentieth century, the church espoused egalitarian ideals, but did little to ensure fair treatment. To break down racial barriers, church leadership should have taken steps such as streamlining the process to ordain Black and Indigenous priests, desegregating its institutions, and preaching against racism and harmful economic policies. They did not. In 1903, a young Belgian missionary named Father Joseph Anciaux took it upon himself to alert the Vatican to racism within the American church. He wrote a document entitled *De Miserabli Conditione Catholicorum Nigorum in America* (Concerning the Wretched Condition of Negro Catholics in America), often just referred to as the Red Book due to the color of its binding. Anciaux enlisted Drexel to help him push the hierarchy for the establishment of a board to run missions for Black Americans. After being rebuked by Rome for their lack of action and prodded by Drexel, who bombarded Archbishop Ryan of Philadelphia with requests to create a centralized office, the bishops established the Catholic Board for Mission Work Among Colored People in 1907, but this board did not institute programs or reforms.[11] Not until the 1920s and 1930s did the American Catholic Church make a more concerted effort to address systemic racism.

Most racial justice work, however, concentrated on fostering goodwill between the races in hopes that warm relations would gradually dismantle racial prejudice. In many cases, however,

---

10 Gary B. Agee, *A Cry for Justice: Daniel Rudd and His Life in Black Catholicism, Journalism, and Activism, 1854–1933* (Fayetteville: University of Arkansas Press, 2011), 22.

11 Davis, *History of Black Catholics*, 198.

unity did not translate into equality. Lofty sentiments about the universality of the church meant little to Black churchgoers forced to sit in the back pews and wait to receive Communion until all whites had received the sacrament. Sr. Mary Gabriella Guidry, a Holy Family Sister, recalled the moment she realized the church did not always act Catholic. In the early 1920s, when she was about ten years old, she and her sisters could not make it to Sacred Heart, the Black parish, for Saturday confession, so they went to Immaculate Conception, the white church, instead. The priest immediately came out of the confessional and accosted the girls, screaming, "Where are you from?" When they replied, he yelled, "This is not your church or parish so don't ever come here again."[12] Another Black Catholic, George Williams, recalled an incident in the 1930s when he entered a Catholic church only to be ejected from his seat. Looking around the sanctuary, "off to one side at the rear I saw room in a pew reserved for some religious brothers or clerics, and thinking they at least would understand, I went over and sat there. Rather than let me share their pew, they got up and stood in the aisle. This final humiliation was too much for me, and I got up and left in the middle of Mass."[13] Sadly, stories such as these were common.

## The Forgotten Philanthropist

Though she is not a household name, Drexel is mentioned at least in passing in most studies of missions to Indigenous people. The same is not true of the literature on Black education. Mother Katharine Drexel's multi-million-dollar investments have been understudied.[14] The Indigenous school system was centralized in

---

12 Guidry, *Southern Negro Nun*, 15.

13 George Hunton, *All of Which I Saw, Part of Which I Was: The Autobiography of George K. Hunton as Told to Gary MacEoin* (Garden City, NY: Doubleday, 1967), 22.

14 A few books have explored individual schools, including Dorothy Ann Blatnica, VSC, *"At the Altar of Their God": African American Catholics in Cleveland, 1922–1961* (New York: Garland, 1995), and Ethel E. Young and Jerome Wilson, *African American Children and Missionary Nuns and Priests in Mississippi: Achievement against Jim Crow Odds* (Bloomington, IN: Authorhouse, 2010). A number of dissertations have also tackled the subject, though mostly also in localized studies. See Loretta M. Butler, "A History of Catholic Elementary

Washington, D.C., but Black education was largely handled on the local and state level. Except for the General Education Board formed in 1902, national task forces were not created, so Catholic and Protestant groups did not battle for control of the federal purse strings. Most American Catholics, therefore, paid little attention to the issue. The Lenten Collection instituted in 1884 raised money for both Black and Indigenous education, but few Catholics took an interest in missionary work in Black communities. BCIM director Rev. William Hughes told a National Catholic Welfare Council representative that his plan to issue a Cardinal Gibbons holy card to raise money for Black causes would fail unless the appeal were made as "the memorial to Cardinal Gibbons because of his interest in the negroes rather than the appeal for the negroes themselves."[15] While Mother Katharine devoted more resources to Black education than she did to Indigenous missions, her work received little attention or support, either during her life or after.

According to Thomas Jesse Jones's 1917 influential report *Negro Education: A Study of the Private and Higher Schools for Colored People in the United States*, the Catholic Board of Missions ran 112 schools with 13,507 students. The Catholic Church was second only to the Black Church Boards, which ran 153 schools and met the needs of 17,299 students.[16] While the total numbers of Protestant and secular institutions exceeded those of the Catholic Church, no single organization sponsored as many schools. Mother Katharine Drexel's money played a large role in

---

Education for Negroes in the Diocese of Lafayette, Louisiana" (Ph.D. diss., The Catholic University of America, 1963); Barbara E. Mattick, "Ministries in Black and White: The Catholic Sisters of St. Augustine, Florida, 1859–1920" (Ph.D. diss., Florida State University, 2008); and Megan Stout Sibbel, "'Reaping the Colored Harvest': The Catholic Mission in the American South" (Ph.D. diss, Loyola University of Chicago, 2013).

15  Rev. William Hughes to Mr. Francis M. Crowly, November 17, 1922, BCIM records, series 1–1, reel 109.

16  Thomas Jesse Jones, ed., "Negro Education: A Study of the Private and Higher Schools for Colored People in the United States," in *Bulletin, 1916* (Washington, DC: Government Printing Office, 1917), reprinted as *Negro Education: A Study of the Private and Higher Schools for Colored People in the United States* (New York: Arno Press and the *New York Times*, 1969), 130–51.

that outreach.[17] Between 1895 and 1928 Mother Katharine donated $2,123,000 for the construction of missions and schools and an additional $3,751,684 for maintenance, salaries, and other expenses.[18] To put this into perspective, the Slater Fund for Black Education had an original endowment of $1,000,000; the Jeanes Fund was similarly endowed, and the Daniel Hand Educational Fund had $1,500,000 at its disposal.[19] The General Education Board, while founded in 1902, gave comparatively little money to Black institutions until well into the 1920s.[20] These numbers prove that Mother Katharine Drexel was one of the most deep-pocketed philanthropists benefiting Black education, yet her contributions are not widely known.

## Calls for Specialization: The Othering of Black Catholic Education

In speeches, Mother Katharine Drexel lamented that white Catholics did not support creating educational programs equivalent to those of the American Missionary Association or the American Baptist Home Mission Society.[21] In most cases, bishops and

---

17  Jones, *Negro Education*, 133.

18  "Contributions of Mother Katharine to Negro and Indian Missions from 1895 to 1928," BCIM records, series 1–1, reel 151, MUA.

19  John E. Fisher, *The John F. Slater Fund: A Nineteenth-Century Affirmative Action for Negro Education* (Lanham, MD: University Press of America, 1986), 6; Lance G. Jones, *The Jeanes Teacher in the United States, 1908–1933* (Chapel Hill: University of North Carolina Press, 1937), 19; Jones, *Negro Education*, 167.

20  Eric Anderson and Alfred A. Moss Jr., *Dangerous Donations: Northern Philanthropy and Southern Black Education, 1902–1930* (Columbia: University of Missouri Press, 1999), 5.

21  Jacqueline Jones, *Soldiers of Light and Love: Northern Teachers and Georgia Blacks, 1865–1873* (Athens and London: Brown Thrasher Books, University of Georgia Press, 1992), and Richardson, *Christian Reconstruction*. Also, Jay Riley Case has argued that the missionary nature of the work of black education kept Northern support for black colleges high even when other educational programs failed. See Case, "From the Native Ministry to the Talented Tenth: The Foreign Missionary Origins of White Support for Black Colleges," in *The Foreign Missionary Enterprise at Home: Explorations in North American Cultural History*, ed. Daniel H. Bays and Grant Wacker (Tuscaloosa: University of Alabama Press, 2003), 73.

archbishops refused to invest diocesan money in Black education; rather, they foisted the responsibility off onto the SBS and other specialized religious groups. Lack of institutional support hindered her work. In one speech she complained that she was asked to open twenty-six missions, but a lack of personnel and money meant she could only launch five.[22] In 1926, Drexel wrote a letter to the American hierarchy warning that the Catholic failure to provide more educational opportunities to Black students would lure people away from the faith. She cautioned that schools such as Howard and Lincoln University required Bible study that could draw Catholics into heresy.[23] She warned that not only would attendance at an institution such as Straight University, run by the American Missionary Association in New Orleans, pull Catholic students away from their faith, but the Protestant mission schools also robbed the church of an opportunity to evangelize to non-Catholics. Drexel reminded the bishops that Catholics believed that secular education left the job of perfecting the human being half done. Drexel knew that the church engaged in massive school building campaigns for white students but rarely invested in Black Catholics. The Vatican urged American prelates to do more to incorporate Black people into the church, but the American hierarchy found pretexts to justify inaction. The hierarchy preferred to "keep battling for its own supremacy in the American Christian landscape rather than do their part to further decenter white supremacy."[24] Mother Katharine had little patience for excuses, and instead launched as many building projects as she could sustain, becoming a one-woman charitable trust.[25]

---

22 Mother Katharine Drexel, "Since the Beginning," 1922 or later, ca. 1926, Collated Writings, MMK Talks, H10J86, vol. 28, folder 1, ASBS.

23 Mother Katharine Drexel to Your Eminences, Most Reverend Archbishops and Right Reverent Bishops, September 11, 1926, *1926 Report, Archdiocese of New Orleans. Mission Work among the Negroes in the Archdiocese of New Orleans*, BCIM records, series 5/2, reports and applications for aid: Archdiocese of New Orleans, reel 9, MUA.

24 O'Connell, *Undoing the Knots*, 92.

25 For more on the contrast between Vatican proclamations and the actions of the American church, see Cyprian Davis, "God of Our Weary Years: Black Catholics in American Catholic History," in *Taking Down Our Harps: Black Catholics in the United States*, ed. Diana Hayes and Cyprian Davis (Maryknoll, NY: Orbis, 1998), 17–46.

From Reconstruction through the end of the nineteenth century, Protestant organizations operated most schools for Black students, particularly in the South, but gradually public schools became more prominent.[26] By 1915, only 4 percent of Black students aged six to fourteen attended private schools.[27] As with Indigenous schools, groups that pushed for government-run schools believed that the schools would retain their religious character even if the missionaries left. Catholics feared this prospect and protested the 1880 Republican platform, which allowed for federal control of education and made provisions for the education of freedmen. Catholics believed that any assertion of government control in education would weaken parochial schools.[28] As a rule, American Catholics did not trust the public school system. At the 1884 meeting of the Third Council of Baltimore, the council moved from issuing exhortations of paternal love to "command[ing] them [parents] with all the authority in our power" to send children to parochial schools unless given permission from the bishops to send their children to public schools. They also ordered all priests to address the issue within two years. While not every parish obeyed, the number of Catholic schools skyrocketed at the end of the nineteenth century and continued to grow in the twentieth. If Catholic schools were responsible for saving the souls of the flock, Mother Katharine Drexel demanded that Black children receive the same opportunities as their white peers.

### Pioneers in Black Catholic Education

Drexel expanded the mission field, but she was the not the first to advocate for Catholic education of Black students; that credit goes to two Black congregations, the Oblate Sisters of Providence and the Sisters of the Holy Family Sisters, which predated the Civil War. The Oblate Sisters of Providence formed in Baltimore in 1829 as the result of the partnership of Elizabeth Lange, a refugee from

---

26 Richardson, *Christian Reconstruction*, 110.
27 Jones, *Negro Education*, 8.
28 James McPherson, *The Abolitionist Legacy: From Reconstruction to the NAACP* (Princeton, NJ: Princeton University Press, 1975), 73.

Haiti, and Suplician priest James Joubert.²⁹ In 1842, Henriette Delille and Juliette Gaudin, two members of the *gens de couleur libre*, New Orleans' free Black population, founded the Holy Family Sisters.³⁰ Both of these communities completed substantial missionary work, all the while battling opposition from "those of their faith who could not imagine a Black woman moral enough to be a religious sister."³¹ The Oblates and Holy Family Sisters dedicated themselves to advancing Black education, but limited finances made large-scale expansion of their work difficult. Their presence in two important Southern Catholic cities meant a tradition of high academic standards for Black students, and the excellence of their schools made students and parents demand more.³²

Several European congregations also staffed many of the church's missions to Black people. In 1871, English priest Herbert Vaughn formed the Mill Hill Fathers, priests dedicated to preaching to the newly emancipated in America.³³ Vaughn also founded the Franciscan Sisters of Mill Hill, a congregation of teaching sisters, and sent them to Baltimore. In 1893, two years after the formation of the SBS, the American branch of the Mill Hill Fathers separated itself from its British parent congregation and became the Society of St. Joseph of the Sacred Heart, commonly referred to as the Josephites. Between 1871 and 1900, the Josephites struggled finan-

---

29  See Diane Batts Morrow, *Persons of Color and Religious at the Same Time: The Oblate Sisters of Providence, 1828–1860* (Chapel Hill: University of North Carolina Press, 2002).

30  See Sister Mary Bernard Deggs, *No Cross, No Crown: Black Nuns in Nineteenth-Century New Orleans*, ed. Virginia Meacham Gould and Charles E. Nolan (Bloomington: Indiana University Press, 2001), and Mary Francis Borgia Hart, *Violets in the King's Garden: A History of the Sisters of the Holy Family of New Orleans* (New Orleans: Sister Mary Francis Borgia Hart, 1976).

31  Diana L. Hayes, "Standing in the Shoes My Mother Made: The Making of a Catholic Womanist Theologian," in *Deeper Shades of Purple: Womanism in Religion and Society*, ed. Stacey M. Floyd-Thomas (New York: New York University Press, 2006), 64.

32  Thaddeus J. Posey, OFM, Cap., "Praying in the Shadows: The Oblate Sisters of Providence, a Look at Nineteenth-Century Black Catholic Spirituality," in *This Far by Faith: Readings in African American Women's Religious Biography*, ed. Judith Weisenfeld and Richard Newman (New York: Routledge, 1996), 80.

33  Shane Leslie, *Letters of Herbert Cardinal Vaughn to Lady Herbert of Lea, 1867–1903* (London: Macmillan, 1942), 240.

cially and founded only eleven parishes.³⁴ The Holy Ghost Fathers, the Society of African Missions, and the Society of the Divine Word Missionaries also established missions that served African American communities, but these international organizations did not focus exclusively on providing education for Black students. Unique among the Catholic organizations serving in the field of Black education, the SBS had the funding to work on a large scale.

## "A Liberal Education": The Educational Philosophy of the SBS

Despite the SBS's professed interest in providing Black students equal access to Catholic education, they did not begin with a color-blind curriculum. They promoted the idea of a "liberal education" that would not be "limited to any one science, or branch of learning; an education which takes a large view of what constitutes the perfect development of man, and which aims to prepare him for life, rather than fit him to make a living."³⁵ They advocated for better educational opportunities, though they eschewed partnership with public schools. Their pedagogical methods, which infused Catholic spirituality into a mixture of industrial and liberal studies, set them apart from both Protestant missions and secular philanthropy.

This mission forced the sisters to negotiate complex educational debates.³⁶ According to Mississippi governor James K. Var-

---

34  St. Joseph's Society of the Sacred Heart, Inc., "Society Annual Report by Year," 3/14/1994, Josephite collection, box 2, Xavier University Archives, New Orleans, Louisiana; hereafter XUA.

35  M. Letterhouse, "What Is a Liberal Education?" *Mission Fields at Home*, November 1928, 23.

36  In recent years, the debate over the methods of perceived accommodationist Booker T. Washington and W. E. B. DuBois has thankfully taken a backseat to more nuanced discussions of education that focus less on ideology and more on conditions at the local level. See Anderson and Moss, *Dangerous Donations*; James D. Anderson, *The Education of Blacks in the South, 1860–1935* (Chapel Hill: University of North Carolina Press, 1988); Margaret A. Diggs, *A Catholic Negro Education in the United States* (Washington, DC: Margaret Diggs, 1936); Adam Fairclough, *Teaching Equality: Black Schools in the Age of Jim Crow* (Athens: University of Georgia Press, 2001); Louis Harlan, *Separate and Unequal: Public School Campaigns and Racism in the Southern Seaboard*

daman's 1904 veto message of a bill to support schools for African Americans, "Literary education—the knowledge of books does not seem to produce any good substantial results with the Negro, but serves to sharpen his cunning, breeds hopes that cannot be gratified . . . promotes indolence, and in turn leads to crime."[37] Many would have agreed with the governor's ugly words. Vardaman's sentiment prevailed in the Catholic theological journal *American Ecclesiastical Review*. In 1898 the journal suggested that Black children did not merit rigorous curriculums: "With these dark children it is not so much the education of books that is needed, as the education of the mind and heart to noble ideas and high moral purposes." The editors concluded, "It may be justly said that, with but few exceptions, these two races [Black and Indigenous] have as yet hardly learned to think or act intelligently." They suggested that the Sisters of the Blessed Sacrament focus their teaching on good housekeeping rather than complex mathematics.[38] Unlike Vardaman and the priests at *American Ecclesiastical Review*, however, the SBS countered, "As if the greater amount of pigmentation precluded capability of mind! The question of mental ability has long since been settled by the intellectual attainments of the colored man himself."[39] Still, the sisters fused academic courses with manual training that they considered a tribute to "esthetic beauty."[40]

### Industrial Education Precedents

Despite limited evidence that Black students could find well-paid work in industrial trades, vocational education became popular in reform circles. In 1890, the year before Drexel launched the

---

*States 1901–1915* (1958; repr. New York: Atheneum, 1969); Mary Hoffschwelle, *The Rosenwald Schools of the American South* (Gainesville: University Press of Florida, 2006); Jones, *Soldiers of Light and Love*; and Jones, *Jeanes Teacher*.

37 Quotation in Fairclough, *Teaching Equality*, 17.
38 "American Foundations of Religious Orders: The Congregation of the Sisters of the Blessed Sacrament for Indians and Colored People," *American Ecclesiastical Review*, 8, no. 1 (January 1898): 7.
39 Theresa V. Reilly, "What Price Education?," *Mission Fields at Home*, January 1933, 60.
40 M. Letterhouse, "The Brain-Side and the Hand-Side in Education," *Mission Fields at Home*, January 1931, 60.

SBS, as many as two-thirds of Hampton Institute students participated in the trade course or night school, which required ten hours of manual labor each day followed by two hours of academic instruction in the evening during the first three years of study.[41] General Samuel Armstrong, Hampton's founder, justified the program, suggesting, "He needs the ten hours' drudgery which he gets in the shops to put him in shape for the struggle of life."[42] Like those in the Indigenous education movement, many prominent thinkers on the subject held to the racist idea that schools needed to instill a strong work ethic in their Black students. The movement gained momentum in the 1880s with the establishment of the John F. Slater Fund, which gave grants to promote industrial education.[43]

In 1891, the Second Mohonk Conference on the Negro Question, a meeting of primarily Protestant, liberal-minded reformers, promoted primary education grounded in common English studies along with industrial work.[44] The movement gained further traction in the twentieth century when it was championed by the General Education Board. Many Black people, however, did not want their educational choices circumscribed by their race. In the nineteenth century, however, industrial education was not only for students of color. Progressive-era reformers such as Jane Addams and John Dewey embraced this pedagogy.[45] Mother Katharine's uncle, Anthony Drexel, founded the Drexel Institute, later Drexel University, in 1891 as one of the premier industrial educational centers in the nation with the goal of training students in applied arts and sciences. He considered vocational education the movement of the

---

41    Robert Francis Engs, *Educating the Disfranchised: Samuel Chapman Armstrong and Hampton Institute, 1839–1893* (Knoxville: University of Tennessee Press, 1999), 157.

42    Samuel Armstrong, "Industrial Training," in *First Mohonk Conference on the Negro Question Held at Lake Mohonk, Ulster County, New York, June 4, 5, 6, 1890*, ed. Isabel C. Barrows (1891; repr. New York: Negro Universities Press, 1969), 15.

43    See Fisher, *John F. Slater Fund*.

44    It is worth noting that neither of conferences on the "Negro Question" invited an African American to attend.

45    Jane Addams, *Democracy and Social Ethics* (New York: Macmillan, 1902), 180–81.

future.[46] Mother Katharine absorbed much of her uncle's enthusiasm for vocational training, as it also tied into prominent Catholic educational thought that celebrated manual labor.

Catholics had a long-standing tradition of promoting manual training. The Pastoral Letter issued by the Second Plenary Council of Baltimore in 1866 cautioned against ornamental education and urged parents to "prepare your children for the duties of the state or condition of life they are likely to be engaged in: do not exhaust your means in bestowing on them an education that may unfit them for these duties."[47] Religious congregations ran industrial schools for girls and boys in almost every U.S. city. Priests and nuns told students to emulate Our Lady and St. Joseph, "who first taught men the loveliness of humble labor."[48] Catholics accepted that a student's gender and class determined what kind of education they received.[49] The SBS adhered to this tradition. Mother Katharine likely based her early institutions on European industrial schools run by monastics. In 1886 and 1887, the Drexel sisters visited Europe and toured many industrial schools before opening their first school, St. Francis Industrial School, which educated orphans of all races. They praised the work of the Christian Brothers, whose schools combined horticulture, apiculture, and agriculture with prayer and scholarship.[50]

In the twentieth century, however, the church tempered its fondness for industrial education. The *Program of Social Reconstruction* issued by the Administrative Committee of the National Catholic War Council in 1919 promoted vocational training for all students but warned teachers not to "deprive the children of the working class of at least the elements of a cultural education."

---

46   James Creese, *A.J. Drexel (1826–1893) and His "Industrial University"* (Princeton, NJ: Newcomen Society, 1949), 8–20.
47   Hugh J. Nolan, ed., "Pastoral Letter Issued by the Second Plenary Council of Baltimore," October 21, 1866, in *Pastoral Letters of the United States Catholic Bishops*, vol. 1, *1792–1940* (Washington, DC: United States Catholic Conference, 2005), 199.
48   Lord, *Our Nuns*, 101.
49   Margaret McGuinness, *Called to Serve: A History of Nuns in America* (New York: New York University Press, 2013), 116.
50   See Duffy, *Katharine Drexel*, 78, and Hurd, "Master Art of a Saint," 50.

The writers added, "A healthy democracy cannot tolerate a purely industrial or trade education for any class of its citizens."[51] Mother Katharine, who likely read the statement, would have agreed. Despite growing up in one of the most affluent families in the country, she spent many hours receiving instruction in domestic arts and sciences. At the convent each sister had to mix classes and prayer with manual labor. Drexel considered labor an essential part of spirituality.[52]

Despite their embrace of some of the tenets of industrial education, Mother Katharine and the SBS did not simply impose "schooling for second-class citizenship."[53] Instead, she usually asked people what they wanted. The *American Catholic Tribune*, a Black Catholic newspaper run by Daniel A. Rudd, frequently printed letters from people in both Northern and Southern cities urging the church to consider founding industrial schools.[54] Rudd himself operated industrial schools specializing in the printing trade in both Cincinnati and Detroit.[55] Rudd formed the Congress of Colored Catholics, a group convened to advocate for Black people in the church.[56] When the Congress met for the first time in 1889, the group's official statement included a push for trade education: "Conscious that one of our greatest and most pressing needs is the establishment of industrial schools, where the hand of our youth may be trained, as well as the mind and heart, we heartily endorse every movement tending to promote such good work."[57] The following year, the Congress formed a committee to

---

51 "Program of Social Reconstruction Issued by the Administrative Committee of the National Catholic War Council, February 12, 1919," in Nolan, *Pastoral Letters of the United States Catholic Bishops*, 1:267.
52 "St. Michael's Convent: It Is Surrounded by Trees and Flowers," *American Catholic Tribune*, September 12, 1891, reprinted from *Catholic News*.
53 Anderson, *Education of Blacks in the South*, 1.
54 See, for example, "Letters to the Editor," *American Catholic Tribune*, December 2, 1887; March 9, 1888; August 31, 1889.
55 For a full biography of Rudd, see Agee, *A Cry for Justice*.
56 For more on the Congresses, see David Spalding, "The Negro Catholic Congresses, 1889–1894," *Catholic Historical Review* 55, no. 3 (October 1969): 337–57.
57 "Address of the Congress to Their Catholic Former Citizens of the United States," *American Catholic Tribune*, January 12, 1889, 2.

petition the U.S. Senate for an industrial school for "colored" Catholics in Washington, D.C.[58] Rudd and his fellow members of the Congress of Colored Catholics were no accommodationists; they also pushed for equal access to schools of higher education, particularly the Catholic University of America.[59] Their repeated demands for Catholic industrial schools, however, show that Mother Katharine did not foist trade schools on the Black community. Rudd and others would have preferred to gain access to existing Catholic schools, but church leaders showed no inclination to eliminate the color barrier. Instead of waiting for the church to rid itself of white supremacy, Mother Katharine built separate schools.

Unlike many who advocated for an industrial curriculum, the SBS also insisted on rigorous academics and fine arts. When Bishop Thomas Sebastian Byrne of Nashville asked Mother Katharine to open a purely industrial school in 1904, she refused, saying,

> I cannot share these views with regard to the education of the Race. I feel that if among our colored people we find individuals gifted with capabilities, with those sterling qualities which constitute character, our Holy Mother the Church who fosters and develops the intellect only that it may give God more glory and be of benefit to others, should also concede to the Negro the privilege of higher education.[60]

Instead of the trade school the bishop requested, the school they opened in Nashville combined academic courses with sewing, cooking, and dressmaking. Within a few years, it grew into an accredited academic high school.[61] The Sisters of the Blessed Sacrament called for a unification of "the Brain-side and the Hand-side in education."[62] Their magazine, *Mission Fields at*

---

58  "The Congress Proceedings," *American Catholic Tribune*, July 19, 1890, 1–2.
59  For example, see "The Congress: Speeches, Letters, and Notes," *American Catholic Tribune*, July 26, 1890, 1.
60  Duffy, *Katharine Drexel*, 254.
61  Lynch, *Sharing the Bread in Service*, 1:145, 147.
62  M. Letterhouse, "The Brain-Side and the Hand-Side in Education," *Mission Fields at Home*, January 1931, 59–60.

*Home*, frequently ran stories on the importance of Black-owned businesses. They designed coursework to help students learn the skills necessary to employ themselves, so they did not have to rely on whites for jobs.[63] This both/and approach makes the SBS theology of education difficult to classify. Their educational philosophy embraced national trends and twisted them to suit a Catholic framework. During their first decade, the SBS founded industrial boarding schools, but as the twentieth century progressed, the sisters transitioned to academically challenging parochial schools.

**Philosophy in Practice: Holy Providence School**

In 1891, when the sisters moved into their temporary convent at St. Michel, the old Drexel estate in Torresdale, Pennsylvania, they took with them ten-year-old Ida May Coffey, who became the first student at Holy Providence School. The school primarily served Black students, but it educated a small number of Indigenous students, as well. Though the school was classified as an orphanage, many of the students had at least one living parent. Students were signed over to the sisters with an indenture contract—a practice not uncommon in the nineteenth century. This contract removed parental control and gave the sisters full authority over the children. Parents signing the indenture contract had to agree that they "will not at any time, demand or receive any compensation for the services of the child during her/his minority, or interfere, in any way whatsoever, with the views or discretion of the Sisters of the Blessed Sacrament in his/her behalf."[64] The practice shows that the early SBS subscribed to the racist idea that in order to be successful, students had to be removed from their home cultures. The SBS also used this system at their school in Rock Castle, Virginia, but they abandoned it in the early twentieth century when parents refused to sign.

---

63 For an example, see James A. Jackson, "Industrial Education as a Basis for Commercial Progress," *Mission Fields at Home*, April 1932, 101; or Thomas E. Purcel, "The Contribution of the Negro to America: Excerpt from an Address given at the Negro in Industry Conference, St. Louis, Missouri," *Mission Fields at Home*, November 1931, 23–24; James A. Jackson, "Outlook in the Business World for the Negro Youth," *Mission Fields at Home*, March 1933, 87–88.

64 "Indenture Contract signed October 12, 1916," in Hurd, "Master Art of a Saint," 105.

Starting with a single ward in 1892, Holy Providence grew to 160 students two years later. Girls stayed until they reached age twenty-one, while boys transferred to the Josephite-run St. Joseph's Home in Wilmington, Delaware, at age thirteen. Students took academic classes in the morning and industrial courses in the afternoon. Boys studied shoemaking, gardening, poultry care, and dairy tending. Their work helped put food on the table of the school and convent. Girls learned sewing, dressmaking, "fancy" laundry (working with high collars, ladies' gowns, and lace), cooking, baking, and hostess skills.[65] Girls sewed and mended their own clothing and helped sisters cook meals. In this way the SBS schools were like other Catholic institutions that catered to the poor; sisters tried to ensure that upon graduation their students would have the skills to earn a living in service jobs.[66] Also, utilizing student labor cut down on costs. In their first industrial boarding schools, the SBS focused on training Black students in fields that had been traditionally open to them rather than on trying to educate them to occupy higher stations. Their first schools did not push societal limits but instead reinforced assimilationist ideas.

## Professionalization of SBS Teaching Staff

Holy Providence was an educational laboratory for the Sisters of the Blessed Sacrament, who received their teaching training there before entering the mission field. Drexel took pedagogy seriously and hired experts from normal schools in New York to train her teachers. Katherine T. Meagher taught the sisters from 1893 to 1896, and Katherine Gorman held the position from 1896 to 1901. SBS sisters took over teacher training as they became more proficient and started obtaining college degrees. In the twentieth century, the congregation's emphasis on higher education shifted SBS schools away from industrial work. By 1924 a visitor to Holy Providence marveled at the students' mathematical prowess, noting, "Then at the blackboard they divided cloth into hundreds of yards, purchased without blinking thousands of tons of coal

---

65  Hurd, "Master Art of a Saint," 106.
66  See Lord, *Our Nuns*, 100–101, 116, and Brown and McKeown, *The Poor Belong to Us*, 13–50.

and unlimited sacks of potatoes, put that mysterious trio, A, B, and C to work for whole periods of time, sent trains on journeys around the globe and ships across the broad ocean, all with a precision and ease that spoke of quick minds stimulated by correct teaching."[67] As at their Indigenous schools, the SBS moved from an industrial model of education to one that embraced a more rigorous academic curriculum, but the process was faster and more comprehensive in their schools for Black students. The shift was subtle rather than done through official proclamation, making it difficult to trace. Likely it came as the result of rising demand from the Black community as well as the sisters' own increasing professionalization.

## "Upon This Rock": The Rock Castle Model of Education

The trajectory from industrial to academic emphasis is best viewed at St. Francis de Sales Academy, commonly called Rock Castle, located in Powhatan County, Virginia. In 1893, Drexel's sister Louise and brother-in-law Edward Morrell built a military-style industrial school for boys in Belmead, Virginia, operated by the Christian Brothers. The Morrells aimed to create a "Catholic Tuskegee," fusing the self-help methods of Booker T. Washington and centuries of Catholic monastic training. Louise and Edward Morrell encouraged Drexel to create a similar school for girls and even purchased an adjoining piece of property in 1895. Construction proved difficult, thanks to the remoteness of its location on the James River, but the SBS opened St. Francis de Sales in 1899 as a year-round industrial boarding school for girls. Like many nineteenth-century schools, Rock Castle opened as an elementary and junior high school, though the sisters planned to grow it into a full-fledged high school. They had to provide preparatory studies because Black students were systematically excluded from quality education in the South. Their first students hailed from the Southeast, primarily Virginia, Maryland, and Washington, D.C., though their reach soon extended deeper into the South and later into the North, as well. During the school's first years, sisters

---

67 Lord, *Our Nuns*, 75.

walked the streets of Richmond telling children about the school. Within a few years, word of mouth gave the school a national reputation.[68] Many students who came had shown academic prowess in their hometowns, where they did not have the ability to continue their education past the eighth grade. For example, priests in Port Arthur, Texas, arranged for Juanita Fletcher to get a scholarship to Rock Castle when she finished elementary school there.[69] Though the sisters referred to the students as "poor," Rock Castle drew students from middle-class Black families who could consider sending their daughters away to school. Writer Ellen Tarry, who attended in the early 1920s, went to Rock Castle after looking at comparable programs at Fisk and Talladega. A childhood friend's recommendation persuaded Tarry to select Rock Castle, and her parents, though non-Catholic, agreed primarily because it cost less than the other schools. During the school's first years, the sisters did not charge tuition. Later, however, they assigned modest fees, far lower than other boarding schools because the school was subsidized by the Drexel fortune.[70]

Girls took English grammar and writing, reading, math, nature study, geography, music, catechism, and Bible history. The sisters emphasized literacy skills. As at Holy Providence, Rock Castle students attended academic classes in the morning and industrial classes in the afternoon. These subjects included sewing, home nursing, laundry, and domestic arts and sciences.[71] Industrial courses followed the curriculum of the Drexel Institute in Philadelphia. The school had a model dining room and laundry where students could hone their domestic skills. Students also had to serve elaborate dinners to guests who visited the school to practice working in high-end dining.[72] Their sewing often garnered

---

68  Nessa Theresa Baskerville Johnson, *A Special Pilgrimage: A History of Black Catholics in Richmond* (Richmond, VA: Diocese of Richmond, 1978), 24–25.

69  Sharon Litwin, "Xavier Alumna Keeps on Battling Barriers," *New Orleans Times Picayune*, December 1, 1985, 44.

70  Ellen Tarry, *The Third Door: The Autobiography of an American Negro Woman* (1955; repr. Tuscaloosa: University of Alabama Press, 1966), 21–30.

71  Hurd, "Master Art of a Saint," 142.

72  Sr. Marie Barat Smith, "A History of St. Emma's Military Academy and St. Francis de Sales High School" (Master's thesis, The Catholic University of America, 1949), 26.

high praise. The SBS entered student handiwork in state competitions, and the school's fine needlework won a gold medal at the Jamestown Exposition in 1907. The organizer of the exhibition lavished praise on the St. Francis exhibit and stated, "The sewing and fancy work of the girls department easily surpasses that of the other schools, and rivals much of the best of the private exhibitors. The school also has a good exhibit of its literary work covering the common school branches and the three year high school course."[73] Much of the early training aimed at producing women capable of either earning a living in domestic service or heading middle-class Christian homes. Twentieth-century students predominantly chose the latter path. A 1948 study of former student occupations found that while many students (58 out of 101) chose to become housewives, none opted for domestic service. Popular occupations included clerical work, nursing, teaching, dressmaking, industrial work, government employment, switchboard operating, beauty salon ownership, and customer service.[74]

In 1902, the sisters added teacher training to the curriculum, and they began high school–level classes in 1904.[75] The SBS considered training teachers to go back out to rural schools across the South a priority. Secondary students studied English, rhetoric, composition, grammar, church history, Latin, algebra, geometry, general science, physiology, chemistry, ancient history, English history, modern history, and civics.[76] By 1915, when Dr. Jesse Jones visited the school as part of his research for his 1917 report on African American education, he counted eighty-eight students in the preparatory department (grades six through eight) and fifty in the secondary program.[77] As women's opportunities in clerical

---

73  Giles B. Jackson and D. Webster Davis, *The Industrial History of the Negro Race of the United States* (Richmond, VA: Giles B. Jackson, 1908), 226.

74  Smith, "History of St. Emma's Military Academy," 55.

75  It is interesting to note that the SBS did not add teacher training to their Indigenous schools until 1919, a difference of nearly twenty years. Documents in the motherhouse do not provide any clues as to why they took so long to start higher education and teacher training in the Indian mission field, but it is possible that language barriers and their adherence to the government school curriculum played a role in this decision.

76  Smith, "History of St. Emma's Military Academy," 27.

77  Jones, *Negro Education*, 327, 653.

fields expanded in the early twentieth century, the sisters started a commercial course in 1918 and offered certificates in typing, shorthand, and "Business English."[78] This move represented a hope that businesses would hire Black women for these roles, though in 1920 only 0.8 percent of Black woman held clerical jobs.[79] The 1914 valedictorian of Rock Castle, Melena Agnes Jones Cass, could find no employment in supposedly enlightened Boston except as a domestic worker.[80] In 1923, the school eliminated classes below the seventh grade, and in 1925, it dropped seventh grade to focus on the state-accredited high school program. Rock Castle continued to offer eighth grade because most Southern public schools only offered Black students a seventh-grade education.

The sisters focused on the high school program because educational opportunities for Black students had increased at the elementary level, while secondary schools lagged. In 1915, Louisiana, for example, did not have a single public high school for Black students.[81] In fact in that year, the entire South had only twenty-one public secondary schools open to Black students. Black-led protests and the concerted efforts of the General Education Board raised that number to 143 by 1925.[82] Ironically, the increase in public funding for Black education threatened the mission of the SBS, who thought public institutions endangered the souls of their students.

The nuns at Rock Castle put increased emphasis on teacher training courses during the early twentieth century. Their goal was to have enough trained lay teachers to extend their reach in rural areas. The SBS wanted their graduates to be, as Mother Katharine put it, "lay apostles," and teach the next generation. The sisters

---

78  Lynch, *Sharing the Bread in Service*, 1:105.
79  John L. Rury, *Education and Women's Work: Female Schooling and the Division of Labor in Urban America, 1870–1930* (Albany: State University of New York Press, 1991), 121.
80  "Cass, Melena Agnes Jones (1896–1978)," in *African American Lives*, ed. Henry Louis Gates and Evelyn Brooks-Higginbotham (Oxford: Oxford University Press, 2004), 150.
81  Jones, *Negro Education*, 34.
82  Anderson and Moss, *Dangerous Donations*, 100.

hoped the religious atmosphere of a school like Rock Castle would aid the spread of Catholic values as their students took over classrooms in both public and Catholic schools. This emphasis on teacher training was rare for Catholic schools, which preferred professed religious teachers. When the SBS tried to open St. Monica's in New Orleans and staff it with lay teachers, Black parents refused to send their students unless nuns came to operate the school.[83] Nevertheless, the SBS continued to train educators and prepare students for college.

In 1930, the school changed its name from St. Francis de Sales Institute to St. Francis de Sales High School. The SBS invested considerable resources and worked to modernize and expand Rock Castle's facilities; it boasted extensive laboratories and a well-stocked library.[84] Juanita Fletcher recalled, "It was at Rock Castle that I first saw a library. They had volumes and volumes of Dickens. I remember precisely what I did. I read Charles Dickens from volume one straight through without stopping. . . . I became a voracious reader."[85] In the 1920s, when Ellen Tarry attended, she found the course work so strenuous that she "had to study harder than ever before."[86] By the 1930s, many of the students at Rock Castle pursued higher education, and the curriculum had to ensure that they could gain college acceptance. A 1931 survey of alumnae from 1925 to 1930 found five working as teachers, six in normal schools, twenty-six in college, two working as nurses, eleven in nurse training school, eleven as married housewives, and fourteen in other professions.[87]

Domestic art and science courses continued, albeit occupying fewer hours per week. Until 1937, most students received both an academic diploma and a home economics certificate upon gradu-

---

83 "Along the Highways and Pathways of the Mission Fields," *Mission Fields at Home*, January 1929, 72.

84 M. Letterhouse, "Ideal in Education," *Mission Fields at Home*, January 1929, 67.

85 Litwin, "Xavier Alumna," 44.

86 *The Third Door*, 45.

87 "Sisters of the Blessed Sacrament: Excerpts from Radio talks, February 2, 9, 16, over station WLWL, New York City by Michael J. Ryan," *Mission Fields at Home*, March 1931, 89.

ation.⁸⁸ According to the sisters' writings, they thought of themselves as operating a large home that needed the labor of all family members; thus, girls worked in the kitchen, laundry, and bakery.⁸⁹ What the students who had to perform such manual labor thought of the arrangement is unclear, though *Mission Fields at Home* published a student essay that suggests that by the 1920s students saw the classes as part of the home economics movement rather than as training for domestic service. The movement, which began in the 1880s as part of manual training pedagogy, became more about protecting the family and the sanctity of the home with the 1908 founding of the American Home Economics Association. By 1920 one-third of all high school women were enrolled in home economics classes.⁹⁰ The young Rock Castle student declared that the students were learning to be "models of every womanly virtue . . . perfect types of womanhood."⁹¹ Another student noted that they received "education of the body, by physical training, play and out-door sports; the education of the mind in the various arts and sciences; the education of the soul in the love and practice of all the virtues, with strong emphasis on the strengthening of the Will."⁹² The shift from preparing students for service work to readying them for college classes reflected an increasing appreciation on the part of the sisters of the capabilities of Black students as well as a willingness to listen to the desires of students and their parents. In addition, they also had to compete with increasing opportunities in higher education offered by both secular and Protestant sources.

## More Souls to Harvest: SBS Shifts to Day School Model

Unlike their work in the Indigenous mission field, in the twentieth century, the SBS shifted their work in Black education from industrial boarding schools to parochial day schools. Most schools started with the first eight grades, and the sisters gradually moved

---

　　88　Smith, "History of St. Emma's Military Academy," 31.
　　89　M. Letterhouse, "Ideals in Education," *Mission Fields at Home*, January 1929, 68.
　　90　See Rury, *Education and Women's Work*, 132–60.
　　91　"The King's Castle," *Mission Fields at Home*, October 1928, 7.
　　92　"The King's Castle," *Mission Fields at Home*, October 1928, 7.

Table 5-1. SBS Schools for Black Students, 1891–1935

| Name | Location | Years in Operation | School Type |
|---|---|---|---|
| Holy Providence | Cornwells Heights, Pa. | 1892–1971 | Industrial Boarding/High School |
| St. Francis de Sales | Rock Castle, Va. | 1899–1983 | Industrial Boarding/High School |
| Immaculate Mother | Nashville, Tenn. | 1905–1954 | 4–12 |
| St. Katharine Hall | Carlisle, Pa. | 1906–1918 | Elementary |
| Our Lady of the Blessed Sacrament | Philadelphia, Pa. | 1908–1972 | Elementary |
| St. Marks | New York, N.Y. | 1909–1967 | Elementary |
| St. Cyprian | Columbus, Ohio | 1912–1958 | Elementary |
| St. Monica | Chicago, Ill. | 1912–1925 | Elementary |
| Our Lady of Lourdes | Atlanta, Ga. | 1913–1974 | Elementary |
| St. Elizabeth | St. Louis, Mo. | 1914–1946 | Elementary |
| St. Ann | Cincinnati, Ohio | 1914–1967 | Elementary |
| St. Peter Claver | Macon, Ga. | 1915–2000* | Elementary-High School |
| St. Catherine's | Germantown, Pa. | 1915–1972 | Elementary |
| Xavier Prep | New Orleans, La. | 1915– | 7–12 |
| Holy Ghost | New Orleans, La. | 1916–1989 | Elementary |
| St. Louis | New Orleans, La. | 1917–1933 | Elementary |
| Our Mother of Sorrows | Biloxi, Miss. | 1917–1973 | Elementary-High School |
| St. John the Baptist | Montgomery, Ala. | 1917–1985 | Elementary-High School |
| Blessed Sacrament | Beaumont, Tex. | 1917–1970 | Elementary-High School |
| St. Benedict the Moor | New York, N.Y. | 1917–1927 | Elementary |
| Blessed Sacrament | New Orleans, La. | 1918–1973 | Elementary |
| St. Edward's | New Iberia, La. | 1918–2004* | Elementary-High School |

(*continued on next page*).

TABLE 5-1. SBS Schools for Black Students, 1891–1935 (continued)

| Name | Location | Years in Operation | School Type |
|---|---|---|---|
| Corpus Christi | New Orleans, La. | 1919–1973 | Elementary |
| St. Peter Claver | New Orleans, La. | 1921–1991 | Elementary |
| St. Peter Claver | Brooklyn, N.Y. | 1922–1937 | Elementary |
| St. Elizabeth | Chicago, Ill. | 1922– | Elementary-High School |
| Our Lady of the Blessed Sacrament | Cleveland, Ohio | 1922–1962 | Elementary |
| St. Augustine | East St. Louis, Mo. | 1922–1927 | Elementary |
| Sacred Heart | Lake Charles, La. | 1922–1989 | Elementary-High School |
| St. Nicholas | St. Louis, Mo. | 1924–1938 | Elementary |
| Xavier University | New Orleans, La. | 1925– | University |
| Holy Savior | Philadelphia, Pa. | 1925–1928 | Catechism |
| Holy Trinity | Cincinnati, Ohio | 1926–1955 | Elementary |
| St. Charles Borromeo | New York, N.Y. | 1926–1941* | Elementary |
| Sacred Heart | Port Arthur, Tex. | 1927–1973 | Elementary-High School |
| Madonna High School | Cincinnati, Ohio | 1927–1962 | High School |
| St. Ignatius | Philadelphia, Ohio | 1982– | Elementary |
| St. Monica | New Orleans, La. | 1930–2005 | Elementary |
| St. Anselm | Chicago, Ill. | 1932–1946 | Elementary |

*These schools remain in operation, though SBS no longer operates them. The closing date represents when the SBS turned administration over to lay staff.

into secondary education. By 1955, the congregation ran more than a dozen high schools. The emphasis on higher education became central to the SBS mission in the South, particularly as public education options improved.

## Religious Instruction at SBS Schools

While students attended SBS schools to gain access to higher education, the sisters kept religious instruction at the forefront. Since the population of Black Catholics was quite small, SBS schools served large numbers of non-Catholic students; their rule stated that they would educate students regardless of denomination. Black Catholics attended SBS schools because the hierarchy preached the evils of secular education, and Protestants often attended because the schools were their best chance at receiving a high-quality education. In her study on Black education in Pointe Coupee Parish, Louisiana, Leola Palmer asserted, "When devout Catholics and Protestants enrolled their children in St. Augustine's Catholic Church (funded but not staffed by the SBS), religious differences no longer existed. Education was the top priority as it guaranteed 9 months of academic instruction for 7 consecutive years."[93]

The SBS imbued the atmosphere of their schools with religion and insisted that all students participate in church activities. At the boarding schools, students went to daily Mass and attended religious retreats. Day-school pupils also attended religious services with their classmates and learned to sing High Mass in Latin. Sisters incorporated faith in their lesson plans, and pupils learned church history and read Bible stories. Like all Catholic schoolchildren, they also celebrated special saints' feast days. Students looked forward to activities such as St. Nicholas visiting in December, St. Patrick's Day celebrations with their Irish nun teachers in March, the May Crowning of Mary, and the Corpus Christi processions in June. Pupils also joined sodalities, or religious clubs, that sponsored activities throughout the year. The

---

93 Leola Palmer, "The Evolution of Education for African-Americans in Pointe Coupee Parish (New Roads, Louisiana): 1889–1969" (Ph.D. diss., Fordham University, 1992), 210.

entire day was ordered around prayer, as students said morning offerings, grace before meals, and evening prayers.

## Conversion and Community Rifts

While sisters claimed they did not try to convert their students, they celebrated the fact that many students did become Catholic. A fictionalized account of the conversion of Florence Estella Lee appeared in *Mission Fields at Home*, which highlights the SBS belief that the presence of the Blessed Sacrament would be enough to draw students to the faith. The story depicts Florence Estella Lee entering the church for the Benediction of the Sacrament—a ceremony when the priest reposes the host that has been on display during Eucharistic Adoration—on her first day at Rock Castle. There she saw a group of girls who all "wore a bright, happy, carefree expression" as they looked toward the priest. Lee gazed at the scene: "The marble altar was resplendent with light and radiance. The priest, vested in white, was facing the people; he held high above his head a beautiful golden Monstrance. In its center gleamed a substance of purest white." Young Florence was so taken with the scene that "she fancied the sister kneeling beside her must hear the beating and throbbing of her heart; it seemed as if it would burst." The article suggests that seeing joyful students experience the power of the Eucharist convinced the girl to request baptism before the end of the school year without the nuns saying a word.[94]

Many students, however, resisted conversion. Rock Castle student Ellen Tarry entered the school as a Congregationalist with strict orders from her family not to join the church, and she resolutely "built up a wall of resistance to the Catholic practices that were a vital part of the daily routine at St. Francis de Sales."[95] Ironically, her father had been a convert to Congregationalism after attending Atlanta University, a missionary college. Despite her determination and her promise to her dying father to become a Congregational missionary to Africa, a school retreat given by Jesuit Abraham Emerick convinced her to convert. To their credit,

---

94 Mary Angela Wedin, "A Gift of God," *Mission Fields at Home*, June 1930, 131–33.

95 Terry, *Third Door*, 44.

the sisters refused to let her enter the church until she received her mother's blessing, a process that took the better part of a year. They also told her that her decision might make her feel a stranger in her own community. Tarry, however, remained adamant, though her conversion caused a rift in her family.

Non-Catholic parents took a risk when they enrolled their children in Catholic schools. In an era of fervent anti-Catholicism, joining the Roman Church made students a double minority. Evelyn Davie's Baptist father and Methodist mother wanted their daughter to receive a better education than the New Orleans public schools could offer, and so they enrolled her in SBS-run Xavier Prep in 1923, but they felt they were "throwing her to the wolves." Davies continued at SBS schools through her master's degree, and though her achievements thrilled her parents, they were devastated and briefly stopped speaking to her when she converted in 1930.[96] Conversion could carry high personal costs, and it put the SBS in the awkward position of dividing families.

Additionally, students embracing the Catholic faith could also cause tensions in the community at large. Mother Katharine once told a story of students at Blessed Sacrament School in Beaumont, Texas, who were stopped by a local Black preacher. The minister invited the students to visit his church, but the children piped up, "Our church is the true church." When he questioned them, the students asked the minister, "Well, if your church is the true church, what are its marks?" When he could not answer, the children ran off laughing at him. The students related the encounter to one of the sisters, and she asked if they had told him the marks—according to doctrine the marks of the church are that it is One, Holy, Catholic, and Apostolic—and they replied, "No, indeed, Sister, we wasn't going to tell him, he'd go and preach that to the people, and fool them into makin' believe he had the marks of the true church, and that his church was the true church."[97]

---

96  Mary Ruth Coffman, OSB, "Evelyn Davie's Dream Deferred," in *Benedict in the World: Portraits of Monastic Oblates*, ed. Linda Kulzer and Roberta Bondi (Collegeville, MN: Order of St. Benedict, 2002), 46.

97  Mother Katharine Drexel, "Talk to NY Auxiliaries 1921," MMK Talks, H 10A, box 30, folder 14, ASBS.

Mother Katharine related the story to highlight the religious knowledge of her pupils, but it shows a schism between the students at the Catholic school and the rest of Beaumont's Black community. Rather than healing this divide, the sisters took pride in it. In a 1921 speech to the Catholic Student Mission Crusade, Mother Katharine used conversions to justify the work of the SBS. She explained, "I have been asked sympathetically by some 'Are you discouraged in the work?' To which I reply how could we *be* discouraged. . . ?" Drexel explained, "Each year, with *God's Help*, our Missions bring their hundreds of converts in the Church, & 5,000 & more children to our schools, thousands & thousands to the Communion Rail; not to speak of the Xian families established and the 46 Colored pupils who have entered two Colored Sisterhoods founded 50 years & more before our own Congregation was in existence."[98] Progress meant more than raising literacy rates, encouraging leaders, and training teachers; the SBS measured success in souls. To do this, they had to extend their reach beyond the classroom.

### Becoming Part of the Community: SBS Visitations

As at their Indigenous schools, the sisters made visitations an integral part of their mission, though the task was easier in the urban schools than on reservations. Sisters went out into the neighborhoods surrounding their schools and visited not only with the parents of their students but also with others nearby. This aided recruitment and helped the sisters get to know the community. Josephite priest Alexis LaPlante credited visitations with the success of the SBS school in Beaumont, remarking that they enabled "the sisters to deal with each child as an individual and not simply as one of a class."[99] On these visits, the sisters distributed religious pamphlets, rosaries, and medals, helped out around the house, or arranged aid from Catholic Services. They served as an important bridge between the Black community and the vast array of Catholic social service organizations, which, while not explicitly segregated, did not advertise their services to the Black community.

---

98  Mother Katharine Drexel, *MMK Writings*, vol. 21, no. 3058, ASBS.
99  Alexis LaPlante to Mother Katharine Drexel, September 10, 1918, ASBS.

The visits built vital personal connections. Unlike the home visits performed by nineteenth-century aid societies, the SBS came not to judge whether families deserved aid but rather to build home-school relationships. In many places, SBS nuns were the only white women making social calls to Black homes on a regular basis, particularly in the South. One sister described a particularly wrenching visit: "We come as friends, interested and congenial. Here we find a mother lying on a bed without sheets. There is a garbage can under the bed into which she has been vomiting. Four little children stand around looking lost. The unwashed dishes are piled on the table. We talk to the sick mother. She had just buried her husband. As we chat, we quietly wash up the dishes, drying them on a pillowcase."[100]

Mother Katharine believed in active participation in the lives and families of her students. Mary Gabriella Guidry, who attended an SBS school in Lake Charles, Louisiana, remembered the sisters coming to her house and being invited to pick their favorite vegetables out of her mother's garden. She recalled the sisters attending most of her family's milestones, including her profession to the Sisters of the Holy Family, her parents' funerals, and her siblings' weddings. These connections between the convent and student homes helped legitimize the white sisters' presence in the Black community.

Conditions in each SBS school varied depending on community support, finances, and personnel, but in general the schools reflected an interest in holistic education. While the first schools were industrial, reflecting their late nineteenth-century foundations, by the twentieth century, the Sisters of the Blessed Sacrament supported rigorous academic coursework rather than the "housekeeping" lessons advocated by some of their fellow Catholics. The sisters kept abreast of educational theory and the philanthropic activities of the General Board of Education and individuals such as Julius Rosenwald, Anna T. Jeanes, and George Peabody, but their pedagogical approach differed. The congregation's combination of the newest trends in education and scientific

---

[100] Sisters of the Blessed Sacrament, *Encounters with the People of God* (Cornwells Heights, PA: Sisters of the Blessed Sacrament, 1967), 53.

philanthropy with the precepts of sacramental salvation made their schools distinctive. They appropriated methodology from both Protestant Mission societies and secular philanthropic boards. They broke significant ground, but they maintained that they did nothing special. After all, they were merely heeding the church's mandate to extend the reach of the Catholic school system. Their mission can be best understood by examining their work in Louisiana, where they put the bulk of their time, talent, and treasure.

CHAPTER 6

# Navigating Race and Religion in Jim Crow Louisiana

"THE LARGE SPACIOUS THREE-STORY BUILDING, formerly Southern University of New Orleans, is undergoing some very radical changes."[1] While the writer in the *Chicago Defender* referred to "carpenters, painters, plasterers, pavers, bricklayers and plumbers" working to repair the school building, the Sisters of the Blessed Sacrament brought radical changes to the South when they entered Louisiana in 1915. Unlike the SBS's previous Southern missions in heavily Protestant Virginia, Georgia, and Tennessee, Louisiana had a rich history of Catholicism. After initial missteps in New Orleans, the Sisters of the Blessed Sacrament expanded from a single high school in New Orleans to dozens of parochial schools and Xavier University, the only historically Black and Catholic college in the country. Their work at Xavier University, the SBS's most ambitious and well-known project, offers glimpses of the SBS vision for an inclusive American Catholicism. The story of the SBS in New Orleans also sheds light on the racial and religious transformation the city underwent in the years following Reconstruction.

## Archbishop Janssens's Vision

At the end of the Civil War, Louisiana boasted the country's highest percentage of Black Catholics. Most lived in the dioceses of Lafayette and New Orleans, in the southern part of the state, often referred to as the French Triangle, which extended from Cameron Parish in the west to Avoyelles Parish in the north and to St.

---

1 "New Sanitarium Ready for Use in Crescent City: Playground Is Dedicated for Children—Inspiring Address by Mayor M. Behrman and Other Distinguished Citizens, New School Building. Mother Katharine Drexel and Her Assistants Help Erect School for the Race—Their Love for Her is Heartfelt—School Opens Soon," *Chicago Defender*, September 11, 1915, 4.

Bernard Parish in the east.² While many enslaved people had been baptized as Catholics, after the Civil War and especially after the collapse of Reconstruction, increasing numbers of Black people deserted the Catholic Church in South Louisiana. By 1890, Black Protestants outnumbered Catholics by roughly two to one.³ Clergy in Louisiana feared this loss of influence. Nothing spurred the hierarchy to action like the specter of losing to Protestants. They called upon Drexel and the SBS to rectify the situation. Archbishop Francis Janssens of New Orleans wasted no time when he learned of the foundation of the Sisters of the Blessed Sacrament.⁴ Janssens, though born in the Netherlands, had spent his entire clerical career in the American South. Concerned with expanding services to Black people in his diocese, Janssens was Drexel's first clerical visitor to the temporary SBS novitiate in Torresdale, Pennsylvania, in 1891.⁵ Rather than seeking donations from people in his own diocese, Janssens turned to Northern philanthropy because he discerned a "dangerous feeling between whites and blacks in many places."⁶ The archbishop explained to Drexel that he already had thirty-two schools and two asylums for Black parishioners, but he wanted to build more.⁷ In 1892, he begged Drexel's assistance in building an asylum for Black children. He complained that doing

---

2  James G. Dauphine, *A Question of Inheritance: Religion, Education, and Louisiana's Cultural Boundary 1880–1940* (Lafayette: Center for Louisiana Studies, University of Southwestern Louisiana, 1993), 20.

3  Ibid., 36.

4  Archbishop Francis Janssens left a mixed legacy for Black Catholics. Born October 17, 1843, in Tilbourg, Holland, he came to the United States as a missionary in 1868. He worked first in Richmond and later in New Orleans and claimed to feel a call to work with African American Catholics. He built many parishes and schools for them, but his insistence on separate churches made him unpopular in the African American community. He also faced a diocese in financial crisis with mounting debts. His appeals to Katharine Drexel often mentioned the sad state of his coffers. See Annemarie Kasteel, *Francis Janssens 1843–1897: A Dutch-American Prelate* (Lafayette: Center for Louisiana Studies, University of Southwestern Louisiana, 1992).

5  The first SBS sisters lived in the old Drexel summer home, St. Michel in Torresdale, until construction was completed on their convent, St. Elizabeth's, in nearby Cornwells Heights in December 1892.

6  Janssens to Archbishop Elder of Cincinnati, February 2, 1889, quoted in Kasteel, *Francis Janssens*, 196.

7  Duffy, *Katharine Drexel*, 312.

anything for Black people in the diocese proved difficult, for "the white people still give 25 cents to a colored asylum when they will give $5 to a white asylum."[8] Drexel responded with the requested money. For several years, she regularly sent the archbishop checks to finance projects for the prelate's Black parishioners.

Both Mother Katharine and the archbishop feared what Janssens termed "leakage" from the Catholic Church. In 1890, he claimed the diocese had only 75,000 Black Catholics, a reduction of 25,000 from an estimated 100,000 in 1865.[9] Historians have since questioned these statistics, asserting instead that New Orleans had no more than 50,000 Black Catholics in 1865 and perhaps as few as 20,000 in 1890. The exact number is hard to gauge, in part because the Census of Religious Bodies only reported those Black Catholics who went to Louisiana's separate churches, while many chose to worship in integrated neighborhood parishes. The first religious census took place in 1906, and it was repeated in 1916, 1926, and 1936. Numbers for Black Catholics are difficult to ascertain from the data collected. Not until the 1936 report was there more of a concerted effort to distinguish between ethnicities within Catholicism. That report concluded that Louisiana had 39 predominantly Black Catholic churches reaching a population of 60,201 parishioners (not including children under six years old). In 1928, Josephite scholar Rev. John Gillard found that 101,258 out of a total of 203,986 Black Catholics in the United States called Louisiana home.[10] Despite questionable data, Janssens perceived a threat from Protestants whom he accused of wooing Black worshipers away from the Catholic Church by building schools. The archbishop of New Orleans believed that the flock would return "when they see greater interest is taken in them."[11]

---

8  Archbishop Janssens to Mother Katharine Drexel, January 14, 1892, Louisiana Corporation Minutes Books, XUA.

9 Donald J. Slawson, "Segregated Catholicism: The Origin of Saint Katherine's Parish, New Orleans," *Vincentian Heritage* 17 (Fall 1996): 151–52.

10  See Bureau of the Census, *Religious Bodies 1936*, vol. 1, *Summary and Detailed Tables*, 882; Gillard, *Catholic Church and the American Negro*, 50.

11  Archbishop Janssens, *Series of Questions to Be Answered by Applicants for Aid from the Commission for the Catholic Missions among the Colored*

In the nadir of race relations, taking an interest, to use the archbishop's language, meant building segregated facilities. Janssens informed Mother Katharine, "There is nothing in my administration of the diocese that worries me more than our Colored People. I cannot find the means to counteract those who try to capture them. In other dioceses they look out for conversion of the Colored People and I have to look out against perversions [accepting the Protestant creed]."¹² In order to combat these "perversions" Janssens urged Drexel to build segregated churches and schools in New Orleans. He believed many Black people left the church due to the poor treatment they received from the hands of white parishioners and that separate facilities would solve racial tensions and thus keep Black Catholics from "those who try to capture them."¹³ He evidently did not consider changing racist policies such as making Black Catholics take Communion last or integrating religious education.

The archbishop acknowledged that he held a minority opinion in New Orleans, confessing to his mentor, Archbishop William Henry Elder of Cincinnati, "Among the priests I stand almost alone in desiring separate churches for them; and yet the more I consider the question, the more I feel the necessity of it in order to keep the *growing-up generation* in the church."¹⁴ His fellow priests had two primary objections. First, many of the French priests believed the church needed to apply its universal creed and avoid extending the color line to houses of worship. Second, the priests did not wish to lose pew rental money from wealthy Black and mixed-race parishioners. Janssens, however, did not listen to their concerns. He wrote to Drexel in early 1892, "It is my decided opinion and advice that your order take charge of this work; to have a school and *church* for the colored populations. . . . It will convince our people and clergy that separate churches

---

*People and the Indians 1890*, BCIM records, series 5/2: reports and applications for aid, Diocese of New Orleans 1889–97, 1899–1903, 1906–7, reel 17, MUA.

12 By "perversions" Janssens means conversions of Catholics to the Protestant faith. Francis Janssens to Mother Katharine Drexel, August 8, 1893, quoted in Duffy, *Katharine Drexel*, 313.

13 Ibid.

14 Francis Janssens to William Henry Elder, February 11, 1889, quoted in Kasteel, *Francis Janssens*, 280, emphasis in the original.

are as necessary as separate schools."¹⁵ The Sisters of the Blessed Sacrament had been established only a year prior to this exchange and were not prepared to take on a mission so far from Pennsylvania. Mother Katharine, therefore, refused his request, but she continued financial support.

Janssens, an outsider to New Orleans, claimed that Black parishioners needed clergy especially devoted to them and warned "the work for the one and for the other is quite different, and it is almost impossible to do much good for the salvation of the Negro whilst engaged in the ministry for the whites."¹⁶ The archbishop also believed that if Black churchgoers continued to sit wherever they wanted in the churches of his city, then whites would desert the faith. He told the Commission for the Catholic Missions Among the Colored People and the Indians, "The feeling between the two races makes such an intermixture impossible, & were we to attempt it, the white people would leave the churches & whilst trying to do some good to one race, much harm would be done to the other."¹⁷ His previous experiences working in Richmond and Natchez little prepared him for the complexities of a three-tier racial and caste structure of New Orleans. Used to negotiating a strict black/white binary, he was unable to see that in the old French sections of the city, blacks and whites proudly attended the same churches. As late as 1908, journalist Ray Stannard Baker was able to observe New Orleans' uniqueness: "In no other city are there any considerable number of Negroes who attend white churches—except a few Catholic Churches. At New Orleans, I have seen white and coloured people worshipping together at the cathedrals."¹⁸ Though they failed to practice social equality or operate integrated schools, within the physical structure of the

---

15   Francis Janssens to Mother Katharine Drexel, March 4, 1892, Louisiana Corporation minutes book, XUA.
16   Quoted in Gillard, *Catholic Church and the American Negro*, 37.
17   Janssens, *Series of Questions to Be Answered by Applicants for Aid from the Commission for the Catholic Missions Among the Colored People and the Indians 1894*, BCIM records, series 5/2: reports and applications for aid, Diocese of New Orleans, reel 17, MUA.
18   Ray Stannard Baker, *Following the Color Line: American Negro Citizenship in the Progressive Era* (1908; repr. New York: Harper Torchbooks, 1964), 122.

church, New Orleans Catholics in the French section did not acknowledge the color line.[19] The Dutch prelate made his observations of prejudice primarily from the churches such as St. Theresa, St. John the Baptist, and St. Alphonsus in the Americanized sector of the city and did not recognize the long-held traditions of biracial worship in the French churches.[20]

Still convinced of the importance of separate parishes, in 1893 Janssens began, with Drexel's money, to create a parish devoted exclusively for Black worshipers. He explained his frustrations to her:

> We are really in an embarrassing dilemma: we see that many of our colored Catholics leave us first because we cannot give them in the church the same accommodations as the whites; that is mix them together, as they desire; for they are driving the whites away owing to the prevailing ideas concerning the two races, and secondly because the real negroes seem to feel more at home in their own (Protestant) churches.[21]

He claimed that he would continue to lose Black members of his flock unless he experimented with separate parishes. The archbishop stressed, "A separate congregation is a trial, and I think here, where we have 2/3 of all the colored Catholics of the U.S., this ought to be given a fair trial."[22] Mother Katharine Drexel did not donate money to interracial parishes for fear that the money would be used for the benefit of whites. Though she was typically well-informed, she, too, failed to appreciate New Orleans's tradi-

---

19   The first Ursuline Sisters to arrive in New Orleans in 1727 set this precedent. They brought women of all races into the Catholic Church and educated free women of color and Indians in the evenings, but they kept these classes separate from the white girls they taught during the day. Emily Clark, "Hail Mary, Down by the Riverside: Black and White Catholic Women in Early America," in *The Religious History of American Women*, ed. Catherine A. Brekus (Chapel Hill: University of North Carolina Press, 2007), 91–107.

20   This argument is fully fleshed out in John Bernard Alberts, "Origins of Black Catholic Parishes in the Archdiocese of New Orleans, 1718–1920" (Ph.D. diss., Louisiana State University, 1998).

21   Francis Janssens to Mother Katharine, November 11, 1893, H 10, box 30, Janssens 1893, ASBS.

22   Ibid.

tion of unified worship. She based her decisions in New Orleans upon the testimony of the archbishop, who misread the racial and religious landscape. Thus, the two embarked on an ill-advised and unpopular plan to build the diocese's first exclusively Black church.

## St. Katherine's Parish

Eager to begin his experiment, Janssens needed a church and priests to run it. When the New Orleans–based Congregation of the Mission priests, popularly known as the Vincentians, erected a new church building for their St. Joseph Parish in 1893, they had no plans for their dilapidated church on Tulane Avenue. Seizing the opportunity, Janssens began negotiations between Drexel and the Vincentians to purchase and refurbish the old building.[23] After lengthy dialogues, Drexel promised five thousand dollars for the extensive renovation project. The plans to create a "Jim Crow church," as its detractors called it, aroused strong passions in New Orleans and received contentious coverage in the Black press.

While some Black Catholics, sick of battling prejudice in their parishes, where they frequently had to sit in special sections and receive Communion after whites, were pleased with plans for the church, others expressed outrage. The *Crusader*, the official publication of the Creole-led New Orleans Comitè des Citoyens that vehemently resisted the drawing of the color line, attacked Drexel directly.[24] Writer and activist Rodolphe Desnudes praised Drexel

---

23 Janssens also saw the need for national parishes to cater to the needs of Italian immigrants, whom he felt needed special attention. In 1892 he asked the Missionary Sisters of the Sacred Heart to open a school and orphanage for Italian immigrants to help them adjust to American life. Kasteel, *Francis Janssens*, 328, and Sr. M. Andree Condon, "The Development of Financial Procedures for the Establishment and Maintenance of Catholic Schools in the Archdiocese of New Orleans, 1727–1958" (Ph.D. diss., Louisiana State University, 1959), 244.

24 The committee formed in 1891 with the purpose of litigating against segregation. It was this group that sued to stop streetcar segregation in *Plessey v. Ferguson* in 1896. Desnudes, the chief author of the newspaper, was born free in 1849. He benefited from Reconstruction and attended law school at Straight University. The Radical Republican later worked for the Customs House. He thus was highly troubled by Reconstruction's repeal and the subsequent onslaught of Jim Crow laws. For more information on Desnudes's the *New Orleans Crusader*,

for her "self-sacrifice, her holy intentions, her practical generosity" but stated that she had made a "grievous mistake," for "as a consequence of the misplaced bounty the color line is perpetuated where it exists already, and introduced with the germ of success where it has not existed before."[25] Desnudes feared separate churches would lead to other forms of segregation. He added, "While Christ has established the Fatherhood of God and the Brotherhood of man, the great Mother's benevolence is being used by destination to destroy that fundamental principle of our religion."[26] Desnudes warned Mother Katharine against promoting separate churches and asked her to rethink her position on segregated schools, as it violated the tenets of the Catholic Church. He accused her of the worst sort of philanthropy and cautioned, "Let her give for God and not for men; let her give for religion, and not for prejudice; let her give for brotherly love and not for caste feeling; let her give for 'liberty and union,' and not for distinctiveness and separation. . . ."[27] Desnudes urged people not to be fooled by Drexel's generosity: "Whether Mother Katherine, or any other philanthropist, will give charity bountifully and humiliation more bountifully, and injury most bountifully, let no one stop at the positive and overlook the superlative."[28]

Janssens angrily responded to the protests, reporting to the Commission on Negro and Indian Missions,

> Whilst here and there we are hampered by the prejudices of the white people; in the city we are hampered by a small portion of the colored people, most of them light mulattoes and politicians, who abuse me in public print for attempting to begin a new church for the colored people. These persons aim at a greater equality with the whites, politically and socially, and also in the churches, and they pretend that

---

see Lester Sullivan, "The Unknown Rodolphe Desnudes: Writings in the New Orleans *Crusader*," *Xavier Review* 10, nos. 1 and 2 (1990): 1–15.

25 "Mother Katherine Drexel and the Color Line," *Daily Crusader*, February 28, 1895, Desnudes Family Collection, *New Orleans Crusader* clippings, Feb. 28–Mar. 5, 1895, XUA.

26 Ibid.

27 Ibid.

28 Ibid.

I wish to accentuate still more the separation between the two races.²⁹

Despite the controversy, St. Katherine's opened on May 19, 1895. At the dedication ceremony, Janssens clarified his position: "It is not intended in opening and dedicating this church to convey the idea that there is a religion for the white people and one for the colored people. The Mother Church accounts them all as her common children, because everyone stands on the same footing before the judgment seat of God." He continued, "It is a church for their own special benefit and occupation. It is for all the colored people of New Orleans, but none of them are compelled to come here. If they prefer to remain in their own parish they are at liberty to do so."³⁰ Most Black Catholics remained in their old parishes. Whether because the bad press kept people away or because St. Katherine's was located far from downtown where most Black people lived, few attended the new church.

At the opening service, Janssens reported, "The building was packed with colored people who seemed delighted," but he misjudged the situation.³¹ When Mother Katharine visited the church in 1904, she reported disappointment in her travel diary: "We attended the ten o'clock Mass. There were about seventy-five devout adults present. The choir was not good. . . . It seems that on Sundays, the Colored prefer to go to Church with the Whites."³² A few years later Fr. Pierre O. Lebeau, a Josephite priest, confirmed, "St. Katherine's is not so well attended either. . . . Many go to the white churches all over the city. They are near them and have free seats in them. I was told they like to go to the white churches. St. Joseph's church is 2 blocks from St. Kather-

---

29 Archbishop Francis Janssens, *Report on Mission Work among the Negroes and Indians: What Is Being Accomplished by Means of the Annual Collection Taken Up for Our Missions* (Baltimore: Foley Bros., 1895), 8.

30 "Church Devoted to Colored Catholics Founded by the Bounty of Mother Katharine Drexel," *Times-Picayune*, May 20, 1895, 10.

31 Janssens, *Series of Questions to be Answered by Applicants for Aid from the Commission for the Catholic Missions Among the Colored People and the Indians 1895*, BCIM series 5/2: reports and applications for aid, Diocese of New Orleans, reel l 17, MUA.

32 Quoted in Duffy, *Katharine Drexel*, 314.

ine's and the same order [Vincentians] attends both and the people attend St. Joseph's also." Not even the staff of the church was loyal, as Lebeau reported, "The organist of St. Katherine's had a requiem mass at St. Joseph's for his wife some time ago."[33]

## A Strategic Withdrawal

Upon Janssens's death in 1897, the Vatican appointed Louis Placide Chapelle as his replacement. Chapelle reverted to the integrationist policies of his French predecessors. This policy was not due to Chapelle's egalitarian ideals but rather because the archdiocese was on the brink of financial ruin. Crippling debt prohibited new building programs. Chapelle demonstrated his disdain of his predecessor's attentions to Black Catholics by ending his support of the Sisters of the Holy Family and cutting off communications with the SBS. Letters from Mother Katharine went unanswered. He stopped requesting funds from the Catholic Missions Among the Colored People.[34] In 1897, the last year of Janssens's report, the diocese operated forty schools for 2,623 Black students. By 1902, after several years of Chapelle's inattention, New Orleans had only thirty-two schools for 1,943 Black students.[35] While Drexel might have seen this as a loss, some historians have suggested that Chapelle's neglect allowed Black New Orleanians to forestall Jim Crow's victory by continuing the practice of mixed parishes.[36]

The ugly controversy over St. Katherine's and the rebuff from Chapelle kept Katharine Drexel and the SBS out of Louisiana for the next twenty years.[37] From this experience she learned to listen to the people she professed to serve. In 1916, for example, when

---

33   P. Lebeau to Justin McCarthy, May 13, 1909, quoted in Alberts, "Origins of Black Catholic Parishes," 269.

34   Alberts, "Origins of Black Catholic Parishes," 275–76.

35   Janssens, *Series of Questions to Be Answered by Applicants for Aid from the Commissions for the Catholic Missions among the Colored People and the Indians 1897 and 1902*, BCIM records, series 5/2: reports and applications for Aid, Diocese of New Orleans, reel 117, MUA.

36   James B. Bennett, *Religion and the Rise of Jim Crow*, 160.

37   John B. Alberts, "Black Catholic Schools: The Josephite Parishes of New Orleans during the Jim Crow Era," *U.S. Catholic Historian* 12, no. 1 (Winter 1994): 84.

the archbishop asked her to donate money to buy an old church in Baton Rouge for the use of Black parishioners, Mother Katharine refused to give a second-hand church. She insisted that before she committed any money to building a new church, the Black population would have to vote on whether they wanted a separate church.[38] Having tasted resistance, she grew more cognizant of the will of the people she professed to help.

Between the St. Katherine's debacle and the SBS's return to New Orleans in the second decade of the twentieth century, the political and religious landscape shifted dramatically for Black people. Not only did they lose political franchise, but new laws curtailed social freedoms and limited educational opportunities. While New Orleans boasted a strong tradition of Black, particularly Afro-Creole, activism, the protesters were unable to stem the tide of Jim Crow legislation. When a second Black parish, St. Dominic's, partially funded by Drexel and staffed by Josephite priests, opened in 1909, there were no protests.[39] Rather than face degrading treatment, limited seating, and refusal of sacraments that had become commonplace in white churches, many in the Black community either abandoned Catholicism or sought their own parishes. In many cases, they based this decision on the prospect of receiving high-quality education for their children. St. Katherine's never flourished as a parish; however, its parochial school attracted many students. It grew steadily from 196 students in 1895 to over 420 students by 1906.[40]

### Education in the Crescent City

Though Black Catholics resented separation in the sanctuary, they sought Catholic educations for their children. Dwindling educational opportunities for Black students in New Orleans brought the SBS back to Louisiana in 1915. Though the city first established a public education system in 1845, the Civil War and the devastation that followed eradicated Crescent City residents' willingness to invest in education for either Blacks or whites. While

---

38  Alberts, "Origins of Black Catholic Parishes," 367.
39  Bennett, *Religion and the Rise of Jim Crow*, 193.
40  Condon, "Development of Financial Procedures," 251.

the 1888 General Public School Act authorized parishes to collect a one- and one-half mill tax, few districts exceeded this small levy, hobbling public education.[41] Not until 1910 did the city adopt compulsory schooling for students between ages eight and fourteen, and it did not become state law until 1916. In 1903, only 34 percent of school-age children of any race attended classes, and the state's illiteracy rate remained above 20 percent until 1930.[42] The situation was worse for Black students.

Despite the fact that New Orleans briefly operated integrated public schools during Reconstruction, after federal authorities pulled out in 1877, those committed to Black education lost political clout.[43] The Louisiana Department of Education announced that each parish had the duty to "afford white and colored children, respectively, equal facilities for their mental instruction and moral training," but this lip service to equality belied the school boards' actions.[44] In 1877, the New Orleans School Board passed a resolution stating, "Whereas: This board, in the performance of its paramount duty; which is to give the best education possible with the means at its disposal to the whole population, without regard to race, color or previous condition, is assured that this end can be best attained by educating the different races in separate schools."[45] The board adhered to its separate schools policy, but it soon forgot its commitment to the "best education possible" for members of all races. In 1881, Black members of the school board were removed, and the all-white New Orleans Parish School Board voted to suspend classes for Black students after the sixth grade.[46]

---

41  A mill is worth 1/1000 of a dollar, or 1/10 of a cent. It is a unit of currency commonly used in referring to property taxes.

42  Dauphine, *A Question of Inheritance*, 90–96.

43  Louis R. Harlan, "Desegregation in New Orleans Public Schools during Reconstruction," *American Historical Review* 67, no. 3 (April 1962): 662–75.

44  Louisiana Department of Education, *Annual Report of the State Superintendent of Public Education for the Year 1877* (New Orleans: Office of the Democrat, 1878), 14.

45  Quoted in Donald E. Devore and Joseph Logsdon, *Crescent City Schools: Public Education in New Orleans 1841–1991* (Lafayette: Center for Louisiana Studies, University of Southwestern Louisiana, 1991), 87.

46  Devore and Logsdon, *Crescent City Schools*, 94.

In 1900, the board further curtailed access to schools by limiting Black education to the first five grades.[47]

The 1880 founding Southern University, which operated elementary and secondary classes on its campus on Magazine Street, softened the blow of the school board's actions. Southern offered a mixture of classical, industrial, and normal education for grades seven through twelve, and it became a fixture in New Orleans' Black community. In 1912, however, the state ordered the relocation of Southern University from New Orleans to Scotlandville, outside of Baton Rouge. Ostensibly the school moved to allow Southern to develop an agricultural curriculum on a more rural campus, but many felt that local whites simply did not want a Black college in their neighborhood.[48] The loss of Southern did not sit well with students and their parents, who fought until 1917 to get New Orleans public schools to offer Black students a secondary curriculum.[49] At the time, New Orleans had several private secondary schools serving Black students, including New Orleans University (Methodist Episcopal), Leland University (Baptist), and Straight University (American Missionary Association), but Black Catholics had preferred to attend the publicly operated Southern. After Southern's relocation, Black Catholics felt they had no access to higher education that would not compromise their religious beliefs.

In response, prominent Black Catholic educator Medard Hillaire Nelson spoke with Archbishop James Hubert Blenk, Chapelle's successor, in hopes of getting the prelate to enlist the aid of Mother Katharine.[50] At the same time, Josephite Father P.

---

47  Devore and Logsdon, *Crescent City Schools*, 118.
48  Sue Lyles Eakin, "The Black Struggle for Education in Louisiana, 1877–1930s" (Ph.D. diss., University of Southwestern Louisiana, 1980), 71, 191. See also Betty Porter, "The History of Negro Education in Louisiana," Master's thesis (Louisiana State University, 1938), 768–75.
49  The board restored sixth grade in 1909, seventh in 1913, and eighth in 1914 but did not build a high school until 1917, when it opened McDonogh 35; see Devore and Logsdon, *Crescent City Schools*, 193.
50  Roland Lagarde, SBS, "A Contemporary Pilgrimage: Personal Testimony of Blessed Katharine's Charism," *U.S. Catholic Historian* 8, no. ½ (Winter–Spring, 1989): 48. Nelson sat on the board of directors for Xavier and was

Lebeau made plans to woo Drexel back to the city. Black Catholics still resented the church's embrace of separate parishes, but parents' desire for quality schools convinced clergy in New Orleans that this time Mother Katharine's work would garner support. When the old Southern University campus came up for sale in 1915, Lebeau recruited Josephite Superior General Justin McCarthy and Archbishop James Hubert Blenk to join him in asking Mother Katherine to bring Black Catholics an option for secondary education.[51]

## The New Southern

Mother Katharine and Mother M. Mercedes, her second in command, traveled south in April 1915 to investigate reopening Southern University as a Catholic school. Knowing that their plan would meet with resistance from the whites who had forced Southern out a few years earlier, the sisters hired lawyer Henry McInery to act as a purchasing agent at the public auction to keep SBS involvement secret. While their lawyer attended the auction, Mother Katharine and Mother Mercedes spent several hours in prayer before the Blessed Sacrament, praying for success. Their ruse worked, and Sisters of the Blessed Sacrament purchased the land and buildings for $18,000. At first, they kept their plans for the school secret, instructing the lawyer to say only that the land had gone to people willing to invest considerable money in New Orleans.[52]

The property took up almost an entire city block on Magazine Street between Constance, Soniat, and Dufasset streets. Southern

---

influential in persuading Mother Katharine to expand into university-level classes. Nelson's influence, too, lived on in Louisiana. One of his daughters taught at Xavier, one served as the registrar of the college, and his grandchild attended the school. His granddaughter, Agnes Gabriel Lagarde, worked in several of the SBS rural schools, including St. Ann's in Malette. Nelson's great-grand-daughter, Sr. Ronald Lagarde, joined the SBS in 1961.

51  Archbishop James Hubert Blenk was born in Bavaria and educated and ordained in Ireland, so he, like Janssens, lacked the French ideal of the universal integrated church. It was under his leadership from 1906 to 1917 that practice of Jim Crow churches became most firmly entrenched.

52  "Southern University Lot Is Sold, Buildings and Lot," *Times Picayune*, April 14, 1915, 6.

was a remarkable find. Mother Mercedes described a large brick school building with classic Grecian columns surrounded by live oak trees. The main building contained a large auditorium, eight classrooms, and several offices. In addition, the property had a mechanical building, a wooden structure, and another small brick classroom building. She added, "Situated in a respectable neighborhood, the central building alone could not be built for $35,000."[53] Since the property had not been occupied for several years, however, the sisters had to spend an additional four thousand dollars for renovations and repairs. One particularly symbolic renovation was the conversion of the old slave shed on the property into a chemistry and physics laboratory.[54]

At first the sisters called the school "Southern University of Louisiana" under the protection of St. Francis Xavier, since they did not want a Catholic name to deter Protestant students from enrolling.[55] Soon, however, nuns and students alike shortened the name to Xavier Prep. The first sisters arrived in early September 1915 and found themselves warmly welcomed. The SBS Louisiana Corporation Annals noted, "The colored people are so delighted to have Southern back again that they are doing everything to help us."[56] The Sisters spent their first few weeks settling into their temporary convent on the third floor of the academic building and readying the school for its grand opening. They printed up a brochure for the new school and took to the streets, meeting with families to explain their new enterprise and to collect names of potential students.

The Sisters also petitioned the archbishop to establish a parish church on school grounds. Blenk agreed and asked Josephite father

---

53  M. Mercedes O'Connor, "Impressions of Mother Mercedes on Her Visitation to Louisiana, 1938," H20A, box 6, folder 7, ASBS.
54  Lynch, *Sharing the Bread in Service*, 1:221.
55  "New Sanitarium Ready for Use in Crescent City," *Chicago Defender*, September 11, 1915, 4.
56  The first sisters at Xavier were Mother Frances Buttell, Mother Mary Paul of the Cross Kinery, Sister M. Barnabas Healy, Sr. Mary Anselm McCann, Sr. Mary Bertha Hoffman, Sr. Mary Angelica Campbell, and Sr. Mary Justin Sullivan. St. Francis Xavier Prep and Convent Annals, 1915–20, copy XUA (originals located ASBS).

John Clarke to pastor Blessed Sacrament Parish. The congregation met in the school auditorium until a new church could be built on a lot across from the school on Constance Street. The following year the sisters opened an elementary school at Blessed Sacrament serving the first six grades. Later, Xavier education students used Blessed Sacrament School as a training school. With Xavier as a base in the city, other SBS-led schools proliferated during the 1910s and 1920s. Corpus Christi, founded in 1919, became the largest Black Catholic parish in the country, and over 1,000 students attended school there.[57] All of the elementary schools served as feeders, first for Xavier Prep and later for Xavier University.

## The Xavier Curriculum

After investigating all of the secondary schools in the New Orleans area, the Sisters finalized their curriculum, which they modeled on the old Southern University catalog. When it first opened, Xavier Prep offered both academic and industrial instruction. In addition to a standard academic course offering, the sisters added religious instruction. The final curriculum was designed by Mary Byrne, a Columbia Teachers' College graduate. During its inaugural year, the school offered sewing, typing, masonry, carpentry, mechanical drawing, English, math, Latin, physical geography, church history, physics, chemistry, plane geometry, and normal training.[58] Not feeling up to the task of operating both a junior high and high school, the sisters, under the leadership of Sister M. Frances (Frances O. Buttell) planned to open with only four grades: seventh, eighth, ninth, and tenth with the intention of adding a grade each year until they had a complete high school. On registration day, however, so many students showed up that they added an eleventh grade and hired an additional teacher. From the start Xavier employed an interracial fac-

---

57 Holy Ghost was founded in 1916, St. Louis in 1918, Blessed Sacrament in 1918, St. Peter Claver in 1921, and St. Monica in 1930. See Lynch, *Sharing the Bread in Service*, 1:228–40.

58 Patricia Marshall, SBS, "Sister Mary Frances Buttell (1884–1877), Visionary for Xavier University," in *Religious Pioneers: Building the Faith in the Archdiocese of New Orleans*, ed. Dorothy Dawes and Charles Nolan (New Orleans: Archdiocese of New Orleans, 2004), 291.

ulty. They began with five Black lay teachers and one white lay teacher in addition to the sisters.[59] During Xavier's first year, the sisters taught more than three hundred students during the day and an additional one hundred in afternoon and evening classes.

For its first ten years, Xavier Prep offered a traditional grammar school course for seventh and eighth grades and gave the older students choices for more advanced studies. Most students chose an academic high school course including English, advanced mathematics, history, Latin, Christian doctrine, Bible, drawing, music, and manual training. Xavier exceeded the white 1915 New Orleans Archdiocesan School Course of Studies, which did not include classical languages.[60] In addition to the academic courses, Xavier also offered clerical and industrial training classes. Xavier students who wanted to go into business chose to take the Commercial Course, a two-year plan of study featuring classes in bookkeeping, phonography, typewriting, English, penmanship, and arithmetic.

Xavier also operated an Industrial Department. Male students chose either the Trade Course or the Teachers' Industrial Course. The four-year Trade Course included classes on tools and materials, shop work, mechanical drawing, math, general science, English, cost estimating, architectural drawing, physics, and chemistry. The Teachers' Industrial Course blended many of the same courses with psychology and pedagogy to prepare students to teach industrial subjects. Female students in the Industrial Department studied home economics and specialized in either Domestic Art (primarily classes relating to sewing and fine dressmaking) or Domestic Science (classes on botany, physiology, food classification, cookery, and household administration). These courses were taken in conjunction with the academic high school diploma program and could be completed in two or three years.

Xavier added a twelfth grade in 1916 and a two-year normal course in 1917. In addition to traditional pedagogy and classroom management classes, Normal Department students also took

---

59  Duffy, *Katharine Drexel*, 325. Their missions rapidly grew, and by 1919 twenty-four sisters lived at the Xavier convent.
60  Eighth Grade Curriculum, *Course of Studies Prepared for the Eight Grades of the Parochial Schools of the Archdiocese of New Orleans*, 1915.

courses in Christian doctrine. Aspiring Xavier educators student-taught at Blessed Sacrament School. After graduation, they were often hired by the SBS to work in their schools, typically elsewhere in Louisiana, but Xavier students also staffed Rock Castle and Belmead in Virginia. In 1918, the sisters petitioned the Louisiana Senate to pass Senate Bill No. 64, which authorized Xavier to confer degrees and grant diplomas. The state approved, and Governor R. Pleasant signed the bill on June 18, 1918. This lent credibility to the institution and made it easier for students to secure jobs, especially in the field of education. The teacher-training program proved so popular that Xavier soon provided two-thirds of the Black teachers in New Orleans.[61]

Though Xavier offered commercial and industrial courses, its classical high school program attracted the most students. In 1920, Xavier awarded thirty-one high school diplomas and six normal certificates. In comparison, it only awarded six commercial certificates and thirteen domestic service diplomas, as well as seven for mechanical drawing, two for manual training, and five for masonry. Sewing, which offered women financial independence, was a popular field, as classes were offered at night. The same year, eighty-five girls and adult women earned certificates in plain sewing, dressmaking, and embroidery.[62] Within a few years, however, Xavier stopped offering domestic service classes, and the number of students in most industrial classes steadily decreased, though sewing remained popular. By the time Xavier University moved to its new campus in 1932, it no longer offered trade courses. The educational goals of the students shaped the curriculum at Xavier as the sisters and lay teachers designed programs to propel students into the middle class.

## From Xavier Prep to Xavier University

Xavier became the congregation's flagship institution. When the Sisters of the Blessed Sacrament created the first historically black

---

61 Shannon Frystak, *Our Minds on Freedom: Women and the Struggle for Black Equality in Louisiana, 1924–1967* (Baton Rouge: Louisiana State University Press, 2009), 61.

62 *Annual Report for 1920*, XUA.

and Catholic university, they transformed Xavier from a local oddity into a national symbol. As the SBS struggled to build a university without significant help from the hierarchy, they expanded their ideas about what a successful product of a Black and Catholic university should look like. They began Xavier with the goal of assimilating students into the white middle class, but experiences in Louisiana led the sisters to design a university that honored Black heritage and emphasized interracial cooperation.

As Xavier Prep became more established in New Orleans, its alumni requested an expansion into collegiate courses. In 1924, the SBS Council debated the efficacy of launching a university. Some sisters feared the financial commitment the college would entail, and others did not believe the Southern Association of Colleges would recognize a Black college "no matter how high its status or broadness of curricula." Despite these reservations, the SBS committed seventy thousand dollars to expand campus facilities, and they announced their intention to begin college classes in 1925. The councilors reasoned that "there was a great need of Catholic leaders among our Colored people and so few Catholic Colleges would admit them." As usual, they left the details to Providence, for "where there was a need God would provide the means and that in some way or other recognition would be given."[63] Their decision reflected the congregation's frustration with segregated Catholic universities. Prior to Xavier's expansion into a degree-granting institution, only a handful of Catholic universities admitted Black students: Duquesne University, Holy Ghost Apostolic College, Creighton University, Fordham University, Loyola University in Chicago, Marquette University, Villanova University, and St. Mary's Seminary, also called Ferndale. Institutions in the border states and in the North began admitting more Black students in the late 1930s, though many remained segregated until after the *Brown* decision. Even though mainstream Catholic publications declared segregation immoral in the 1940s, Catholic colleges resisted integration. Xavier would become the only historically Black and Catholic university in the country and the only Catholic college to admit Black students in

---

63 *Annals of the SBS*, 21:153, ASBS.

the South.⁶⁴ Rather than fighting a church that in general refused to open its doors to Black students, the SBS built a university. The irony of this position was that Xavier also offered white institutions an out: they did not have to accept Black students if the students had a place at Xavier.

The SBS tried to interest the rest of the Catholic Church in their mission, but they were rebuffed. As she fundraised for the new college, Mother Katharine elicited the help of the United States Catholic hierarchy, whom she wanted to endorse and fund the school in the same way they had done with the Catholic University of America several decades earlier. In September 1926, she began her campaign by sending documents detailing their plans, dispatching telegrams to the members of the hierarchy, and getting onto the agenda for the prelate's meeting in Philadelphia. She filled her report with statistics that showed "colored Catholic high school graduates who aspire to a college education are compelled to matriculate either in an avowedly Protestant institution or in a non-sectarian one in which they find themselves in a completely Protestant environment, unless, indeed, they seek admission to Northern colleges for white people." In the North, she complained, students "find their way to non-sectarian and Protestant colleges and universities, for with rare exceptions Catholic colleges refuse to admit them." Drexel begged the bishops and archbishops to make her university a priority.⁶⁵ They refused. Cardinal Dougherty replied to Drexel, stating, "Evidently, there has been some misunderstanding; because the matter trusted of by yourself and Archbishop Shaw is not one for the entire Hierarchy, but rather for the Board of Indian and Negro Missions."⁶⁶ What Drexel believed essential for the good of the entire Roman Catholic Church, the hierarchy wanted to foist off to a mission board. Despite the lack of interest and financial support, however, the SBS pursued their plan.

---

64   See Richard J. Roche, OMI, "Catholic Colleges and the Negro Student" (Ph.D. diss., The Catholic University of America, 1948).

65   Convent of the Blessed Sacrament to Your Eminences, Most Reverend Archbishops and Right Reverend Bishops September 14, 1926, in BCIM records, series 5/2, reports and applications for aid, reel 9, MUA.

66   Archbishop Dennis Dougherty to Mother Katharine Drexel, September 22, 1926, BCIM records, series 5/2, applications for aid, reel 9, MUA.

The SBS constructed the Xavier Annex with seven new classrooms, separate laboratories for physics, chemistry, and biology, a domestic science kitchen, and a small library.[67] In 1925, the sisters turned the Normal Department into a teachers' college and opened a small college of arts and sciences, though Louisiana did not recognize it as a four-year college until 1928. Though they still taught some industrial classes such as sewing, the sisters made academics the top priority of the new college. Admissions requirements included a high school diploma or exam as well as previous course work in English, Latin, algebra, plane geometry, Greek or modern language, science, history, and electives. Xavier's four-year curriculum emphasized apologetics, philosophy, and theology. They also offered a two-year pre-medical program with extensive science courses.[68] Many Xavier students went on to medical school at Meharry Medical College in Nashville. In 1927, Xavier added a College of Pharmacy. While doors closed to those in the legal and medical professions, pharmacy offered ample opportunities. Sr. M. Frances Buttell seized on the idea when she found that no schools in Louisiana offered pharmacy training to Black students and convinced Drexel that Xavier needed the program; she even held bake sales to help pay for supplies.[69] An article in *Mission Fields at Home* celebrated the first graduating class from the school of pharmacy, stating, "The eight who go forth as graduate pharmacists feel well qualified to meet the exigencies of their profession in a scientifically accurate way. Best of all, they have been formed in Catholic Ethics, and the formation will play a vital part in their business endeavors and in all future social contacts."[70] Professors at Xavier stressed entrepreneurship because self-employed students did not have to rely on white business owners for job opportunities.

An occupational survey taken of Xavier graduates from 1925 to 1941 shows Xavier students found work. Out of the 660

---

67 *Annual Report Louisiana Corporation of the Sisters of the Blessed Sacrament 1924*, Louisiana Corporation Minutes Books, XUA.
68 Ibid.
69 Marshall, "Sister Mary Frances Buttell," 291.
70 Theresa V. O'Reilly, "June Days in New Orleans," *Mission Fields at Home*, July–August 1930, 154.

respondents, the most popular career was education. Three hundred and four students, or 46 percent, worked in schools. An additional forty-four alumni were pursuing advanced degrees either at Xavier or in other institutions at the time of the survey. Other popular occupations included pharmacy, office work, music, and journalism. Thirty chose careers in the armed forces. While many women entered the workforce, eighty-six identified themselves as housewives. The sisters, given their focus on spiritual growth, might have been most gratified by the twenty-two women and one man who entered religious life.[71]

Academics formed the core of the Xavier experience, but the school also worked to provide recreational opportunities and extracurriculars. The pages of the *Xavier Herald*, the school's newspaper, are filled with articles on club meetings, dances, field days, community service activities, music recitals, celebrations, and sporting events. These extracurricular activities included the League of the Sacred Heart, the People's Eucharistic League, the Forensic Club, Literary Society, Glee Club, and the Student Orchestra. Xavier also produced a literary magazine called the *Xaverian*. Extracurriculars built pride and shaped the institution's identity. The school song offers a glimpse of the institution's values. It concludes by referencing the school's ultimate purpose, the salvation of souls: "Xavier ever be our guide / And lead us on the way; / Through life's journey, onward, upward, / To the eternal day."[72] Presumably sung at school events, the song reflects the SBS desire for students to use Xavier, and by extension the Catholic Church, as a "haven pier" in their journey into the American middle class. To accomplish this, the school had to be more than simply a classroom.

## On the Athletic Fields

Sports helped Xavier develop a national profile. Students fielded teams in baseball, basketball, and football. The football team,

---

71  All figures are taken from Mary Josephina Kenney, "Contributions of the Sisters of the Blessed Sacrament for Indians and Colored People to Catholic Negro Education in the State of Louisiana" (Master's thesis, The Catholic University of America,1942), Table IX.

72  "Xavier," *Mission Fields at Home*, June 1929, 147.

initiated by Josephite priest Father Hugh Conahan, initially scandalized members of the Xavier community. Father Conahan aspired to form a "Negro Notre Dame" and went on recruiting trips all over the South to find players, often basing his decisions on size and brute strength. He brought his unruly brood, who, according to his fellow Josephite Father Edward Murphy, looked "like higher education in reverse" back to campus, despite Xavier having no dormitories. The school had to scramble to find places for them.[73] Despite these inauspicious beginnings, sports became an integral part of Xavier student life and helped Xavier develop a strong reputation across the city and the nation. Just as the Notre Dame football team became a symbol of Catholic inclusion in the American Dream, so the Xavier sports teams became a statement about the legitimacy of Black Catholics. In June 1929, the SBS made a financial commitment to athletics and bought land to construct a new stadium. They enlisted the help of the entire community, which rallied behind the plan to build a stadium to accommodate over one thousand people. For years the completed stadium served as a gathering place for all Black athletes in the city. During the fundraising campaign, a sister explained, "Xavier needs a stadium, but the Negro youth of New Orleans need it more."[74]

Athletics also gave students a safe space to contest racism. Students and coaches made no secret of their wish to challenge the lily-white Notre Dame team. They faced white Catholic opponents when they played Manhattan College and LaSalle University in special exhibition games.[75] The Xavier community wanted a chance to outperform their white counterparts. The stadium itself proved a contentious space. As one of the most impressive sports arenas in the South, it often hosted non-Xavier events. In 1935, the *Times-Picayune* sponsored the Brutes-Pirates game and sought to host it in Xavier's stadium. The paper demanded that a special

---

73   Edward F. Murphy, *Yankee Priest: An Autobiographical Journey with Certain Detours, from Salem to New Orleans* (Garden City, NY: Doubleday, 1952), 210.
74   Neal R. Owens, "Xavier Stadium," *Mission Fields at Home*, November 1930, 24.
75   Chester L. Washington, "Ches' Sez: Gold Rush Stirs South," *Pittsburgh Courier*, October 19, 1935, A4.

section be roped off and reserved for whites. The school balked and refused to segregate its own stadium.[76]

## Making a Joyful Noise: Xavier's Fine Arts Program

The sisters stressed education for the whole person, so in addition to academics and athletics, Xavier established a strong fine arts department, adding a music school in 1926. In 1930, Xavier launched a band program, the first for Black students in New Orleans, and in 1931 it started a school orchestra.[77] Father Murphy put on revues to showcase student talent. The first one, titled *The Footlight Parade*, featured original songs, sketches, the Xavier Yellow Jackets Band, dance numbers, and stepping. The pious priest wanted to add some high culture to the show, so he made the students perform the bridal lullaby from Mendelssohn's *Midsummer Night's Dream*. The singers, however, had a little fun with the number. The bride was a light-skinned, blonde-haired girl and the groom a very dark boy. A practical joker thought it would be funny to have her father holding a shotgun at the wedding. The entire audience dissolved into hysterics, for as Father Murphy reported, "The satire of the thing—the very idea of a southern colonel forcing his daughter to marry a Negro—simply 'made' *Footlight Parade*. But it almost 'unmade' me."[78] The arts program gave Xavier students the creative space to work out the complexities and absurdities of their lives in the Jim Crow South.

The talent uncovered in the early revues led Sister M. Elise Sisson to begin Xavier's world-renowned opera program in 1934. Noting that New Orleans had no opera company and Black arts patrons were banned from traveling performances, she decided that Xavier students would bring opera to the Big Easy. They began with an elaborate production of *Faust* in 1935 and developed a fan base in New Orleans and beyond.[79] The students were

---

76 "Xavier Stops Plan for Segregation in Own Stadium," *Chicago Defender*, December 21, 1935, 15.
77 *Annual Reports 1925–1930*, XUA.
78 Murphy, *Yankee Priest*, 214.
79 "Sister Mary Elise, 84, Dies; Founder Opera Company," *Afro-American*, August 7, 1982, 8. After a lengthy tenure at Xavier (1934–69), Sister Elise

invited to be the Ethiopian chorus in *Aida* at the Municipal Auditorium but were later uninvited when people complained that Black and white voices should not mix on stage. Turning anger into inspiration, Sister Elise put on her own production of *Aida*, which went on to win more critical acclaim than the production that had shunned her students.[80]

## Campus Religious Life

The college developed the typical trappings of most universities, but Xavier also promoted Catholic clubs and activities. Central to the college's social life were confraternities and sodalities. The SBS mission magazine bragged in 1929, "Not the least in importance among Xavier student activities is the Apostleship of Prayer."[81] Students joined the Catechetical Guild to teach Sunday School classes in Black parishes, the Evidence Guild to write pamphlets spreading the faith, and the Convert League to evangelize to others in the community. The college served as an important religious hub for Black Catholics by helping to educate members of the Holy Family Sisters and the Oblate Sisters of Providence. During the 1920s, when states began requiring increasing professionalization and education for teachers, these nuns had a distinct disadvantage of not being able to attend Catholic universities.[82] Several Holy Family Sisters attended Xavier each year, and many more came for summer sessions. In addition, the university opened a small Xavier Extension in Baltimore, headquarters of the Oblate Sisters of Providence. Until more Catholic universities desegregated, Xavier provided Black sisters the an opportunity to

---

went on to found Opera South in conjunction with Jackson State College, Utica Junior College, and Tougaloo College. In the 1970s she helped develop Opera Ebony, a national black touring company.

80 Murphy, *Yankee Priest*, 216.

81 M. Letterhouse, "Negro Higher Education," *Mission Fields at Home*, July 1929, 150.

82 Drexel and the Jesuit John LaFarge were among those who lobbied the Catholic University of America to open its doors to Blacks, especially those in religious life. CUA agreed and offered a special summer school starting in 1933. It is not surprising that when CUA admitted three Black students in 1936, two of them were Xavier graduates. "Students Enter Catholic Univ. Local Girl Enrolled. Officials Still Decline to Make Any Statement," *Afro-American*, October 10, 1936, 1.

obtain higher education in a religious setting. The influence of the sister-students added to Xavier's religious milieu.[83]

Xavier was even the site of an alleged miracle in 1927. An apparition of St. Therese the Little Flower appeared in a window of a classroom at Xavier Prep, drawing crowds from all over the city. Sr. Mary of Grace Cavanaugh explained in a letter to her fellow sisters, "There are 12 panes in the window. In the last two, in the lower, right hand corner, there seemed to be a figure, the piece of wood dividing the two panes running almost through the center of the same. The face could not be seen feature by feature, but the expression was wonderfully sweet. . . . The eyes seemed to be looking directly at you, but I do not mean to say one could see them clearly."[84] This appearance immediately drew criticism from white Catholics, which aroused Sr. Mary of Grace's ire: "And will you please listen to this!!!!! Quite a number of people have said, why should she appear in a lowly, humble, Colored church? If I were permitted to use slang, I would tell you what I would like to have answered."[85] Even without the miracles, the Xavier campus was one where religion was intertwined in all activities.

## A New Campus

By 1929, the university was bursting at the seams. Drexel and Duplian Rhodes, a 1918 graduate, scoured the city to purchase a lot for the new campus. Again, she had difficulty purchasing property, since white owners protested when they learned the purpose for which she intended the land. Finally, she acquired a tract of land in an unzoned area between two canals on Washington Avenue at a cost of $105,691.00.[86] The SBS first constructed the Xavier University Stadium, which opened in October 1930. Not until the following year did building begin on the academic and administrative build-

---

83  A few Holy Family Sisters have written about attending Xavier. See, for example, Sr. Mary Gabriella Guidry, *The Southern Negro Nun*, and Mary Francis Borgia Hart, *Violets in the King's Garden*.

84  Sr. Mary of Grace to SBS Sisters, October 15, 1927, Xavier University and Convent Annals and Related Correspondence 1915–45, St. Francis Xavier Prep and Convent Annals 1927–45 (copies), XUA.

85  Ibid.

86  Duffy, *Katharine Drexel*, 327.

ings. As was her custom, Drexel insisted on employing local Black builders.[87] Drexel knew that every decision she made for her school was also a political act. For this reason, she spared no expense on the new campus, which cost over a half million dollars and took sixty-four railroad cars of Indiana limestone. Her attention to detail was not lost on Malcolm Barrios, a member of the class of 1934, who rejoiced, "Nothing but the best will be Xavier's."[88]

The imposing limestone structures Mother Katharine erected became a concrete manifestation of the Catholic Church's interest in Black education. To put it in theological terms, they saw it as an outward sign of grace of the church—of course, the sisters received little help from the hierarchy and financed the bulk of the half-million-dollar construction project with the Drexel fortune. Still, the symbolic importance of the gleaming Gothic structures cannot be overstated. The New Unit, as it was called for many years, represented progress to some and a dangerous precedent to others. Jesuit Reverend John LaFarge called the opening of the new plant "a turning point in the history of the Catholic Church in the United States."[89]

The Black press took interest in Xavier's opening. When the *Philadelphia Tribune*, a Black newspaper, produced its yearly honor roll for 1932, the Drexel family joined the esteemed company of Mordecai Johnson (president of Howard University) and John Hope (president of Morehouse University) for their contributions to Black education, and it placed Xavier in the upper echelon of historically Black colleges and universities.[90] Drexel's dedication to advancing higher education opportunities brought the Sisters of the Blessed Sacrament new credibility in the Black community, which had previously looked at Catholic efforts with ambiguity. A writer for the *Atlanta Daily World* told his readers, "Okey, Xavier, you should see it—this school some day will be one of the strongest financially and educationally in the race. . . .

---

87 "Mission Field from Xavier," *Mission Fields at Home*, March 1932, 92.
88 Malcolm Barrios, "The Greater Xavier," *Mission Fields at Home*, November 1932, 23.
89 John LaFarge, "Doing the Truth," *Interracial Review* 11 (November 1932): 218.
90 Joseph Baker, "Yesterdays Look Backward with a Smile as 1932 Delivers Its Roll of Honor," *Philadelphia Tribune*, January 5, 1933, 12.

My prediction is that it will be the Notre Dame of the South someday."[91] A writer for the *Pittsburgh Courier* was similarly impressed and remarked, "The first view of Xavier is one which usually lives long in the observer's memory. It is one of the largest and most composite educational structures in the entire South, and its modern type, light gray color and immaculate appearance makes it an imposing edifice."[92] The stately structures advertised the work of the SBS and put them, as Dr. Thomas W. Turner, head of the Federated Colored Catholics of the United States, explained, in the company of philanthropists such as Annie T. Jeanes, Julius Rosenwald, and the Phelps Stokes Foundation.[93]

While they failed to either open the doors of Catholic universities or to financially support the creation of Xavier, members of the hierarchy turned up when it came time to take pictures at its opening. Cardinal Dennis Joseph Dougherty of Philadelphia and New Orleans Archbishop John William Shaw formally dedicated the New Unit at a well-attended ceremony on October 12, 1932. The speakers of the day repeatedly commented on the power of Catholic schooling to uplift. Rev. John B. Morris of Little Rock called the university "a triumph for the church in this Southland" and added, "There is reason indeed for the enthusiasm of the Colored race of New Orleans which is so apparent in all their faces today when they find themselves beginning to see the light which the Most High God sheds in their souls through the divinity of a Catholic education."[94] Father Kerry O'Connor Keane echoed these sentiments, noting, "This dedication marks the wake or funeral of that monstrous injustice to Negro Youth who wanted to obtain higher education and still remain a practical Catholic."[95] It also gave the church an excuse to avoid desegregating their other institutions.

---

91 J. Chunn, "Chunn Discovers New Orleans is a Nice Place," *Atlanta Daily World*, October 20, 1934, 5.

92 Washington, "Ches' Sez," A4.

93 Thomas W. Turner, "Visit to Catholic New Orleans," *Chronicle: Official Organ of the Federated Colored Catholics of the United States*, March 1932, 52.

94 Quoted in Kenney, "Contributions of the Sisters of the Blessed Sacrament," 58.

95 "New Xavier Unit Is Finest of Its Kind in South," *Xavier Herald*, November 1932, 1.

While the Catholic clergy focused on Xavier as an instrument of the faith, the secular media understood Xavier's potential to challenge Southern society. *Time* magazine noted, "Many a white Southern college would look shabby beside Xavier with its solid copper gutters, chromium equipment in the laboratory and home economics kitchen, auditorium with expensive indirect lighting and full stage, and half of the $3,000,000 Drexel library."[96] Father Edward Murphy explained the attention to aesthetics, writing, "The handsome Indiana limestone structure indicated that Mother Katherine deemed charity too beautiful a virtue to be rendered unbeautifully and that she was giving her best to a people who so often received the opposite from others."[97] One student intuited this and noted, "You can't imagine what it meant to walk in and see those shiny floors!"[98]

Not everyone appreciated Drexel's attention to fine detail, however. *Time* reported resentment by white Louisianans and claimed those living around Xavier suggested the college motto should be "Is Yo' Did Yo' Greek Y it?" This common racist trope mocked the desire of African Americans for a classical education and suggested that they master the rudiments of English first. In the magazine's next issue, the story provoked several letters to the editor. Louise Drexel Morrell wrote to correct some factual inaccuracies in the story, such as its assertion that only Catholics were admitted and that the school had an endowment. Another was written by Horace M. Bond, a leader in Black education. He mockingly suggested that, given the state of education for Louisiana whites, the motto "Ain't you-all done that thar Latting yit?" might be fitting for the region's white schools. He concluded, "The writer, a Protestant negro, ineligible to attend or teach at New Orleans' Xavier, [this is incorrect] invokes Protestant blessings on the enterprise, thanks God for Mother Katharine Drexel whose Catholic philanthropy promises to give Louisiana Negros

---

96   The school did not, in fact, get the Drexel library. In fact, it struggled until 1938 to install a real collegiate library on the campus. Otherwise, however, the facilities did rival or exceed those at white schools. "Religion: For the Tenth Man," *Time*, October 24, 1932.
97   Murphy, *Yankee Priest*, 191.
98   Marshall, "Sister Mary Frances Buttell," 292.

what their State refuses to give."[99] The editors at *Time*, however, were not the only ones who questioned the need for such a school. At the dedication a priest, shocked at the state-of-the-art buildings, muttered in Latin, "What a waste!"[100] In addition, one woman at the ceremony was heard whispering, "That college called Xavier is a shame. Higher education for Negroes! Robbing us of our servants—that's what I call it."[101] Xavier threatened the status quo. While bishops talked, Drexel and the SBS erected buildings.

**The Master Art: Building Catholic Leaders**

The cornerstone of the new building read, "God's greatest work on earth is man. Man's master art is the leading of man to God." The sisters, priests, and lay teachers at the university prided themselves on building a Catholic community and relished bringing students to the "true faith." Winning souls meant little if they did not also empower students to be worldly leaders. The president of Xavier, Mother Agatha Ryan, wrote, "The missionary must not only convert souls, but he must raise up among the people for whom he labors, leaders of their own flesh and blood who can guide and direct their own in a way that even the missionary is powerless to do.... The Sisters firmly believe that from the growing student body would come undoubtedly the race leaders who will do much to mold the opinion of Colored America."[102] To create this leadership class, the sisters instilled racial pride in their students. Former Xavier pupil Gertrude Guidry remembered Sister M. Frances Buttell standing in the doorway each morning bellowing, "Shoulders back, heads up. And don't shuffle your feet. You are as good as anyone that walks God's earth, and never forget it!" Guidry claimed, "She wouldn't let you forget—she'd burn that in you, day after day. 'You are as good as anybody. You are created in God's image.'"[103] The SBS backed

---

99 "Religion: For the Tenth Man"; "Letters," *Time*, November 7, 1932.
100 Lynch, *Sharing the Bread in Service*, 225.
101 Murphy, *Yankee Priest*, 196.
102 M. M. Agatha Ryan, *Proposed Sketch for Catholic History*, 7, in St. Francis Xavier Convent Annals, ASBS.
103 Quoted in Marshall, "Sister Mary Frances Buttell," 287.

these verbal reminders with a curriculum crafted to foster pride in Black history and culture.

## Avoiding "Mis-education" and Embracing African American History

Aware of the work of Carter G. Woodson and his Association for the Study of Negro Life and History, the sisters moved to make the study of Black history an integral part of studies at Xavier. Woodson, whose parents had been enslaved, earned his doctorate in history from Harvard and devoted his scholarly life to popularizing Black history.[104] He urged, "Instead of going to others to find something to admire, begin to appreciate yourselves."[105] Woodson believed that education without embracing African and African American culture was a disservice, and he disdained the "educated Negroes" who "insist they are not different."[106] He complained, after scouring catalogs of leading Historically Black Colleges and Universities, that while they taught Greek and Latin, philosophy, and ancient history, they failed to teach African history, art, or music. Woodson labeled these white-washed curriculums "mis-education."[107]

The SBS heard Woodson's message, and in 1925, the sisters established the Negro History Association at Xavier. Following Woodson's lead, in February 1926, Xavier began celebrating Negro History Week, a national program common at many Black colleges and universities. In 1927, for example, activities included performances of spirituals by the glee club and the singing group the Osceola Five. Xavier students also heard lectures on African history, famous Black Americans, and slavery. The school news-

---

104 For a biography, see Jacqueline Goggin, *Carter G. Woodson: A Life in Black History* (Baton Rouge: Louisiana State University Press, 1993).
105 Carter G. Woodson, "What the Negro Has to Dramatize," press release, February 17, 1932, quoted in Goggin, *Carter G. Woodson*, 156.
106 Carter G. Woodson, "The Director Speaks," *Journal of Negro History* 16, no. 3 (July 1931): 345.
107 Carter G. Woodson, *The Mis-Education of the Negro* (Philadelphia: Harkin Press, 1931). He also published a synopsis of the work in the NAACP organ *The Crisis*: Carter G. Woodson, "The Mis-Education of the Negro," *Crisis* 38 (August 1931), 266–67.

paper editorialized, "The aim of Negro History Week would be defeated if from the celebration we did not carry away a new confidence and a stronger pride in the History of our people. Ours is a history not to be ignored, but to be studied with admiration and conscious pride. There are many lessons we might carry away from it."[108] In 1929, the celebration focused on the works of writers of the Harlem Renaissance Paul Laurence Dunbar and Countee Cullen, and the paper urged students to "remember the jewels of our race's history. . . . Let it be a source of inspiration. Burn into your innermost fibers the guiding principles so vividly personified by our countless heroes and heroines."[109]

Wishing to center the study of Black history and culture all year rather than doing lip service by celebrating for a week, in 1933, the college launched a Negro History Department. The department featured courses on Black Americans in Slavery and the Civil War, Reconstruction, Post-Reconstruction, Sources of Negro History, and a course in Ethnological Backgrounds of the American Negro.[110] Led by Father Hugh Conahan and Rev. Dr. Edward Murphy, along with lecturer David Jackson, the Negro History Department examined the African past as well as the contributions of Black Americans to the Catholic Church. In 1934, the department introduced Elementary and Secondary Methods in Negro History as well as pedagogy classes on how to teach Black history. Xavier-trained teachers were expected to teach Black history to their students. They also organized a class called The Negro in American Literature that featured "readings from the representative writers in the fields of Fiction, Drama, Poetry, Spirituals, Blues, Labor Songs, Essays, History and Biography."[111] The new courses received praise from the Black press, as well, adding to Xavier's national reputation.[112]

---

108   Helena Baptists, "Editorial," *Xavier Herald*, March 1927, 2.
109   Rene Roussene, "Negro History Week," *Xavier Herald*, February 1929, 1.
110   *Xavier College Bulletin*, 1933–34.
111   *Xavier College Bulletin*, 1934–35.
112   See, for example, Negro Councilman, "Negro History Course Taught at Xavier 'U,'" *Philadelphia Tribune*, September 6, 1934, 14; and Negro Councilman, "Xavier University Has Big Enrollment," *Philadelphia Tribune*, November 1, 1934, 5.

To procure teachers for these courses, the SBS financed graduate education for Black scholars. One of the first students sent for graduate work was David Jackson. He graduated Xavier with a bachelor's degree in education in 1932, and the Sisters of the Blessed Sacrament then hired him to teach Negro history and English literature in 1933. In 1934, they sent him to the Department of Records and Research in New Orleans to apply his training to sociological research, and in 1935, the sisters paid for him to attend Howard University for graduate work. Howard, formerly home to Carter G. Woodson, was the epicenter of research in African American history, grounded in the scholarship of Alain Locke and Kelly Miller, who established courses on "inter-racial history" as early as 1915.[113] From 1935 to 1936, Jackson worked on his master's degree at Howard in African history under Professor Leo H. Hansberry. Jackson wrote a thesis entitled "The Catholic Church and the New Orleans Negro," and during his time in Washington he maintained a close connection with the dean of Xavier, Sr. M. Madeline Sophie Ryan, who provided him with research materials. He reinforced the nuns' belief in the importance of Catholic education for Black students when he complained of a spirit of anti-Catholicism pervading the predominantly Protestant Howard University campus and wrote to Sr. Madeline Sophie, "Scholastic philosophy is unheard of at Howard. As I mentioned to Father Murphy in many of my courses the Catholic Church is made the worst of all evils of Medieval Europe and of present day America."[114]

Upon the completion of his degree, Jackson wrote to Mother M. Agatha Ryan, Xavier's president, assuring her that "on my return to Xavier as a *Master of Arts in History*, I shall work as previously for the Greater Honor and Glory of God, and for the best interest of Xavier University and the cause which it represents (emphasis in original)."[115] During his tenure he taught classes on

---

113 Rayford Whittingham Logan, *Howard University: The First Hundred Years, 1867–1967* (New York: New York University Press, 1969), 171.
114 David Jackson to M. Madeline Sophie, October 13, 1935, David J. Jackson collection, box 1, folder: Biographic Data on David J. Jackson, XUA.
115 David Jackson to Mother M. Agatha, May 21, 1936, personnel file, Jackson David. J., XUA. Sadly, the relationship did not remain positive, as Jackson repeatedly ran into financial trouble and asked for loans from the university.

Ancient African Kingdoms and the History of Ethiopia and Egypt, as well as New Negro History, which included a section on Problems of the Negro in the Economic History of the United States. He also took the Negro Historical Association under his wing with its purpose "to foster a deeper interest in historical study and research; to encourage creative writing of historical short stories, plays, etc., and to train students in the arrangements of programs for national celebrations."[116] As an active member of the NAACP and the Federation of Colored Catholics (FCC), Jackson taught students to take pride in both their race and their faith and to hold society accountable to standards of justice.

In addition to offering African and African American history, the university took a holistic cultural approach. The Music Department, which had previously focused on subjects such as Gregorian chant and classical music, began teaching a course called The Negro and Music in the 1930s. In addition, the newly formed Fine Arts Department developed a class called The Negro in Art and Architectures.[117] This interest in African and African American cultures also guided library book procurement. The school collected books about and by Black Americans and gathered early records and archival materials such as birth records, baptismal certificates, and marriage contracts. These collections gathered under the auspices of the Negro Historical Association were intended to make Xavier a research center for Black life, especially along the Gulf Coast.[118]

---

When creditors began contacting the university, his contract was not renewed. In 1940 he migrated to New York City, where he found a job teaching in public schools, although he did not teach African American history specifically. Upon his departure the Department of Negro History merged with the History Department, but without a qualified teacher the classes were eventually canceled in favor of U.S. and European history classes. Not until the 1960s was the program restored. Jackson did, however, leave his mark on the school through his large collection of newspaper clippings on Black Americans, which has become part of the university archives.

    116   *Xavier Bulletin*, 1935–36.
    117   *Xavier Bulletin*, 1934–35.
    118   "Books . . . Rare Books . . . Precious Books . . . God's Book . . . And Why Xavier University Is Concerned About Them," *Mission Fields at Home*, January–February 1936, 3–4.

This curricular emphasis on Black history and culture drew the attention of the Father of Black History. Woodson visited Xavier in November 1934; during a speech there he affirmed the students, saying, "God did not make the Negro inferior. To believe that is unchristian. Take your color . . . and make of it a brighter future for tomorrow."[119] Woodson praised the university and reported back to Father Murphy, "I am still thinking of the enjoyable stay at Xavier. I could not but feel buoyant in that Christian atmosphere. You made me think that the spirit of Jesus Christ has not yet departed from the earth."[120]

## Making Change: The School of Social Work Opens

In order to preserve the spirit of Christ in the world, Xavier faculty knew that they had to train students to go out into the world and advocate for justice. To accomplish this work, they opened the School of Social Work in 1934. Xavier University's School of Social Work combined Progressive Era ideas about scientific management of social ills with the distinctive agenda of the Catholic social teachings advocated by Pope Leo XIII in *Rerum Novarum* (1891) and Pius XI in *Quadragesimo Anno* (1931). The foundation of the School of Social Work yet again signaled that the SBS believed that the social justice doctrines advanced by the hierarchy applied to people of all races. Interested in eradicating poverty and injustice, the Catholic social reformers such as Fr. John Ryan and Fr. William Kerby, who started the National Catholic Welfare Council, also insisted that "there is a distinct Catholic morality, a distinct Catholic philosophy of life and faith, a distinct scale of social and moral valuations, a distinct view of sin, of social responsibility and a distinct type of conscience due to the sacramental ministry and religious training."[121] Very few Catholics at the time applied Catholic social teachings to racial issues, but the founding School of Social Work at Xavier sent a message that justice meant little if it were not applied across the color line.

---

119  *Xavier Herald*, November 1934.
120  Quotation in *Annual Report for 1934*, XUA.
121  William Joseph Kerby, *The Social Mission of Charity: A Study of Points of View in Catholic Charities* (New York: Macmillan, 1921), 155.

In 1931 Sr. M. Francis Xavier gave a talk to the student body urging students to use their education to serve others, telling them "to do their share in furthering the kingdom of God on earth."[122] One of Mother M. Agatha's proudest accomplishments while president of Xavier was the cooperation she fostered between Xavier students and those in the city's parochial schools. She explained, "As Xavier students under the guidance of a Xavier professor aid in the development and supervision of these projects . . . indirectly, leadership and good citizenship are fostered, and in the Xavier graduate is inculcated the idea of community helpfulness and responsibility."[123] This community responsibility would lead to agitation for social justice during the long civil rights movement. Xavier graduates developed a reputation in New Orleans for leading the fight for Black rights. Many students and professors joined their fellow Catholics in leading interracial masses and meetings in the city.[124] Xavier alumna also occupied prominent positions in New Orleans public schools and centers for social work, empowering them to aid the Black community.

## "An Xavier Family"

Though the congregation acted largely without the help of the Catholic hierarchy, with Xavier University, it thrust the Roman Church's evangelization of Black Americans into the public eye. The gray Indiana limestone buildings made a concrete statement of the nuns' commitment to mitigating the effects of race prejudice. The school was more than symbol, however. Each year the sisters celebrated Baby's Day and invited alumni to come back to campus with their children. Remarking on the celebration in 1930, one sister remarked, "The future of the College, as far as

---

122 "Inspiring Illustrated Lecture Delivered to General Assembly: Students Exhorted to Become Lay Apostles," *Xavier Herald*, December 1931, 2.

123 M. Agatha Ryan, "Catholic Education and the Negro" (pamphlet) (Washington, DC: The Catholic University of America Press, 1942), 15.

124 R. Bentley Anderson points out that Xavier graduates were the first to integrate professional schools at Loyola. He stresses, "Catholic interracialists did not engage in mass protests or acts of civil disobedience to challenge racial segregation; rather they attempted to convert the hearts and minds of their coreligionists to bring about change." Anderson, *Black, White, and Catholic: New Orleans Interracialism, 1947–1956* (Nashville: Vanderbilt University Press, 2005), 11.

the student body is concerned, is assured if the plans of these mothers materialize."[125] That sister was prophetic, for the sisters frequently taught the children and later grandchildren of their first students. Generations of New Orleans families made the institution flourish, and it inspired loyalty in many. Journalist Warren Brown noted simply, "Ours was a Xavier family."[126] Brown's father had attended the college and later taught for the SBS in New Iberia. His mother worked as Xavier's switchboard operator for forty years. All five children in his family attended the university. In fact, his sisters bore the names of nuns who influenced his parents. When Brown had a daughter, he united his pride in his African heritage with his appreciation for the SBS and named his daughter Kafi Drexel Brown. To the nuns who founded Xavier in 1915, their work could not have a more fitting legacy. Using Xavier University as a central command post, the SBS attempted to expand their work through the rural South.

---

125 "Along the Highways and Pathways of the Mission Fields," *Mission Fields at Home*, June 1930, 142.

126 Martha McNeill Hamilton and Warren Brown, *Black and White and Red All Over: The Story of a Friendship* (New York: Public Affairs, 2002), 37; Warren Brown, "Canonization Is Close to Home for One Family: Mother Katharine Drexel Inspired, Helped Blacks, Native Americans," *Washington Post*, September 30, 2000.

CHAPTER 7

# The Catholic Rosenwald

## Mother Katharine Schools in Rural Louisiana

IN 1918 MOTHER KATHARINE and Mother M. Ignatius Ryan set off on a meandering trip through the rural South that would shape SBS policy for generations. The two nuns visited more than a dozen locations from Virginia to Texas, but Louisiana impressed Mother Katharine most as a mission field ripe for expansion. During this tour she met the eccentric Father J. Girault de la Corgnais, an old French Jesuit. Girault based his mission at St. Thomas Church in Pointe-a-la-Hache, Louisiana, but he spent most of his time motoring around the bayous in a small boat dubbed the *St. Thomas*, saying Mass wherever he found willing congregants. His zeal convinced the wealthy nun to donate the money for a school in the community of City Price, where previously Black students received only one month of schooling per year. In the spring of 1921, Girault asked Mother Katharine to take a river boat tour with him so she could see conditions for herself.[1] As she toured the school Girault had built with her money, she was impressed by the quality of the instruction and the students' capacity, not capabilities to learn.[2] Continuing through the bayou, she saw that other crudely built rural schools needed improvement. At one, the teacher's desk was two old altars lashed together, and the chalkboard balanced on an old pew. Some enterprising teachers in Klotzville had cobbled together a school from the reclaimed lumber of the area's old abandoned Catholic missions.[3] After completing the wild boat trip, during which she and Father Girault came perilously close

---

1 Duffy, *Katharine Drexel*, 333.
2 Mother Katharine Drexel, "Trip to New Orleans and Rural South, 1921," H10 A, box 30, folder 7, ASBS.
3 Ibid.

to plunging off the *St. Thomas*, Drexel decided to make a greater effort to solve what she saw as a regional educational crisis. Mother Katharine began a campaign to build and administer a rural Catholic school system in the Diocese of Lafayette. Although she had provided funding for schools throughout the U.S. for decades and had in fact paid for several schools in southwestern Louisiana already, her donations had been ad hoc rather than systemic. Her 1921 tour of bayou communities convinced her of the need for a well-planned, centrally organized rural school system for Black students. Though never large or well-funded enough, these schools aimed to do the work that both the state government and local dioceses refused to do.

The Sisters of the Blessed Sacrament intended this rural school system to create a ladder of Catholic education from elementary to postgraduate schools. This concept was not new to Catholics, but the Euro-American-dominated church had not extended it to non-white students before. After purchasing land and erecting the schools, the SBS paid the salaries of the lay teachers, typically recent graduates of Xavier and other SBS schools, hired to staff them. Xavier University offered scholarships to students who agreed to serve in a rural school for at least two years after completing teacher training. Mother M. Mercedes, Drexel's successor as superior general, explained that the system allowed the SBS to reach both the middle class students in New Orleans and the desperately poor: "Both poles of the system meet, as it were, in the rural school where the graduate of Xavier is teaching the country children the rudiments of knowledge and the elements of religion, heart and soul intent on her task."[4] The teachers who staffed rural schools needed all the help they could get.

## Rural School Problems

In the rural sections of the state, schooling for Black students was almost nonexistent. Louisiana organized a public school system in 1899, but it did not pass a mandatory attendance law until 1916. Even then, municipalities made little effort to establish schools for

---

4 "Impression of Mother M. Mercedes on her Visitation of Louisiana, 1938," Mother M. Mercedes correspondence, box 6, folder 7, ASBS.

Black students among the plantations and bayous. Those that were organized were, according to the State Agent of Rural Schools for Negroes, "scattered in their aims, wretched in their squalor, utterly inadequate and inefficient as to methods and results."[5] The 1923-24 Special Report of Negro Schools admitted, "At the present rate of improvement in the State, however, it will be a long time before the Negro children of the state will be reasonably supplied with school facilities."[6] Until 1935, schools were controlled on a local rather than state basis, which meant that rural areas would have had to levy higher taxes than urban districts to achieve the same results. Most rural areas lacked the will to accomplish this.[7] In 1918, Leo Favrot, the state agent of Rural Schools for Negroes, claimed that 52 percent of Black students had not enrolled in public school and that 47 percent did not attend any school.[8] As in New Orleans, most rural schools for Black students only offered grades one through six. In 1915, the year the SBS opened Xavier, the state did not have a single fully accredited public high school for Black students, and by 1935 it had only thirty-five, located in primarily in cities.[9]

Whites stymied efforts. Corrupt school boards stole money that should have gone to Black schools. In 1912, in parishes that were between 10 and 25 percent Black, white schools had a per capita expenditure of $10.18 and Black schools $2.42. In districts where the Black population was between 25 and 50 percent of the total, white schools spent $14.18 and Black schools $.91. Those districts composed of 75 or more percent of Black students spent a generous $28.89 on their white students and merely $.87 on Black students.[10] By 1930, the situation had improved slightly; Louisiana spent $64.47 on white students and $16.54 on Black

---

5   Favrot, "Aims and Needs in Negro Public Education in Louisiana," *Bulletin Number Two*, 1918, 3-4.
6   A. Lewis and W. Sizemore, "1923-1924 Special Report of Negro Schools," in *Report to 1923-1924 Legislative Session* (Baton Rouge, LA, 1924); quoted in Eakin, "Black Struggle for Education in Louisiana," 33.
7   Dauphine, *A Question of Inheritance*, 12.
8   Favrot, "Aims and Needs in Negro Public Education in Louisiana," 4.
9   State Department of Education of Louisiana, *Eighty-Seventh Annual Report, for the Session 1935-36*, 188-89.
10  Favrot, "Aims and Needs in Negro Public Education in Louisiana," 16.

students, though disparity remained the rule.[11] Black tax dollars paid for schools that barred their entrance.[12] The limited funding for Black schools, combined with a desire to have students work the fields, led to shortened school years. In 1916–17 the school year for Black students lasted only 89 days, or roughly four months, while white students attended 140 days, an arrangement that continued through the 1930s. In 1922, the state passed a law mandating a 140-day school year for all students between the ages of seven and fourteen, but this was widely ignored.[13] Many families kept their children out to work on the farms during harvest time, further eroding the school term.[14] In rural parishes where the economy depended on plantation labor, the school year for Black students was structured around the cotton and sugar seasons. For example, in Pointe Coupee Parish, the Black schools started six weeks after the white ones to facilitate the cotton harvest.[15]

Rural schools also lacked qualified teachers. In the 1916–17 school year, only 551 out of 1,439, or 38 percent, of teachers in Black schools held either college degrees or normal certificates. Another 227, or 16 percent, had second-grade certificates, while the remainder held third-grade certificates, meaning they only had to prove mastery of the sixth-grade elementary curriculum.[16] By 1930, teacher training had not much improved. For example, in St. James Parish, 11 percent of teachers in Black schools had graduated college or normal school, 44 percent had finished high school, and another 44 percent had not finished high school. Jefferson County, closer to New Orleans, fared better with 52 percent of Black teachers having degrees, 47 percent having com-

---

11   Clark Foreman, *Environmental Factors in Negro Elementary Education* (New York: Julius Rosenwald Fund by W. Norton, 1932), 25.

12   Louis Harlan's study *Separate and Unequal* shows that Louisiana was not alone in this practice; the counties in North and South Carolina, Virginia, and Georgia with the highest percentage of black students spent the least on their education.

13   State Department of Education of Louisiana, *Fifteenth Compilation of School Laws* (Baton Rouge: 1936), 203.

14   Favrot, "Aims and Needs in Negro Public Education in Louisiana," 23.

15   Palmer, "Evolution of Education for African-Americans," 186.

16   Calculated from figures in Favrot, "Aims and Needs of Negro Public Education in Louisiana," 23–24.

pleted high school, and only .35 percent without a diploma.[17] The situation in southern Louisiana was critical. Katharine Drexel believed that the Catholic Church needed to step in. Not only would high-quality education provide Black students with an important asset that might lift them out of poverty, but the SBS was also convinced that it "will go far toward winning a cheerful cooperation of White and Colored in striving for a better and larger future."[18] To accomplish this goal, the Sisters of the Blessed Sacrament set their sights on the Diocese of Lafayette, where they knew they would have to begin by training teachers.

## Work Begins in Lafayette

Carved out of the Diocese of New Orleans in 1918, the Diocese of Lafayette, which included Acadia, Allen, Beauregard, Calcasieu, Cameron, Evangeline, Landry, Iberia, Jefferson, Lafayette, St. Martin, St. Mary, and Vermilion parishes, had the largest population of Black Catholics in the country. In 1922, Bishop Jules Benjamin Jeanmard estimated that his diocese had 100,000 Black residents, including 40,000 practicing Catholics.[19] This number would have been higher a generation earlier. The newly appointed Bishop Jeanmard, much like Janssens, fretted over this decline. He warned of Protestant societies planning to "invade" the region unless the church invested in schools. He accused Methodists and Baptists of poaching Black Catholics. Jeanmard wrote to the American Board of Catholic Missions in exasperation "that this method was successful our missionaries in charge of the colored work have precise knowledge. 'I can show you,' writes one of our priests, 'six Baptist churches, where every member from the preacher to the sexton is a baptized Catholic." He despaired: "In one civic parish with a Negro population of 35,000 of whom

---

17 Foreman, *Environmental Factors in Negro Elementary Education*, table 2.
18 M. Letterhouse, "The Bayou Teche and the Prairies of Fair Opelousas," *Mission Fields at Home*, April 1929, 116.
19 "Application for Aid Presented to the Commission for the Catholic Missions among the Colored People and the Indians," August 12, 1922, BCIM records, series 5/2: reports and applications for aid, Diocese of Lafayette, Louisiana, reel 6, MUA.

27,000 are baptized Catholics, there was not, in 1920, a single Catholic teacher in the public schools. These public schools are left entirely to the teachers to give whatever lead they please to the pupils."[20] Jeanmard viewed the increase of public schools as a threat and lamented, "The State is doing more and more for the education for the negro and, by learning English as they do in Public schools (our Catholics are mostly French-speaking), they are becoming a more easy prey for our preachers."[21] Jeanmard did not wish to deny Black students the right to learn English. Instead, he wanted English lessons to come with Catholic theology. Catholic schools, he hoped, would solve his problem. Once again, his solution was to build separate schools rather than to address the systemic racism within the churches in his diocese.

## Building on the Work of the Black Community

Black families had been working on building Catholic schools long before Jeanmard. For example, in 1908 only one Catholic church served the Lake Charles community, but it was located several miles from the primarily Black section of town. Black parishioners often met and walked to church together. On these walks, they discussed the lack of educational opportunities. Backed by ten families, businessman Louis Adams and his associate Gilbert Rochon went to Monsignor Hubert Cramers, the pastor of Immaculate Conception Church, asking for a Catholic school as well as a separate parish located closer to their homes. Cramers consulted his fellow priests as well as the Holy Family Sisters, who provided the name of a respected lay teacher who might be interested in establishing a school. On October 8, 1908, Adams and Rochon organized the school board, and Eleanora Figaro, a graduate of St. Paul's School in Lafayette, began holding classes in the tiny and unfinished Greene Hall until 1910, when they built a small wood-frame building. Rapid growth made the

---

20  Jules B. Jeanmard, "Colored Missions Needs for Lafayette," in *Report of the American Board of Catholic Missions to the American Episcopate from July 1, 1928–July 17, 1929* (Chicago: American Board of Catholic Missions, 1929), 81–83.

21  Bishop Jules B. Jeanmard to the Rev. J. Tennelly, SS, DD, February 4, 1926, BCIM records, series 5/2: reports and applications for aid, reel 26, MUA.

hiring of a second teacher a necessity.[22] Not until 1919 did the Holy Ghost Fathers gather the funds to construct Sacred Heart Parish for Black parishioners. At that point they converted the private school into a parish-affiliated one. Black families repeatedly sought a Catholic education for their children, both because they valued the religious instruction and because Catholic schools, unlike their public counterparts, went beyond the sixth grade.

## Sacred Heart Becomes Xavier Extension

In 1920, Mother Katharine, impressed with Sacred Heart, provided some of the money to construct a new state-of-the-art school, and in 1922 SBS sisters arrived to help the lay teachers expand the school.[23] The SBS had the resources to add a high school and normal department. By 1933, they linked Sacred Heart with Xavier and offered university extension classes at the Lake Charles campus.[24] Sacred Heart students took classes in religion, math, English, social studies, science, Latin, French, industry, and teacher training.[25] As at Xavier, teacher training drew the most students. Of the forty graduates between 1927 and 1933, eighteen became teachers. These graduates also produced one nurse, six housewives, two insurance agents, ten who continued to college, one nun, and one junior seminarian.[26]

SBS sisters made sure their students compared favorably to the students at Lake Charles' white Catholic school, St. Charles Academy. In 1923, Mother M. Amadeus noted that at Sacred Heart's closing exercise, "The children all wore white dresses with white ribbons and their parents spared nothing to make them look nice.

---

22  Gloria P. Ambrose and Bernadine B. Proctor, "Sacred Heart School," in *The First Hundred Years: 1882–1992; The Centennial of Catholic Education in "Imperial" Calcasieu*, ed. Donald J. Millet Sr. and Elaine B. Bodin (Lake Charles, LA: Alta, 1982).

23  Figaro remained a fixture at Sacred Heart until her death in 1953. In 1949 Pope Pius XII honored her with the Pro Ecclesia et Pontifice award, the highest honor awarded to a member of the laity. Figaro was the first African American to receive this honor.

24  Butler, "History of Catholic Elementary Education for Negroes," 82–84.

25  Kenney, "Contributions of the Sisters of the Blessed Sacrament," 46.

26  See Butler, "History of Catholic Elementary Education," 152.

They were given a regulation length for skirts, sleeves and necks which they obeyed and consequently looked pretty and modest. I was pleased to know this was remarked when they were contrasted with the academy girls [from the all-white Catholic school]."[27] She noted that Father Hackett, Sacred Heart's priest, delighted in the fact that the sisters from St. Charles came to the ceremonies, "because their entertainments used to annoy him so, when, intending to introduce something funny, they always pictured the most disgusting type of Negro with protruding red lips and clownish attire."[28] The act of conforming to ancient Catholic traditions and prudish modesty standards that could be seen as oppression in this case was a protest against racism. The sisters tried to prove that their students were more pious than those in white schools. The SBS, with its extensive financial resources, was able to do work the poor rural families could not have accomplished, but they succeeded because they built on a foundation firmly established by Black families. As she expanded her work in the rural South, Mother Katharine preferred to sponsor schools at locations where community leaders had already begun the work.

## St. Edward's, Another Building Block in the Rural School System

In 1918, St. Edward's School in New Iberia became the third foundation stone for the SBS rural school program. That year the SBS partnered with the Holy Ghost Fathers and contributed ten thousand dollars to build a new school. The sisters faced unique challenges in New Iberia, as students lacked educational foundations. Sr. Gervase, who taught at St. Edward's from 1924 to 1930, recalled one seventeen-year-old boy who arrived in her class with no previous schooling.[29] The school started with five grades, but the sisters soon added a high school and normal program. In 1924, the high school received state accreditation.[30] Only three years later, St. Edward's placed first in the state examination conducted

---

    27  Mother M. Amadeus to Mother Katharine, 28 July 1923, *Annals of the SBS*, vol. 21 (1923), 54, ASBS.
    28  Ibid., 56–57.
    29  Lynch, *Sharing the Bread in Service*, 1:245.
    30  Butler, "History of Catholic Elementary Education," 91.

by the superintendent of Colored Schools.[31] By 1935, the school achieved high ratings from the Louisiana Department of Education, receiving 945 out of a possible 1,000 points in a state assessment.[32] As at Xavier, the sisters also sponsored the Negro History Club and Negro Literature Club. Students began each day by singing the Black National Anthem, "Lift Every Voice and Sing."

During St. Edward's first years, the curriculum featured classes in religion, math, English, social science, science, and teacher training. After 1935, however, St. Edwards began offering more courses such as home economics, shop work, and physical education, though at the same time they added Latin and French.[33] This enhancement of the industrial curriculum while they were creating a first-class university for Black students a few hours away seems incongruous. The addition of the domestic training courses could have been, however, a subtle way of ensuring that the students in a poor community received food and clothing during the Depression. In 1936, the students used the domestic science room to prepare a hot lunch for the entire school, possibly the only hot meal they received all day.[34] As at other SBS schools, the teacher training program at New Iberia proved one of its most popular courses. The establishment of the SBS's three teacher-training programs—Xavier, Sacred Heart, and St. Edward's—supplied the raw talent to implement their rural school agenda. Without these lay teachers, the SBS could not have extended themselves so rapidly.

## Building in the Bayous

Once the SBS had a pipeline of lay teachers, they began to construct and staff rural schools. Drexel asked Bishop Jeanmard to help her select sites for her schools. The two toured the diocese together during Holy Week in 1923. Location, even in the bayou,

---

31   Fr. John C. Glade to Rt. Reverend Jules B. Jeanmard, DD, bishop of Lafayette, August 28, 1928, BCIM records, series 5/2: reports and applications for aid, Diocese of Lafayette, Louisiana, reel 6, MUA.
32   Fr. A. Walsh, CSSp., to Rt. Rev. Jules B. Jeanmard, September 18, 1935, BCIM records 5/2: reports and applications for aid, Diocese of Lafayette, Louisiana, reel 6, MUA.
33   Kenney, "Contributions of the Sisters of the Blessed Sacrament," 51–52.
34   Lynch, *Sharing the Bread in Service*, 250.

is everything. When selecting a site, Drexel first made certain she had the support of the local priest. To secure her investment, the pastor had to agree to supervise the schools and provide the sacraments to the students and their families. Additionally, she required priests to find accommodations for the teachers with local families. Wary after the controversy surrounding St. Katherine's in New Orleans, Drexel also made local pastors conduct a survey to ascertain interest in a Catholic school. In some towns, wealthy Black families or sympathetic whites donated the land for a school, while in other areas the SBS or the American Board for Colored Missions purchased it. Drexel worked with an architect on plans for one- and two-room schoolhouses that could be constructed for between two and four thousand dollars. When possible, she hired Black construction crews to build them. In addition to construction costs, the SBS also paid the teacher salaries.

Graduates from SBS teacher training programs staffed the rural schools. Sisters based at St. Edward's supervised the rural teachers and held additional training seminars at the New Iberia campus. Drexel paid teachers between $47.50 and $55 per month depending on experience. As a comparison, in 1920 the state of Louisiana paid Black teachers $379 per year, or roughly $41.56 per month, based on a nine-month term.[35] Though the SBS offered a just wage, teachers could have received considerably higher pay working in public schools in New Orleans. In 1922, teachers'

---

35  Monroe N. Work, ed., *The Negro Year Book 1921–1922* (Tuskegee, AL: Negro Yearbook Company, 1922), 240. By 1929 the average Black teacher's salary was $496 a year, or roughly $55 per month, though it was considerably lower in rural areas. See Monroe N. Work, ed., *The Negro Year Book 1931–1932* (Tuskegee, AL: Tuskegee Institute, 1931), 206. It is also worth noting that while the salaries Mother Katharine paid were on par with Black public-school wages, they were considerably less than white teachers in public schools earned. For example, in 1931 the average salary for a white teacher in Louisiana was $1,050 per year, or roughly $117 per month. Leander L. Boykin, "The Status and Trends of Differentials Between White and Negro Teachers' Salaries in the Southern States, 1900–1946," *Journal of Negro Education* 18, no. 1 (Winter 1949): 41. In fairness, the salary Drexel paid out was more than the diocese paid for nuns to work in schools, which amounted to only $350 per year, or $29 per month. Sisters rarely ever saw this full amount, however. Condon, "Development of the Financial Procedures," 269.

salaries in the city rose to between $100 and $124 a month. With all her other expenses, Mother Katharine could not match these salaries. Rural school salaries, however, did include room and board with local Catholic families. The sisters often checked up on housing arrangements made for their teachers because they wanted to ensure both their physical and moral safety. Initially Drexel worried that parents would balk at letting their city-educated children live in the primitive conditions of rural communities, but Bertha Thomas Antonio, the first Xavier graduate placed in the rural schools, reported that her mother exclaimed, "If we won't help our own people, who will?"[36]

For the first few years of the rural school program, Xavier provided most of the teachers, but eventually Xavier teachers primarily staffed schools in New Orleans, while Sacred Heart and St. Edward's alumni taught in the outlying areas.[37] Between 1920 and 1939, the SBS built and staffed twenty-four such rural schools and aided more than sixty others through donations of land, buildings, teacher's salaries, or supplies. These schools, often called "Mother Katharine schools," typically offered grades one through eight, employed one to four teachers, and accommodated between 60 and 250 students. Between 1921 and 1935, the number of Black students attending Catholic schools in the Diocese of Lafayette doubled.[38]

Most of the schools continued through the eighth grade, while public schools only offered a sixth-grade education to Black students. Some graduates went on to attend one of the SBS high schools, but the congregation could not provide high schools in every rural location. The schools offered a basic grammar school curriculum featuring heavy doses of reading, writing, and arithmetic as well as classes on history, health, and arts.

---

36   Quoted in Lynch, *Sharing the Bread in Service*, 1:263.
37   Ibid., 263.
38   According to the *Report on Negro Work and Application for Aid*, in 1921 the Diocese of Lafayette boasted thirteen schools with a total of 2,357 students, while in 1935 it had twenty-seven schools and 4,503 students. BCIM records, series 5/2: reports and applications for aid, Diocese of Lafayette, Louisiana, reel 6, MUA.

TABLE 7-1. SBS Rural Schools

| School | Location | Year Founded |
| --- | --- | --- |
| St. Paulinus | City Price | 1920 |
| St. Thomas | Pointe-á-la-Hache | 1922 |
| St. Joseph | Broussard | 1922 |
| St. Peter | Glencoe | 1922 |
| Our Mother of Mercy | Rayne | 1923 |
| St. Peter | Julien Hill | 1923 |
| Our Lady of Lourdes | Abbeville | 1923 |
| St. Benedict | Bertrandville | 1923 |
| St. Luke | Thibodaux | 1923 |
| St. Katherine | Coulee Crouche | 1924 |
| Our Lady of the Assumption | Carencro | 1924 |
| St. Leo | Leonville | 1925 |
| St. Elizabeth | Prairie Basse | 1926 |
| Our Mother of Mercy | Church Point | 1928 |
| St. Ann | Mallet | 1928 |
| St. Benedict the Moor | Duson | 1928 |
| Our Lady of Grace | Reserve | 1930 |
| Little Flower | Mamou | 1930 |
| Notre Dame | St. Martinville | 1931 |
| St. Jude | West Point-á-la-Hache | 1933 |
| St. Monica | Tyrone | 1935 |
| St. John the Baptist | Edgard | 1938 |
| St. Mathilda | Eunice | 1939 |

Despite the presence of non-Catholics, all schools taught Christian doctrine as the first class of the day, and each student received preparation for Holy Communion. The remote locations of the schools, combined with the chronic shortages of priests, meant that schools doubled as churches and the teachers as catechetical leaders.

## Small Schools, Large Problems

The SBS made sure all the teachers in the Mother Katharine Schools received at least a first-grade certificate, but teachers faced challenges for which the model classrooms and laboratory schools had not prepared them. Despite Mother Katharine's support, money was always short. Bishop Jeanmard lamented, "Our financial problems are even greater than are our spiritual ones."[39] He blamed the decline of cotton prices, insects, underwater mortgages, and especially the devastating flood of 1927 for the chronic shortage of money in these parishes. Although the SBS and other donors paid for construction of buildings and the salaries of the teachers, schools had other expenses that had to be met locally, which proved difficult during lean years.

Drexel's standard rural school contract dictated that the local priest had to make all repairs. These often went uncompleted as a result of budget shortfalls or negligence. Even though they had signed contracts promising to handle maintenance, many priests demanded that Drexel pay for building upkeep because, as they pointed out, "They are your schools."[40] Conditions shocked visiting SBS supervisors. Some priests did not properly administer the schools, and Mother Katharine eventually refused to send funds until "on receipt of the annual report of money expended someone would be appointed to investigate as to whether the pastor really had the painting and repairing done."[41] Inspecting the rural schools and keeping them in working order became an unruly task. Drexel appointed a sister based in Lake Charles to commit to full-time work as a superintendent of the rural schools, a job that entailed listening to litanies of complaints. In Pointe-á-La Hache, a sister found the school in ill repair and reported, "The teachers were teaching in a building whose roof was leaking to such an extent that on rainy days it was necessary to keep a child sweeping out the water." Her note that "the two teachers at this school are doing good work" must have come as little consolation to the educators and students who labored in the mire.[42] Though Drexel built a new school in Rayne, she left the priest in charge of securing furnishings. Lamenting the poor quality of the desks his poverty forced him to buy, he suggested, "Free-sitting is a positive

---

39 Jules B. Jeanmard, "Missionary Problems of the Young Diocese of Lafayette," *Report of the American Board of Catholic Missions, July 1, 1931 to July 1, 1932* (Chicago: American Board of Catholic Missions, 1932), 79.
40 Mother M. Amadeus to Mother Katharine, July 28, 1923, in *Annals of the SBS 1923*, 21:59, ASBS.
41 Mother Katharine Drexel to Jules B. Jeanmard, April 23, 1933, quoted in Lynch, *Sharing the Bread in Service*, 1:267.
42 *Annual Report 1933*, Louisiana Corporation Minutes, XUA.

comfort compared to what our present so-called school desks afford."⁴³ At Scotville, seventy students shared eight desks. Pupils had to kneel on the floor to write on wooden benches.⁴⁴ Cracks in the walls, holes in the floor, poor lighting, and inadequate heating marred the Julien Hill School. Despite this, children barred from the public school system poured in.⁴⁵

Drexel also had difficulty with clerics who refused to honor their agreements to provide students with sacraments. Drexel penned many missives to Bishop Jeanmard about errant priests and asked that he insist upon more frequent services at the schools. For example, the priest in Leonville refused to visit the students at St. Leo's because he feared "the people [whites] would be jealous."⁴⁶ At Mother of Mercy in Rayne, Father Doutre did not want to rile his white parishioners by letting Black parishioners attend Mass on Sundays; instead, he offered to say Mass for the schoolchildren on Thursday. Mother Eucharia Robb, rural school supervisor, sarcastically replied, "That would be a very good arrangement if we could prevail upon the Holy Father to dispense these people from hearing Holy Mass on Sunday and transfer the obligation to Thursday." Bishop Jeanmard caught wind of the exchange and assured Mother Eucharia, "Mother, the children will have Mass on Sundays. I will see to that."⁴⁷ The diocesan priests relied on the Sunday collections to provide their livelihoods, and whatever their feelings on their Black parishioners, many bowed to the racist demands of their white churchgoers. Even when local priests fully cooperated, however, myriad problems plagued the rural schools.

---

43   Rev. R. Auclair, SSJ, to Right Rev. and Dear Bishop [Jeanmard], August 22, 1930, in *Report on Negro Work and Application for Aid Presented to the Commission for the Catholic Missions Among the Colored People and the Indians 1930*, BCIM records, series 5/2: reports and applications for aid, Diocese of Lafayette, Louisiana, reel 6, MUA.

44   Theresa V. O'Reilly, "Shakespearean Art and Jesuit Bend," *Mission Fields at Home*, September 1929, 178.

45   M. Letterhouse, "The Bayou Teche and the Prairies of Fair Opelousas," *Mission Fields at Home*, March 1929, 116.

46   Mother Katharine to My very dear daughters in the Blessed Sacrament, April 30, 1925, in *Annals of the SBS 1925*, 22:111, ASBS.

47   Mother Eucharia Robb to Mother Katharine, October 18, 1923, in *Annals of the SBS 1923*, 21:76, ASBS.

Rural schools relied upon charitable donations that dried up in hard times. During the Depression, when students often arrived at school clad in rags or stayed home because they lacked shoes, collecting tuition seemed unreasonable. Some schools assessed a nominal tuition, payable in penny increments. Though Governor Huey Long had arranged for Catholic schools to receive free textbooks starting in 1929, the poor rural schools seldom had the funds to provide additional literature for their students. Much like today, some teachers dipped into their own money to provide resources for their students. Mother Katharine wrote of one such teacher, whom she dubbed an "Xavier lay apostle," at the school in Church Point, "One of them out of her own salary, is subscribing to a modern encyclopedia, so as to give her 7th and 8th grade pupils literary information, for they have no books in the school whatsoever, except for their school books."[48] Local communities also rallied around the schools despite dire economic conditions. Parents held fairs and concerts to raise money for supplies, built furniture, and provided students with hot meals.

In addition to monetary woes, many city-educated teachers faced a language barrier, as most of the children entering their classrooms spoke Creole, a patois of French. As one of the sisters insensitively explained, "The melodious drollery and grotesqueness of this dialect are known to literary students as the mold into which much of Louisiana humorous song and verse is cast."[49] When St. Joseph's opened in Broussard in 1932, the teachers had trouble getting their students to speak *American* and announced a prize for English proficiency to inspire students to learn the language.[50] As at the Indigenous schools, teachers had to start with remedial language lessons before advancing to the suggested elementary curriculum.

Since they hesitated to turn students away, teachers also faced overcrowding. In 1929, the school in Leonville had 137 students

---

48 Mother Katharine Drexel to All Sisters, May 5, 1930, *St. Francis Xavier Prep and Convent Annals 1927–1945* (copies), XUA.

49 M. Letterhouse, "The Bayous Teche and the Prairies of Fair Opelousas," *Mission Fields at Home*, April 1929, 115.

50 "Rural Schools—Louisiana," *Mission Fields at Home*, December 1932, 47.

in a room with a single teacher; Julien Hill had 126 pupils. At St. Martinsville teachers planned for 100 students, but on the first day of school 246 students attempted to cram themselves into the two-room schoolhouse, leaving the teachers scrambling.[51] Chronic overcrowding, common to rural schools across the country, was complicated by the fact that enrollment swelled midway through the year after the public school's term for Black students ended. In a strange marriage of church and state, in some locations, teachers received public funding for part of the year while Mother Katharine paid their salaries for the rest of the time. In Scotville, for example, the school was "public four months and Catholic the other five."[52] While increased enrollments meant helping additional students, it made school administration a logistical nightmare.

In addition to chronic poverty and overcrowding, students and teachers in rural schools endured racist attacks and the bigotry of the townspeople. Most Catholic schools in the country formed in conjunction with parishes and typically had the support of both clergy and the people in the pews. The SBS rural schools, on the other hand, often lacked parish support. In 1925, the priest at Leonville explained his absence from the school, saying, "The Curè who was here before me buried a saintly, old colored woman near the graves for the whites and blessed it. He had to fly for his life, so you see one must be prudent." He asked Drexel to build a separate entrance to the church for Black parishioners, recounting an incident when a group of white men ejected a Black man who tried to receive the Eucharist at the same time as white parishioners. He explained to Mother Katharine that he believed the man had the right to receive the sacrament but that what he did was not "prudent." In the name of prudence, therefore, he advocated segregation. Drexel refused.[53] That same year in Glencoe, an integrated church, a white crowd attacked one Black boy for putting his finger in the Holy Water before a white woman and

---

51   M. Letterhouse, "St. Martinsville, LA," *Mission Fields at Home*, December 1931, 36–37.

52   O'Reilly, "Shakespearean Art and Jesuit Bend," 179.

53   Drexel to My Very Dear Daughters in the Blessed Sacrament, April 30, 1925, *Annals of SBS 1925*, 22:111–12.

another for accidently brushing past a white woman. At Church Point in 1928, teacher Theresa LeBlanc had to hide a student from a mob that threatened to kill him for an alleged impropriety with a white woman. Later the teacher spirited him away to New Orleans hidden under a blanket in her car.[54] These incidents and countless others added to the burdens of Drexel's "Lay Apostles."

Despite the difficulties, the sisters felt that the system was one of their finest achievements. Drexel frequently spoke of the program and praised the zeal of the teachers during fundraising talks. In a 1925 speech to the Carroll Club in New York City, she recounted the teachers' sacrifices and added, "I have often wondered since if a parallel case would be found amongst their fairer sisters."[55] In some of the tiny hamlets of southwestern Louisiana, the SBS and their lay teachers often provided the only education available to Black children during the 1920s and 1930s. Especially during the years of the Depression, the rural school plan provided jobs not only for teachers, but for construction workers and contractors, as well. Sr. Patricia Lynch, the congregation's historian, also points out the cultural influence the schools had on the small villages, saying, "In many a crossroad community these teachers were the only college-educated residents, black or white, and were a constant reminder to their students that they could follow the same path."[56] Heartened by the results of the system developed in the Diocese of Lafayette, the SBS employed similar plans in Tuscaloosa, Alabama, Ridge, Maryland, Cross-Roads, West Virginia, and East Texas. Though the payment of lay teachers cost the SBS more than sixty thousand dollars a year, when asked if it was worth the expense, Mother Katharine erupted, "*Is it worth while?* A look at the Tabernacle, a thought of why Christ is there, a thought suggested by the crucifix that hangs above it answers the question—'Is it worth while?'"[57]

---

54   Lynch, *Sharing the Bread in Service*, 1:268–69.
55   Mother Katherine Drexel, "Carroll Club Talk, 1925," H 10 A, box 30, folder 14, ASBS.
56   Lynch, *Sharing the Bread in Service*, 1:271.
57   "The Growth of the Congregation," *Mission Fields at Home*, October 1928, 10.

## A Catholic Rosenwald?

Inevitable comparisons arise between Drexel's foundation of a string of rural schools and the work undertaken by the Julius Rosenwald Fund. While both philanthropists deployed similar tactics, they had different aims. Julius Rosenwald, the wealthy Sears and Roebuck president, preached the gospel of a "fair chance" for Black Americans.[58] Spurred to action by inequality in Southern schools, in 1912 he started his school construction campaign by giving Booker T. Washington $25,000 to build Tuskegee offshoots in rural Alabama. Though tweaked over the years, the basic plan engineered by Washington and Rosenwald entailed giving grants to build small public schools in rural communities contingent upon the ability of the local people to match the funds. This system aimed to strengthen rural public schools by working with local communities. The "Plan for the Erection of Rural Schoolhouses" operated out of Tuskegee until 1920, when Rosenwald reorganized the foundation. Starting in 1920, Rosenwald emphasized bigger "model" schools rather than the one- and two-teacher plans that had originally been the hallmark of the program. This ideological change often put new schools out of the reach of the poorest communities. Drexel, on the other hand, exclusively built small one- to two-room buildings. In 1927, when Edwin Embree took over the helm of the Rosenwald Fund, the board phased out building grants. Rosenwald's program, which ran from 1912 to 1932, helped finance the construction of 5,358 schools.

At the most basic level, the Drexel and Rosenwald plans differed in scale. While Drexel founded and staffed twenty-three rural schools and aided an additional sixty in the state, the larger fund constructed more than sixty times as many. The Rosenwald Fund focused almost exclusively on school construction, while, in addition to building costs, Drexel also had to pay for teacher salaries each month. Additionally, she covered the expenditures associated with running fifty-one convents, forty-nine elementary schools, twelve high schools, and one university, as well as covering incidental expenses of at least another hundred schools. Drexel's empire of benevolence had a large but limited budget.

---

58  Hoffschwelle, *Rosenwald Schools*, 29.

Also, the Rosenwald Fund required matching donations from the communities, while Drexel did not.

Both Drexel and Rosenwald believed in the connection between building high-quality structures and achieving educational success. Like Rosenwald, Drexel used the finest materials when constructing her buildings because she believed that children from the poorest communities deserved quality. Though simple in comparison to the elaborate architecture of Xavier in New Orleans or St. Francis de Sales in Rock Castle, Virginia, the rural schools were designed to be buildings the community could take pride in. The school at Broussard was "delightfully airy and light," and sisters described Glencoe as "a beautiful little school."[59] Mother Katharine boasted that the school in Point-á-La Hache "is a much better schoolhouse than the whites have in this part of the country."[60] Rosenwald, too, emphasized the quality of his school designs and included modern sanitation.[61] While the schools were built to educate Black students, local white populations envied the facilities constructed by Drexel and Rosenwald. The special designation of a school as a "Mother Katharine School" or a "Rosenwald School" sent a message about its quality.

Both schools inspired community pride and a commitment to education. They differed, however, on their definitions of community. For Mother Katharine, community always meant preserving ties to the Catholic Church. Though SBS schools opened their doors to students regardless of religious creed, their purpose remained evangelization. The rural schools aimed to reclaim lapsed Catholics, and many of the sites eventually grew from mission outposts into parish churches and larger schools. Often when priests established parishes near the Mother Katharine Schools, the church took over school management, as was the case in City Price and Point-á-la-Hache. Other times, as schools grew, groups of religious sisters joined the lay teachers. When they expanded,

---

59 Report of Mother M. Eucharia on Rural Schools, letter to Mother Katharine, October 18, 1923, *Annals of the SBS*, 21:72–78.
60 Mother Katharine Drexel, "Trip to New Orleans and the Rural South 1921," H10, box 30, folder 7, ASBS.
61 Hoffschwelle, *Rosenwald Schools*, 111.

SBS sisters assumed charge of operations at Notre Dame School in St. Martinville, Our Mother of Mercy in Church Point, St. Mathilde in Eunice, and Our Mother of Mercy in Rayne.[62] The schools served as gateways for the church into rural communities.

Unlike the Rosenwald schools, which partnered with public school systems, Mother Katharine Schools intended to subvert the public system, which the SBS saw as a threat to the faith. In a letter written to the teachers and children of Little Flower of Jesus School in Ville Platte, Mother Katharine explained that the rural schools were created so all students "may be brought to know and love God with all their heart and soul." She added, "Someday you will be a saint, each of you."[63] Written during a time when many white priests would not even allow Black children in their churches, her claim that Black children would become revered saints demonstrates her belief in Catholic education as the great societal leveler. Making saints, educating children, empowering the laity, and challenging social customs all intertwined in the SBS missions.

Drexel, had she lived to see it, might have measured her success by the fact that the rural Louisiana schools produced four Black bishops: Harold R. Perry, auxiliary bishop of New Orleans, attended Sacred Heart; Raymond Caesar, bishop of Goroko, Papua New Guinea, went to St. Mathilda's in Eunice; Curtis John Guillroy, bishop of Beaumont, received his earliest education at St. Ann's in Mallet; and Leonard Olivier, auxiliary bishop of Washington, D.C., got his start at Sacred Heart in Lake Charles. Though students of all religious backgrounds flocked to the rural schools, at their heart, the Mother Katharine Schools aimed to create distinctly Catholic communities. They also served to remind the broader Catholic populace—whether it was "prudent" or not—of its duties and responsibilities to all children.

---

62 Lynch, *Sharing the Bread in Service*, 1:270–71, 2:37–51, and Butler, "History of Catholic Elementary Education for Negroes," 176.

63 Mother Katharine Drexel, "Writings #2300 Mother Katharine to Teachers and Children of Little Flower of Jesus School in Ville Platte, LA, January 14, 1943," ASBS.

CHAPTER 8

# From Spiritual to Temporal Needs

## The Evolution of the Sisters of the Blessed Sacrament and Catholic Social Justice

"SISTERS, GET OUT AND VOTE? Most of the women are too lazy to go out and vote. Are you registered?"[1] Most Reverend Albert T. Daeger's shocked response to the SBS's 1928 request to vote demonstrates the church's unease with the sisters' embrace of worldly solutions to accomplish spiritual aims. Prayer and education remained the SBS's primary weapons in their campaigns to improve the social and economic position of Black and Indigenous people, but by the 1920s and 1930s, the sisters turned to politics and media campaigns. Mother Katharine kept her involvement with the National Association for the Advancement of Colored People (NAACP) and the congregation's political lobbying quiet, and little of this work has come to light. As such, Mother Katharine is typically depicted as a demure holy woman rather than as a savvy political operator who used both prayer and petitions to advance racial justice. Mother Katharine mirrored trends in American Catholic social thought that called for Catholics to take a more active role in society. When the church did not act, however, she also used secular methods to push for reform.

### Spiritual or Temporal Needs?

The SBS was created to right societal wrongs perpetrated against Indigenous and Black communities, but Mother Katharine's published writings and speeches often focused exclusively on the work she did for the spiritual welfare of these groups. Her main busi-

---

1 Mother Stanislaus to Mother Katharine Drexel, *Annals of the SBS* 25 (1928), 214.

ness, after all, was the salvation of souls. Only after years of witnessing deplorable conditions in pueblos, bayous, and inner cities did she publicly push for reform. In 1907, Father William Ketcham, then director of the Bureau of Catholic Indian Missions, ran an article about the SBS in the *Indian Sentinel* that asserted that the congregation sought to improve the "spiritual and temporal welfare" of Black and Indigenous people. When she read an advance copy, Drexel objected to the use of the word "temporal," insisting that the order existed principally to offer spiritual aid. BCIM secretary Charles Lusk attempted change her mind, insisting, "Now, it seems to me that to insert 'spiritual' and leave out 'temporal' would not state fully the aim and scope of your work." He elaborated, "The purpose of your Community is to elevate the Indian and Negro races, and in carrying out this purpose you have established and are carrying on schools where not only religious but a secular education is given, including an industrial training." Lusk argued, "A secular and industrial training is surely temporal, and while not as essential as a religious training, it is necessary if we expect the Indians and Negroes to be fitted to become good citizens and to hold their own in the race of life." Lusk asked Drexel to change her mind about the wording, concluding, "All this being fact, and I do not think it can be gainsaid, is not your Community devoted to both the temporal and spiritual welfare of the Indians and Negroes?"[2] Drexel remained adamant that she and her sisters were above *temporal* concerns. It is not clear if she genuinely believed this or if she wanted to deflect the same type of criticism other groups—such as the St. Joseph Sisters of Peace—received when they advocated for reform.[3] She carefully guarded the congregation's reputation, which depended on the good will of the ecclesiastical authorities.

Drexel shied away from recognition of her material aid to secular groups and preferred to work in the shadows. Since her death, the church has downplayed her commitment to justice in favor of emphasizing her piety. The depiction of Drexel as a model

---

2 Charles Lusk to Katharine Drexel, January 6, 1907, BCIM records, series 1–1, box 55, folder 6, MUA.

3 Lusk had his way, but Drexel protested his decision. "The Sisters of the Blessed Sacrament for Indians and Colored People," *Indian Sentinel*, 1907, 4–18.

of personal holiness has obscured her secular activism. The Vatican's official investigation into her sanctity looked for proof of heroic spirituality instead of highlighting her worldly activities. Those interviewed about Drexel's career focused on her abdication of her social station and her fortune. Journalist Kenneth L. Woodward has pointed out that Saint Katharine Drexel's *positio*, the multivolume document testifying to her sanctity, offers scant evidence that, outside of funding segregated schools and the Bureau of Catholic Indian Missions, "Mother Drexel did or said anything of a 'heroic' or 'prophetic' nature in opposition to racial segregation or in favor of civil rights for blacks."[4] Instead, the *positio* focused on her obedience to church authority.[5]

As a result, few know about her extensive petitioning and lobbying and her financial support of the NAACP. Contrary to her image as a meek religious figure, Mother Katharine Drexel possessed a radical—or at least radically Catholic—vision of American society. Though she valued obedience, she looked outside the church and engaged with the political establishment when necessary. In 1907 Drexel hesitated to use the word "temporal," but by 1921, when the Cardinal James Gibbons announced, "And what do the Negroes and the Indians ask? Nothing but the Faith, the benefits of which you know so well," the sisters knew that faith required action.[6]

## Drexel's Political Education

Growing up in a wealthy, elite white family, Drexel understood power. She saw the necessity of cultivating political relationships to achieve holy ends. Despite her vows to remove herself from the world, she kept abreast of events in Washington. Family connections aided this effort. Her sister Louise's husband, Colonel

---

4 Kenneth L. Woodward, *Making Saints: How the Catholic Church Determines Who Becomes a Saint, Who Doesn't, and Why* (New York: Simon and Schuster, 1990), 235.
5 Cummings, *A Saint of Our Own*, 194.
6 James Cardinal Gibbons, Archbishop Dennis Dougherty, and Archbishop Patrick Hayes, "An Appeal in Behalf of the Negro and Indian Missions," *Report on Mission Work among the Negroes and the Indians*, 1921, 4.

Edward Morrell, served in the House of Representatives between 1900 and 1907. During his tenure, Morrell introduced a bill designed to prevent racial discrimination on railroads. In addition, he acted to reverse the Browning ruling in 1902 and helped win the fight to restore rations to Indigenous children in Catholic schools in 1903.[7] Drexel frequently wrote to him for advice and to keep tabs on Congress. Her older sister Elizabeth's husband, Walter George Smith, presided over the American Bar Association (ABA), represented the Southwest on the U.S. Board of Indian Commissioners, and had contacts in many levels of government. Smith, a prominent Republican, also counted President Warren G. Harding as a friend.[8] He handled much of the legal work for the SBS, including writing contracts, deeds, and agreements for novices and postulants. He also used his contacts through the ABA to help Drexel find sympathetic lawyers across the country. Her close relationships with her brothers-in-law gave her insider knowledge of action on Capitol Hill. In addition, her work with the Bureau of Catholic Indian Missions meant that she had eyes and ears in Washington.

Under the tutelage of Monsignors Joseph A. Stephan and William Ketcham, Mother Katharine developed a keen understanding of the political system. Their correspondence kept her abreast of Congressional developments.[9] The directors of the BCIM kept her well versed on government contract provisions, the use of tribal funds, the machinations of the Board of Indian Commissioners, and all legislation relating to Indigenous people. She had to use her political connections to establish St. Michael's

---

[7] Prucha, *Churches and the Indian Schools*, 66–80. For Edward Morrell's efforts, see Morell, *Rations to Indian School Children: Argument of Cong. Edward Morrell, 1903* (Washington, DC: Bureau of Catholic Indian Missions, 1903).

[8] Thomas A. Bryson, *Walter George Smith* (Washington, DC: The Catholic University of America Press, 1977).

[9] Stephan in particular was strident in his use of politics for religious reasons. In 1892, the year after Drexel formed the SBS, he engaged in all-out war with President Benjamin Harrison and published a report on the administration's purportedly anti-Catholic activities. He sent a letter to every priest in the country advising them to "take off their coats and defeat Harrison." George J. Marlin, *The American Catholic Voter: 200 Years of Political Impact* (South Bend, IN: St. Augustine's Press, 2004), 119–20.

School and Mission in Arizona.[10] Mother Katharine and the BCIM appealed to her brother-in-law to pull strings and get the SBS land deal pushed through Congress and marked as "Special."[11] Long before the Nineteenth Amendment gave her the right to vote, Drexel wielded political power. By 1900, she had been thoroughly schooled in the ways of politics both by her family and her connections at the BCIM. She even engaged in an ill-fated effort to install a family friend as U.S. surgeon general.[12]

Despite her penchant for politics, in the early years of the congregation, Drexel asked the men she worked with to assert her agenda rather than storming the capital herself. Through the early 1920s, Drexel remained wary of overt political action. In 1922, the superior of the New York convent asked Mother Katharine if she would approve of the sisters signing a petition for the Dyer Anti-Lynching Bill proposed in Congress. Hesitant to sign a public petition, Drexel wrote her brother-in-law Walter George Smith for advice. Drexel expressed unease, telling Smith, "Of course, in itself we know that lynching is a most barbarous thing, but I feel that perhaps there might be some political intrigue back of this and would not wish the Sisters to commit themselves by their signatures without being assured from you as to whether you think they should sign such a petition or not."[13] Smith's response has

---

10 See Mother Katharine Drexel to Charles Lusk, March 3, 1898; Mother Katharine Drexel to Charles Lusk, March 13, 1898; Charles Lusk to Mother Katharine Drexel, April 16, 1898: BCIM records, series 1–1, box 36, folder 17, MUA.

11 Father William Ketcham to Edward Morrell, April 21, 1902, BCIM records, series 1–1, box 42, folder 21, MUA.

12 Upon the retirement of Dr. Robert M. O'Reilly, Mother Katharine tried to lobby for a family friend, Lt. Col. Louis Bruchemin. Not only did Mother Katharine write to Senator Joel Cook of Pennsylvania, she prevailed upon Ketcham to write to President Roosevelt and a half dozen senators. Despite her best effort, Bruchemin did not receive the appointment. Mother Katharine Drexel to Fr. William Ketcham, September 11, 1908, BCIM records, series 1–1, box 60, folder 1; Fr. William Ketcham to President Roosevelt, November 19, 1908, BCIM records, series 1–1, box 60, folder 3; Mother Katharine Drexel to Fr. William Ketcham, November 11, 1908, BCIM records, series 1–1, box 60, folder 3; Fr. William Ketcham to Mother Katharine Drexel, November 12, 1908, BCIM records, series 1–1, box 60, folder 3, MUA.

13 Katharine Drexel to Walter George Smith, May 22, 1922, MMK letters, H10 A, box 26, ASBS.

been lost, but likely, Mother Katharine did not have the sisters sign to avoid damaging political entanglements.

Though some sisters expressed interest in politics during the early 1920s, it is not clear that they voted until 1928. The presidential candidacy of Catholic Alfred E. Smith spurred them, and many other Catholic sisters, to action. The archbishop of Philadelphia, Dennis Joseph Cardinal Dougherty, said Catholics had a religious duty to help elect a Catholic, and Drexel set about to do her part. In August 1928, Drexel sent a letter telling each convent to register all sisters.[14] Drexel and the General Council also allotted funds to cover the poll tax in Southern states. Every eligible sister voted.[15] The sisters took great interest in the election, pasting newspaper articles and surveys regarding the race into their annals. This foray into participatory democracy would not be their last. The SBS were not the only sisters who voted, but their turn to political participation shows that through the 1920s and 1930s, the SBS increasingly committed itself to temporal action.

## The SBS and Catholic Interracial Reform

In the 1920s, the SBS began working with Catholic interracial groups on media campaigns to better the economic and legal status of Black Americans. For instance, Mother Katharine promoted the radio program "The Interracial Hour" on the Paulist radio station WLWL. In an era when few superior generals allowed sisters access to the media, Mother Katharine asked each convent to "listen in." Mary Ewens, OP, has stated that sisters in the 1920s, 1930s, and 1940s suffered from "cloister mentality," which meant that "sisters were warned to restrict contact with the outside world as much as possible. Newspapers, radios, libraries, and so on were seen as dangerous distractions, as were various kinds of public events and meetings. The eyes of the sisters were turned inward and the world outside the content walls was full of snares."[16] While this mentality

---

14  *Annals of the SBS* 25 (1928), 212, ASBS.
15  *Annals of the SBS* 25 (1928), 214, ASBS.
16  Mother Katharine Drexel to Reverend Mother, December 12, 1932, H40, A83C, ASBS. Mary Ewens, "Women in the Convent," in Kennelly, *American Catholic Women*, 33.

seems to have been the case in many congregations, Drexel was media savvy and understood that worldly means were necessary to get out her message. The sisters' magazine frequently reprinted WLWL radio talks on issues of social justice and urged their readers to tune in. Drexel's sister Louise Morrell also appeared on the program in Mother Katharine's name in 1934 to condemn lynching, promote desegregation of Catholic schools, and speak out for economic justice.[17] In the 1930s the SBS hired Manhattan lawyer George K. Hunton to raise publicity and to break "through the curtain of prejudice and in getting a better image of the Negro across to the American public, or at least to the American Catholic public."[18] Though Mother Katharine and the sisters shunned individual attention, they understood the power of media as an agent of change.

As they turned to "natural means," Mother Katharine and the SBS supported Catholic effort at interracial reform. One of Drexel's most important collaborators was Jesuit John LaFarge. LaFarge's interest in Black Catholics stemmed from his tenure as a priest in Maryland, where he saw the effects of racism. In 1924, LaFarge engaged Mother Katharine to help him establish the Cardinal Gibbons Institute in Ridge, Maryland, an industrial school for Black students. The school closed in 1933, but LaFarge's interest in interracial reform work continued. He appealed to Drexel to aid the Federated Colored Catholics (FCC), a group dedicated to improving race relations in the church, which she did in 1933.[19]

---

17 "The Laity and the Negro Mission Field: Radio Talk by Mrs. Edward Morrell Over Station WLWL, New York City," *Mission Fields at Home*, February 1934, 68–69.
18 Hunton, *All of Which I Saw*, 55.
19 Mother Katharine to Rev. John LaFarge, SJ, November 30, 1933, Interracial Letters, box H40, A 73 C, ASBS. The Federation of Colored Catholics was founded by Dr. Thomas Wyatt Turner in 1925 to secure rights to black Catholics such as advocating for a black clergy, integration of Catholic colleges, and representation in church governance. When white priests John LaFarge and William Markoe became involved in the early 1930s, they pushed to make the group more interracial and less confrontational. In 1932 Turner was deposed by those in LaFarge's camp, and the council dissolved in 1933. While the priests felt an all-black group absolved whites from dealing with the very real racism of the church, the group's president, Dr. Turner, saw the white clerical presence as a means of

After the FCC splintered in late 1933, LaFarge created the Catholic Interracial Council (CIC), which also relied heavily on subsidies from Drexel. The CIC led interracial prayer services and meetings, sponsored lectures, and worked to desegregate Catholic colleges. It published the Manhattanville Resolutions in 1933, which called for Catholic Action on racial issues.[20]

Though she funded some of these efforts, Drexel disliked donating to committees that lacked concrete action plans. In a July 1933 meeting, Drexel repeatedly asked LaFarge exactly what the committee would do to improve the lives of Black people, and he failed to provide a clear answer. She was concerned that the committee would not produce tangible results and expressed little interest in the idea. In a memo following their meeting, LaFarge noted that Drexel would not be involved with the committee in any practical way. He complained, "Her views and methods are crystalized, and her thoughts revolve in a sphere of her own."[21] LaFarge was correct. Drexel was a woman of action, not of talk. Empowered by the proclamation of Catholic Action and social justice, Drexel used her resources to turn rhetoric into rights with or without official sanction from the Catholic Church. Her work with the NAACP represented a shift in her thinking about what it meant to serve the Black community.

## Partnership with the NAACP

The SBS had shied away from signing petitions in 1922, but a few years later they partnered with the National Association for the

---

robbing the African American Catholics of their agency. See David Southern, *John LaFarge and the Limits of Catholic Interracialism, 1911–1963* (Baton Rouge and London: Louisiana State University Press, 1996), 78, and Marilyn Wenzke Nickels, *Black Catholic Protest and the Federated Colored Catholics, 1917–1933: Three Perspectives on Racial Justice* (New York: Garland, 1988), 97–135.

20 Hunton, *All of Which I Saw*, 95. See also Thomas J. Harte, CSsR, "Catholic Organizations Promoting Negro-White Race Relations in the United States" (Ph.D. diss., The Catholic University of America, 1947). Harte suggests that the councils were primarily exclusive groups catering to educated, middle-class blacks and whites that favored gradual approaches to racial problems.

21 Rev. John LaFarge, "Memo of Conversation with Rev. Mother Katharine, Cornwells, July 15, 1933," Interracial Letters, box H 40 A, 73 C, ASBS.

Advancement of Colored People (NAACP). Drexel's connection with the NAACP originated in 1924 when Isadore Martin, president of the Philadelphia branch, wrote her a letter explaining the goals of the NAACP and asking for her help.[22] He stressed, "It is not a charitable organization but one that stands for a square deal for all men regardless of color or race." Martin added, "It is opposed to the Ku Klux Klan and furnished the data to the *New York World* which exposed the Klan. It is fighting lynching, all forms of discrimination and all forms of injustice."[23] Constantly besieged with requests for money, Drexel nonetheless sent the organization a check for twenty-five dollars, an amount roughly equal to the average worker's weekly pay. She continued small but regular donations to the Philadelphia chapter. Over time, she drew the attention of the national NAACP secretary, Walter White. Beginning in the early 1930s, Drexel and White exchanged letters, phone calls, telegrams, and visits. Though Drexel contributed annually to the NAACP, she played a significant role in three campaigns: the Scottsboro Defense, the Mississippi Flood Control Project labor investigations, and the pursuit of federal anti-lynching legislation. Close examination of these crusades reveals a shift in the SBS from spiritual to temporal action.

## SBS and the Scottsboro Defense

When the train screeched to a halt in Paint Rock, Alabama, on March 25, 1931, few could have predicted that the events of the day would launch protests, inflame the Communist Party, and arouse the passions of an elderly Catholic nun. Two white women, Victoria Price and Ruby Bates, had jumped aboard the train in Chattanooga dressed as males, along with several white men. When twenty to thirty Black men boarded the train at Stevenson, Alabama, tensions rose. The white men were either physically

---

22   Vincent P. Franklin, *The Education of Black Philadelphia: The Social and Educational History of a Minority Community, 1900–1950* (Philadelphia: University of Pennsylvania Press, 1979), 68.

23   In 1921 the *New York World* ran a series of articles exposing the Ku Klux Klan as a racist and unlawful organization. The articles aimed to destroy the Klan but had the ironic effect of causing a surge in membership. Isadore Martin to Katharine Drexel, May 29, 1924, H 80 B, box 8, folder NAACP, ASBS.

forced off the train or left of their own accord. Once off the train, they contacted the authorities in Stevenson and telephoned the police in Paint Rock, the next stop. When the train arrived, only nine Black men remained. Authorities discovered the two white women, Victoria Price and Ruby Bates, on board posing as male laborers and charged the Black men with rape. The indictment came despite Price and Bates's denials that the crime had occurred and the lack of any forensic evidence. Facts mattered little, and the nine, except for the youngest, Roy Wright, were tried, convicted, and sentenced to death in a Scottsboro courtroom.

The legal battle to free the young men lasted over a decade and reached the Supreme Court twice. The case also legitimized the Communist Party in the eyes of the Black community, as it was the International Labor Defense who first came to the aid of the young men and their families. Many who defended the Scottsboro Boys, as they came to be known, did so partly because they feared the Communist Party. NAACP secretary Walter White wrote, "There is but one effective and intelligent way in which to counteract Communist efforts at proselyting among American Negroes, and that method is drastic revision of the almost chronic American indifference to the Negro's plight."[24]

Mother Katharine's involvement started when Isadore Martin approached Drexel in June 1931, asking her to contribute to the Scottsboro Boys' Defense Fund. Martin included graphic details of the original trial to prevail upon Mother Katharine. He wrote, "When the first so-called trial came up, a noisy mob on the outside of the courthouse influenced the jury to bring a verdict of guilty. . . . When the verdict was brought in, a brass band was called in as music appropriate for a joyous holiday was played."[25] This description must have captured Drexel's attention, for to the side she scrawled, "What do you think of this?" When Martin informed her that the Rosenwald Fund would donate $1,000 a

---

24 Walter White, "The Negro and the Communists," *Harper's Magazine*, December 1931, 3–13. Also see Clarence Darrow, "Scottsboro," *Crisis*, March 1932, n.p.

25 Isadore Martin to Mother Katharine Drexel, June 5, 1931, H-80, box 8, folder NAACP, ASBS.

year for three years if they got at least four matching donations, she sent $1,000 to the NAACP Legal Defense Fund.[26]

Drexel and the SBS held up the specter of communism as a consequence of racial justice deferred. Around the time of their involvement with the Scottsboro case, the SBS published a pamphlet called *Missionaries of the Right*.[27] They warned, "Two magnetic alternatives face the intelligent American Negro of today in his pursuit of the happiness which the Constitution of his country guarantees him." On the one hand, they asserted, communism offered "social determination and social equality," but the sisters claimed that the church "also offers social determination and social equality" in addition to "something in addition to these, something more vital, more precious than either of them—a peace of spirit." The "missionaries" of communism offered freedom from oppression, a promise, the SBS warned, that appealed to Black Americans.[28] They countered, however, that the church "puts spiritual determination first and shows that the material benefits of social justice can be properly and permanently realized only through correct and adequate adjustment of each individual soul."[29] If civil rights were not granted, they predicted dire consequences.

After contributing to the fund, Drexel followed developments in the case through correspondence with Walter White and Isadore Martin. By 1934, two things about the Scottsboro case

---

26 Isadore Martin to Mother Katharine Drexel, October 8, 1931, H-80, box 8, folder NAACP, ASBS.

27 Houston, quoted in Patricia Sullivan, *Days of Hope: Race and Democracy in the New Deal Era* (Chapel Hill: University of North Carolina Press, 1996), 88.

28 In the 1930s, the Communist Party made inroads in the Black community by promising social equality and solidarity. While most African Americans did not embrace the economic tenets of socialism, they appreciated the message of respect as well as the willingness to expose the corruption of the economic and judicial system, especially in the South. See Harvard Sitkoff, *A New Deal for Blacks: The Emergence of Civil Rights as a National Issue; The Depression Decade* (New York: Oxford University Press, 1978), 143–47, and Glenda Elizabeth Gilmore, *Defying Dixie: The Radical Roots of Civil Rights 1919–1950* (New York: Norton, 2008), 15–66.

29 "Missionaries of the Right," SBS vocation booklet, ca. 1930s, H 40, A7, Social Justice, ASBS.

were clear: justice proved elusive, and the communists were gaining support. The American Scottsboro Committee, an interracial board of Protestants, Catholics, and Jews, formed in 1934 with the dual purpose of freeing the wrongly incarcerated and protesting communist involvement. Drexel joined the committee, which included fellow Catholics John LaFarge, SJ, and George Hunton, Dr. George Edmund Haynes of the Race Relations Division of the Federal Council of the Churches of Christ, Rev. Fred L. Brownless of the American Missionary Association, and William H. Davis of the *Amsterdam News*.[30] Members organized churches to raise awareness and funds to defray legal costs for the defendants. They also sponsored Scottsboro Boys Day on November 25, 1934.[31] The American Scottsboro Committee did not last long. The Communist Party urged the committee to join the Scottsboro Joint Action Committee to present a united front, but rather than join with the communists, the group disbanded in December 1935. The NAACP handled the case poorly, and the American Scottsboro Committee group accomplished little, but Drexel's public participation shows a shift in her understanding of her mission and a willingness to engage in work for justice in this world in addition to salvation in the next.[32]

---

30 "Outline of and Purpose and Plan of the American Scottsboro Committee, Inc.," H 80 B, box 8, folder NAACP, ASBS.

31 George E. Haynes, "Scottsboro Appeal," *Philadelphia Tribune*, January 17, 1935, 4; "American Scottsboro Committee Asks Public to Wait for Court Clarification of Controversy," *New Journal and Guide*, December 1, 1934, 9.

32 The defendants' ordeal did not end with the disbanding of the American Scottsboro Committee. While charges were dropped against Olen Montgomery, Willie Roberson, Eugene Williams, and Roy Wright in 1937, the others remained in jail under life sentences. Charlie Weems was paroled in 1943, Roy Wright in 1944. Clarence Norris was briefly paroled in 1944 but then re-jailed until 1946. Ozie Powell got out of jail in 1946. Haywood Patterson escaped from prison in 1948 only to be caught in Michigan in 1950, though Michigan refused to extradite him to Alabama. Patterson was arrested a few months later on an unrelated charge and died in prison on August 24, 1952. All of the men bore the stain of a rape conviction until 1976, when Governor George C. Wallace finally pardoned Clarence Norris. James R. Acker, *Scottsboro and Its Legacy: The Cases That Challenged American Legal and Social Justice* (Westport, CT: Praeger, 2008), 185. On November 21, 2013, the State of Alabama finally issued posthumous pardons for the remaining defendants.

## Mississippi Flood Control Project Investigation

In the 1930s, Mother Katharine collaborated with the NAACP to advance the economic rights of Southern laborers on the Mississippi Flood Control Project. In 1927 disaster struck the Mississippi Delta. A flood inundated 16,570,627 acres across seven states, destroyed crops worth $102,562,395, wiped out 41,487 buildings, damaged an additional 162,017 structures, displaced at least 325,554 people, and killed between 250 and 500 people.[33] These staggering numbers, however, tell only part of the story. In the aftermath of the natural disaster, lawmakers, engineers, and contractors vied to ensure such devastating flooding could never again jeopardize the Mississippi Delta. Congress transferred the authority for river reconstruction from the states to the Army Corps of Engineers and, on May 15, 1928, passed a flood control act authorizing $325 million for the Mississippi Flood Control Project.[34] The program promised to aid the South, but it did so by exploiting Black labor.

Prefiguring the large-scale public works of the New Deal, this federal project relied heavily on local contractors under the control of the U.S. War Department. Seeking to minimize costs and line their own pockets, contractors hired Black men whom they could pay less. The NAACP pronounced, "The great river down which the slaves were sold is the scene of a new and terrible slavery today. The slavery of 1932, like that before the Civil War, is rooted in the exploitation of black men's labor, the mistreatment of their bodies, and the denial to them of the primary decencies that civilization owes all human beings."[35] Though conditions

---

33   Pete Daniel, *Deep'n as It Come: The 1927 Mississippi River Flood* (Fayetteville: University of Arkansas Press, 1996), 8.

34   Daniel, *Deep'n as It Come*, 208. For a technical analysis of the works project, see House Committee on Flood Control, *Progress and Present Status of Flood Control on the Mississippi River and Its Tributaries: Hearings before the Committee on Flood Control*, House of Representatives, Seventy-Third Congress, First Session, March 30 and May 12, 1933 (Washington, DC: United States Government Printing Office, 1933).

35   Press Department of the National Association for the Advancement of Colored People, "Mississippi River Slavery... 1932," *Papers of the NAACP Part 10: Peonage and Labor and the New Deal, 1913–1939*, reel 13.

were arguably not worse than debt peonage operations in the South, the fact that federal dollars financed the project gave White and others hope of finding redress.[36] As word of deplorable treatment began to seep out of the labor camps along the river, the American Federation of Labor (AFL) launched an investigation. In December 1931, Holt Ross and Thomas Carroll of the AFL examined labor practices in the Delta, and they published their report in March 1932.[37] Backlash followed. Holt Ross lost his position with the AFL, the files related to the article were suppressed, and workers who talked to Ross and Carroll were beaten or fired.[38]

The NAACP sent activist and former Red Cross worker Helen Boardman to investigate in August 1932. She found workers reticent to speak. Nevertheless, she visited twenty-two labor camps between New Orleans and Memphis and conducted hundreds of interviews, though she omitted or changed the names of the workers in her report. Boardman found troubling practices in the Delta. Most camps instituted a twelve- to fourteen-hour workday and paid men less than ten cents per hour. Companies forced workers to spend their meager wages at company stores, which charged exorbitant prices, double or triple the market rate. Some contractors charged workers for potable water. Employees who did not buy supplies from company stores were dismissed without pay. Boardman also found that white overseers routinely whipped workers. These conditions reminiscent of slavery enraged and inspired the NAACP. Report in hand, Walter White leapt into action.

White sent copies of Boardman's report to President Herbert Hoover, Secretary of War Patrick Hurley, Attorney General William D. Mitchell, and twenty-five United States senators. Hoover did not respond but forwarded it to the War Department.

---

36 Mary White Ovington, *The Walls Came Tumbling Down* (New York: Harcourt, Brace, 1947), 245.

37 Holt Ross and Thomas Carroll, "Levees, Labor, and Liberty," *Federationist*, March 1932, 292.

38 Helen Boardman, "Report by the NAACP on Conditions on the Mississippi Flood Control Project," *Papers of the NAACP Part 10: Peonage, Labor and the New Deal, 1913–1939*, reel 13.

Secretary of War Patrick J. Hurley promised White an investigation.[39] On September 22, 1932, Brigadier General George B. Pillsbury questioned Boardman in his Washington office, but he dismissed her evidence.[40] Although the investigation was still ongoing, the NAACP believed it was "purely perfunctory and that there [would] be 'whitewashing.'"[41] White sent urgent pleas to President Hoover and Senator Robert Wagner, a liberal pro-labor and civil rights legislator representing New York.[42] Feeling pressured, Hoover tapped Robert Moton, Booker T. Washington's successor at the Tuskegee Institute, to form a committee to investigate. This committee received no funding, though, and the cause faltered.[43]

The NAACP had to gather more evidence. The difficulty, as White explained, was, "We cannot ask the poor devils down there to do this, for reprisals in the form of discharge from their jobs, beatings, and even death would be the price exacted of them."[44] Instead, the NAACP planned to send several members to infiltrate the camps. Unfortunately, the organization had run out of money. Revenue in 1932 had dropped more than $8,000 from the previous year, and by November, the NAACP had only $215 in the bank and bills exceeding $13,000.[45] White had to reduce his staff and

---

39 Patrick J. Hurley to Walter White, August 31, 1932, Papers *of the NAACP Part 10*, reel 13.

40 Quotations in this paragraph come from NAACP, "Investigation of Labor Camps Along the Mississippi Flood Control Project," September 30, 1932, Papers *of the NAACP Part 10*, reel 13.

41 Ibid.

42 Wagner served in the Senate from 1927 to 1949 and championed the causes of labor and civil rights. An enthusiastic architect of the New Deal, Wagner is best known for the Wagner Act of 1935, which legitimated labor unions and his support of the Costigan-Wagner Anti-Lynching legislation that called national attention to the crime. For a biography of Wagner, see J. Joseph Huthmacher, *Senator Robert F. Wagner and the Rise of Urban Liberalism* (New York: Athenaeum, 1968).

43 Press Bureau of the NAACP, "No Funds for Hoover Committee Probe N.A.A.C.P. Pushes Wagner Resolution," New York, November 25, 1932, Papers *of the NAACP Part 10*, reel 14.

44 Walter White to Helen G. Murray, September 30, 1932, *Papers of the NAACP, Part 6: The Scottsboro Case, 1931–1950*, reel 5.

45 Sullivan, *Lift Every Voice*, 163.

cut wages to stay afloat.⁴⁶ The NAACP issued desperate public pleas to raise the $2,500 necessary to mount the investigation in the fall of 1932, warning if they did not receive the funds "one of the greatest battles for economic justice to the Negro may be lost."⁴⁷ When the public fundraising campaign failed, White turned to Mother Katharine Drexel and her sister Louise Drexel Morrell.

In October and November 1932, White made a series of telephone calls to the Drexel sisters to discuss strategies for the investigation. Their goal, in addition to raising wages and ending the inhumane working conditions, was to increase the flow of federal dollars and jobs to Black workers in the Delta. Crunching the numbers, the NAACP stated that workers in Memphis, Vicksburg, and New Orleans were losing $1,412,226 a year—the difference between what they were being paid and the prevailing wage law. White calculated that their success could mean an additional ten million dollars in earnings over ten years.⁴⁸ In early November 1932, Walter White visited St. Elizabeth's Convent. There he met with Mother Katharine's second in command, Mother Mercedes, who gave White one thousand dollars to start the investigation. At the end of the month, Drexel sent White another check for one thousand dollars. Mother Katharine had already allocated the money for Xavier University, but when she heard of the abuses on the Mississippi Flood Control Project, she shifted funds to free up money for White. Years later, White recalled that when he spoke to her, she said, "I had promised Xavier some steel filing cases but they will have to wait another year because human lives are more important than filing cases."⁴⁹ Only a month prior to this, the new addition of Xavier had been dedicated, making 1932 one of the most expensive years in SBS history. That she found additional money for the NAACP is

---

46 "Horrors of Camps in Delta Bared: N.A.A.C.P. Report Describes Peonage," *New York Amsterdam News*, January 11, 1933, 3.

47 "NAACP Asks for $2,500 Immediately: Need Funds Right Now to Fight," *Atlanta Daily World*, September 27, 1932, 1; Walter White, "N.A.A.C.P. Asks Nation to Give It $2,500 at Once," *Afro American*, October 1, 1932, 3.

48 NAACP Press Department, "Mississippi River Slavery . . . 1932," November 1932, *Papers of the NAACP, Part 10,* reel 13.

49 Walter White to Mother Katharine Drexel, October 30, 1940, H-80, box 8, folder NAACP, ASBS.

indicative of her understanding of its importance. Louise Drexel Morrell also sent the NAACP five hundred dollars in early December. This $2,500 represented the entire budget for the dangerous infiltration operation.[50]

White wrote Mother Mercedes a few days later, saying, "I feel a greater strength for and a greater hope in the work after my visit to Cornwells Heights."[51] He told Mother Katharine, "Your prayers and your sacrifice of school equipment to supply the funds to help correct this grievous situation have brought joy and happiness where before there was only a fear that we might not be able to help those so sorely in need of help."[52] Shortly after their meeting, White contacted NAACP president Joel Spingarn, suggesting that Mother Katharine be offered a position on the board; whether they extended the offer is unclear. Drexel, though she remained an ardent supporter, never joined the board.[53] Flush with cash and raised spirits, White began to put his energies into forcing a Senate hearing. In December 1932, White sent out a press release urging individuals to write to their senators to assure passage of Senator Robert Wagner's resolution demanding an investigation into the conditions of the labor camps. Mother Katharine contacted Pennsylvania Senator David Reed, asking him to support Wagner. She also urged the sisters in Louisiana to send letters to their senators. Senator Reed responded evasively to Drexel, so she took him to task in January 1933 and applied further pressure.[54]

Roy Wilkins, then the assistant secretary of the NAACP, used Drexel's money to infiltrate the camps. Upon his return to New

---

50  In 1932 $2,500 was a considerable sum. The average annual income in the United States that year was $3,006.05. Internal Revenue Service, *Statistics of Income for 1932* (Washington, DC: Government Printing Office, 1934), 65.
51  Walter White to Mother Mercedes, November 4, 1932, box H-80, NAACP, ASBS.
52  Walter White to Mother Katharine Drexel, November 7, 1932, H-80, box 8, folder NAACP, ASBS.
53  Walter White to Joel Spingarn, November 5, 1932, *Papers of the NAACP, Part 1*, reel 25.
54  Walter White to Mother Katharine Drexel, January 16, 1933, H-80, box 8, folder NAACP, ASBS.

York, he regaled Mother Katharine with a vivid description of his adventures.⁵⁵ Wilkins embarked on his journey with George S. Schuyler, an investigative journalist from the *New York Evening Post*. They traveled to Memphis, where they changed into work clothes and attempted to sneak into the Delta. Simply changing garments, however, did not make these educated men from New York City blend in.⁵⁶ The team experienced a setback when Vicksburg police arrested Schuyler on December 29. Authorities released him, but they warned him "to leave town without waiting for the next train."⁵⁷ Wilkins and Schuyler reconnected in January and visited nine camps before police once again discovered them and commanded them to leave Mississippi. Wilkins expressed disappointment to Mother Katharine that the men in the camps were "reluctant to discuss this phase of life (brutality) in the camps, since they were in peril of retaliatory action." Despite the awful conditions, the workers did not want to jeopardize their only source of income. Wilkins told Drexel, "They know they are being exploited, but many of them cannot help themselves. They must eat and they must have a place to sleep." He did find, however, that "the people are hoping and praying for some power outside their own area to expose their condition and rectify the evils to which they are subjected."⁵⁸ Wilkins believed that his clandestine journey would satisfy the commission's appetite for specifics.⁵⁹

On January 10, 1933, Senator Wagner introduced Senate Resolution 300, "Authorizing Investigation of Labor Conditions Prevailing upon the Mississippi Flood-Control Project." The resolution passed and went to the Senate Finance Committee. Members of the committee tried to block the investigations, so on February 10, Wagner again went before the Senate and asked for action on the

---

55 Wilkins also published his findings in the NAACP organ the *Crisis*. Roy Wilkins, "Mississippi Slavery in 1933," *Crisis*, April 1933, 81–82.

56 "Horrors of Camps in Delta Bared," *New York Amsterdam News*, January 11, 1933, 3.

57 "Dixie Policemen Missed $22 in Schuyler Sock," *Afro American*, January 21, 1933, 8.

58 Roy Wilkins to Mother Katharine Drexel, January 14, 1933, H-80, box 8, folder NAACP, ASBS.

59 Wilkins also published an account of his trip; see Wilkins, "Mississippi Slavery in 1933," *Crisis*, April 1933, 81–82.

resolution.⁶⁰ The Finance Committee slashed the investigation budget, but the watered-down resolution passed on February 22, and a committee was named.⁶¹ Thanks to the pressure applied by the NAACP and its supporters like the Drexel sisters, the Senate hearings proved unnecessary. Realizing that the Department of War did not want to undergo such scrutiny, Secretary of War George H. Dern contacted White and promised reform.⁶² Further, Dern promised that the War Department would inspect the labor camps to check for compliance. June marked further good news for the organization, as a clause prohibiting discrimination by race, creed, or color was placed in the $3.3 billion Public Works Program.

Investigation of the new Contractors' Code showed its limitations, though. It included a Grandfather Clause that stated that in locations where the minimum wage was less than forty cents an hour on July 15, 1932, it would now be thirty cents an hour.⁶³ This allowed contractors to continue paying low wages in the South. In addition, the new code did not pertain to laborers on emergency projects such as levee building. Drexel learned the details of the new code while traveling in the West, and she sent a hasty telegram to Mother Mercedes asking her to forward a message to Franklin Roosevelt. Drexel informed the president:

> I hereby protest against the discriminatory provisions of the Contractors' Code which has been just submitted to the NRA because it does not in any way benefit or improve the condition of the thirty thousand Negro laborers on the Mississippi Flood Control project. . . . We rely on you to see that the tenth part of our population shall not be discriminated against in the New Deal and that your efforts to give everyone the benefit of shorter hours and a living wage be not frustrated.⁶⁴

---

60   *Congressional Record, Senate*, February 10, 1933, 76:3750.

61   *Congressional Record, Senate*, February 22, 1933, 76:4691–4692, and *Congressional Record, Senate*, vol. 77, part 2, 1321–22.

62   Quoted in Walter White to Mother Katharine, June 6, 1933, *NAACP Papers, Part 10*, reel 14.

63   "NAACP Fights Dixie Levee Work Code," *Afro American*, September 23, 1933, 14.

64   Mother Katharine Drexel to Franklin Roosevelt, September 16, 1933, box H-80, NAACP, ASBS. Response from the White House came in the form of

The pressure on Washington paid off, and conditions improved. Wages rose to forty cents per hour, and workers were guaranteed a thirty-hour work week.[65] In October 1933, the board of directors of the NAACP drafted a formal resolution thanking Mother Katharine and Louise Morrell for their participation in the project. It read in part, "Due to their generosity . . . some 30,000 men instead of working from sixty to ninety hours a week for nine dollars will receive a minimum of twelve dollars a week for thirty hours of work, an increase of between $75,000 and $90,000 per week."[66] White promised Drexel that the work would continue and that he planned on following up to make sure contractors were obeying the new laws.[67]

The following summer, White reported back to Mother Katharine that he noted improvements in camp conditions after making his own trip to Delta. He told Drexel, "I know that you would have been happy indeed could you have seen as we did the results of the work which you made possible. We found that the thirty-hour week was being strictly enforced. We also found that the minimum wage of forty cents an hour is being rigidly adhered to."[68]

---

a letter from A. Forbush, the chief of the Correspondence Division of the National Recovery Administration, who politely thanked her for her telegram and said, "We have noted with interest your protest concerning the Contractor's Code, and we are routing your letter to the Deputy Administrator in charge, where we are sure it will have due weight." A. Forbush to Mother Katharine Drexel, September 20 1933, box 40 A, folder 83 c, ASBS. Publicly, Roosevelt responded to Drexel, the NAACP, and others, saying, "It is not the purpose of this Administration to impair Southern industry by refusing to recognize traditional differentials." Quotation in Raymond Wolters, *Negroes and the Great Depression: The Problem of Economic Recovery* (Westport, CT: Greenwood, 1970), 145.

65 "Levee Camp Workers to Get Higher Pay, Shorter Hours: Payroll Rise of $75,000 Weekly," *Pittsburgh Courier*, October 14, 1933, A1.

66 Walter White to Mother Katharine, October 18, 1933, *Papers of the NAACP, Part 10*, reel 14. While the board knew of Drexel's involvement with the campaign, Drexel refused to let White publicly acknowledge her role. Though he asked several times to give her credit for her help, she always demanded that he keep her involvement secret.

67 Walter White to Mother Katharine Drexel, November 28, 1933, *Papers of the NAACP, Part 10*, reel 14.

68 Walter White to Mother Katharine Drexel, July 10, 1934, *Papers of the NAACP, Part 10*, reel 14.

He also noted fewer company stores, better sanitation, and more hygienic living and working conditions. In a typically understated response, Mother Katharine explained that she acted because "it seems only just."[69] The following year she reported to White, "I am happy to have been able to aid the worthy cause and thank God that some good has come to our people through your efforts to obtain relief so greatly needed."[70]

## SBS Joins Anti-Lynching Campaign

Better working conditions meant little, however, when Black men and women lived in fear of their lives. Overcoming her earlier fear of political entanglements, Drexel joined the fight to pass the Costigan-Wagner Anti-Lynching Bill in 1934, despite Catholic opposition to the legislation. In 1930, for example, an editorial for the Jesuit weekly *America* stated that while Catholics opposed lynching on moral principle, the real solution for the problem "cannot be had at the hands of a legislature" but instead would come with the reintroduction of religion into schools.[71] By late 1934, however, Drexel's experience on the Mississippi Flood Control had shown her the power of the federal government to make change, and she endorsed the Costigan-Wagner Bill.

In December 1934, White wrote Drexel with details of the brutal lynching of Claude Neal that had occurred in Florida on October 26.[72] The case reanimated the anti-lynching movement, and White hoped to use it to push a bill through the Senate. He asked Drexel for money to print a pamphlet to send to 100,000 religious leaders. Drexel wrote a check. In addition, she engaged

---

69 Mother Katharine Drexel, February 24, 1933, *Papers of the NAACP*, Part 10, reel 14.
70 Mother Katharine Drexel to Walter White, July 23, 1934, *Papers of the NAAP*, Part 10, reel 14.
71 "Investigating Lynching," *America*, October 18, 1930, 30.
72 Neal had been kidnapped in Florida by an Alabama mob, which cut off his fingers and toes, castrated him, and then made him eat his genitals. The proceeded to torture him with a red-hot poker and finally hanged him on a tree near the county courthouse. The brutality of the lynching bought the debate over federal legislation into the forefront. See Sitkoff, *A New Deal for Blacks*, 286–95.

the entire congregation in the fight. On Christmas Eve letters went to each house asking the superior to write a personalized letter to President Roosevelt in support of the anti-lynching bill.[73] These letters asked the president how they could hope to educate patriotic Black girls and boys if he refused to condemn atrocities against them. The letter from Xavier Prep in New Orleans stated, "It is our daily effort to instill in them [Black students] loyalty and devotion to our beloved country. This is made a very difficult task when such events occur as the recent torturing and lynching of a Negro by a mob of white people in Florida."[74] Mother Juliana's letter from Sacred Heart School in Lake Charles, Louisiana, expressed similar themes: "Every day I hear the Negro children in Sacred Heart School . . . saluting the American Flag. Their soft voices 'pledge allegiance to the flag . . . with liberty and justice for all.' In the name of JUSTICE I beg you to use your mighty influence for the prompt passage of Congress of the Costigan-Wagner Anti-Lynching Bill."[75] The sisters all questioned how the president could expect them to produce loyal American citizens if he did not protect their students' fundamental human rights.

Taking a different tack, the letter from Corpus Christi Convent in New Orleans appealed to religion and decency to urge the passage of the bill. The letter told Roosevelt of the 1,400 students attending the school and pleaded, "In their name, in the name of our common humanity, and in the name of the Divine Child, whose Birthday we celebrate tomorrow, I beg you to urge upon Congress the speedy passage of the Costigan Wagner Anti-Lynching Bill."[76] Letters from St. John the Baptist in Montgomery and from Xavier University also appealed to the president's morality and even his vanity; the Xavier letter implored, "In these days which try men's souls, the reputation is justly yours that no

---

73 Motherhouse to Mother M. Dorothea at Xavier Prep, December 24, 1934, H 40, B 5, box 2, Anti-Lynching Bill, ASBS.

74 Xavier Prep to Franklin Roosevelt, December 24, 1934, H 40, B 5, box 5, Anti-Lynching Bill, ASBS.

75 Mother Juliana of Sacred Heart School, Lake Charles, Louisiana, to Franklin Roosevelt, December 24, 1934, H 40 B, box 5, Anti-Lynching Bill, ASBS.

76 Mother Camilla of Corpus Christi Convent, New Orleans, to Franklin Roosevelt, December 24, 1934, H 40 B, box 5, Anti-Lynching Bill, ASBS.

request brought to you is disregarded."⁷⁷ In addition to the letters to the president, Drexel asked each superior of a local house to contact their congressmen. Another letter to the White House and telegram followed from the motherhouse.⁷⁸ Despite pressure from the SBS and many other groups, the bill failed. Though the NAACP and other groups continued to push for the anti-lynching bill for more than a decade, Congress failed to enact federal anti-lynching legislation until the Emmett Till Act of 2021. Still, the work in the 1930s drew attention to the crisis and embarrassed the South; as a result, lynching declined.⁷⁹

Drexel was not the only Catholic to advocate for the bill. Father Gillard, a Josephite from Baltimore, sent letters to hundreds of parish priests to urge them to support the NAACP in the initiative, and the newly formed Catholic Interracial Council also spoke up for Costigan-Wagner. The Catholic hierarchy, however, did not advocate for the legislation. Drexel's financial contributions and the SBS letter writing campaigns put them in the minority of Catholics willing to take a public stand.

## Xavier as NAACP Recruiting Ground

SBS involvement with the NAACP also influenced Xavier students. In 1935, White sent Daisy Lampkin, the field director of the NAACP, to Xavier University on a recruitment drive. They eagerly responded, and twenty-three students became an integral part of New Orleans' NAACP junior division. Xavier students took on leadership positions in the organization, including first vice president, first assistant secretary, and assistant treasurer; another student garnered a space on the executive board.⁸⁰ The *Xavier Herald* reported, "In her talk Mrs. Lampkin made frequent

---

77  President Xavier University to Franklin Roosevelt, December 24, 1934, H 40, A 7, box 3 C, Interracial Letters from Sister Katharine Drexel, ASBS.
78  *Annals of the SBS 1935*, 14, ASBS.
79  Sitkoff, *A New Deal for Blacks*, 281. For a complete history of the fight for anti-lynching legislation, see Robert L. Zangrando, *The NAACP Crusade against Lynching, 1909–1950* (Philadelphia: Temple University Press, 1980).
80  "Xavier Students Well Represented in N.A.A.C.P.," *Xavier Herald*, May 1935, 1.

references to the noted Dr. DuBois and our own Reverend Mother Katharine Drexel who, she said, was one of the most energetic and consistent contributors to the support of the Association and one of its most noteworthy members."[81] Xavier frequently hosted NAACP meetings, and Walter White thanked Drexel for the hospitality he always received on campus.[82] Though she saw prayer as her primary weapon against the evils of racism, Mother Katharine knew that practical methods such as protest and media campaigns must be used, as well.

On November 13, 1958, several years after Mother Katharine's death, the Catholic bishops distributed a letter calling for a celebration of Mother Katharine's birthday. In response, Roy Wilkins, who succeeded White as the executive secretary of the NAACP, mailed a letter to the convent offering the NAACP's official thanks for Mother Katharine's role in the campaigns of the 1930s. Wilkins stated, "Her spirit is with all who seek to do right and who reach out with love and helpfulness to their fellow men." He concluded, "She was a believer that a determination upon the right and a follow-up in faith and prayer and earnest work would accomplish the goals sought—not overnight but surely."[83] Wilkins understood Drexel. Neither she nor the Sisters of the Blessed Sacrament were radicals in the traditional sense of the word. The SBS wore the heavy habit of the church. They professed their vows to a hierarchical and patriarchal institution. They lived within the rules of a rigid society that valued white supremacy over justice. Yet, over time they began using their voices to call for justice and took senators and presidents to task, even while most in the church sat on the sidelines. Drexel and the Sisters of the Blessed Sacrament labored in the shadows of the nascent Civil Rights movement. They did not lead campaigns; they paid for them. They did not march in the streets; they wrote letters. They did not publicize their work; they prayed, and they voted.

---

81 "The Field Director of the N.A.A.C.P. Visits Students; Mrs. Daisy Lampkin Gives Spirited Talk on Race Progress," *Xavier Herald*, May 1935, 2.

82 Walter White to Mother Katharine Drexel, May 16, 1938, H 80 A, folder NAACP, ASBS.

83 Roy Wilkins to Mother Mary Timothy, November 25, 1958, box H-80, ASBS.

CHAPTER 9

# "These Kluxes Are All Wrought Up"

## Battling the "Catholic Problem" and Conflicting Visions of America

MOTHER KATHARINE liked to tell audiences that she entered the religious life because she experienced "the call of God and country."[1] Her seemingly innocuous vision created strong backlash. A few months after the founding of the Sisters of the Blessed Sacrament, Father Augustus Tolton, one of the first Black priests, wrote to Mother Katharine, commiserating with her over the hostility they both faced, reporting, "The south is looking on with angry eyes, the north in many places is criticizing every act, just as it is watching every move I make. . . . They watch us, just the same as the Pharisees did our Lord. They watched him."[2] Today Mother Katharine's face adorns stained glass windows and 24 Carat gold holy medals, but when she began training sisters to combat the effects of bigotry and challenge conceptions of who was worthy of American citizenship, she did something unpopular and dangerous. Her sainthood has erased the risk inherent in her work. In a 2001 reference work on Catholic women, Drexel is referred to as one of the "good women" in Catholic history, a statement that belies the controversial nature of her work.[3] The SBS outreach to Black Americans caused outrage from many sources—mainstream Protestants, Black Americans, poor white Catholics, and the Ku Klux Klan.

---

1 Mother Katharine Drexel, "Since the Beginning," 1922, Collated Writings, MMK talks, H 10J86, vol. 28, folder 1, ASBS.
2 Quotation in Davis, "God of Our Weary Years," 33.
3 Paula Kane, "General Introduction," in *Gender Identities in American Catholicism*, ed. Paula Kane, James Kenneally, and Karen Kennelly (Maryknoll, NY: Orbis, 2001), xxii.

## Battling Anti-Catholicism

Dubbed "the last acceptable prejudice" by Jesuit scholar Mark Massa, anti-Catholicism has a long history in the United States. The Sisters of the Blessed Sacrament regularly found themselves in communities that distrusted the church and regarded their vocations as sinister. While the U.S. Constitution prohibits the establishment of an American church, for years the nation cherished a Protestant civil religion, which meant other religions were perceived as un-American.[4] Mocked as a hierarchical and superstitious relic of a European past, Catholicism did not have a public platform on which to push for social reform. The First Vatican Council's 1870 decree of papal infallibility gave Protestants further ammunition against the church. Social gospel adherents such as Josiah Strong labeled Catholics a threat. Strong's arguments stemmed from the notion that Catholics maintained loyalty to a foreign pope as well as a dislike of public schools. He explained, "When, therefore, the Catholic hierarchy and press assert that the only way to make a good Catholic out of a child is to keep him out of the public school and separate him from American children, it is an acknowledgement that Romanism is un-American and represents an alien civilization."[5] Nativist groups arose in the 1880s. By 1895, the largest anti-Catholic organization, the American Protective Association, boasted 500,000 members.

Anti-Catholic rhetoric and literature peaked in the first three decades of the twentieth century. Newspapers such as the *Liberator* and the *Menace* arrived on thousands of American doorsteps each week, spreading such vitriol as "A Menace Battle Hymn," which urged vigilance on Protestants for "Rome never sleeps—she changes not, / Her creed has ever been a plot / 'Gainst human Liberty / She dulls the conscience, dwarfs the mind, / with superstition's fetters binds / All souls that own her sway."[6] Catholics,

---

4   Mark S. Massa, SJ, *Anti-Catholicism in America: The Last Acceptable Prejudice* (New York: Crossroad, 2001), 3.

5   Josiah Strong, *Our Country, Its Possible Future, and Its Present Crisis*, rev. ed. (New York: Baker and Taylor, 1891), 97.

6   Quotation in Justin Nordstrom, *Danger on the Doorstep: Anti-Catholicism and American Print Culture in the Progressive Era* (Notre Dame, IN: University of Notre Dame Press, 2006), appendix, n.p.

these papers asserted, could not be true Americans. Catholics such as the Sisters of the Blessed Sacrament who sought to Americanize others were looked at with suspicion and contempt. What could people beholden to a papal monarchy know of democracy?

As Catholics sought to assert themselves politically in the 1920s, anti-Catholicism grew more virulent. The church, sisters included, countered by stressing its place in American history. The 1913 SBS entry in a book designed to help young women discern which congregation they wanted to join called the Sisters of the Blessed Sacrament a "distinctly American congregation."[7] Drexel's first biographer felt the need to foreground Mother Katharine's American bona fides, offering readers reassurance: "This is her story, the story of a loyal American whose roots go back to the earliest days of American history and whose life and deeds may continue to affect generations of Americans yet unborn."[8] Growing up in Philadelphia during the nation's centennial had a profound impact on Drexel, and she took pride that her Catholic family draped their house in the largest flag on the street.[9] Mother Katharine and her ilk believed that Catholics had something to offer American society—they would Americanize others. This assertive Catholicism made the nativist Anglo-Saxon Protestant population anxious and paved the way for conflict, for, as one historian has put it, "Being fully Catholic and fully American was not for the fainthearted."[10]

Anti-Catholic organizations viewed all members of the church with varying degrees of mistrust, but they reserved a special hatred for priests and nuns. The anti-Catholic press proclaimed them guilty of treason and wrote about revolting acts of lasciviousness. Many viewed religious sisters as miscreants perverting notions of True Womanhood. Early nineteenth-century nuns feared wearing

---

7  Dehey, *Religious Orders of Women in the United States*, 298.
8  Duffy, *Katharine Drexel*, 15. Duffy repeatedly refers to Drexel's unique American spirit, saying, "She loved God, she loved America. She wanted the American Indian and Colored to be drawn to God and to share all the privileges of life in this land of the free." Ibid., 99.
9  Burton, *Golden Door*, 39.
10  Edward R. Kantowicz, *Corporation Sole: Mundelein and Chicago Catholicism* (Notre Dame, IN: University of Notre Dame Press, 1983), 32.

their habits in public and sometimes traveled clandestinely. Heated discourse flared into violence in 1834, when a mob burned and desecrated Mount Benedict, an Ursuline convent in Charlestown, Massachusetts.[11] The publication of inflammatory (and falsified) convent exposés such as Maria Monk's *Awful Disclosures of the Hotel Dieu Nunnery*, which sold more than 300,000 copies before the Civil War, cast religious sisters as treacherous and licentious women.[12] Commendable service in the Civil War raised the status of religious sisters in the years that followed, but firebrands such as Georgia populist Tom Watson kept images of vice-ridden nuns in the public eye well into the twentieth century. Watson, despite sending his own daughter to a convent school, alternately labeled the convent a dungeon or a house of prostitution.[13] The 1919 publication of Helen Jackson's *Convent Cruelties, or My Life in a Convent*, further fanned the flames of hatred against nuns.[14] Catholic sisters often had to combat fear and prejudice when they ventured out of the convent.[15] If all sisters faced discrimination, habited white women living in Black neighborhoods and visiting Black homes like the SBS attracted hostility and prejudice.

## Fear and Anger from the Black Community

After the failure of St. Katharine's in New Orleans, the SBS made it a policy to make sure they were welcome before they moved in. Nevertheless, when the SBS moved into a new city, they often encountered fear and hostility from their new Black neighbors. Sisters reported that children in Montgomery, Alabama, ran and

---

    11   See Nancy Lusignan Schultz, *Fire and Roses: The Burning of the Charlestown Convent, 1834* (New York: Free Press, 2000).

    12   Maria Monk, *Awful Disclosures of the Hotel Dieu Nunnery*, ed. Ray Allen Billington (Hamden, CT: Archon, 1962 [facsimile of the 1836 edition]).

    13   Thomas E. Watson, *The Inevitable Crimes of Celibacy: The Vices of Convents and Monasteries, Priests and Nuns* (Thompson, GA: Press of the Jeffersonian Pub. Co., 1916), 16–17, 21–22.

    14   Kelly J. Baker, *Gospel According to the Klan: The KKK's Appeal to Protestant America, 1915–1930* (Lawrence: University of Kansas Press, 2011), 142.

    15   Andrew S. Moore, *The South's Tolerable Alien: Roman Catholic in Alabama and Georgia 1945–1970* (Baton Rouge: Louisiana State University Press, 2007), 1, 12, 25.

hid from them because they believed the sisters would cause their teeth to fall out.[16] Having never seen nuns before, the children thought the habited sisters were ghosts and otherworldly spirits. In 1917, the priest in Beaumont, Texas, informed Mother Katharine, "The colored are a little afraid to meet the Sisters," but he consoled, "They will come gradually."[17] He also noted that the families that attended Blessed Sacrament Parish faced "the taunts of the ministers and their devotees."[18] He noted that neither the Black nor the white population knew quite what to make of the enterprise and blamed all problems on "the unusualness in the city to have a Catholic school for the Colored."[19] In Nashville, Black ministers used their pulpits to rail against the sisters and tried to get their congregations to shun the Catholic school.[20] The sisters combated these misconceptions by walking the streets, passing out flyers, and visiting homes. Black parents might have had prejudices against Catholic nuns, but their desire to educate their children trumped their fears of a Roman conspiracy or ghoulish nuns.

In the North, where the color line was less explicit, the Sisters of the Blessed Sacrament faced harsher opposition from the Black community. Some in the Black press accused them of creating segregation where none had existed before and disparaged them in the papers. For example, the *Chicago Defender* ran an angry piece in April 1913 when the SBS opened St. Monica's School. The headline screamed, "Catholics Must Not Separate Races in Schools: Recent Idea of This Heretofore Broad-Minded Religious Body to 'Jim Crow' the Races in Their Schools Does Not Please the Masses."[21] The *Defender* resented the imposition of separate schools especially, as Illinois public schools did not segregate. The writer insisted, "We are of the same tongue, having no special

---

16   Lynch, *Sharing the Bread in Service*, 1:198.
17   Alexis LaPlante to Mother Katharine Drexel, August 27, 1917, H10B, box 22, folder 21, ASBS.
18   Alexis LaPlante to Mother Katharine Drexel, August 9, 1915, H10B, box 22, folder 21, ASBS.
19   Alexis LaPlante to Mother Katharine Drexel, December 18, 1917, H10B box 22, folder 21, ASBS.
20   Duffy, *Katharine Drexel*, 260.
21   "Catholics Must Not Separate Races in Schools," *Chicago Defender*, April 5, 1913, 1.

desire to be anything other than Americans."²² Placing blame on Father John S. Morris for segregating the mission and thus starting "Jim Crowism in Illinois," the *Defender* demanded that the archbishop investigate. The archbishop, however, four years later made unofficial policy official when he announced, "Now I desire St. Monica's to be reserved entirely for the Colored Catholics of Chicago. . . . All other Catholics of whatever race or color are to be requested not to intrude."²³ While the Diocese of Chicago was divided into territorial parishes of roughly a square mile each, in reality, parishes formed around ethnic lines. In 1916, 65 percent of Chicago's Catholics worshiped in ethnic parishes.²⁴ The practice of separating parishioners by ethnicity made sense to many Catholics, but the *Defender* resented the imposition of the color line, since the establishment of St. Monica's meant Black students could no longer attend nearby St. James's School. Black Catholics had not received much of a welcome at St. James because white opposition kept many Black students from enrolling. Still, the SBS built a segregated school where one had not existed, and this led the white school to kick out Black students. While she did not leave behind a specific explanation, one can infer that Mother Katharine built schools like St. Monica's in Chicago because she thought more students would enroll in Catholic school if they were not treated like second-class citizens. Evidence does show that SBS schools filled quickly once they were built. Within a few years, the *Defender* had altered its position. In 1919, it ran a story announcing, "The good Sisters of this society do great work throughout the country for children. All the Catholic children should be sent to St. Monica School."²⁵ By 1925 the school had an enrollment of more than 1,000 pupils, and the SBS built three more schools in the city.²⁶ Though they resented the church's move to segregation, many Black parents swallowed their anger to get their children a good education.

---

22   Ibid.
23   "St. Monica's Church Again the Scene of Discrimination," *Chicago Defender*, November 17, 1917, 1.
24   Kantowicz, *Corporation Sole*, 82.
25   "St. Monica's Catholic School Opens Again, Tuesday, Sept. 2," *Chicago Defender*, August 30, 1919, 17.
26   Hoy, *Good Hearts*, 89.

## White Catholic Opposition

While Black Catholics sometimes took umbrage with the Sisters of the Blessed Sacrament, whites were the primary source of opposition. Mother Katharine knew that many found her interracial work distasteful. In the novitiate instructions, she warned incoming postulants, "Our work in the eyes of the idiot world is a dishonorable one. A certain stigma falls upon those who choose it." She reassured them, however, "But in God's eyes, it bears a mark of high nobility. In the eyes of Jesus hanging on the cross it is more than honorable, it is sweetly divine."[27] The thought of heavenly approbation, however, did not save the sisters from worldly malice.

One of the first attacks on the congregation came from white Catholics who believed that Mother Katharine was wasting her fortune on people who did not deserve it. In 1891, the Memphis publication *Adam: The Catholic Journal of the New South* wrote an editorial criticizing Drexel for giving money to blacks at the expense of "neglected and suffering white people." The editors argued, "This negro conversion is all well enough in theory for Northerners to descant upon, but it assumes quite a different aspect in cold reality to those who know where of they speak." They contended, "It is a waste of time and money to endeavor to inculcate the doctrines of Catholicity into the cranium of a full grown darkey."[28] On a 1904 trip through the South, Mother Katharine encountered a priest who asked her about her work. When she told him about the SBS, he responded, "It's not so bad, I suppose, with the Indians, but the other fellows can't keep the Faith." She retorted, "They are not one bit worse than those Our Lord and His Apostles preached to."[29] The racist priest's attitude prevailed in the church.

The South did not have a monopoly on complaints, however. In 1894, a few years after the congregation's foundation, Father Walter Eliot, a priest from New York City who had peti-

---

27 "The Sisters of the Blessed Sacrament for Indians and Colored People," *Indian Sentinel*, 1907, 13.
28 Reprinted in *American Catholic Tribune*, February 7, 1891, 2.
29 Burton, *Golden Door*, 187.

tioned Drexel to aid his mostly white congregation, angrily remembered her refusal, recalling that "she said in effect 'no poor white trash need apply.' Only black and red are the team they [the SBS] will back."[30] Despite the fact that the name of her congregation indicated that they sought to aid Black and Indigenous people, he felt entitled to her money. She responded to the criticism of an unnamed priest, saying, "Do you think, Rev. Father, that I have no charity in my heart for the whites? You are mistaken, I wish them all temporal & spiritual blessings, but not at the expense in any age or time of the poorest of God's creatures in the United States."[31] Many Catholics believed Mother Katharine had abandoned the white race, and Drexel had to defend herself from the charge of being a race traitor. Hostility from her coreligionists, however, paled in comparison to that from non-Catholic sources.

**Threats to the Congregation**

A few months after her profession, a reporter asked Mother Katharine if she anticipated trouble given the controversial nature of her work, and she replied, "I presume we will find some obstacles in our way, but we expect this. Our Lord found them while on earth sowing the seeds of the Gospel and we can hardly hope to escape what he did not."[32] While she responded piously to the question, she took practical precautions. The celebration of the laying of the cornerstone of the motherhouse in July 1891 caused a stir in Philadelphia. The day before the ceremony a worker found a stick of dynamite near the dais, and rumors of an attack on the convent swirled around town. Mother Katharine employed a plainclothes policeman to keep an eye out for trouble. Her architect, Charles M. Burnes, crafted a fake box of explosives to warn people away from the dais. While the motherhouse remained safe, the close call sent a message to the first sisters that their work would be unpopular.[33] It would not be the last time the mother-

---

30 Quoted in Hoy, *Good Hearts*, 87–88.
31 Mother Katharine Drexel, *Writings 3161*, undated but pre-1891, ASBS.
32 "St. Michael's Convent, It Is Surrounded by Trees and Flowers," *American Catholic Tribune*, September 12, 1891, 1.
33 Lynch, *Sharing the Bread in Service*, 1:53.

house came under attack: a 1904 break-in frightened the sisters so badly that they bought two .38 caliber revolvers and a police whistle to protect the chapel, and in July 1926, the Ku Klux Klan burned a cross by the convent grounds.[34]

## Not in My Back Yard: Neighborhoods Block SBS Plans

Most opposition was less dramatic than threats to blow up the motherhouse. It often came from bankers and men in nice suits. Whites who did not want Black schools in their neighborhoods complicated Mother Katharine's real estate transactions. When Drexel sent a priest to approach a bank for a loan to build a school, "the banker said he would have to know on what property the mortgage was to be placed, and when Father told him its location, the man said he would not have any 'nigger' school in that locality."[35] They struggled to find acceptable places to construct schools because Drexel insisted on building in well-respected neighborhoods. By doing this, Mother Katharine asserted that Black students had a right to occupy important places in city landscapes. As such, Drexel resorted to subterfuge and third-party buyers.

A detailed examination of the foundation of Immaculate Mother School in Nashville, Tennessee, demonstrates the hostility SBS work engendered and highlights Mother Katharine's skillful handling of controversy. In 1905, Drexel decided to purchase Mile End, a spacious antebellum mansion located at Central and Seventh Avenue for her new Nashville school. Bishop Thomas Byrne heard grumblings from the neighbors and took precautions to disguise the sisters' plans. When Mother Katharine and Sister M. Josephine McLoughlin traveled to Nashville to meet with Bishop Byrne to discuss the proposition, the prelate escorted them to the property in an enclosed carriage. They had to view the house through half-closed blinds, fearing that onlookers would glimpse their habits and surmise their plans. The nuns only had a few minutes to assess the property from across the street before

---

34 *Original Annals of the SBS 1904–1905*, 41, ASBS.
35 Mother Katharine to the Sisters of the Blessed Sacrament, May 13, 1921, ASBS.

the bishop felt it prudent to spur on the horses lest the party draw attention to itself.[36]

Although their harried circumstances meant the sisters got only a cursory glance at the property, Drexel decided to purchase it for $25,000.[37] Fearing that the owner, Samuel Keith, would not sell to the sisters, especially if he knew it would be used for a school for Black girls, Drexel conducted the transaction through a purchasing agent, Thomas J. Tyne, who then transferred the building title to the congregation.[38] The *Nashville Banner* uncovered the real owners of the story and ran a story on February 13 about the new school, which would offer academic and industrial work to Black girls, and controversy erupted. When he realized to whom he had sold his house, the owner launched a furious campaign to stop the SBS. His virulent objection might have stemmed from the fact that the press named him as the property owner.[39] Keith, a Methodist, was the president of the Fourth National Bank of Nashville, and he served on several prominent cultural and philanthropic boards in the city. He had a reputation to protect. Additionally, he feared that a Black school would drive down neighborhood property values, a concern, as he still owned several pieces of land in the area.[40] Keith offered to refund the money if the SBS renounced its plans for the school. Drexel refused to yield.

On February 27, 1905, Keith wrote a letter to the editor of the *Banner* announcing that he sold the property to an agent and had not known the real buyer's identity. He pled ignorance and insisted, "I did not desire that my old home should be used for that purpose, and I knew that my neighbors would object to it."[41]

---

36 *Original Annals of the SBS, 1905*, 5, ASBS.
37 She had first offered $18,000, and when the owner, Samuel Keith, rejected the offer, she announced that she refused to pay more than $24,000 for the house. When Mr. Keith would not accept a penny less than $25,000, the bishop offered to pitch in $1,000. *Original Annals of the SBS 1905*, 7, ASBS.
38 *Original Annals of the SBS 1905*, 7, ASBS.
39 See "Mother Drexel's Bounty: To Found Industrial School for Negro Girls in Nashville," *New York Times*, February 14, 1904, 10.
40 Steven Hoskins, "A Restless Landscape: Building Nashville History and Seventh and Drexel" (Ph.D. diss., Middle Tennessee State University, 2008), 52, 78.
41 *Original Annals 1905*, 9–10, ASBS.

Keith also composed a letter to the agent Thomas Tyne trying to get him to reverse the sale. Getting no satisfaction from Tyne, Keith turned to Bishop Byrne and warned that the school would send property values plummeting and would destroy the neighborhood. He angrily asserted, "The place has been the residence of myself and my family for nearly twenty-five years, and I would not have been willing upon any conditions to see it used for that purpose, nor would I have been willing to sell it for a purpose that would be either offensive to the sentiments of my neighbors or damaging to their property."[42] He even offered to donate additional money if Byrne would donate the property to the Little Sisters of the Poor, a congregation formed in France in 1842 with the purpose of caring for the underprivileged elderly. While nuns in general were unpopular, those that taught Black students were not welcome in Keith's neighborhood.[43]

When Keith wrote to Drexel asking her to rescind the sale, she responded politely but firmly. She ignored his real concern about the race of the students and instead told Keith that the inhabitants of the property would be nuns, who she promised would be on their best behavior. Mother Katharine insisted that the sisters would treat the neighbors with respect and added, "We have every reason to hope we may receive from our white neighbors the cordial courtesy for which the Southern people are so justly noted."[44] She also informed him that she had scouted the neighborhood and found many houses in the surrounding area belonging to Black families, suggesting that elite whites no longer dominated the neighborhood and thus had lost the authority to dictate its makeup.[45] Addressing Keith's concern that his family home would be sullied, she urged him to remember that his physical house paled in comparison to the heavenly home

---

42  Ibid., 12.
43  Keith also did not understand that upon the final sale, the land belonged to the Sisters of the Blessed Sacrament and not the Diocese of Nashville. Byrne, though he had to give approval to the sisters' work in his diocese, did not have any authority over the building site itself.
44  *Original Annals 1905*, 16, ASBS.
45  Indeed, Keith was one of the last old families to leave. Most elites had fled to West Nashville, away from encroaching industrialization. Hoskins, "Restless Landscape," 66.

awaiting him after death: "There is but one home, strictly speaking, that eternal home where we all hope to meet our own, and where there will be no *separation* any more."[46] She refused to acknowledge his concerns about race, property values, or other temporal issues.

Unplacated, Keith decided that he would rather lose the property and his money than see his family home become a school for Black girls. He schemed to get the city of Nashville to run Central Street through the middle of his property in accordance with pre–Civil War city plans. The city refused to pursue Keith's fancy. Bishop Byrne stepped in to mollify Keith by assuring him that his fears were ungrounded. He assured Keith that the sisters "are women of good birth and breeding, of culture and refinement, and of a high and delicate sense of what is due to those by whom they are surrounded or with whom they come in contact." His defense of the sisters' good breeding is more than a little disingenuous, as Keith had greater issue with the race of the students than the manners of the nuns. Byrne did, however, also inform Keith that the young Black girls who would attend the school would "compare favorably with the young girls of any institution in Nashville."[47]

Despite the bishop's assurances, Keith continued to stir up trouble with the city council and his former neighbors. Fifty people petitioned the mayor to stop the development of Immaculate Mother School. In June 1905, a group of white women living in the surrounding area organized the Stevenson Avenue Ladies Group and petitioned Mother Katharine to move the school. They suggested that the SBS relocate the academy to a rundown section of the city. When Drexel told them she intended to continue with her plans, they published their complaint in the *Nashville Banner*. An accompanying editorial suggested that the elite white women had the right to decide who got to live in their neighborhood. The editorial writer, Patrick Henry, stated, "[These women] are the offspring of the men who gave us a white man's government under a constitution that guarantees the protection of our property

---

46 *Original Annals 1905*, 16, ASBS.
47 Ibid., 22.

rights and which never contemplated this injury of those rights by any species of legal fraud or unfriendly legislation against their inalienable and God given inheritance."[48] The city's white, Protestant elite believed that it could dictate the geography of the city. Drexel's purchase of a prominent antebellum mansion, a symbol of the group's power, for the purpose of educating Black women was too much.

Byrne assured Mother Katharine that "the better class are with us," but bitter conflict continued through the summer of 1905.[49] Tensions remained so high that only one agent could be found who would insure the property because many feared arson.[50] In exasperation, Drexel vented: "My God! How much light can be wasted when the darkness does not comprehend it."[51] She consoled herself in Eucharistic language, though, and told Byrne, "It is certainly encouraging to meet some opposition in your work and ours. It is so appropriate for Convent of the Blessed Sacrament—Christ dwelling with us—and the School of the Immaculate Mother, to have people of the city have no room for our previous Charge."[52] Despite the protests, the school opened with twenty-nine students in September 1905 and grew so quickly that the SBS had to erect a new building the following year. By 1907, Byrne reported to the Commission for Catholic Missions among the Colored People and the Indians that the sisters filled every seat at their school, and he announced, "The bitter opposition of a few years ago has almost disappeared."[53] In 1909, the sisters completed their conquest of Nashville: demolition balls razed Mile End, and an Italianate convent rose from the antebellum mansion's foundations. In a city dubbed the

---

48 "The Keith Property Transaction," *Nashville Banner*, July 1, 1905, quoted in Hoskins, "A Restless Landscape," 82.

49 *Original Annals 1905*, 24.

50 Bishop Thomas S. Byrne reported the story almost twenty years later in *Report on Mission Work among the Negroes and the Indians: What Is Being Accomplished by Means of the Annual Collection for our Missions 1923*, 28.

51 Duffy, *Katharine Drexel*, 259.

52 Ibid., 258.

53 Application for Aid Presented to the Commission for the Catholic Missions among the Colored People and the Indians, 1907, Bureau of Catholic Indian Mission Records, Series 5/2, reel 16, MUA.

Protestant Vatican, the Sisters of the Blessed Sacrament trod on dangerous ground.[54]

## Legal Hurdles

In addition to battling public opinion and wary property owners, the SBS faced challenges from Southern state houses that wanted to shut down their work. Southern state legislatures debated bills in the decade of the 1910s including convent inspection acts, "anti-garb" bills (which banned sisters clad in habits from teaching in public schools, a common practice especially in smaller towns), prohibition of sacramental wine, and laws banning the reading of a non–King James Bible.[55] In July 1915, for example, Georgia State Senator J. B. Way introduced a bill "to prohibit the teaching, by any white teacher, in any school for colored pupils of this State, or the teaching by any colored teacher in any school for white pupils of the State, whether the said school or schools be or not a part of or belonging to and subject to the public school system of this State."[56] The *Chicago Defender*, which opined that "the state of Georgia can always be depended upon to do the wrong thing whenever the opportunity presents itself," labeled the bill un-American.[57] No doubt spurred by Tom Watson's press crusade against the enemies of the New South—the Catholic Church, Jews, and African Americans—Georgia became hostile territory for the SBS.[58]

The proposed law threatened the sisters' work at Our Lady of Lourdes School (established 1913) in Atlanta, as well as at St. Peter Claver School (established 1915) in Macon. Archbishop Edmund Francis Prendergast had a hard time puzzling out the pri-

---

54 Ironically, despite the initial rancor, Drexel and the SBS proved so popular in the African American community that students and their families petitioned to change the name Central Street to Drexel Street sometime before 1914. Hoskins, "A Restless Landscape," 85.

55 Mattick, "Ministries in Black and White," 163.

56 *SBS Annals 1915*, 81–82, ASBS.

57 "Keeping Up Their Reputation," *Chicago Defender*, July 24, 1915, 8, and "That Georgia Bill," *Chicago Defender*, July 31, 1915, 8.

58 Charleton Mosely, "Latent Klanism in Georgia, 1890–1915," *Georgia Historical Quarterly* 56 (Fall 1972): 365–86. Mosely credits Watson and his paper the *Jeffersonian* with fanning the flames of prejudice in the region.

mary motive of the law and mused to Mother Katharine, "Is the motive plain bigotry against the Church or is race prejudice the source of it?" He asked Drexel to deploy her political connections to ensure that they would not have to close the schools. Mother Katharine's brother-in-law, Walter George Smith, former president of the American Bar Association, had the resources to find powerful Catholic (or sympathetic) attorneys to influence the lawmakers. The bill passed the state senate, but it ultimately foundered in the house. The sisters' annals credited protest drummed up by Smith's contacts with sinking the bill. Though not ultimately successful, the bill and similar legislation ratcheted up the tension in the Southern schools, where the white community labeled the sisters "race traitors."

## The Klan Threatens SBS Work

The 1915 reconstitution of the Ku Klux Klan heightened resistance to Drexel's plans to build churches and schools for Black people. Inspired by the 1915 D. W. Griffith film *Birth of a Nation*, William Joseph Simmons chartered the new Ku Klux Klan in Georgia. The Klan claimed that its purpose was to enforce the morals of the community, especially defending the "chastity of womanhood and the exemplification of a pure and practical patriotism."[59] Part of this defense of morality included virulent racism, anti-Catholicism, and anti-Semitism. When Hiram Wesley Evans became imperial wizard of the Klan in November 1922, he touted the secret society as the champion of Americanism.[60] He viewed the Klan as a "patriotic, benevolent, and Christian order."[61] The Catholic Church represented a threat to this order, and Evans viewed it as "the most dangerous alien power."[62] Evans questioned whether Catholics could be American citizens. Thus, he argued, Catholics, such as the Sisters of the Blessed Sacrament,

---

59   "Ku Klux 'Empress' Comes Here to Shop," *New York Times*, September 11, 1921, 22.
60   Hiram Wesley Evans, "The Klan: Defender of Americanism," *Forum* 74, no. 6 (December 1925), 805.
61   Baker, *Gospel According to the Klan*, 37.
62   Hiram Wesley Evans, "The Klan's Fight for Americanism," *North American Review* 223, no. 830 (March 1, 1926): 45.

could not teach Americanism to others, for the result would "at best produce only confusion of thought."[63] Klan ideology held that the conversion of Black people to Catholicism would welcome the "horrors of Hayti and San Domingo" to American soil. They believed that the Catholic Church was "after the negro as one of its major steps in dominating the American republic."[64] Accordingly, missions such as those financed by the SBS had to be stopped. While the SBS faced Klan persecution in multiple locations, the conflict in Beaumont, Texas, an oil-refining city near the Louisiana border, exemplifies the dangers of their mission.

### Beaumont: A "Truly Lawless Town"

In 1915, Josephite priest Alexis LaPlante convinced the SBS to finance the construction of a church and school for Black Catholics. Four sisters arrived to staff Blessed Sacrament School in 1917, and it quickly reached full capacity. This growth fueled resentment in the community. Father LaPlante and the Sisters of the Blessed Sacrament faced opposition to their mission from the Ku Klux Klan and ambivalence from Beaumont law enforcement. Mother Mary of the Visitation Leary, the local superior, complained to Mother Katharine, saying that Beaumont "is a truly lawless town. No punishment is meted out to offenders unless they be poor Negroes who only looked crooked. They need not do that most times, to be lodged in jail. All kinds of crimes go almost unnoticed, unless it be a case where a colored man does some even slight act to a white man, then the law is disturbed about the violation."[65] Prejudice in the community was such that when mob rule threatened the church and lives of their students, authorities—both legal and ecclesiastical—stood idly by.

Chartered by George B. Kimbro in 1920, the Beaumont Klan, Texas's seventh chapter, kept busy. They seemed to have two

---

63 Ibid., 46.

64 *Searchlight*, August 1922, quoted in Nancy MacLean, *Behind the Mask of Chivalry: The Making of the Second Ku Klux Klan* (New York: Oxford University Press, 1994), 140.

65 Mother Mary of the Visitation Leary to Mother Katharine Drexel, March 21, 1922, quoted in Lynch, *Sharing the Bread in Service*, 1:209.

goals: to monitor morals in the oil fields and to make sure the town's large Black population knew their place.[66] On March 1, 1922, Charles Blunt, a Black porter at the Plaza Hotel, was flogged in Port Arthur, and on March 18 the Klan abducted, flogged, and tarred and feathered Dick Richards, another Black porter from the Crosby Hotel who was a member of Blessed Sacrament. The *Beaumont Enterprise* reported that Richards might have been targeted because "he is said to have accumulated quite a fortune through tips."[67] He also owned his own car, which must have seemed like an affront to Klan members. Mother Katharine believed he was a target because his daughter was a Sister of the Holy Family Sisters.[68] On March 20 the Klan flogged, tarred, and feathered white Judge J. A. Pelt, who had spoken out against the vigilante group. On the same day, the Klan organized a parade aimed to intimidate anyone who threatened the Protestant Christian order. The parade marched past the Blessed Sacrament convent. Mother Mary of the Visitation believed that Blessed Sacrament was targeted because its parish rosters included a high percentage of Black professionals, including four doctors and three dentists.

The following day, the Klan threatened the church. On March 21, a sign appeared on the door reading "To the pastor of this Church: We want an end to the services here. We will not stand for any white priest consorting with nigger wenches in the face of our families. We will give you one week to suppress it or a flogging and a tar and feather will follow."[69] The note reflected an old trope that priests used the confessional to violate women. In this case, the Klan combined their fears of predatory priests with their hatred of miscegenation and stereotypes of Black women. The next day another note appeared promising to bring the structure down with dynamite. Despite the threats, Father Alexis LaPlante

---

66  Thomas E. Kroutter, "The Ku Klux Klan in Jefferson County, TX, 1921–1924" (Master's thesis, Lamar University, 1972), 11.

67  *Beaumont Enterprise*, March 21, 1922, 2.

68  Mother Katharine Drexel to Josephine Drexel, May 8, 1922, Mother Katharine Correspondence #2887, vol. 20, ASBS.

69  Lynch, *Sharing the Bread in Service*, 1:209. Also see "Threat to Bomb Catholic Church Posted on Door; Matter Brought to Light When Citizens Made Appeal to City and County Authorities," *Beaumont Enterprise*, March 22, 1922, 1.

continued to celebrate Mass and Lenten devotionals each evening. Drexel later bragged to her cousin Josephine, "The priest held his ground & so did the Sisters and the Congregation. Just go on as usual. It was so brave of the Colored to attend the night services of Lent, notwithstanding the threat."[70] Attending services did require fortitude, for Mother Mary of the Visitation complained, "No civic protection can be hoped for, because all the officials here belong to the infamous party. Our Lord of course can stay it all, and we pray after Mass and will pray, but at the same time, natural means must be used too."[71]

Some local officials did denounce the Klan. The headlines of the *Beaumont Enterprise* of March 22 screamed, "Mayor Advocated Vigorous Methods to End Whippings" and "City Commission Goes on Record against Tar Parties and Police Are Asked to Get on Their Necks; Detectives May Be Employed to Stamp Out Such Practices." City Council Member Joe C. Clemmons said, "Word has gotten out on the street that the entire city administration as well as the police department are members of the Ku Klux Klan. That impression must be changed, and I heartily endorse the action [a reward for the capture of the party guilty of the assault and threat on the church] taken by Mayor Steinhagen."[72] Mother Mary of the Visitation, who harbored deep suspicions of local law enforcement, scoffed when the sheriff came to the church to offer his aid: "It is almost a certified fact that this worthy gent is a Klansman himself. He told Father to let him know if anything happened and he would see to it. Imagine!"[73]

The threat to bomb the church and maim its priest also produced a reaction from Beaumont citizens. Several prominent white men sent a letter to the *Beaumont Enterprise* denouncing "the outrages committed by the cowardly anarchists who placed the

---

70 Mother Katharine Drexel to Josephine Drexel (Seton-Henry), May 8, 1922, Mother Katharine Correspondence, vol. 20, #2887, ASBS.

71 Mother Mary of the Visitation to Mother Katharine Drexel, March 21, 1922, quoted in Lynch, *Sharing the Bread in Service*, 1:210.

72 "Mayor Advocated Vigorous Methods to End Whippings," *Beaumont Enterprise*, March 22, 1922, 1.

73 Mother Mary of the Visitation to Mother Katharine Drexel, March 22, 1922, ASBS.

two notices signed KKK on the doors of the Blessed Sacrament Catholic Church." They added, "We have every confidence in our county and city officials and demand of them that they do not permit these outrages to be committed."[74] Why they had this confidence, however, is unclear, for the sisters believed that the sheriff, Tom Garner, and the chief of police, B.B. Johnson, were Klan members.

The next day, the local whites-only Catholic fraternal organization, the Knights of Columbus, sent a letter to the editor of the *Enterprise* insisting that the "KKK are morally responsible for all such acts of unlawfulness as they established the precedent of taking the law in their own hands."[75] The Knights of Columbus were infuriated at the attack on a Catholic church, and they offered to protect Father Alexis LaPlante. Two brothers, J. Barry and H. Barry, brought him a revolver and spent the night in the rectory, "armed and ready to shoot without notice any masked people that may come."[76] A student patrolled the church grounds. Mother Mary of the Visitation reported, "The Knights are after the KKK and say they are going to make them stand for their signature on the two signs posted on the door."[77] Black Protestants also collected five dollars to bolster church and convent security. Despite the support from the Knights and their neighbors, Catholic clerics did not aid LaPlante and the sisters. LaPlante reported, "Father Kelly, of the white parish, upon hearing the news went away for two days."[78] Mother Mary of the Visitation pointed out that the city's rabbi offered aid while the Catholic church stood by: "The stranger [the rabbi] came and up to this writing not one of St. Anthony's [the white parish] priests has made his appearance and even Fr. Hardy, who came to town yesterday (and has always stopped at Father's when he did) passed by without a word."[79]

---

74 "Letter to the Editor," *Beaumont Enterprise*, March 22, 1922.
75 "Letter to Editor," *Beaumont Enterprise*, March 24, 1922, 8.
76 Alexis LaPlante to Mother Katharine Drexel, March 28, 1922, ASBS.
77 Mother Mary of the Visitation to Mother Katharine Drexel, March 27, 1922, ASBS.
78 Ibid.
79 Mother Mary of the Visitation to Mother Katharine Drexel, March 22, 1922, ASBS.

The media coverage caused some local judges and leaders to call an anti-Klan meeting that attracted 1,600 citizens. The city launched an official grand jury investigation, calling Father LaPlante and Mother Mary of the Visitation to testify, but it did not return a single indictment. Mayor Steinhagen, who Mother Mary of the Visitation was convinced was also a Klansman, wrote an appeal to the citizens of Beaumont urging them to "cut out all this foolishness."[80] He promised to purge the city payroll of any Ku Klux Klan members. Not surprisingly, the investigation failed to yield a single Klan member. Mother Mary of the Visitation confided to Mother Katherine, "I don't feel satisfied yet, dear Mother, and these Kluxes are all wrought up and will do much more I'm afraid, if something very radical is not done to prevent them. The officials here all said they were not members of the Klan, but it is almost proven they are."[81] A few months later, her fears were confirmed when the post-election newspaper headlines announced, "Jefferson County Ku Klux Klan ticket is swept into office; take all offices by a wide margin in landslide."[82]

Despite a decline in Klan activity after 1924, the group continued to threaten the work of the SBS. In 1926, the Josephite priest at neighboring Port Arthur, Texas, roughly sixteen miles from Beaumont, begged Mother Katharine to open a school because he could not trust the local public schools. He informed her, "With one exception these teachers are anti-Catholic. I objected to the Ku Klux superintendent, but my protest was ignored."[83] The relationship between the Black Catholic Church and the public school system further deteriorated, and he wrote Mother Katharine of a violent altercation with the school superintendent: "Recently I had the pleasure of kicking this scoundrel out of my room. Now he says he'll blow out my brains." Father Joseph A. Lally sardonically concluded, "That would make it

---

80 "Letter from Mayor Steinhagen," *Beaumont Enterprise*, March 30, 1922, 1.
81 Mother Mary of the Visitation to Mother Katharine Drexel, April 24, 1922, in Lynch, *Sharing the Bread in Service*, 1:213.
82 *Beaumont Journal*, July 24, 1922, 1.
83 Joseph A. Lally to Mother Katharine Drexel, February 6, 1926, H10, B33, box 33, folder 10, ASBS.

mighty inconvenient for me."[84] The work had dangerous detractors, and priests and sisters risked their lives when they established schools and convents.

## Dangerous Beliefs

While they used traditional religious language, the Sisters of the Blessed Sacrament had unpopular beliefs and faced opposition from multiple factions. Drexel wrote that she wanted Americans to come to "a realization that out of every ten people in this country one is a Negro, and that everyone has an immortal soul made to the image and likeness of God which is made for Heaven and redeemed by Christ's Passion and Death. He shares in the common dignity of a human being regardless of his nationality or race."[85] Their missions for Indigenous people did not face as much opposition, but all their work put them outside of acceptable societal boundaries. The sisters practiced the politics of respectability and preached chastity, modesty, and humility, but they broke with gender and racial norms. It is no wonder they riled up the "Kluxes" and others who believed they had the monopoly on the American Dream.

---

84 Lally to Mother Katharine Drexel, April 12, 1926, H10, B33, box 33, folder 10, ASBS.
85 *Annals of the SBS 1932*, 177, ASBS.

# Conclusion

ON A RAINY OCTOBER MORNING IN 2000, crowds braved torrential downpours and flocked to St. Peter's Square to witness Pope John Paul II declare Mother Katharine Drexel a saint. Her March 3 feast day makes Drexel a fixture in the Catholic calendar. Children read about her on Sunday mornings in parish religious education classes; men and women can purchase statues and relics and pray for her intercession. On eBay the faithful can purchase St. Katharine dolls, medals, stamps, and coloring books. Becoming a saint has made her a woman for all time, but it has removed her from her own. As sociologist Pierre Delooz has suggested, "All saints are more or less *constructed* in that, being necessarily saints *for other people*, they are remodeled in the collective representation which is made of them. It often happens, even, that they are so remodeled that nothing of the real original is left."[1] Canonization has not completely obscured the real Mother Katharine, though it has softened her at the edges and oversimplified the complicated history of the Sisters of the Blessed Sacrament.

The physical legacy of the SBS is easy to identify; maps delineate the landscapes Mother Katharine reshaped. By 1935, when a massive heart attack forced Mother Katharine to cease her active leadership of the Sisters of the Blessed Sacrament, the congregation operated seven boarding schools, thirty-seven day schools, one university, three social settlements, one house of study, and one shrine. They also supervised more than twenty rural schools in Louisiana and funded dozens more schools across the country. At the time of Mother Katharine's death in 1955, the congregation had opened an additional twenty-two missions. While her habit of anonymous giving makes coming up with a definitive

---

1 Pierre Delooz, "Towards a Sociological Study of Canonized Sainthood in the Catholic Church," in *Saints and Their Cults: Studies in Religious Sociology, Folklore and History*, ed. Stephen Wilson (Cambridge: Cambridge University Press, 1983), 194.

amount that Drexel donated to Black and Indigenous missions difficult, a reasonable estimate would be between fifteen and twenty million dollars—more than 400 million in today's dollars. Mother Katharine's considerable financial investment in Black and Indigenous Catholic education changed the religious landscape of the United States.

To view Mother Katharine only as a self-sacrificing philanthropist, the ATM of the Catholic home mission system, however, does her and her fellow Sisters of the Blessed Sacrament a disservice. As the nuns crisscrossed the country founding schools and social settlement centers, they fostered cross-cultural connections that were messy and complicated. When the SBS started their mission to education and evangelize, their assimilationist aims were often shrouded in racist ideas and white supremacy. Over time, they became some of the first Catholics to seek social and economic justice for Black and Indigenous groups, though they sometimes acted for rather than with the people they wanted to help. Putting the sisters on pedestals and admiring them as paragons of virtue obscures the reality that they at times perpetuated racism and at other times challenged the church to address inequality. Mother Katharine and the sisters signed letters to prelates with the fawning line, "Bowing to Kiss the Sacred Purple," but they never hesitated to offer opinions on what the church needed to do to live out its mission.

By building churches and schools across the country, the SBS engaged in more than raising brick-and-mortar structures. Guided by an inclusive interpretation of Catholic doctrine, the Sisters of the Blessed Sacrament set out, like many of their Protestant counterparts, to win America for Christ. Catherine L. Albanese has written that the complex and messy cultural interchanges that make up the story of religion on the continent can be seen as gift exchanges. She likens the gift-giving process to a dance: sometimes "the choreography is danced out in a more or less lightly inflected theme: exchanges have been smooth and easy; gifts have been given and received with delight." This is not always the case, however, and "at other times the dance has looked more like a martial arts 'push hands' demonstration between opposing but intimately connected actors." Other times, she notes, "one or another dancing partner has gone down.

The gift has been smashed . . . there are cuts and bruises, twisted knees, and more."[2] The gift exchange metaphor seems particularly apt when applied to the work of Mother Katharine Drexel and the Sisters of the Blessed Sacrament. The sisters believed their purpose was to share their spiritual gifts with others who were not yet received into the Mystical Body of Christ. They do not seem to have questioned whether these gifts were wanted.

SBS gift-giving did sometimes lead to "cuts and bruises, twisted knees and more." Black Power activists such as Father Lawrence Lucas, who attended SBS schools in New York City in the 1950s, claim that while the schools offered excellent academics, it was at the price of lowered self-esteem. He noted, "Every day I went to that all-colored school, I learned how smart white people were and how dumb colored people were."[3] With each passing year new and more horrifying pictures arise of the impact boarding schools had on Indigenous people. Many Indigenous families view Catholic missions as places of cultural genocide and remember boarding schools as cold and institutional. The sisters, however, believed that they were doing God's work by giving their faith to others.

The personal contact that accompanied these cultural exchanges changed the sisters. Contrary to the image of solitary nuns spending their days in prayer behind the heavy iron cloister grates, American sisters in general and the Sisters of the Blessed Sacrament in particular were women on the go. Though they could travel nowhere without permission and obeyed strict curfews, the SBS were characterized by movement. Mother Katharine logged thousands of miles each year as she visited not only her own missions but also those she funded. Sisters in the mission field also did considerable traveling. Those stationed at Indigenous missions journeyed to the remotest parts of the reservations, talking to and breaking bread with the people they met. Sisters staffing schools or settlements in Black neighborhoods found themselves taking pontoon boats through the bayous of Louisiana or going door to door

---

2   Catherine L. Albanese, "Exchanging Selves, Exchanging Souls: Contact, Combination, and American Religious History," In *Retelling U.S. Religious History*, ed. Thomas A. Tweed (Berkeley: University of California Press, 1997), 225.
3   Lucas, *Black Priest/White Church*, 19.

in Harlem and Chicago. One sister suggested putting up recruiting posters with the slogan "See America First with the S.B.S."[4] By visiting homes and crossing thresholds into places traditionally off-limits for white women, the sisters used their faith to push boundaries and to challenge economic and political structures.

Sisters who set out from the motherhouse trained in the latest pedagogy expected to impart their knowledge on the poor and downtrodden. Instead, they found themselves learning as much as they taught. Thomas A. Tweed has suggested, "When it's effective, teaching—and learning—means moving back and forth between the familiar and the strange, and the familiarization of the other generates a limited but transformative empathy."[5] Transformative empathy did not erode the sisters' conviction that their way—leading souls to God through the Roman Catholic Church and exposing students to middle-class white culture—was the best way to empower the oppressed. It did, however, force the Sisters of the Blessed Sacrament to become holistic problem solvers. Their students needed sacraments and school readers, but their parents also needed jobs, their relatives needed control of their land, and they needed to be safe from lynch mobs. The SBS thus were some of the first Catholic women to tackle issues of racial justice. Mother Katharine's fortune insulated them from clerical control and allowed them to push their ministry further than other groups could in the early twentieth century.

Their work has since been overshadowed by the work of "New Nuns" in the Civil Rights Movement and the aftermath of Vatican II. During the 1960s, sisters, responding to the Vatican's call to renewal, the feminist movement, and social justice doctrines of the time, began to leave their traditional posts as teachers and nurses and take up work with the poor and with racial minorities.[6] Images of sisters marching in Selma have become

---

4   Sr. Eletta Maris, "S.B.S. Diary," *Mission Fields at Home*, January@-February 1949, 7.

5   Tweed, *Crossing and Dwelling*, 180.

6   Much has been written on the changing identity of American sisters. Many scholars cite Leon Joseph Cardinal Suenens's book *The Nun in the World* as one of the influences that pushed sisters from parochial schools into inner cities. Suenens, *The Nun in the World: Religious and the Apostolate*, trans. Geoffrey

iconic. Unlike many congregations, the Sisters of the Blessed Sacrament continued their work in schools. Their protests against segregation were less dramatic than some of their fellow sisters. For example, in 1961, they took out a large advertisement in the *Times-Picayune* that made the Catholic case for eliminating prejudice. They noted, "The fundamental principles of justice . . . are equally binding and applicable to all men. Forced segregation violates both Justice and Charity." They scolded their fellow Christians by adding, "Biblical scholars know there is no scriptural foundation for segregation."[7] These were strong words, but in the context of the 1960s they seemed tame. In 1965 then Superior General Mother M. David suggested that Mother Katharine would have wanted the congregation to continue to focus on education because "human needs are not met or entirely satisfied by news articles, platform speeches and vehement declarations."[8] This course of action was less flashy than marching in the streets.

The work of the Sisters of the Blessed Sacrament changed in scope and scale after two important events in the mid-1950s. The 1954 *Brown v. Board of Education* decision, which eventually led to school desegregation, made some SBS schools obsolete. While implementation of desegregation took decades and was never complete, in some locations the SBS closed schools once they saw that Black students could get a good education in integrated Catholic schools. For example, Immaculate Mother School in Nashville closed in 1954 when Bishop William Lawrence Adrian announced that Black students would be welcomed in any diocesan school.[9] By the early 1970s, many SBS schools had closed or merged with white Catholic schools.

---

Stevens (Wheathampstead, Hertfordshire: Anthony Clarke, 1962). I draw here from Carole Garibaldi Rogers, *Habits of Change: An Oral History of American Nuns* (Oxford: Oxford University Press, 2011); Kennelly, *American Catholic Women*; and Amy L. Koehlinger, *The New Nuns: Racial Justice and Religious Reform in the 1960s* (Cambridge, MA: Harvard University Press, 2007).
    7  "The Sisters of the Blessed Sacrament Issue a Call to Catholic New Orleans," *Times-Picayune*, February 12, 1961, 13.
    8  Lynch, *Sharing the Bread in Service*, 2:116.
    9  Hoskins, "Restless Landscape," 91.

More than the *Brown* decision, however, Mother Katharine's death at the age of ninety-seven on March 3, 1955, affected the sisters' ability to operate and expand their mission work. According to the instructions of her father's will, if all three sisters died without any heirs, the money would revert to the charities he named in his will. Mother Katharine's death marked the end of the SBS income from his trust, which at that point amounted to $410,000 a year. This was a financial blow to the SBS. Archbishop John O'Hara of Philadelphia petitioned Pope Pius XII to allow the SBS to receive any money the charities named in Francis Drexel's will did not need. He set up the Drexel Trust to manage the roughly $12,913,799 left in the Drexel fortune, and he added the SBS to the list of beneficiaries. This provided SBS some financial support for roughly a decade after Mother Katharine's death.[10] Still, the congregation no longer had the financial means drive new mission and reform efforts. For these reasons, the SBS lost its prominence at the same time as others in the church began to take real interest in issues of social and racial justice.

In an era when religious sisters have congressional lobbying organizations, chain themselves to nuclear facilities, launch campaigns to end the death penalty, and live and serve, as a matter of course, in the poorest neighborhoods, Drexel's ideas seem quaint. In 1891, however, her vision of professed Catholic women crossing the color line with the express purpose of extending the church's social teachings to two groups who were at that time either reviled or ignored by most whites made her a unique figure in both American Catholicism and American social history. In the years after the codification of canon law in 1917, a period in which scholars have lamented, "Religious communities of women religious calcified under the weight of ecclesiastical hegemony," the SBS took increasing interest in social and economic justice and used the media and political influence to effect change.[11]

The sisters lacked a nuanced understanding of the people they professed to serve. Particularly in their first years of operation, they viewed Indigenous people as a monolithic group and failed to

---

10 Lynch, *Sharing the Bread in Service*, 2:78.
11 Coburn and Smith, *Spirited Lives*, 225.

appreciate the three-tiered caste system in New Orleans. They also saw Black and Indigenous people as objects of pity rather than as people with their own ideas and agendas. The congregation formed because Eastern white women "burned with a desire to go to those 'other' brethren and bring them to the King."[12] While the lack of nuance and cultural understanding caused pain and misunderstandings, their work was based on a simple yet radical idea. SBS novices learned, "In God's sight their souls are as valuable as the souls of kings, perhaps more so, for with God, there was, or is, no distinction in creating souls."[13] This position allowed little room for subtlety. In 1928, Mother Katharine admonished her fellow sisters not to be complacent: "Voluntary tepidity causes a lessening of the life of Jesus in us."[14] She believed that failure to act would betray their religious beliefs. At the same time, Mother Katharine and the SBS did not issue radical pronouncements; they worked within the accepted language of the hierarchical church. The sisters employed Eucharistic theology to justify an innovative mission for the church, and they used Drexel's fortune to force the church's hand.

During her life, the press ran stories calling Drexel the woman "who gives $1,000 a day to charity," and the institutional church praised her loyalty, self-sacrifice, and obedience. Today, her Saint of the Day reflection on Franciscan Media stresses her relatability: "Saints have always said the same thing: Pray, be humble, accept the cross, love and forgive. But it is good to hear these things in the American idiom from one who, for instance, had her ears pierced as a teenager, who resolved to have 'no cake, no preserves,' who wore a watch, was interviewed by the press, traveled by train, and could concern herself with the proper size of pipe for a new mission."[15] All of these stories about Drexel are true. None of these get at the legacy Mother Katharine wanted the SBS to

---

12 "Saint Catharine's Indian School, Santa Fe, New Mexico," *Indian Sentinel*, 1903–4, 13.
13 "Sisters of the Blessed Sacrament," *Indian Sentinel*, 1907, 13.
14 Mother Katharine Drexel, "Reading of the Spirit of the Apostolate," Rev. Mother Lectures 1928, Collated Writings, MMK talks, H10J8B vol. 28, folder 9, ASBS.
15 Franciscan Media, "Saint Katharine Drexel," *Saint of the Day*, March 3, 2021, accessed June 15, 2022, https://www.franciscanmedia.org/saint-of-the-day/saint-katharine-drexel.

have. Juanita Fletcher, who won the Alumnus of the Year award from Xavier in 1985, had a different assessment of their work that would have resonated with Drexel. When she spoke of Xavier, she said, "It strengthens the pride and self-image of young black people. It enables them to look all people straight in the eyes and let them know that they are first and foremost Americans, that they are on an equal footing with anybody."[16] The history of race, gender, and religion in America is a complicated one that has kept scholars busy for years unpacking nuances and deconstructing meaning. Drexel and the SBS saw things more simply. They witnessed inequality and prejudice and sought to use their Catholic faith to expand the definition of who got to be an American. It was other people who made it complicated.

---

16 Sharon Litwin, "Xavier Alumna Keeps on Battling Barriers," *Times-Picayune*, December 1, 1985, 44.

# Bibliography

## Archival Collections

### Beaumont, Texas
Beaumont Historical Society

### Bensalem, Pennsylvania
Archives of the Sisters of the Blessed Sacrament (Now housed at the Catholic Historical Research Center, Archdiocese of Philadelphia, Philadelphia, Pennsylvania)

### Galveston, Texas
Diocese of Houston/Galveston Archives

### Milwaukee, Wisconsin
Marquette University Archives, Bureau of Catholic Indian Missions Correspondence
Marquette University Archives, Bureau of Catholic Indian Missions, Mission Reports
Marquette University Archives, Commission for the Catholic Missions Among the Colored People and the Indians, Reports and Applications for Aid

### New Orleans, Louisiana
Xavier University Archives, David J. Jackson Collection
Xavier University Archives, Josephite Collection
Xavier University Archives, Xavier Bulletin and Course Catalogues

### Washington, DC
Library of Congress, NAACP Administrative File. Subject File: Congressional Action—Costigan Wagner Bill 1933–36. Text-fiche.
Library of Congress, Papers of the NAACP Part 7: The Anti-Lynching Campaign, 1916–55, Series B: Legislative and Publicity Files. Text-fiche.

Library of Congress, Papers of the NAACP Part 10: Peonage, Labor, and the New Deal, 1913–39. Text-fiche.
Library of Congress, Papers of the NAACP. Part 6: Scottsboro Case, 1931–50. Text-fiche.
Library of Congress, Personal Correspondence. Walter White 1919–39. Text-fiche.

## Newspapers and Magazines

*Afro-American* (Baltimore)
*Atlanta Daily World*
*America*
*American Catholic Tribune*
*American Ecclesiastical Review*
*Beaumont Enterprise*
*Beaumont Journal*
*Catholic Mind*
*Catholic Worker*
*Catholic World*
*Chicago Defender*
*Colored Harvest*
*Commonweal*
*Crisis*
*Daily Crusader*
*Freedman's Journal*
*Indian Sentinel*
*Interracial Review*
*Josephite Missions*
*Little Bronzed Angel*
*Mission Fields at Home*
*New Journal and Guide* (Norfolk, Virginia)
*New Orleans Times Picayune*
*New York Amsterdam News*
*New York Times*
*Philadelphia Tribune*
*Pittsburgh Courier*
*Queen's Work*
*Time Magazine*
*Washington Post*
*Xavier Herald*

## Papal Encyclicals

Leo XIII. *Rerum Novarum* (1891).
Pius X. *Sacra Tridentina Synodus* (1905).
Pius XI. *Rerum Ecclesiae* (1926).
———. *Divini Illius Magistri* (1929).
———. *Quadragesimo Anno* (1931).
———. *Sertum Laetitae* (1939).
Pius XII. *Mystici Corporis Christi* (1943).

## Government Documents

Board of Indian Commissioners. "Indian Education." In *Twelfth Annual Report of the Board of Indian Commissioners*, 1880.
Bureau of the Census. Special Reports. *Religious Bodies: 1906*. Part I, *Summary and General Tables*. Washington, DC: Government Printing Office, 1910.
———. *Religious Bodies: 1906*. Part II, *Separate Denominations: History, Description, and Statistics*. Washington, DC: Government Printing Office, 1910.
———. *Religious Bodies: 1916*. Part I, *Summary and General Tables*. Washington, DC: Government Printing Office: 1919.
———. *Religious Bodies1916*. Part II, *Separate Denominations: History, Description, and Statistics*. Washington, DC: Government Printing Office, 1919.
———. *Religious Bodies: 1926*. Vol. 1, *Summary and Detailed Tables*. Washington, DC: Government Printing Office, 1930.
———. *Religious Bodies: 1926*. Vol. II, *Separate Denominations Statistics, History, Doctrine, Organization and Work*. Washington, DC: Government Printing Office, 1929.
———. *Religious Bodies 1936*. Vol. 1, *Summary and Detailed Tables*. Washington, DC: Government Printing Office, 1941.
———. *Religious Bodies 1936*. Vol. II, Part II, *Denominations K to—, Statistics, History, Doctrine, Organization and Work*. Washington, DC: Government Printing Office, 1941.
House Committee on Flood Control. *Progress and Present Status of Flood Control on the Mississippi River and Its Tributaries: Hearings before the Committee on Flood Control*. House of Representatives, Seventy-Third Congress, First Session, March 30 and May 12, 1933. Washington, DC: United States Government Printing Office, 1933.
Internal Revenue Service. *Statistics of Income for 1932*. Washington, DC: Government Printing Office, 1934.

*Report 1064. "Authorizing Investigation of Labor Conditions Prevailing upon Mississippi Flood Control Project."* 72nd Congress, Second Session. January 10, 1933.

## Primary Sources

"American Foundation of Religious Orders: The Congregation of the Sisters of the Blessed Sacrament for Indians and Colored People." *American Ecclesiastical Review* 13 (January 1898): 1–13.

Anderson, Beverly Jacques. *Cherished Memories: Snapshots of Life and Lessons from a 1950s New Orleans Creole Village.* Bloomington, IN: iUniverse, 2011.

Baker, Ray Stannard. *Following the Color Line: American Negro Citizenship in the Progressive Era.* New York: Harper Torchbooks, 1964. Originally published in 1908.

Barrows, Isabel C., ed. *First Mohonk Conference on the Negro Question Held at Lake Mohonk, Ulster County, New York, June 4,5,6, 1890.* New York: Negro Universities Press, 1891. Reprint 1969.

Beecher, Lyman. *A Plea for the West.* Cincinnati: Truman and Smith, 1835.

Belloc, Hillaire. *The Contrast.* New York: Robert M. McBride, 1924.

Bureau of Catholic Indian Missions. *An Appeal in Behalf of Catholic Indian Mission Schools.* Washington, DC: BCIM, 1902.

———. *The Bureau of Catholic Indian Missions: The Work of the Decade, Ending December 31, 1883.* Washington, DC: BCIM, 1884.

———. *The Bureau of Catholic Indian Missions 1874–1895.* Washington, DC: Church News, 1895.

———. *Report of the Catholic Indian Missions for the Year Ending October 1, 1898.* Washington, DC: BCIM, 1898.

———. *Report of the Bureau of Catholic Indian Missions for Year Ending October 1, 1899.* Washington, DC: BCIM, 1899.

———. *Report of the Bureau of Catholic Indian Missions for 1900–01 and 1901–02.* Washington, DC: BCIM, 1902.

———. *Report of the Director of the Bureau of Catholic Indian Missions for 1903–04.* Washington, DC: BCIM, 1904.

———. *Report of the Director of the Bureau of Catholic Indian Missions for 1904–1905.* Washington, DC: BCIM, 1905.

———. *Report of the Director of the Bureau of Catholic Indian Missions for 1905–1906.* Washington, DC: BCIM, 1906.

———. *Report of the Director of the Bureau of Catholic Indian Missions for 1906.* Washington, DC: BCIM, 1906.

———. *Report of the Director of the Bureau of Catholic Indian Missions for 1907*. Washington, DC: BCIM, 1907.
———. *Report of the Director of the Bureau of Catholic Indian Missions for 1908*. Washington, DC: Press of Byron S. Adams, 1908.
———. *Report of the Director of the Bureau of Catholic Indian Missions for 1909*. Washington, DC: BCIM, 1909.
———. *Report of the Director of the Bureau of Catholic Indian Missions for 1910*. Washington, DC: BCIM, 1910.
Burgess, Larry E., ed. *The Lake Mohonk Conference of Friends of the Indian: Guide to the Annual Reports*. New York: Clearwater, 1975.
Burns, J., Bernard J. Kohlbrenner, and John B. Peterson. *A History of Catholic Education in the United States: A Textbook for Normal Schools and Teachers' Colleges*. New York: Benziger Brothers, 1937.
Butsch, Joseph. "Catholics and the Negro." *Journal of Negro History* 2, no. 4 (October 1917): 393–410.
Coffin, Ernest W. "On the Education of Backward Races: A Preliminary Study." *Pedagogical Seminary* 15, no. 1 (March 1908): 1–62.
*Course of Studies Prepared for the Eight Grades of the Parochial Schools of the Archdiocese of New Orleans*, 1915.
Crow Dog, Mary, and Richard Erodes. *Lakota Woman*. New York: HarperPerennial, 1991.
Cusack, Mary Francis. *The Nun of Kenmare: An Autobiography*. London: Hodder and Stoughton, 1889.
Deggs, Mary Bernard. *No Cross, No Crown: Black Nuns in Nineteenth-Century New Orleans*. Edited by Virginia Meacham Gould and Charles E. Nolan. Bloomington: Indiana University Press, 2001.
DuBois, W. E. B. "Does the Negro Need Separate Schools?" *Journal of Negro Education* 4, no. 3 (July 1935): 328–35.
———. *The Philadelphia Negro: A Social Study*. Philadelphia: University of Pennsylvania Press, 1996.
———. *The Souls of Black Folk*. Oxford: Oxford University Press, 2007. Originally published in 1903.
Durier, Bishop Anthony. *Report on Mission Work among the Negroes and the Indians: What Is Being Accomplished by Means of the Annual Collection Taken Up for our Missions*. Clayton, DE: Press of St. Joseph's Industrial School, 1900.
Eadie, Betty J. *Embraced by the Light*. Placerville, CA: Gold Leaf Press, 1992.
Ellis, John Tracy. *Documents of American Catholic History*. Vol. 2. Wilmington, DE: Michael Glazier, 1987.

Evans, Hiram W. *The Rising Storm: An Analysis of the Growing Conflict Over the Political Dilemma of Roman Catholics in America.* New York: Arno Press, 1977. Originally published in 1930.

Fahs, Sophie Lyon. *Racial Relations and the Christian Ideal: A Discussion Course for College Students.* New York: Committee on Christian World Education, 1923.

Favrot, Leo M. "Aims and Needs in Negro Public Education in Louisiana." *Bulletin Number Two,* 1918.

Foreman, Clark. *Environmental Factors in Negro Elementary Education.* New York: Julius Rosenwald Fund and W. W. Norton, 1932.

Fortunate Eagle, Adam. *Pipestone: My Life in an Indian Boarding School.* Norman: University of Oklahoma Press, 2010.

Furfey, Paul Hanly. *Fire on the Earth.* New York: Macmillan, 1936.

Geser, Fintan, OSB. *The Canon Law Governing Communities of Sisters.* St. Louis: B. Herder, 1938.

Gillard, John T., SSJ. *The Catholic Church and the American Negro.* Baltimore: St. Joseph's Society Press, 1929.

———. *Colored Catholics in the United States.* Baltimore: Josephite Press, 1941.

Guidry, Mary Gabriella. *The Southern Negro Nun.* New York: Exposition Press, 1974.

Hamilton, Martha McNeill, and Warren Brown. *Black and White and Red All Over: The Story of a Friendship.* New York: Public Affairs, 2002.

Haskin, Sara Estelle. *Women and Missions in the Methodist Episcopal Church, South.* Nashville: Publishing House of the M. Church, 1920.

Hoxie, Frederick E., ed. *Talking Back to Civilization: Indian Voices from the Progressive Era.* Boston: Bedford St. Martin's, 2001.

Hughes, William. *Opportunities for Service by Catholics among American Indians.* Pamphlet. Washington, DC: Bureau of Catholic Indian Missions, 1931.

———. *Indians on a New Trail.* Pamphlet. Washington, DC: Bureau of Catholic Indian Missions, 1934.

Hunton, George. *All of Which I Saw, Part of Which I Was: The Autobiography of George K. Hunton as Told to Gary MacEoin.* Garden City, NY: Doubleday, 1967.

Janssens, Archbishop Francis. *Report of the American Board of Catholic Missions, July 1, 1931 to July 1, 1932.* Chicago: American Board of Catholic Missions, 1932.

Jeanmard, Jules B. "Colored Missions Needs for Lafayette." In *Report of the American Board of Catholic Missions to the American Episcopate from July 1, 1928–July 17, 1929,* 81–83. Chicago: American Board of Catholic Missions, 1929.

———. "Missionary Problems of the Young Diocese of Lafayette." In *Report of the American Board of Catholic Missions, July 1, 1931 to July 1, 1932*. Chicago: American Board of Catholic Missions, 1932.
Johnston, Basil H. *Indian School Days*. Norman: University of Oklahoma Press, 1988.
Jones, Thomas Jesse, ed. "Negro Education: A Study of the Private and Higher Schools for Colored People in the United States." In *Bulletin, 1916*. Washington, DC: Government Printing Office, 1917.
Kerby, William Joseph. *The Social Mission of Charity: A Study of Points of View in Catholic Charities*. New York: Macmillan, 1921.
Ketcham, William H. *Rev. WM. H. Ketcham, Our Catholic Indian Missions: A Paper Read Before the Catholic Missionary Congress, Chicago, November 16, 1908*. Washington, DC: Byron S. Adams, 1908.
Kilpatrick, William H., ed. *The Educational Frontier*. New York: Century, 1933.
LaFarge, John. *The Race Question and the Negro: A Study of the Catholic Doctrine on Interracial Justice*. New York: Longmans, Green, 1943.
———. *The Catholic Viewpoint on Race Relations*. Garden City, NY: Hanover House, 1960.
Lanslots, D. I., OSB. *Handbook of Canon Law for Congregations of Women under Simple Vows*. New York: Fr. Pustet, 1909.
Lord, Daniel A., SJ. *Our Nuns: Their Varied and Vital Service for God and Country*. New York: Benziger Brothers, 1924.
———. *Our Part in the Mystical Body*. St. Louis: Queen's Work, 1935.
Louisiana Department of Education. *Annual Report of the State Superintendent of Public Education for the Year 1877*. New Orleans: Office of the Democrat, 1878.
Lynch, Patricia, SBS. *Sharing the Bread in Service: Sisters of the Blessed Sacrament, 1891–1991*. 2 vols. Bensalem, PA: Sisters of the Blessed Sacrament, 1998.
Manna, Paolo. *The Conversion of the Pagan World: A Treatise upon Catholic Foreign Missions*. Translated by Joseph F. McGlinchey. Boston: Society for the Propagation of the Faith, 1921.
Markoe, William M. *The Slave of the Negroes*. Chicago: Loyola University Press, 1920.
Meriam, Lewis. *The Problem of Indian Administration*. Institute for Government Research. Baltimore: Johns Hopkins University Press, 1928.
*Mission Work among the Negroes and the Indians: What Is Being Accomplished by Means of the Annual Collection Taken Up for Our Missions*. Baltimore: Sun Book and Job Printing Office, 1889.

*Mission Work among the Negroes and the Indians: What Is Being Accomplished by Means of the Annual Collection Taken up for Our Missions.* Clayton, DE: Press of St. Joseph Industrial School, 1910.

Monk, Maria. *Awful Disclosures of the Hotel Dieu Nunnery.* Introduction by Ray Allen Billington. Hamden, CT: Archon, 1962. [Facsimile of 1836 edition.]

Morrell, Edward. *Rations to Indian School Children: Argument of Cong. Edward Morrell.* Pamphlet. Washington, DC: Bureau of Catholic Indian Missions, 1903.

Murphy, Edward F. *The Tenth Man.* Philadelphia: Dolphin Press, 1937.

———. *Yankee Priest: An Autobiographical Journey with Certain Detours, from Salem to New Orleans.* Garden City, NY: Doubleday, 1952.

Nolan, Hugh J., ed. *Pastoral Letters of the United States Catholic Bishops.* Vol. 1, *1792–1940.* Washington, DC: United States Catholic Conference, 2005.

O'Brien, David, and Thomas A. Shannon, eds. *Catholic Social Thought: The Documentary Heritage.* 10th ed. Maryknoll, NY: Orbis, 2003.

Ovington, Mary White. *The Walls Came Tumbling Down.* New York: Harcourt, Brace, 1947.

Petra, Mary. *Blossoms Gathered from the Lower Branches: Or a Little Work of an Oblate Sister of Providence.* Baltimore: Oblate Sisters of Providence, 1914.

Pratt, Richard Henry. "The Advantages of Mingling Indians with Whites." *Official Report of the Nineteenth Annual Conference of Charities and Correction,* 1892.

———. *Battlefield and Classroom: Four Decades with the American Indian, 1867–1904.* Edited by Robert M. Utley. Norman: University of Oklahoma Press, 2003.

Pumphery, Stanley. *Indian Civilization: A Lecture by Stanley Pumphery with an Introduction by John G. Whittier.* Philadelphia: Bible and Tract Distributing Society, 1877. Reprint Ann Arbor: University of Michigan Library, 2005.

Reily, John T. *Passing Events in the Life of Cardinal Gibbons.* Martinsburg, W.VA: John T. Reily, 1890.

*Report of the American Board of Catholic Missions to the American Episcopate from July 1, 1928–July 17, 1929.* Chicago: American Board of Catholic Missions, 1929.

*Report on Mission Work among the Negroes and Indians: What Is Being Accomplished by Means of the Annual Collection Taken Up for Our Missions.* Baltimore: Foley Bros., 1895.

Rogers, Carole Garibaldi. *Habits of Change: An Oral History of American Nuns.* New York: Oxford University Press, 2011.

Ryan, John A., and Joseph Husslein, eds. *The Church and Labor*. New York: Macmillan, 1924.
Ryan, M. Agatha. "Catholic Education and the Negro." Pamphlet. Washington, DC: The Catholic University of America Press, 1942.
Schmidlin, Josef, SVD. *Catholic Mission Theory*. Translated by Matthias Braun, SVD. Techny, Ill.: Mission Press, 1931.
Segale, Sister Blandina. *At the End of the Santa Fe Trail*. Milwaukee: Bruce, 1948.
Shields, Thomas Edward. *Philosophy of Education*. Washington, DC: The Catholic Education Press, 1921.
Sisters of the Blessed Sacrament. *Navajo Adventure*. Cornwells Heights, PA: Sisters of the Blessed Sacrament, 1952.
———. *Encounters with the People of God*. Cornwells Heights, PA: Sisters of the Blessed Sacrament, 1967.
Society for the Propagation of the Faith. *The Mission Apostolate: A Study of the Mission Activity of the Roman Catholic Church and the Story of the Foundation and Development of Various Mission-Aid Organizations in the United States*. New York: Paulist Press, 1942.
Stephan, James. "Report by Rev. J. A. Stephan, Director, to Rt. Rev. Bishop M. Marty, President of the Bureau of Catholic Indian Missions for the Year 1891–1892." Washington, DC: BCIM, 1892.
Strong, William. "Remarks on Indian Reform." *Proceedings of the Third Annual Meeting of the Lake Mohonk Conference*. 1885.
Tarry, Ellen. *The Third Door: The Autobiography of an American Negro Woman*. Tuscaloosa: University of Alabama Press, 1966. Originally published in 1955.
Wald, Lillian. *The House on Henry Street*. New York: Henry Holt, 1915.
Watson, Thomas E. *The Inevitable Crimes of Celibacy: The Vices of Convents and Monasteries, Priests and Nuns*. Thompson, GA: Press of the Jeffersonian Pub. Co., 1916.
Weber, Anselm, OFM. *The Navajo Indians: A Statement of Facts*. Pamphlet. 1914.
———. "Fall 1900: Students to Santa Fe, Headmen to Cienega." In *The Navajos as Seen by the Franciscans, 1898–1921: A Sourcebook*, edited by Howard M. Bahr. 72–85. Lanham, MD: Scarecrow, 2004.
White, Walter. *A Man Called White: The Autobiography of Walter White*. Athens, GA: Thrasher, 1948.
Woodson, Carter G. "The Director Speaks." *Journal of Negro History* 16, no. 3 (July 1931): 344–48.
Work, Monroe N. ed. *The Negro Year Book 1921–1922*. Tuskegee, AL: Negro Yearbook Company, 1922.
Zitkala-Ša. *American Indian Stories*. Washington, DC: Hayward, 1921.

## Secondary Sources

### Books

Abell, Aaron L. *American Catholicism and Social Action: A Search for Social Justice, 1865–1950*. Garden City, NY: Hanover House, 1960.

———, ed. *American Catholic Thought on Social Questions*. Indianapolis: Bobbs-Merrill, 1968.

Acker, James R. *Scottsboro and Its Legacy: The Cases that Challenged American Legal and Social Justice*. Westport, CT: Praeger, 2008.

Adams, David Wallace. *Education for Extinction: American Indians and the Boarding School Experience, 1875–1928*. Lawrence: University of Kansas Press, 1995.

———. "Beyond Bleakness: The Brighter Side of Indian Boarding Schools, 1870–1940." In *Boarding School Blues: Revisiting American Indian Educational Experiences*, edited by Clifford Traafzer, Jean A. Keller, and Loene Sisquoc. Lincoln: University of Nebraska Press, 2006.

Agee, Gary B. *A Cry for Justice: Daniel Rudd and His Life in Black Catholicism, Journalism, and Activism, 1854–1933*. Fayetteville: University of Arkansas Press, 2011.

Albanese, Catherine L. "Exchanging Selves, Exchanging Souls: Contact, Combination, and American Religious History." In *Retelling U.S. Religious History*, edited by Thomas A. Tweed, 200–226. Berkeley: University of California Press, 1997.

Alexander, Charles C. *The Ku Klux Klan in the Southwest*. Lexington: University of Kentucky Press, 1965.

Allen, Robert L. *Reluctant Reformers: Racism and Social Reform Movements in the United States*. Washington, DC: Howard University Press, 1974.

Ambrose, Gloria P., and Bernadine B. Proctor. "Sacred Heart School." In *The First Hundred Years: 1882–1992; The Centennial of Catholic Education in "Imperial" Calcasieu*, edited by Donald J. Millet Sr. and Elaine B. Bodin. Lake Charles, LA: Alta, 1982.

Anderson, Eric, and Alfred A. Moss Jr. *Dangerous Donations: Northern Philanthropy and Southern Black Education, 1902–1930*. Columbia: University of Missouri Press, 1999.

Anderson, James D. "The Historical Development of Black Vocational Education." In *Work, Youth, and Schooling: Historical Perspectives on Vocationalism in American Education*, edited by Harvey Kantor and David B. Tyack, 180–222. Stanford, CA: Stanford University Press, 1982.

———. *The Education of Blacks in the South, 1860–1935*. Chapel Hill: University of North Carolina Press, 1988.
Anderson, R. Bentley. *Black, White, and Catholic: New Orleans Interracialism, 1947–1956*. Nashville: Vanderbilt University Press, 2005.
Appleby, R. Scott. *"Church and Age Unite!" The Modernist Impulse in American Catholicism*. Notre Dame, IN: University of Notre Dame Press, 1992.
Appleby, R. Scott, Patricia Byrne, and William L. Portier, eds. *Creative Fidelity: American Catholic Intellectual Traditions*. Maryknoll, NY: Orbis, 2004.
Archambault, Marie Therese, Mark G. Thiel, and Christopher Vecsey, eds. *The Crossing of Two Roads: Being Catholic and Native in the United States*. Maryknoll, NY: Orbis, 2003.
Bahr, Howard M., ed. *The Navajo as Seen by the Franciscans, 1898–1920: A Sourcebook*. Lanham, MD: Scarecrow Press, 2004.
Baker, Kelly J. *Gospel According to the Klan: The KKK's Appeal to Protestant America, 1915–1930*. Lawrence: University of Kansas Press, 2011.
Baldwin, Lou. *Saint Katharine Drexel: Apostle to the Oppressed*. Philadelphia: Catholic Standard and Times, 2000.
Barker, Debra K. S. "Kill the Indian, Save the Child." In *American Indian Studies: An Interdiscplinary Approach to Contemporary Issues*, edited by Dane Morrison, 47–78. New York: Peter Lang, 1997.
Barry, John M. *Rising Tide: The Great Mississippi Flood of 1927 and How It Changed America*. New York: Simon and Schuster, 1997.
Baudier, Roger. *The Catholic Church in Louisiana*. New Orleans: Louisiana Library Association Public Library Section, 1939.
Bays, Daniel H., and Grant Wacker. *The Foreign Missionary Enterprise at Home: Explorations in North American Cultural History*. Tuscaloosa: University of Alabama Press, 2003.
Beaver, R. Pierce. *Church, State, and the American Indians: Two and a Half Centuries of Partnership in Missions between Protestant Churches and Government*. Saint Louis: Concordia, 1966.
———. *All Loves Excelling: American Protestant Women in World Mission*. Grand Rapids, MI: Eerdmans, 1968.
Bennett, James B. *Religion and the Rise of Jim Crow in New Orleans*. Princeton, NJ: Princeton University Press, 2005.
Bergland, Betty Ann. "Settler Colonists, 'Christian Citizenship' and the Women's Missionary Federation at the Bethany Indian Mission in Wittenberg, Wisconsin, 1884–1934." In *Competing Kingdoms: Women, Mission, Nation, and the American Protestant Empire, 1812–1960*, edited by Barbara Reeves-Ellington, Kathryn Kish

Sklar, and Connie A. Shemo, 167–94. Durham, NC: Duke University Press, 2010.
Blatnica, Dorothy Ann, VSC. *"At the Altar of Their God": African American Catholics in Cleveland, 1922–1961*. New York: Garland, 1995.
Bodo, Fr. Murray, OFM, ed. and trans. *Tales of an Endishodi: Father Berard Haile and the Navajos, 1900–1961*. Albuquerque: University of New Mexico Press, 1998.
Bowden, Henry Warner. *American Indians and Christian Missions: Studies in Cultural Conflict*. Chicago: University of Chicago Press, 1981.
Brandewie, Ernest. *In the Light of the Word: Divine Word Missionaries of North America*. Maryknoll, NY: Orbis, 2000.
Brekus, Catherine A. "Introduction: Searching for Women in Narratives of American Religious History." In *The Religious History of American Women: Reimagining the Past*, edited by Catherine A. Brekus, 1–50. Chapel Hill: University of North Carolina Press, 2007.
Brewer, Eileen Mary. *Nuns and the Education of American Catholic Women, 1860–1920*. Chicago: Loyola University Press, 1987.
Brooks-Higginbotham, Evelyn. *Righteous Discontent: The Women's Movement in the Black Baptist Church, 1880–1920*. Cambridge, MA: Harvard University Press, 1993.
Brown, Dorothy M., and Elizabeth McKeown. *The Poor Belong to Us: Catholic Charities and American Welfare*. Cambridge, MA: Harvard University Press, 1997.
Bryson, Thomas A. *Walter George Smith*. Washington, DC: The Catholic University of America Press, 1977.
Burch, Susan. *Committed: Remembering Native Kinship in and beyond Institutions*. Chapel Hill: University of North Carolina Press, 2021.
Burton, Katherine. *The Golden Door: The Life of Katharine Drexel*. New York: P. J. Kenedy and Sons, 1957.
Butler, Anne. "Mother Katharine Drexel: Spiritual Visionary for the West." In *By Grit and Grace: Eleven Women Who Shaped the American West*, edited by Glenda Riley and Richard W. Etulain, 198–220. Golden, CO: Fulcrum, 1997.
———. *Across God's Frontiers: Catholic Sisters in the American West, 1850–1920*. Chapel Hill: University of North Carolina Press, 2012.
Butler, Anne, Michael E. Engh, SJ, and Thomas W. Spalding, CFX, eds. *The Frontiers and Catholic Identities*. Maryknoll, NY: Orbis, 1999.
Butler, Jon. "Historiographical Heresy: Catholicism as a Model for American Religious History." In *Belief in History: Innovative Approaches to European and American Religion*, edited by Thomas Kselman, 286–309. Notre Dame, IN: University of Notre Dame Press, 1991.

Byrne, Patricia. "In the Parish but Not of It: Sisters." In *Transforming Parish Ministry: The Changing Roles of Catholic Clergy, Laity and Women Religious*, edited by Jay P. Dolan, R. Scott Appleby, Patricia Byrne, and Debra Campbell, 109–200. New York: Crossroad, 1989.

Campbell, Debra. "Reformers and Activists." In *American Catholic Women: A Historical Exploration*, ed. Karen Kennelly, CSJ, 152–81. New York: Macmillan, 1989.

Carroll, James T. *Seeds of Faith: Catholic Indian Boarding Schools*. New York: Garland, 2000.

Carson, Mary Eisenman. *Blackrobe for the Yankton Sioux: Fr. Sylvester Eisenman, OSB (1891–1948)*. Chamberlain, SD: Tipi Press, 1989.

Case, Jay Riley. "From the Native Ministry to the Talented Tenth: The Foreign Missionary Origins of White Support for Black Colleges." In *The Foreign Missionary Enterprise at Home: Explorations in North American Cultural History*, edited by Daniel H. Bays and Grant Wacker, 60–74. Tuscaloosa: University of Alabama Press, 2003.

Chafe, William H. "Women's History and Political History: Some Thoughts on Progressivism and the New Deal." In *Visible Women: New Essays on American Activism*, edited by Nancy A. Hewitt and Suzanne Lebsock, 101–18. Urbana: University of Illinois Press, 1993.

Chang, Derek. "Imperial Encounters at Home: Women, Empire, and the Home Mission Project in Late Nineteenth Century America." In *Competing Kingdoms: Women, Mission, Nation, and the American Protestant Empire, 1812–1960*, edited by Barbara Reeves-Ellington, Kathryn Kish Sklar, and Connie A. Shemo, 293–317. Durham, NC: Duke University Press, 2010.

Chappell, David L. *A Stone of Hope: Prophetic Religion and the Death of Jim Crow*. Chapel Hill: University of North Carolina Press, 2004.

Chermie, Deany M. "Sifting Through Fifty Years of Change: Writing Program Administration at an Historically Black University." In *Historical Studies of Writing Program Administration: Individuals, Communities, and the Formation of a Discipline*, edited by Barbara L'Eplathenier, and Lisa Mastrangelo, 145–66. West Lafayette, IN: Parlor Press, 2004.

Child, Brenda. *Boarding School Seasons: American Indian Families, 1900–1940*. Lincoln: University of Nebraska Press, 1998.

Chinnici, Joseph P., OFM. *Living Stones: The History and Structure of Catholic Spiritual Life in the United States*. New York: Macmillan, 1989.

Chinnici, Joseph P., OFM, and Angelyn Dries, eds. *Prayer and Practice in the American Catholic Community*. Maryknoll, NY: Orbis, 2000.

Clark, Emily. "Peculiar Professionals: The Financial Strategies of the New Orleans Ursulines." In *Neither Lady nor Slave: Working Women of the Old South*, edited by Susanna Delfino and Michele Gillespie, 198–220. Chapel Hill and London: University of North Carolina Press, 2002.

———. "Hail Mary Down by the Riverside: Black and White Catholic Women in Early America." In *The Religious History of American Women: Reimagining the Past*, edited by Catherine A. Brekus, 91–107. Chapel Hill: University of North Carolina Press, 2007.

———. *Masterless Mistresses: The New Orleans Ursulines and the Development of a New World Society, 1727–1834*. Chapel Hill: University of North Carolina Press, 2007.

Clatterbuck, Mark. *Demons, Saints, and Patriots: Catholic Visions of Native America through the "Indian Sentinel," 1902–1962*. Milwaukee: Marquette University Press, 2009.

Coburn, Carol K., and Martha Smith. *Spirited Lives: How Nuns Shaped Catholic Culture and American Life, 1836–1920*. Chapel Hill: University of North Carolina Press, 1999.

Coffman, Mary Ruth, OSB. "Evelyn Davie's Dream Deferred." In *Benedict in the World: Portraits of Monastic Oblates*, edited by Linda Kulzer and Roberta Bondi, 45–53. Collegeville, MN: Order of St. Benedict, 2002.

Collum, Danny Duncan. *Black and Catholic in the Jim Crow South: The Stuff That Makes Community*. New York: Paulist Press, 2006.

Conrad, Glenn R., ed. *Cross, Crozier and Crucible: A Volume Celebrating the Bicentennial of a Catholic Diocese in Louisiana*. Lafayette: Archdiocese of New Orleans with Center for Louisiana Studies, 1993.

Copeland, M. Shawn. *The Subversive Power of Love: The Vision of Henriette Delille*. New York: Paulist Press, 2009.

Cordier, Mary Hurlbut. *Schoolwomen of the Prairies and Plains: Personal Narratives from Iowa, Kansas, and Nebraska, 1860s–1920s*. Albuquerque: University of New Mexico Press, 1992.

Cremin, Lawrence A. *The Transformation of the School: Progressivism in American Education, 1876–1957*. New York: Alfred A. Knopf, 1961.

Creese, James. *A.J. Drexel (1826-1893) and His "Industrial University."* Princeton, NJ: Newcomen Society, 1949.

Cummings, Kathleen Sprows. "The 'New Woman' at the 'University': Gender and American Catholic Identity in the Progressive Era." In *The Religious History of American Women: Reimaginging the Past*, edited by Catherine A. Brekus, 206–31. Chapel Hill: University of North Carolina Press, 2007.

———. *New Women of the Old Faith: Gender and American Catholicism in the Progressive Era*. Chapel Hill: University of North Carolina Press, 2009.

———. *A Saint of Our Own: How the Quest for a Holy Hero Helped Catholics Become American*. Chapel Hill: University of North Carolina Press, 2019.

Curtis, Sarah A. *Civilizing Habits: Women Missionaries and the Revival of French Empire*. Oxford: Oxford University Press, 2010.

Curtis, Susan. *A Consuming Faith: The Social Gospel and Modern American Culture*. Baltimore: Johns Hopkins University Press, 1991.

Daigler, Mary Jeremy. *Through the Windows: A History of the Work of Higher Education among the Sisters of Mercy of the Americas*. Scranton. PA: University of Scranton Press, 2001.

Daniel, Pete. *Deep'n As It Come: The 1927 Mississippi River Flood*. Fayetteville: University of Arkansas Press, 1996.

Dauphine, James G. *A Question of Inheritance: Religion, Education, and Louisiana's Cultural Boundary, 1880–1940*. Lafayette: Center for Louisiana Studies, University of Southwestern Louisiana, 1993.

Davis, Cyprian. *The History of Black Catholics in the United States*. New York: Crossroad, 1991.

———. "God of Our Weary Years: Black Catholics in American Catholic History." In *Taking Down Our Harps: Black Catholics in the United States*, edited by Diana Hayes and Cyprian Davis, 17–46. Maryknoll, NY: Orbis, 1998.

Dehey, Elinor Tong. *Religious Orders of Women in the United States: Accounts of Their Origin and of the Most Important Institutions*. Hammond, IN: W. B. Conhey, 1913.

Deloria, Vine, Jr. *Custer Died for Your Sins: An Indian Manifesto*. New York: Macmillan, 1969.

Delpit, Lisa D. "Act Your Age, Not Your Color." In *Growing Up African American in Catholic Schools*, edited by Jacqueline Jordan Irvine and Michele Foster, 116–25. New York: Teachers' College Press, 1996.

De Jong, Greta. *A Different Day: African American Struggles for Justice in Rural Louisiana, 1900–1970*. Chapel Hill: University of North Carolina Press, 2002.

Delooz, Pierre. "Towards a Sociological Study of Canonized Sainthood in the Catholic Church." In *Saints and Their Cults: Studies in Religious Sociology, Folklore and History*, edited by Stephen Wilson, 189–216. Cambridge: Cambridge University Press, 1983.

Deutsch, Stephanie. *You Need a Schoolhouse: Booker T. Washington, Julius Rosenwald, and the Building of Schools for the Segregated South*. Evanston, IL: Northwestern University Press, 2011.

Devore, Donald E., and Joseph Logsdon. *Crescent City Schools: Public Education in New Orleans, 1841–1991*. Lafayette: Center of Louisiana Studies, University of Southwestern Louisiana, 1991.

Dichtl, John R. *Frontiers of Faith: Bringing Catholicism to the West in the Early Republic*. Lexington: University Press of Kentucky, 2008.

Diggs, Margaret A. *Catholic Negro Education in the United States*. Washington, DC: Margaret A. Diggs, 1936.

Dolan, Jay P. *Catholic Revivalism: The American Experience, 1830–1900*. Notre Dame, IN: University of Notre Dame Press, 1978.

———. *The America Catholic Experience: A History from Colonial Times to the Present*. Garden City, NY: Doubleday, 1985.

———. *In Search of an American Catholicism: A History of Religion and Culture in Tension*. New York: Oxford University Press, 2002.

Dolan, Jay P., R. Scott Appleby, Patricia Byrne, and Debra Campbell. *Transforming Parish Ministry: The Changing Roles of Catholic Clergy, Laity and Women Religious*. New York: Crossroad, 1989.

Donovan, Mary Ann. *Sisterhood as Power: The Past and Passion of Ecclesial Women*. New York: Crossroad, 1989.

Dries, Angelyn, OSF. "The Americanization of Religious Life: Women Religious, 1872–1922." *U.S. Catholic Historian* 10, no. 1/2 (1991–92): 13–24.

———. *The Missionary Movement in American Catholic History*. Maryknoll, NY: Orbis, 1998.

Duffy, Consuela Marie, SBS. *Katharine Drexel: A Biography*. Philadelphia: Peter Reilly, 1966.

Edwards, Wendy J. Deichmann, and Carolyn De Swarte Gifford, eds. *Gender and the Social Gospel*. Urbana and Chicago: University of Illinois Press, 2003.

Ellis, Clyde. "'We Had a Lot of Fun, but of Course, That Wasn't the School Part': Life at the Rainy Mountain Boarding School, 1893–1920." In *Boarding School Blues: Revisiting American Indian Educational Experiences*, edited by Clifford Traafzer, Jean A. Keller, and Leone Sisquoc, 76–77. Lincoln: University of Nebraska Press, 2006.

Engs, Robert Francis. *Educating the Disfranchised and Disinherited: Samuel Chapman Armstrong and Hampton Institute, 1839–1893*. Knoxville: University of Tennessee Press, 1999.

Enoch, Jessica. *Refiguring Rhetorical Education: Women Teaching African American, Native American, and Chicano/a Students, 1865–1900*. Carbondale: Southern Illinois University Press, 2008.

Enochs, Ross. *The Jesuit Mission to the Lakota Sioux: A Study of Pastoral Ministry, 1886–1945*. Kansas City, MO: Sheed and Ward, 1996.

Evans, Sara M. "Women's History and Political Theory: Toward a Feminist Approach to Public Life." In *Visible Women: New Essays on American Activism*, edited by Nancy A. Hewitt and Suzanne Lebsock. 119–40. Urbana: University of Illinois Press, 1993.
Ewens, Mary. *The Role of the Nun in Nineteenth-Century America*. New York: Arno Press, 1978.
———. "Political Activity of American Sisters Before 1970." In *Between God and Caesar: Priests, Sisters, and Political Office in the United States*, edited by Madonna Kolbenschlag, 30–51. New York: Paulist Press, 1985.
Fairclough, Adam. *Race & Democracy: The Civil Rights Struggle in Louisiana, 1915–1982*. Athens: University of Georgia Press, 1995.
———. *Teaching Equality: Black Schools in the Age of Jim Crow*. Athens: University of Georgia Press, 2001.
Fisher, James Terrence. *The Catholic Counterculture in America, 1933–1962*. Chapel Hill: University of North Carolina Press, 1989.
Fisher, John E. *The John F. Slater Fund: A Nineteenth-Century Affirmative Action for Negro Education*. Lanham, MD: University Press of America, 1986.
Flanagan, Maureen A. *America Reformed: Progressives and Progressivisms 1890s-1920s*. New York: Oxford University Press, 2007.
Foley, Albert S. *God's Men of Color*. New York: Arno Press, 1969.
Foley, Thomas W. *Father Francis M. Craft: Missionary to the Sioux*. Lincoln: University of Nebraska Press, 2002.
Franklin, Vincent P. *The Education of Black Philadelphia: The Social and Educational History of a Minority Community, 1900–1950*. Philadelphia: University of Pennsylvania Press, 1979.
Frystak, Shannon. *Our Minds on Freedom: Women and the Struggle for Black Equality in Louisiana, 1924–1967*. Baton Rouge: Louisiana State University Press, 2009.
Gannon, Michael V. *Rebel Bishop: The Life and Era of Augustin Verot*. Milwaukee: Bruce, 1954.
Gates, Henry Louis, and Evelyn Brooks-Higginbotham, eds. *African American Lives*. Oxford: Oxford University Press, 2004.
Giago, Tim. *The Aboriginal Sin: Reflections on the Holy Rosary Indian Mission School (Red Cloud Indian School)*. San Francisco: Indian History Press, 1978.
Gifford, Carolyn De Swarte, ed. *The American Deaconess Movement in the Early Twentieth Century*. New York: Garland, 1987.
Gilmore, Glenda Elizabeth. *Gender and Jim Crow: Women and the Politics of White Supremacy, 1896–1920*. Chapel Hill: University of North Carolina Press, 1996.

———. *Defying Dixie: The Radical Roots of Civil Rights, 1919–1950.* New York: W. W. Norton, 2008.

Ginzburg, Lori. *Women and the Work of Benevolence: Morality, Politics, and Class in the Nineteenth-Century United States.* New Haven, CT: Yale University Press, 1990.

Goggin, Jacqueline. *Carter G. Woodson: A Life in Black History.* Baton Rouge: Louisiana State University Press, 1993.

Griffin, Sr. M. Julian, VSC. *Tomorrow Comes the Song: The Story of Catholicism among the Black Population of South Georgia, 1850–1978.* Savannah, GA: Sister M. Julian, 1978.

Guilday, Peter. *A History of the Councils of Baltimore, 1791–1884.* New York: Arno Press, 1969.

Hale, Grace Elizabeth. *Making Whiteness: The Culture of Segregation in the South, 1890–1940.* New York: Pantheon, 1998.

Hall, David D., ed. *Lived Religion in America: Toward a History of Practice.* Princeton, NJ: Princeton University Press, 1997.

Hall, Jacquelyn Dowd. *Revolt against Chivalry: Jessie Daniel Ames and the Women's Campaign against Lynching.* New York: Columbia University Press, 1979.

Halsey, William M. *The Survival of American Innocence: Catholicism in an Era of Disillusionment, 1920–1940.* Notre Dame, IN: University of Notre Dame Press, 1980.

Handy, Robert T., ed. *The Social Gospel in America, 1870–1920: Gladden, Ely, and Rauschenbusch.* New York: Oxford University Press, 1996.

Harlan, Louis R. *Separate and Unequal: Public School Campaigns and Racism in the Southern Seaboard States 1901–1915.* New York: Atheneum, 1969. Originally published in 1958.

Hart, Mary Francis Borgia. *Violets in the King's Garden: A History of the Sisters of the Holy Family of New Orleans.* New Orleans: Sister Mary Francis Borgia Hart, 1976.

Hayes, Diana L. "Standing in the Shoes My Mother Made: The Making of a Catholic Womanist Theologian." In *Deeper Shades of Purple: Womanism in Religion and Society*, edited by Stacey M. Floyd-Thomas, 55–76. New York: New York University Press, 2006.

Hill, Patricia. *The World Their Household: The American Woman's Foreign Mission Movement and Cultural Transformation, 1870–1920.* Ann Arbor: University of Michigan Press, 1985.

Hoffschwelle, Mary S. *The Rosenwald Schools of the American South.* Gainesville: University Press of Florida, 2006.

Holt, Marilyn Irvin. *Indian Orphanages.* Lawrence: University Press of Kansas, 2001.

Hoxie, Frederick E. *A Final Promise: The Campaign to Assimilate the Indians, 1880–1920*. Lincoln: University of Nebraska Press, 1984.
Hoy, Suellen. *Good Hearts: Catholic Sisters in Chicago's Past*. Urbana: University of Illinois Press, 2006.
Hughes, Cheryl C. D. *Katharine Drexel: The Riches-to-Rags Story of an American Catholic* Saint. Grand Rapids, MI: Eerdmans, 2014.
Hunter, Jane H. "Women's Mission in Historical Perspective: American Identity and Christian Internationalism." In *Competing Kingdoms: Women, Mission, Nation, and the American Protestant Empires, 1812–1960*, edited by Barbara Reeves-Ellington, Kathryn Kish Sklar, and Connie Schemo, 19–42. Durham, NC: Duke University Press, 2010.
Huthmacher, J. Joseph. *Senator Robert F. Wagner and the Rise of Urban Liberalism*. New York: Athenaeum, 1968.
Jackson, Giles B., and D. Webster Davis. *The Industrial History of the Negro Race of the United States*. Richmond, VA: Giles B. Jackson, 1908.
Jackson, Helen Hunt. *Century of Dishonor: A Sketch of the U.S. Government's Dealings with Some of the Tribes*. Boston: Roberts Brothers, 1895. Originally published in 1889.
Jacobs, Margaret D. *White Mother to a Dark Race: Settler Colonialism, Maternalism, and the Removal of Indigenous Children in the American West and Australia, 1880–1940*. Lincoln: University of Nebraska Press, 2009.
Jacobson, Matthew Frye. *Barbarian Virtues: The United States Encounters Foreign Peoples at Home and Abroad, 1876–1917*. New York: Hill and Wang, 2000.
Janiewski, Dolores. "Giving Women a Future: Alice Fletcher, the 'Woman Question,' and 'Indian Reform." In *Visible Women: New Essays on American Activism*, edited by Nancy A. Hewitt and Suzanne Lebsock, 325–44. Urbana: University of Illinois Press, 1993.
Janken, Kenneth Robert. *White: The Biography of Walter White, Mr. NAACP*. New York: New Press, 2003.
Johnson, Nessa Theresa Baskerville. *A Special Pilgrimage: A History of Black Catholics in Richmond*. Richmond, VA: Diocese of Richmond, 1978.
Jones, Edward A. *A Candle in the Dark: A History of Morehouse College*. Valley Forge, PA: Judson Press, 1967.
Jones, Jacqueline. *Soldiers of Light and Love: Northern Teachers and Georgia Blacks, 1865–1873*. Athens and London: Brown Thrasher Books, University of Georgia Press, 1992.

Jones, Lance G. *The Jeanes Teacher in the United States, 1908–1933*. Chapel Hill: University of North Carolina Press, 1937.
Jones, Robert P. *White Too Long: The Legacy of White Supremacy in American Christianity*. New York: Simon and Schuster Paperbacks, 2020.
Jones, Thomas Jesse, ed. *Negro Education: A Study of the Private and Higher Schools for Colored People in the United States*. New York: Arno Press and the *New York Times*, 1969.
Josephite Fathers. *The Josephites: A Century of Evangelization in the African American Community*. Baltimore: St. Joseph's Society of the Sacred Heart, 1993.
Kane, Paula, James Kenneally, and Karen Kennelly, eds. *Gender Identities in American Catholicism*. Maryknoll, NY: Orbis, 2001.
Kantor, Harvey, and David B. Tyack, eds. *Work, Youth, and Schooling: Historical Perspectives on Vocationalism in American Education*. Stanford, CA: Stanford University Press, 1982.
Kantowicz, Edward R. *Corporation Sole: Cardinal Mundelein and Chicago Catholicism*. Notre Dame, IN: University of Notre Dame Press, 1983.
Kaplan, Amy. *The Anarchy of Empire in the Making of U.S. Culture*. Cambridge, MA: Harvard University Press, 2002.
Kasteel, Annemarie. *Francis Janssens, 1843–1897: A Dutch American Prelate*. Lafayette: Center for Louisiana Studies, University of Southwestern Louisiana, 1992.
Keller, Robert H. *American Protestantism and the United States Indian Policy, 1869–82*. Lincoln: University of Nebraska Press, 1983.
Kendi, Ibram X. *Stamped from the Beginning: The Definitive History of Racist Ideas in America*. New York: Nation, 2016.
Kenneally, James J. *The History of American Catholic Women*. New York: Crossroad, 1990.
Kennelly, Karen, CSJ, ed. *American Catholic Women: A Historical Exploration*. New York: Macmillan, 1989.
Kinzer, Donald. *An Episode in Anti-Catholicism: The American Protective Association*. Seattle: University of Washington Press, 1964.
Kirby, Jack Temple. *Darkness at the Dawning: Race and Reform in the Progressive South*. Philadelphia: J. Lippincott, 1971.
Kirlin, J. *The Life of Most Reverend Patrick John Ryan, D.D., L.L.D. Archbishop of Philadelphia and Record of His Golden Jubilee*. Part 1. Philadelphia: Gibbons, 1903.
Knecht, Sharon C. *Oblate Sisters of Providence: A Pictorial History*. Virginia Beach, VA: Donning, 2007.
Kobes Du Mez, Kristin. *Jesus and John Wayne: How White Evangelicals Corrupted a Faith and Fractured a Nation*. New York: Liveright, 2021.

Koehlinger, Amy L. "'Are You the White Sisters or the Black Sisters?': Women Confounding Categories of Race and Gender." In *The Religious History of American Women: Reimagining the Past*, edited by Catherine A. Brekus, 253–78. Chapel Hill: University of North Carolina Press, 2007.

———. *The New Nuns: Racial Justice and Religious Reform in the 1960s*. Cambridge, MA: Harvard University Press, 2007.

Koren, Henry J., CSSp. *The Serpent and the Dove: A History of the Congregation of the Holy Ghost in the United States, 1745–1984*. Pittsburgh: Spiritus Press, 1985.

Koven, Seth, and Sonya Michel, eds. *Mothers of a New World: Maternalist Politics and the Origins of Welfare States*. New York: Routledge, 1993.

Kuhns, Elizabeth. *The Habit: A History of the Clothing of Catholic Nuns*. New York: Doubleday, 2003.

Labbé, Dolores Egger. *Jim Crow Comes to Church*. New York: Arno Press, 1978.

Lanigan, Paul Joseph. *Society of Saint Joseph of the Sacred Heart 1893–1943*. Baltimore: Josephite Press, 1943.

Lears, Jackson. *Rebirth of a Nation: The Making of Modern America, 1877–1920*. New York: HarperPerennial, 2009.

Leslie, Shane. *Letters of Herbert Cardinal Vaughn to Lady Herbert of Lea, 1867–1903*. London: Macmillan, 1942.

Lisio, Donald J. *Hoover, Blacks, & Lily-Whites: A Study of Southern Strategies*. Chapel Hill: University of North Carolina Press, 1985.

Logan, Rayford Whittingham. *Howard University: The First Hundred Years, 1867–1967*. New York: New York University Press, 1969.

Lomawaima, K. Tisianina. *They Called It Prairie Light: The Story of Chilocco Indian School*. Lincoln: University of Nebraska Press, 1994.

Lorde, Audre. *Zami: A New Spelling of My Name*. Berkeley, CA: Crossing Press, 1982.

Lucas, Lawrence. *Black Priest/White Church: Catholics and Racism*. New York: Random House, 1970.

Luker, Ralph E. *The Social Gospel in Black and White: American Racial Reform, 1885–1912*. Chapel Hill: University of North Carolina Press, 1991.

Lynch, Patricia, SBS. "Mother Katharine Drexel's Rural Schools: Education and Evangelization through Lay Leadership." In *Cross, Crozier and Crucible: A Volume Celebrating the Bicentennial of a Catholic Diocese in Louisiana*, edited by Glenn R. Conrad, 262–74. Lafayette: Archdiocese of New Orleans with the Center for Louisiana Studies, 1993.

MacLean, Nancy. *Behind the Mask of Chivalry: The Making of the Second Ku Klux Klan*. New York: Oxford University Press, 1994.

Mahoney, Irene, OSU. *Lady Blackrobes: Missionaries in the Heart of Indian Country*. Golden, CO: Fulcrum, 2006.

Mann, Kristen Dutcher. *The Power of Song: Music and Dance in Mission Communities of Northern New Spain, 1590–1810*. Stanford, CA: Stanford University Press, 2010.

Marlin, George J. *The American Catholic Voter: 200 Years of Political Impact*. South Bend, IN: St. Augustine's Press, 2004.

Marriot, Alice Lee. *María: The Potter of San Ildefonso*. Norman: University of Oklahoma Press, 1948.

Marshall, Patricia, SBS. "Sister Mary Francess Buttell (1884–1977), Visionary for Xavier University." In *Religious Pioneers: Building the Faith in the Archdiocese of New Orleans*, edited by Dorothy Dawes and Charles Nolan, 287–98. New Orleans: Archdiocese of New Orleans, 2004.

Massa, Mark S. *Catholics and American Culture: Fulton Sheen, Dorothy Day, and the Notre Dame Football Team*. New York: Crossroad, 1999.

———. *Anti-Catholicism in America: The Last Acceptable Prejudice*. New York: Crossroad, 2003.

Massingale, Bryan N. *Racial Justice and the Catholic Church*. Maryknoll, NY: Orbis, 2010.

McBeth, Sally. *Ethnic Identity and the Boarding School Experience of West Central Oklahoma American Indians*. Washington, DC: University Press of America, 1983.

McDannell, Colleen. *The Christian Home in Victorian America, 1840–1900*. Bloomington: Indiana University Press, 1986.

———. *Material Christianity: Religion and Popular Culture in America*. New Haven, CT: Yale University Press, 1995.

McGerr, Michael. *A Fierce Discontent: The Rise and Fall of the Progressive Movement in America*. New York: Oxford University Press, 2003.

McGreevy, John T. *Parish Boundaries: The Catholic Encounter with Race in the Twentieth-Century Urban North*. Chicago: University of Chicago Press, 1996.

———. *Catholicism and American Freedom: A History*. New York: W. W. Norton, 2003.

McGuinness, Margaret M. *Called to Serve: A History of Nuns in America*. New York: New York University Press, 2013.

McGuire, Meredith B. *Lived Religion: Faith and Practice in Everyday Life*. New York: Oxford University Press, 2008.

McNamara, Jo Ann Kay. *Sisters in Arms: Catholic Nuns through Two Millennia.* Cambridge, MA: Harvard University Press, 1996.
McShane, Joseph M. *"Sufficiently Radical": Catholicism, Progressivism, and the Bishops' Program of 1919.* Washington, DC: The Catholic University of America Press, 1986.
McSheffery, Daniel. *Saint Katharine Drexel: Pioneer for Human Rights.* Totowa, NJ: Resurrection Press, 2002.
Meyers, Bertrande. *The Education of Sisters: A Plan for Integrating the Religious, Social, Cultural and Professional Training of Sisters.* New York: Sheed and Ward, 1941.
Moore, Andrew S. *The South's Tolerable Alien: Roman Catholics in Alabama and Georgia 1945–1970.* Baton Rouge: Louisiana State University Press, 2007.
Moore, James T. *Acts of Faith: The Catholic Church in Texas 1900–1950.* College Station: Texas A&M Press, 2002.
Morrison, Dane, ed. *American Indian Studies: An Interdisciplinary Approach to Contemporary Issues.* New York: Peter Lang, 1997.
Morrow, Diane Batts. "Faith and Frugality in Antebellum Baltimore: The Economic Credo of the Oblate Sisters of Providence." In *Neither Lady nor Slave: Working Women of the Old South,* edited by Susanna Delfino and Michele Gillespie, 221–45. Chapel Hill: University of North Carolina Press, 2002.
———. *Persons of Color and Religious at the Same Time: The Oblate Sisters of Providence, 1828–1860.* Chapel Hill: University of North Carolina Press, 2002.
Moslener, Sarah. *Virgin Nation: Sexual Purity and American Adolescence.* Oxford: Oxford University Press, 2015.
Mosely, Charleton. "Latent Klanism in Georgia, 1890–1915." *Georgia Historical Quarterly* 56 (Fall 1972): 365–86.
Nickels, Marilyn Wenzke. *Black Catholic Protest and the Federated Colored Catholics, 1917–1933: Three Perspectives on Racial Justice.* New York: Garland, 1988.
Nordstrom, Justin. *Danger on the Doorstep: Anti-Catholicism and American Print Culture in the Progressive Era.* Notre Dame, IN: University of Notre Dame Press, 2006.
Oates, Mary J., ed. *Higher Education for Catholic Women: An Historical Anthology.* New York: Garland, 1987.
———. *The Catholic Philanthropic Tradition in America.* Bloomington: Indiana University Press, 1995.
O'Brien, David J., and Thomas A. Shannon. *Catholic Social Thought: The Documentary Heritage.* Maryknoll, NY: Orbis, 2003.

O'Connell, Marvin R. *John Ireland and the American Catholic Church*. St. Paul: Minnesota Historical Society Press, 1988.

O'Connell, Maureen H. *Undoing the Knots: Five Generations of American Catholic Anti-Blackness*. Boston: Beacon Press, 2021.

Ochs, Stephen J. *Desegregating the Altar: The Josephites and the Struggle for Black Priests, 1871–1960*. Baton Rouge: Louisiana State University Press, 1990.

Orsi, Robert A. *Thank You, St. Jude: Women's Devotion to the Patron Saint of Hopeless Causes*. New Haven, CT: Yale University Press, 1996.

———. "Everyday Miracles: The Study of Lived Religion." In *Lived Religion in America: Toward a History of Practice*, edited by David D. Hall, 3–21. Princeton, NJ: Princeton University Press, 1997.

———. *The Madonna of 115th Street: Faith and Community in Italian Harlem, 1880–1950*. 2nd ed. New Haven, CT: Yale University Press, 2002.

———. *Between Heaven and Earth: The Religious Worlds People Make and the Scholars Who Study Them*. Princeton, NJ: Princeton University Press, 2005.

Osborne, William A. *The Segregated Covenant: Race Relations and American Catholics*. New York: Herder and Herder, 1967.

Peterman, Thomas Joseph. *The Cutting Edge: The Life of Thomas Andrew Becker, 1831–1899, First Bishop of Wilmington, Delaware, Sixth Bishop of Savannah, Georgia*. Devon, PA: Wm. T. Cooke, 1982.

Polite, Vernon C. "Making a Way Out of No Way: The Oblate Sisters of Providence and St. Frances Academy in Baltimore, Maryland, 1828 to the Present." In *Growing Up African American in Catholic Schools*, edited by Jacqueline Jordan Irvine and Micehle Foster, 62–75. New York: Teachers' College Press, 1996.

Posey, Thaddeus J. "Praying in the Shadows: The Oblate Sisters of Providence, a Look at Nineteenth-Century Black Catholic Spirituality." In *This Far by Faith: Readings in African-American Women's Religious Biography*, edited by Judith Weisenfeld and Richard Newman, 73–93. New York: Routledge, 1996.

Prucha, Francis Paul. *American Indian Policy in the Formative Years: The Indian Trade and Intercourse Acts 1790–1834*. Cambridge, MA: Harvard University Press, 1962.

———. *Americanizing the American Indians: Writings of the "Friends of the Indian" 1880–1900*. Cambridge, MA: Harvard University Press, 1973.

———. *The Churches and the Indian Schools, 1888–1912*. Lincoln: University of Nebraska Press, 1979.

———. *The Great Father: The United States Government and the American Indians*. Lincoln: University of Nebraska Press, 1984.
Raboteau, Albert J. *A Fire in the Bones: Reflections on African American Religious History*. Boston: Beacon Press, 1995.
Rahill, Peter J. *The Catholic Indian Missions and Grant's Peace Policy, 1870–1884*. Washington, DC: The Catholic University of America Press, 1953.
Rathbun, Tanya. "Hail Mary: The Catholic Experience at St. Boniface." In *Boarding School Blues: Revisiting America Indian Educational Experiences*, edited by Clifford Traafzer, Jean A. Keller, and Loene Sisquoc, 156. Lincoln: University of Nebraska Press, 2006.
Read, Florence Matilda. *The Story of Spelman College*. Atlanta: Princeton University Press, 1961.
Reeves-Ellington, Barbara, Kathryn Kish Sklar, and Connie A. Shemo, eds. *Competing Kingdoms: Women, Mission, Nation, and the American Protestant Empire, 1812–1960*. Durham, NC: Duke University Press, 2010.
Richardson, Joe M. *Christian Reconstruction: The American Missionary Association and Southern Blacks, 1861–1890*. Athens: University of Georgia Press, 1986.
Riley, Glenda. *Confronting Race: Women and Indians on the Frontier, 1815–1915*. Albuquerque: University of New Mexico Press, 2004.
Robert, Dana Lee. *American Women in Mission: A Social History of Their Thought and Practice*. Macon, GA: Mercer University Press, 1996.
———, ed. *Gospel Bearers, Gender Barriers: Missionary Women in the Twentieth Century*. Maryknoll, NY: Orbis, 2002.
Rury, John L. *Education and Women's Work: Female Schooling and the Division of Labor in Urban America, 1870–1930*. Albany: State University of New York Press, 1991.
Ruswick, Brent. *Almost Worthy: The Poor, Paupers, and the Science of Charity in America, 1877–1917*. Bloomington: Indiana University Press, 2013.
Scharf, Lois. *To Work and To Wed: Female Employment, Feminism, and the Great Depression*. Westport, CT: Greenwood Press, 1980.
Schuck, Michael J. *That They May Be One: The Social Teachings of the Papal Encyclicals, 1740–1989*. Washington, DC: Georgetown University Press, 1991.
Schultz, Nancy Lusignan, ed. *Veil of Fear: Nineteenth-Century Convent Tales*. West Lafayette, IN: Purdue University Press, 1999.
———. *Fire and Roses: The Burning of the Charleston Convent, 1834*. New York: Free Press, 2000.

Scott, Anne Firor. *Natural Allies: Women's Associations in American History*. Urbana: University of Illinois Press, 1991.

Sealander, Judith. *Private Wealth and Public Life: Foundation Philanthropy and the Reshaping of American Social Policy from the Progressive Era to the New Deal*. Baltimore: Johns Hopkins University Press, 1997.

Semple, Rhonda Ann. *Missionary Women: Gender, Professionalism and the Victorian Idea of Christian Mission*. Suffolk: Boydell Press, 2003.

Sernett, Milton C. *Bound for the Promised Land: African American Religion and the Great Migration*. Durham, NC: Duke University Press, 1997.

Sheen, Fulton J. *The Mystical Body of Christ*. London: Sheed and Ward, 1935.

Sitkoff, Harvard. *A New Deal for Blacks: The Emergence of Civil Rights as a National Issue: The Depression Decade*. New York: Oxford University Press, 1978.

Skok, Deborah A. *More Than Neighbors: Catholic Settlements and Day Nurseries in Chicago, 1893–1930*. DeKalb: Southern Illinois University Press, 2007.

Smithson, Sandra O. *To Be the Bridge: A Commentary on Black/White Catholicism in America*. Nashville: Winston-Derek, 1984.

Southern, David W. *John LaFarge and the Limits of Catholic Interracialism, 1913–1963*. Baton Rouge: Louisiana State University Press, 1996.

Spivey, Donald. *Schooling for the New Slavery: Black Industrial Education, 1868–1915*. Westport, CT: Greenwood Press, 1978.

Strong, Josiah. *Our Country, Its Possible Future, and Its Present Crisis*. Rev. ed. New York: Baker and Taylor, 1891.

Suenens, Leon Joseph Cardinal. *The Nun in the World: Religious and the Apostolate*. Translated by Geoffery Stevens. Wheathampstead, Hertfordshire: Anthony Clarke, 1962.

Sullivan, Patricia. *Days of Hope: Race and Democracy in the New Deal Era*. Chapel Hill: University of North Carolina Press, 1996.

———. *Lift Every Voice: The NAACP and the Making of the Civil Rights Movement*. New York: New Press, 2009.

Szaz, Margaret Connell. *Education and the American Indian: The Road to Self-Determination since 1928*. Albuquerque: University of New Mexico Press, 1974.

———. *Between Indian and White Worlds: The Cultural Broker*. Norman: University of Oklahoma Press, 1994.

Tarry, Ellen. *Katharine Drexel, Friend of the Oppressed*. San Francisco: Ignatius Press, 1958.

Taves, Ann. *The Household of Faith: Roman Catholic Devotions in Mid-Nineteenth Century America*. Notre Dame, IN: University of Notre Dame Press, 1986.
Thompson, Margaret Susan. "Philemon's Dilemma: Nuns and the Black Community in Nineteenth-Century America: Some Findings." In *The American Catholic Religious Life: Selected Historical Essays*, edited by Joseph M. White, 81–96. New York: Garland, 1988.
———. "Women, Feminism and the New Religious History: Catholic Sisters as a Case Study." In *Belief and Behavior: Essays in the New Religious History*, edited by. Philip R. Vandermeer and Robert P. Swierenga, 136–63. New Brunswick, NJ: Rutgers University Press, 1991.
Tilley, Terrence W. *Inventing Catholic Tradition*. Maryknoll, NY: Orbis, 2000.
Tinker, George E. *Missionary Conquest: The Gospel and Native American Cultural Genocide*. Minneapolis: Fortress Press, 1993.
Traafzer, Clifford, Jean A. Keller, and Loene Sisquoc, eds. *Boarding School Blues: Revisiting American Indian Educational Experiences*. Lincoln: University of Nebraska Press, 2006.
Trawick, Robert. "Dorothy Day and the Social Gospel Movement: Different Theologies, Common Concerns." In *Gender and the Social Gospel*, edited by Wendy J. Deichmann and Carolyn De Swarte Gifford, 139–49. Urbana: University of Illinois Press, 2003.
Trennert, Robert A. *The Phoenix Indian School: Forced Assimilation in Arizona, 1891–1935*. Norman: University of Oklahoma Press, 1988.
Turner, George J. "The Josephites and Catholic Education in the United States." Ph.D. diss., Fordham University, 1957.
Tweed, Thomas A. ed. *Retelling U.S. Religious History*. Berkeley: University of California Press, 1997.
———. *Crossing and Dwelling: A Theory of Religion*. Cambridge, MA: Harvard University Press, 2006.
Tyrell, Ian. "Women, Missions, and Empire: New Approaches to American Cultural Expansion." In *Competing Kingdoms: Women, Mission, Nation, and the American Protestant Empire*, edited by Barbara Reeves-Ellington, Kathryn Kish Sklar, and Connie A. Shemo, 43–66. Durham, NC: Duke University Press, 2010.
Vanderholt, James F., Carolyn B. Martinez, and Karen A. Gilman. *The Diocese of Beaumont: The Catholic Story of Southeast Texas*. Beaumont: East Texas Catholic, 1991.
Vadermeer, Philip R., and Robert P. Swierenga, eds. *Belief and Behavior: Essays in the New Religious History*. New Brunswick, NJ: Rutgers University Press, 1991.

Van Nuys, Frank. *Americanizing the West: Race, Immigrants, and Citizenship, 1890–1930.* Lawrence: University of Kansas Press, 2002.

Vecsey, Christopher. *On the Padre's Trail.* Notre Dame, IN: University of Notre Dame Press, 1996.

———. *The Paths of Kateri's Kin.* Notre Dame, IN: University of Notre Dame Press, 1997.

———. *Where the Two Roads Meet.* Notre Dame, IN: University of Notre Dame Press, 1999.

Verney, Kevern, and Lee Sartain, eds. *Long Is the Way and Hard: One Hundred Years of the NAACP.* Fayetteville: University of Arkansas Press, 2009.

Vidulich, Dorothy. *Peace Pays a Price: A Study of Margaret Anna Cusak, the Nun of Kenmare.* Teaneck, NJ: Garden State Press, 1975.

Walch, Timothy. *Parish School: American Catholic Parochial Education from Colonial Times to the Present.* New York: Crossroad-Herder, 1996.

Weaver, Mary Jo. *New Catholic Women: A Contemporary Challenge to Traditional Religious Authority.* San Francisco: Harper and Row, 1986.

Weisenfeld, Judith, and Richard Newman, eds. *This Far by Faith: Readings in African-American Women's Religious Biography.* New York: Routledge, 1996.

Weisiger, Marsha. *Dreaming of Sheep in Navajo Country.* Seattle: University of Washington Press, 2009.

White, Joseph M., ed. *The American Catholic Religious Life: Selected Historical Essays.* New York: Garland, 1988.

White, Ronald Jr. *Liberty and Justice for All: Racial Reform and the Social Gospel (1877–1925).* Louisville, Ky.: Westminster John Knox Press, 2002.

Wilken, Robert L. *Anselm Weber, O.F.M.: Missionary to the Navaho, 1898–1921.* Milwaukee: Bruce, 1955.

Wittenberg, Patricia. *The Rise and Fall of Catholic Religious Orders: A Social Movement Perspective.* Albany: State University of New York Press, 1994.

Wolters, Raymond. *Negroes and the Great Depression: The Problem of Economic Recovery.* Westport, CT: Greenwood, 1970.

Woods, James M. *A History of the Catholic Church in the American South, 1513–1900.* Gainesville: University Press of Florida, 2011.

Woods, Thomas E., Jr. *The Church Confronts Modernity: Catholic Intellectuals and the Progressive Era.* New York: Columbia University Press, 2004.

Woodson, Carter G. *The Mis-Education of the Negro.* Philadelphia: Harkin Press, 1931.

Woodward, C. Vann. *Tom Watson: Agrarian Rebel.* New York: Oxford University Press, 1963.
Woodward, Kenneth L. *Making Saints: How the Catholic Church Determines Who Becomes a Saint, Who Doesn't and Why.* New York: Simon and Schuster, 1990.
Yohn, Susan A. *A Contest of Faiths: Missionary Women and Pluralism in the American Southwest.* Ithaca, NY: Cornell University Press, 1995.
York, Darlene Eleanor. "The Academic Achievement of African Americans in Catholic Schools: A Review of the Literature." In *Growing Up African American in Catholic Schools*, edited by Jacqueline Jordan Irvine and Micehle Foster, 11–46. New York: Teachers' College Press, 1996.
Young, Ethel E., and Jerome Wilson. *African American Children and Missionary Nuns and Priests in Mississippi: An Achievement against Jim Crow Odds.* Bloomington, IN: Authorhouse, 2010.
Zangrando, Robert L. *The NAACP Crusade against Lynching, 1909–1950.* Philadelphia: Temple University Press, 1980.

## Journal Essays

Alberts, John B. "Black Catholic Schools: The Josephite Parishes of New Orleans during the Jim Crow Era." *U.S. Catholic Historian* 12 (Winter 1994): 77–98.
Anderson, Christine M. "Catholic Nuns and the Invention of Social Work: The Sisters of the Santa Maria Institute of Cincinnati, Ohio, 1897 through the 1920s." *Journal of Women's History* 12, no. 1 (Spring 2000): 60–88.
Banner, Lois. "Religious Benevolence as Social Control: A Critique of an Interpretation." *Journal of American History* 60, no. 1 (June 1973): 23–41.
Boykin, Leander L. "The Status and Trends of Differentials between White and Negro Teachers' Salaries in the Southern United States, 1900–1946." *Journal of Negro Education* 18, no. 1 (Winter 1949): 40–47.
Butler, Anne. "Western Spaces, Catholic Places." *U.S. Catholic Historian* 18, no. 4 (Fall 2000): 25–39.
Dunch, Ryan. "Beyond Cultural Imperialism: Cultural Theory, Christian Missions, and Global Modernity." *History and Theory* 41 (2002): 301–25.
Fichter, Joseph, H. "The White Church and the Black Sisters." *U.S. Catholic Historian* 12, no. 1 (Winter 1994): 31–48.

Freedman, Estelle. "Separatism as Strategy: Female Institution Building and American Feminism, 1870–1930." *Feminist Studies* 5, no. 3 (1979): 512–29.
Garneau, James F. "Saint Katharine Drexel in the Light of the New Evangelization." *Josephinum Journal of Theology* 10, no. 1 (Jan. 2003): 122–31.
Harlan, Louis R. "Desegregation in New Orleans Public Schools during Reconstruction." *American Historical Review* 67, no. 3 (April 1962): 663–75.
Kaplan, Amy. "Manifest Domesticity." *American Literature* 70, no. 3 (1998): 581–606.
Lagarde, Roland, SBS. "A Contemporary Pilgrimage: Personal Testimony of Blessed Katherine Drexel's Charism." *U.S. Catholic Historian* 8, nos. 1–2 (Winter–Spring, 1989): 47–50.
Lynch, Patricia, SBS. "Collective Biography: Founding Women of the Sisters of the Blessed Sacrament." *U.S. Catholic Historian* 10, nos. 1–2 (1991/1992): 101–6.
McNally, Michael J. "A Peculiar Institution: Catholic Parish Life and the Pastoral Mission to the Blacks in the Southeast, 1850–1980." *U.S. Catholic Historian* 5, no. 1 (1986): 67–80.
Peterson, Susan. "A Widening Horizon: Catholic Sisterhoods on the Northern Plains, 1874–1910." *Great Plains Quarterly* 5, no. 3 (Spring 1985), 125–32.
Slawson, Donald J. "Segregated Catholicism: The Origin of Saint Katherine's Parish, New Orleans." *Vincentian Heritage* 17 (Fall 1996): 141–84.
Spalding, David. "The Negro Catholic Congresses, 1889–1894." *Catholic Historical Review* 55, no. 3 (October 1969): 337–57.
Sullivan, Lester. "The Unknown Randolphe Desnudes: Writings in the New Orleans *Crusader*." *Xavier Review* 10, nos. 1–2 (1990): 1–15.
Sze, Corinne P. "Gone but Not Forgotten: St. Catherine's Industrial Indian School." *Bulletin of the Historic Santa Fe Foundation* 30, no. 1 (Spring 2003), 1–24.
———. "Interview with Patrick Toya: 'Roots that are Very, Very Deep.'" *Bulletin of the Historic Santa Fe Foundation* 30, no. 1 (Spring 2003), 25–31.
Tentler, Leslie Woodcock. "On the Margins: The State of American Catholic History." *American Quarterly* 45, no. 1 (March 1993): 104–27.
Thompson, Margaret Susan. "Sisterhood and Power: Class, Culture, and Ethnicity in the American Convent." *Colby Quarterly* 25, no. 3 (September 1989): 149–75.

Treviño, Roberto R. "Facing Jim Crow: Catholic Sisters and the 'Mexican Problem' in Texas." *Western Historical Quarterly* 34, no. 2 (Summer 2003): 139–64.
Tristano, Richard M. "Holy Family Parish: The Genesis of an African-American Catholic Community in Natchez, Mississippi." *Journal of Negro History* 83, no. 4 (Autumn 1988): 258–83.
Zens, Sister M. Serena, OSB. "The Educational Work of the Catholic Church among the Indians of South Dakota from the Beginning to 1935." *South Dakota Historical Collections* 20, no. 1 (1940): 299–356.

## Theses and Dissertations

Alberts, John B. "Origins of Black Catholic Parishes in the Archdiocese of New Orleans, 1718–1920." Ph.D. diss., Louisiana State University, 1998.
Bland, Sister Joan, SNDN. "*Hibernian Crusade: The Story of the Catholic Total Abstinence Union of America.*" Ph.D. diss., The Catholic University of America, 1951.
Butler, Kristie Lee. "Along the Padres' Trail: The History of St. Michael's Mission to the Navajo (1898–1939)." Master's thesis, Arizona State University, 1991.
Butler, Loretta M. "A History of Catholic Elementary Education for Negroes in the Diocese of Lafayette, Louisiana." Ph.D. diss., The Catholic University of America, 1963.
Collier, Brian S. "St. Catherine Indian School, Santa Fe, 1887–2006: Catholic Indian Education in New Mexico." Ph.D. diss., Arizona State University, 2007.
Condon, Sr. M. Andree. "The Development of the Financial Procedures for the Establishment and Maintenance of Catholic Schools in the Archdiocese of New Orleans, 1727–1958." Ph.D. diss., Louisiana State University, 1959.
Eakin, Sue Lyles. "The Black Struggle for Education in Louisiana, 1877–1930s." Ph.D. diss., University of Southwestern Louisiana, 1980.
Harte, Thomas J., CSsR. "Catholic Organizations Promoting Negro-White Race Relations in the United States." Ph.D. diss., The Catholic University of America, 1947.
Hoskins, Steven. "A Restless Landscape: Building Nashville History and Seventh and Drexel." Ph.D. diss., Middle Tennessee State University, 2008.
Hurd, Nicole Farmer. "The Master Art of a Saint: Katharine Drexel and Her Theology of Education." Ph.D. diss., University of Virginia, 2002.

Kenney, Mary Josephina. "Contributions of the Sisters of the Blessed Sacrament for Indians and Colored People to Catholic Negro Education in the State of Louisiana." Master's thesis, The Catholic University of America, 1942.

Kroutter, Thomas. "The Ku Klux Klan in Jefferson County, TX, 1921–1924." Master's thesis, Lamar University, 1972.

Markmann, Margaret Mary. "Katharine Drexel: Educational Reformer and Institution Builder." Ph.D. diss., Temple University, 2012.

Mattick, Barbara E. "Ministries in Black and White: The Catholic Sisters of St. Augustine, Florida, 1859–1920." Ph.D. diss., Florida State University, 2008.

McLaughlin, Raymond. "A History of State Legislation Affecting Private Elementary and Secondary Schools in the United States, 1870–1945." Ph.D. diss., The Catholic University of America, 1946.

Misch, Edward J. "The American Bishops and the Negro from the Civil War to the Third Plenary Council of Baltimore (1865–1884)." Ph.D. diss., Gregorian Pontifical University, 1968.

Murphy, John C. "An Analysis of the Attitudes of American Catholics Toward the Immigrant and the Negro, 1825–1925." Ph.D. diss., The Catholic University of America, 1940.

Palmer, Leola. "The Evolution of Education for African-Americans in Pointe Coupee Parish (New Roads, Louisiana): 1889–1969." Ph.D. diss., Fordham University, 1992.

Pochè, Justin D. "Religion, Race, and Rights in Catholic Louisiana, 1938–1970." Ph.D. diss., University of Notre Dame, 2007.

Porter, Betty. "The History of Negro Education in Louisiana." Master's thesis, Louisiana State University, 1938.

Riggs, Sister Francis Mary, SBS. "Attitudes of Missionary Sisters toward American Indian Acculturation." Ph.D. diss., Catholic University of America, 1967.

Roche, Richard J., OMI. "Catholic Colleges and the Negro Student." Ph.D. diss., Catholic University of America, 1948.

Rousseve, Theresa Vincent. "The Educational Activities of the Sisters of the Holy Family of New Orleans, Louisiana, 1842–1955." Masters' thesis, The Catholic University of America, 1955.

Sibbel, Megan Stout. "'Reaping the Colored Harvest': The Catholic Mission in the American South." Ph.D. diss, Loyola University of Chicago, 2013.

Smith, Sr. Mary Barat. "A History of St. Emma's Military Academy and St. Francis De Sales High School." Master's thesis, The Catholic University of America, 1949.

# Index

## A
Addams, Jane, 148
Amadeus, Mother M. SBS, 213, 214 n., 219 n.
American Baptist Home Mission Society, 142
American Board for Catholic Missions, 67, 211, 216
American Federation of Labor, 240
American Missionary Association, 5, 142–43, 181, 238
American Protective Association, 252
American Scottsboro Committee, 238
Americanization, 4–5, 14, 58, 68, 85, 96, 253
Anciaux, Father Joseph, 139
anti-Catholicism, 5, 59, 164, 201, 252–54, 264–65
Armstrong, Samuel, 148
Association of Holy Childhood, 52
Atlanta University, 163

## B
Bayley, J. Roosevelt, 51
black education, 147–52, 179–82, 185, 208–11
Blenk, Archbishop James Hubert, 181, 183
Blessed Sacrament School, Beaumont, TX, 164, 255, 266–70
Blessed Sacrament School, New Orleans, LA 184, 186
Boardman, Helen, 240–41
Board of Indian Commissioners, 49–50
Bonin, Gertrude, 96, 100, 118
Bouvier, Emma. See Drexel, Emma
Brown, Warren, 205
*Brown v. Board* decision, 187, 277–78
Browning, Daniel M., 59–60

Bureau of Catholic Indian Missions, 13, 23–24, 45–46, 58, 229–30; creation of, 51; funding of, 52, 60; Drexel donations to, 52–58, 61–63, 80
Bureau of Indian Affairs, 58
Burton, Sister Elizabeth, SBS, 37
Buttell, Sister M. Frances, SBS, 184, 189, 198
Byrne, Bishop Thomas S., 138, 151, 259, 261–63
Byrne, Mary, 184

## C
Cabrini, Mother Frances, 9
Carlisle Indian School, 49, 58–59, 65–66, 100, 105
Catholic Church; ethnic parishes, 256; immigration, 3, 138; mission work with African Americans, 11, 26, 28, 135–40; mission work with Indigenous groups, 11, 47–52; missionaries, 5–6; opposition to Drexel, 257–74; racial justice work, 278; rivalry with Protestants, 7, 9, 59–60, 67–68

Catholic Interracial Council, 234, 249
Catholic Missions Among the Colored People, 139, 141, 178
Catholic Students Mission Crusade, 21, 105
Catholic University of America, 23, 35, 40, 126, 151, 188
Catholic Women, 8–10

Chapelle, Archbishop Louis Placide, 178, 181
Chappo, Michael, 112
Chavez, Nat, 106, 108
Chin Lee, AZ 57, 65

313

Christian Brothers, 149, 154
Coffey, Ida May, 152
Collier, John, 81
Comitè des Citoyens, 175
Conahan, Father Hugh, SSJ, 191, 200
Congress of Colored Catholics, 150–51
Contractor's Code, 245
Corrigan, Archbishop Michael, 12
Costigan-Wagner Anti-Lynching Act, 12, 247–49
Craft, Father Francis, SJ, 15
Crow Dog, Mary, 102
Cusack, Mother Mary Francis, CSJP, 11–12

**D**

Daniel Hand Educational Fund, 142
Davie, Evelyn, 164
Dawes Severalty Act, 52, 105
De Miserabli Conditione Catholicorum Nigorum in America, 142
Delille, Henriette, 145
Desnudes, Rodolphe, 175–76
Dewey, John, 148
Dorsey, Father John, SSJ, 32
Dougherty, Cardinal Dennis, 71, 72, 188, 196, 232
Drexel Institute, 35, 148, 155
Drexel Morrell, Louise, 18, 23, 36, 154, 197, 229, 233, 242–43, 246
Drexel Smith, Elizabeth, 17, 23, 54, 97, 230
Drexel, Anthony, 35, 148
Drexel, Emma Bouvier, 18–20
Drexel, Francis Anthony, 17–18, 22, 54; will of, 22, 78, 278
Drexel, Hannah Jane Langstroth, 17–18
Drexel, Mother M. Katharine, SBS; American identity, 253; business practices, 68–74; comparison to Julius Rosenwald, 195–96, 224–26; contributions to Black education, 140–42; discerning a vocation, 23–26; early life, 17–22; education of, 20, 35; first philanthropy, 22–23; founding the SBS, 27; income tax exemption, 79; joins Sisters of Mercy convent, 26; limitations to philanthropy, 74–80; missionary agenda of, 11; NAACP collaboration, 234–50; partnership with Bureau of Catholic Indian Missions, 23, 45–46; political education of 229–32; *Positio of*, 229; sainthood of, 13, 46, 229, 251, 273; shift from spiritual to temporal concerns, 228–29, 276; subsidies to BCIM, 63–65, 77–78; views on race, 11, 29–32; views on voting, 3, 15, 232; waning influence at BCIM, 80–84
Dyer Anti-Lynching Bill, 231

**E**

Eadie, Betty J., 96, 102
Eisenman, Sylvester OSB, 72, 89–90, 104, 107
Ellis, Clyde, 102
Eucharist, 27, 40–42, 111, 135, 163, 222, 263, 279
Evans, Hiram Wesley, 265–66
Ewing, Charles, 51

**F**

Federated Colored Catholics, 196, 233–34
Fletcher, Juanita, 155, 158, 280
Flizigai, Zita, 119
Fort Defiance, AZ, 65–66, 88, 93
Fortunate Eagle, Adam, 68, 96, 102
Franciscan Sisters of Mill Hill, 29, 145
Friends of the Indian, 5, 15, 49

**G**

Gaudin, Juliette, SSF, 145
General Education Board, 141–42, 148, 157, 166
Giago, Tim, 102, 120
Gibbons, Cardinal James, 8, 32, 141
Gillard, John, SSJ, 31, 136, 171, 249

Girault de la Corgnais, Father J., 207
Gorman, Katherine, 153
Grant, Margaret, 106
Grant, Ulysses S., 50–51
Guidry, Gertrude, 198
Guidry, Sister Mary Gabriella, SSF, 135, 140, 166

**H**

Haile, Father Berard, OSF 47, 112
Hampton Institute, 148
Handmaids of Mary, 37
Harding, Warren G., 230
Holy Family Sisters, 37–38, 135, 144–45, 166, 193, 212, 267
Holy Ghost Fathers, 146, 213–14
Holy Name Society, 115
Holy Providence School, Torresdale, PA 38, 152–53
Hoover, Herbert, 240–41
Howard University, 143, 195, 201
Hughes, Rev. William, 63, 66–67, 69–80, 83, 90–91, 98, 122, 141
Hunt, Wilber, 116
Hunton, George K., 140, 233, 238

**I**

Immaculate Mother School, Nashville, TN, 259–64, 277
Indian Rights Association, 5
*Indian Sentinel*, 13, 63–64, 96–97, 121, 124, 127, 228
industrial education, 147–52

**J**

Jackson, David, 201–2
Jackson, Helen Hunt, 20–21, 48–49
Janssens, Archbishop Francis, 169–78, 182, 211
Jeanes Fund, 142
Jeanes, Anna T., 166
Jeanmard, Bishop Jean Jules, 211–12, 215, 218, 220
Johnson-O'Malley Act, 84
Josephites, See Society of Saint Joseph
Joubert, James SSP, 145

**K**

Keith, Samuel, 260–62
Ketcham, Father William, 45, 47, 59–61, 63, 67–69, 73–75, 78–80, 110, 228, 230, 231
Kinlichini, Gertrude, 121
Knights of Columbus, 269
Ku Klux Klan, 235, 251, 259, 265–71

**L**

LaFarge, John, SJ, 31, 195, 233–34, 238
Lally, Father Joseph A. SSJ, 270–71
Lampkin, Daisy, 249–50
Lange, Elizabeth, OSP, 144
LaPlante, Father Alexis, SSJ, 165, 266–70
Leary, Mother Mary of the Visitation, SBS, 266–70
Lebeau, Fr. Pierre O. SSJ, 177–78, 182
Lenten Collection for Indian and African American Missions, 52, 62, 79, 137, 141
Leo XIII, 6–7, 9, 23, 203
Lusk, Charles, 55, 70, 72, 228, 231

**M**

Manhattanville Resolutions, 234
Marquette League, 52
Martin, Isadore, 235–37
Martínez, María Montoya, 120
Marty, Martin, 53–54
Mary Knoll Sisters, 38
McCarthy, Justin SSJ, 178, 182
Meagher, Katherine T., 153
Medicine Men, 94, 117, 131
Mercedes, Mother M. SBS, 182, 208, 242–45
Merriam Report, 80–81
Mill Hill Fathers, 148, *See* Society of Saint Joseph
*Mission Fields at Home*, 41–42, 109, 124, 127–32, 151, 163
Missionaries, 3–5, 9–10, 38–39
Missionary Congregation Servants of the Holy Spirit, 29

Missionary Sisters of the Sacred Heart of Jesus, 9, 175
Mississippi Flood Control Project, 12, 239–47
Mohonk Conference on the Negro Question, 15
Morgan, Thomas Jefferson, 48, 58, 114–15
Morrell, Edward, 36, 54, 154, 230
Morrell, Louise, See Drexel, Louise Morrell
Mother Katharine Schools, 217, 218; comparison to Rosenwald Schools, 224–26; physical conditions, 219–20; teachers at, 223
Moton, Robert, 241
Murphy, Father Edward, SSJ, 191–92, 197, 200, 203
Mystical Body of Christ, 3, 14–15, 40–42, 78, 275

**N**

NAACP. See National Association for the Advancement of Colored People
National Association for the Advancement of Colored People, 12–13, 202, 227, 229, 234–50
National Catholic Welfare Council, 141, 203
Navajo, 88–95, 103, 105, 110–12, 121–22, 125, 127–33
Neal, Claude, 247
Negro History Week, 199–200
Nelson, Medard Hillaire, 181
Neri, Sister Philip, SBS, 127
New Women, 8, 11

**O**

Oblate Sisters of Providence, 37–38, 144–45, 193
Oblate Sisters of the Blessed Sacrament, 37
O'Connor, Bishop James, 23–25, 34, 53, 89
Osage, 55, 75–78, 97

Our Lady of Lourdes School, Atlanta, GA, 264

**P**

Peabody, George, 166
Peace Policy, 50–51
Phelps Stokes Foundation, 196
Pius X, 39–40
Pius XI, 7, 203
Pius XII, 278
Pratt, Richard Henry, 49, 58, 115
Progressive Era, 3, 5, 11, 120, 148, 203
Propaganda Fide, 9
Pueblo, 55, 81, 86, 88–92, 111, 116–18, 120, 124–30, 133

**Q**

Quadragesimo Anno, 7, 203
*Quick Bear v. Leupp*, 60

**R**

Red Cloud, 53
Rock Castle, See Saint Francis de Sales School
Rerum Novarum, 7, 15, 203
Roosevelt, Franklin, 12, 81, 231, 245–49
Rosenwald Fund, 224, 236
Rosenwald, Julius, 166, 196, 224–26
Ross, Holt, 240
Rudd, Daniel, 136, 139, 150–51
Ryan, Archbishop John Patrick, 25–27, 33, 36, 139
Ryan, Mother M. Agatha, SBS, 198, 201, 204
Ryan, Mother M. Ignatius, SBS, 207
Ryan, Sister M. Madeline Sophie, SBS, 201

**S**

Sacra Tridentina Synodus, 39
Sacred Heart School, St. Charles, LA, 135, 140, 213–15, 217, 226, 248
Santa Fe Indian School, Santa Fe, NM 65

Saint Augustine's, Winnebago, NE, 85, 89, 91
Saint Catherine's Indian School, Santa Fe, NM, 81, 83, 85–89, 91–93, 99, 101, 103, 106–8, 110–11, 115–20, 122
Saint Dominic's School, New Orleans, LA, 179
Saint Edward's School, New Iberia, LA, 214–17
Saint Francis de Sales School, Rock Castle, VA, 152–59, 163–64, 225
Saint Francis Industrial School, Eddington, PA, 23, 149
Saint Joseph Sisters of Peace, 11–12, 228
Saint Katherine's Parish, New Orleans, LA, 175–79, 254
Saint Labre School, Ashland, MT, 70, 73
Saint Louis Industrial School, Pawhauska, OK, 53, 75–78
Saint Michael's, St. Michael's, AZ, 47, 66, 85, 88–89, 93–95, 97–98, 100, 103–11, 118–19, 122–23, 128, 231
Saint Monica's School, Chicago, IL 255–56
Saint Monica's School, New Orleans, LA, 158
Saint Paul's, Marty, SD, 72, 85, 89–90, 95, 99, 101, 104–5, 107, 121
Saint Peter Claver School, Macon, GA, 264
Saint Peter Claver School, Philadelphia, 38
Schuyler, George S., 244
Scottsboro Boys, 12, 235
Scottsboro Defense Committee, 12, 235–38
Segale, Sister Blandina SC, 87
Senora, Laurentia, 116–17
Shaw, Archbishop John William, 188, 196
Shuysua, George Raphael, 111, 119
Sioux, 89–91, 104, 118

Sisson, Sister M. Elise SBS, 192–93
Sisters of the Blessed Sacrament; attracting students, 90–95; changing views on Indigenous culture, 123–27; comparison to government schools, 119–20; conversion of students, 163–65; cooperation with government schools, 64–68; discipline at SBS schools 101–4; first sisters 33–39; founding of, 27; interracial reform, 232–35, 257; legal troubles, 264–65; medical missions of, 122; mission of, 2–3, 114–17, 120–22; partnership with NAACP, 12–13, 234–50; pedagogy, 104–6, 153–59; political activities of, 12–13; publications of,124–27; racism and, 222–23, 274; religious instruction of students, 162–63; response to Civil Rights Movement, 276–77; rule of, 27; shift to day schools, 159, 162; sisters as missionaries, 9–13; sisters of color, 36–38; student experiences at SBS schools, 95–104, 106–9, 117–20, 275; threats to organization, 258–59; use of media, 232–33; visitations of, 91, 165–66, 275–76; voting 227, 232
Sisters of Charity, 87
Sisters of Loretto, 75–77, 86–87
Sisters of Mercy, 33, 34, 36, 54
Sisters of St. Francis of Glen Riddle, 75
Sisters of St. Joseph of Carandolet, 28
Sitting Bull, 53
Slater Fund, 142, 148
Slattery, Father John SSJ, 36
Smith, Elizabeth, See Drexel, Elizabeth Smith
Smith, Walter George, 230–31, 265
Social Gospel, 3, 6, 252
Society for the Preservation of the Faith among Indian Children, 52, 63
Society of African Missions, 115

Society of Saint Joseph, 145, 148
Society of the Divine Word, 29, 32, 146
Sodality of Mary, 119
Southern University, New Orleans, 181–82, 184
Stephan, Monsignor Joseph, 37, 51, 53, 55, 58, 73, 78, 80, 87, 88, 230
Straight University, 175, 181
Strong, Josiah, 252

**T**
Tarry, Ellen, 155, 158, 163–64
Tekakwitha House, 63
Tennelly, Father J.B., 71–72
Third Council of Baltimore, 147
Tolton, Father Augustus, 251
Turner, Thomas W., 196
Tuskegee Institute, 224, 241

**V**
Vardaman, James K., 147
Vatican II, 11, 276
Vaughn, Cardinal Herbert, 145

**W**
Wagner, Robert, 241, 243–44
Washington, Booker T., 154, 224, 241
Watson, Tom, 254, 264

Weatua, Josephine, 111
Weber, Father Anselm, OFM, 35, 47, 93–94, 103, 105, 110
White, Walter, 235–37, 240, 242–47, 250
Wilkins, Roy, 243–44, 250
Williams, George, 140
Women and reform movements, 5–9

Woodson, Carter G., 199, 201, 203
Wounded Knee, 15

**X**
Xavier Prep, New Orleans, LA, 164, 187, 248; curriculum of, 184–86; founding of, 182–84
Xavier University, New Orleans, LA 169, 208, 213, 215, 225, 242, 248, 280; athletics 190–92; curriculum of, 189–90, 199–203; fine arts programming, 192–93; founding of, 186–89; NAACP recruitment at, 249–50; new campus, 194–98; religious life of, 193–94; School of Social Work 203–4

**Z**
Zitkala Ša. *See* Bonin, Gertrude

www.ingramcontent.com/pod-product-compliance
Lightning Source LLC
Chambersburg PA
CBHW020315010526
44107CB00054B/1850